Virtue, Commerce, and History

IDEAS IN CONTEXT

Edited by Richard Rorty, J. B. Schneewind, and Quentin Skinner

The books in this series will discuss the emergence of intellectual traditions and of related new disciplines. The procedures, aims, and vocabularies that were generated will be set in the context of the alternatives available within the contemporary frameworks of ideas and institutions. Through detailed studies of the evolution of such traditions, and their modification by different audiences, it is hoped that a new picture will form of the development of ideas in their concrete contexts. By this means, artificial distinctions between the history of philosophy, of the various sciences, of society and politics, and of literature may be seen to dissolve.

Forthcoming titles include the following:

Richard Rorty, J. B. Schneewind, and Quentin Skinner (eds.),
Philosophy in History: Essays in the Historiography of Philosophy
David Lieberman, *The Province of Legislation Determined*
Noel Malcolm, *Hobbes and Voluntarism*
Quentin Skinner, *Studies in Early Modern Intellectual History*
Edmund Leites (ed.), *Conscience and Casuistry in Early Modern Europe*
Lynn Joy, *Gassendi the Atomist: Advocate of History in an Age of Science*
Mark Goldie, *The Tory Ideology: Politics and Ideas in Restoration England*

This series is published with the support of the Exxon Education Foundation.

Virtue, Commerce, and History

Essays on Political Thought and History,
Chiefly in the Eighteenth Century

J. G. A. POCOCK

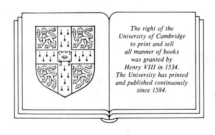

The right of the
University of Cambridge
to print and sell
all manner of books
was granted by
Henry VIII in 1534.
The University has printed
and published continuously
since 1584.

CAMBRIDGE UNIVERSITY PRESS

Cambridge

London   New York   New Rochelle

Melbourne   Sydney

Published by the Press Syndicate of the University of Cambridge
The Pitt Building, Trumpington Street, Cambridge CB2 1RP
32 East 57th Street, New York, NY 10022, USA
10 Stamford Road, Oakleigh, Melbourne 3166, Australia

First published 1985
Reprinted 1986

Printed in the United States of America

Library of Congress Cataloging in Publication Data
Pocock, J. G. A. (John Greville Agard), 1924–
Virtue, commerce, and history.
(Ideas in context)
Chiefly reprints of essays originally
published 1976–1982.
Includes bibliographies and index.
1. Political science – Great Britain – History – 18th
century – Addresses, essays, lectures. 2. Political
science – United States – History – 18th century –
Addresses, essays, lectures. I. Title. II. Series.
JA84.G7P635 1985   320′.01   84–15626
ISBN 0 521 25701 8 hard covers
ISBN 0 521 27660 8 paperback

To my colleagues and friends in the
Conference for the Study of Political Thought

Contents

PART III

1

◁══▷

Introduction
The state of the art

I

Of the ten essays that compose the remainder of this volume, nine were originally published between 1976 and 1982, though one or two were written for spoken delivery substantially earlier than their appearance in print. The last, which constitutes the whole of Part III, receives separate introduction. As a constellation they represent work on the history of political discourse in England, Scotland, and America, chiefly between the English Revolution of 1688 and the French Revolution of 1789, though Part III pursues the intimations of this history into the half-century following the latter event. This work has been done at a time when perceptions of "British history" are continuing to change, perhaps more drastically than for some time past, and when perceptions of what constitutes "the history of political thought" have been undergoing intensive scrutiny and restatement. Though the present volume is intended as a contribution to the practice, not the theory, of its branch of historiography, it is necessary to introduce it with a statement of where it stands in the process of change regarding the history of political thought. To describe a practice and its entailments, however, especially when these are understood to be in process of change, cannot be done without employing, and to some degree exploring, the language of theory.

I have already used two terms, the history of political thought and the history of political discourse, which are discernibly not identical. The former term is retained here, and in the nomenclature of learned institutions and journals, because it is familiar and conventional and serves to mobilize our energies in the right directions, and also because it is by no means inappropriate. The activities it directs us to study are visibly those of men and women thinking; the speech they employ is self-critical and self-refining, and regularly ascends toward levels of theory, philosophy, and science. Nevertheless, the change that has come over this branch of historiography in the past two decades may be characterized as a movement away from emphasizing history of thought (and even more sharply, "of ideas") toward emphasizing something rather different, for which "history of speech" or "history of discourse," although neither of them unproblematic or irreproachable, may be the best terminology so far found. To show how this movement has come about, and what it entails, is necessary in order to introduce its practice.

In a Cambridge-centered retrospect, some of this movement's origins may be discovered in the linguistic analysis favored by philosophers in the 1950s, which tended to present thoughts as propositions appealing to a limited number of modes of validation; others in the speech-act theories developed in Oxford and elsewhere about the same time, which tended to present thoughts as utterances performing upon those who heard them, and indeed upon those who uttered them. Both tended to focus attention upon the great variety of things that could be said or seen to have been said, and upon the diversity of linguistic contexts that went to determine what could be said but were at the same time acted upon by what was said. It is obvious enough what the historians of political thought have been doing with the perceptions thus offered them; but it is curious, in retrospect – and perhaps evidence of the difficulty of getting philosophers to talk about the same things as historians – that the series *Philosophy, Politics and Society,* which Peter Laslett began to edit in 1956, devoted itself almost wholly to the analysis and exploration of political statements and problems, and hardly at all to determining their historical status or to the historiography of political argument.[1] Paradoxically, at the very same time that Laslett was announcing that "for the moment, anyway, political philosophy is dead,"[2] the history of political thought, including philosophy (if philosophy can be included in anything) was about to undergo a fairly dramatic revival, due in large part to Laslett himself. It was Laslett's editorial work on Filmer and Locke[3] that taught others, including the present writer, the frameworks, both theoretical and historical, in which they should set their researches.

There began to take shape a historiography, with characteristic emphases: first on the variety of idioms, or "languages" as they came to be known, in which political argument might be conducted (an example might be the language of

---

[1] The three exceptions that may be said to prove this rule are J. G. A. Pocock, "The History of Political Thought: A Methodological Enquiry," in *Philosophy, Politics and Society: Second Series,* ed. Peter Laslett and W. G. Runciman (Oxford, 1962); Quentin Skinner, " 'Social Meaning' and the Explanation of Social Action," and John Dunn, "The Identity of the History of Ideas," both in *Philosophy, Politics and Society: Fourth Series,* ed. Peter Laslett, W. G. Runciman, and Quentin Skinner (Oxford, 1972).

[2] Peter Laslett, ed., *Philosophy, Politics and Society* (Oxford, 1956), p. vii.

[3] *Patriarcha and Other Political Works of Sir Robert Filmer* (Oxford, 1949); *John Locke: Two Treatises of Government* (Cambridge, 1960; rev. ed., 1963).

the common law as a constituent of what we now know as ancient constitution-alism)[4] and second, on the participants in political argument as historical actors, responding to one another in a diversity of linguistic and other political and historical contexts that gave the recoverable history of their argument a very rich texture. The republication of Filmer's writings in 1679 was seen to have evoked responses as linguistically diverse as Locke's *First* from his *Second Treatise,* or Algernon Sidney's *Discourses on Government* from either, and at the same time to have evoked, from those concerned to reply to the *Freeholder's Grand Inquest*[5] rather than to *Patriarcha,* responses of yet another kind: the controversy between Petyt and Brady, or the revision of Harrington by his associate Henry Neville.[6] All these threads in the history of argument could be followed as they diverged and converged again; there began to emerge a history of actors uttering and responding in a shared yet diverse linguistic context. The question why all this looked like a revolution in the historiography of political thought requires one to describe the state of the art before all this happened, and it is difficult to do so without setting up straw men. The immediate point is that there has ever since been a felt (and answered) need to redescribe the historiography of political thought and its entailments, and to define its practice in terms more rigorously historical.

It has been usual to suggest that *in illo tempore* the disciplines of political theory and the history of political thought had become confounded, and that the advent of an analytic and linguistic philosophy that was severely ahistorical helped greatly to disentangle them. But if the linguistic philosophers did not concern themselves with the writing of history, the historians were slow to draw upon or to contribute to the philosophy of speech acts and propositions. The present writer is aware that he did not so much learn from the contributors to *Philosophy, Politics and Society* as discover that he had been learning from them; it was left to the practice to discover its own entailments. The analysis of scientific inquiry in the turbulent passage from Popper to Kuhn and beyond had its importance, but it was only in the middle 1960s, with the first appearance of writings by Quentin Skinner, that historians of political thought began to state the logic of their own inquiry and pursue it into fields where it encountered the philosophy of language. There began a discussion that continues to produce a vigorous and extensive literature.[7] It would be difficult, and might not be useful, to trace all its intri-

---

[4] J. G. A. Pocock, *The Ancient Constitution and the Feudal Law: English Historical Thought in the Seventeenth Century* (Cambridge, 1957).

[5] James Tyrrell and William Petyt regarded this work as of the same tendency as the writings published under Filmer's name, and I do not therefore enter into the present controversy regarding its authorship. See Corinne Comstock Weston, "The Authorship of the *Freeholder's Grand Inquest,*" *English Historical Review* XCV, 1 (1980), pp. 74–98.

[6] Caroline Robbins, ed., *Two English Republican Tracts* (Cambridge, 1969).

[7] Bibliographies complete to the moment of their compilation may be found in Quentin Skinner, *The Foundations of Modern Political Thought,* 2 vols. (Cambridge, 1978), vol. 1, *The Renaissance,* pp. 285–6; Lotte Mulligan, Judith Richards, and John K. Graham, "Intentions and Conventions: A

cacies or attempt to write its history; yet the need to describe the present state of the art obliges us to give an account of its chief characteristics.

Professor Skinner is known for having made, at different times, two pronouncements on the objectives which a historian of this kind should pursue. The earlier of these stressed the importance of recovering the intentions which an author was carrying out in his text; the objections that have been made to this proposal have not destroyed it, but have rather pointed out the need in some respects to go beyond it. For example, it has been asked whether we can recover the author's intentions from his text without becoming imprisoned in the hermeneutic circle. The answer is that this may indeed be a danger when we have no evidence regarding the intentions other than the text itself; in practice, this is sometimes the case but not always. There may be evidence, unreliable and treacherous but still usable, from the author's other writings or his private correspondence; an admirable habit of preserving the letters of learned men has prevailed among antiquaries for hundreds of years. The more evidence the historian can mobilize in the construction of hypotheses regarding the author's intentions, which can be then be applied to or tested against the text itself, the better his chances of escaping from the hermeneutic circle, or the more circles of this kind his critics will have to construct in the attempt to dismount him.

A more penetrating objection has been that which asks whether a *mens auctoris* can be said to exist independently of his *sermo*, that is, whether a set of intentions can be isolated as existing in the author's mind, to which he then proceeds to give effect in writing and publishing his text. Do not the intentions come into being only as they are effected in the text? How can he know what he thinks, or what he wanted to say, until he sees what he has said? Self-knowledge is retrospective, and every author is his own owl of Minerva. Evidence of the kind mentioned in the preceding paragraph can still be mobilized, on occasion, in order to point out that an author of whom enough is known can be said to have had before him a number of possible actions, giving effect to a variety of intentions, and that the act he did perform, and the intentions to which he did give effect, may have differed from some other act he could have performed and may even have meditated performing. But the objection with which we are dealing cuts deeper than this. It asks not only whether intentions can exist before being artic-

Critique of Quentin Skinner's Method for the Study of the History of Ideas," *Political Studies* XXVI, 1 (1979), pp. 84–98; J. G. A. Pocock, *"The Machiavellian Moment* Revisited: A Study in History and Ideology," *Journal of Modern History* LIII, 1 (1981), pp. 50–1 n. 9; James H. Tully, "The Pen Is a Mighty Sword: Quentin Skinner's Analysis of Politics," *British Journal of Political Science* XIII, 4 (1983), pp. 489–509.

It should be mentioned that there are said to be levels of language – having to do with computer technology, market research, or something of the kind – at which the phrase "state of the art" has taken on some short-lived significance. The present author has no desire to be read in that sense. He believes himself to be practicing an art whose present state can be reflectively examined, and he hopes that this note may be of interest to historians.

ulated in a text, but whether they can be said to exist apart from the language in which the text is to be constructed. The author inhabits a historically given world that is apprehensible only in the ways rendered available by a number of historically given languages; the modes of speech available to him give him the intentions he can have, by giving him the means he can have of performing them. At this point the objection has raised the question of *langue* as well as *parole,* of language context as well as of speech act.

This had, of course, been part of Skinner's contention. His insistence on the recovery of intentions had been to some degree destructive in its purpose; it was aimed at eliminating from consideration those intentions an author could not have conceived or carried into effect, because he lacked the language in which they could have been expressed and employed some other, articulating and performing other intentions. Skinner's method, therefore, has impelled us toward the recovery of an author's language no less than of his intentions, toward treating him as inhabiting a universe of *langues* that give meaning to the *paroles* he performs in them. This by no means has the effect of reducing the author to the mere mouthpiece of his own language; the more complex, even the more contradictory, the language context in which he is situated, the richer and more ambivalent become the speech acts he is capable of performing, and the greater becomes the likelihood that these acts will perform upon the context itself and induce modification and change within it. At this point the history of political thought becomes a history of speech and discourse, of the interactions of *langue* and *parole;* the claim is made not only that its history is one of discourse, but that it has a history by virtue of becoming discourse.

There seems no doubt, however, that the focus of attention has moved in some measure from the concept of intention toward that of performance. At one level of theory, this is reflected in Professor Skinner's writings on speech acts and related matters; at one level of practice, in his dictum – to be seen in *The Foundations of Modern Political Thought* and forming the second of those pronouncements mentioned earlier – that if we are to have a history of political thought constructed on authentically historical principles, we must have means of knowing what an author "was doing"[8] when he wrote, or published, a text. The two words quoted prove to contain a wealth of meanings. In colloquial English, to ask what an actor "was doing" is often to ask "what he was up to," that is, what he was "playing at " or "getting at." What, in short, was the (sometimes concealed) purposive strategy of his actions? The notion of intention has certainly not been abandoned, as is evident also in the idiom – a favorite one with Skinner – that speaks of an author as performing this or that "move." But we also find it

[8] Skinner, *Foundations,* vol. 1, p. xi (the approach "might begin to give us a history of political theory with a genuinely historical character") and p. xiii ("it enables us to characterise what their authors were *doing* in writing" the classic texts).

possible to ask whether an actor "knew what he was doing," implying the possibility of a gap between intention and effect, or between consciousness of the effect and the effect itself; to ask this is to ask what the effect was, to whom and at what point in time it became apparent, and to confront the fact that actions performed in an open-ended time context produce an open-ended series of effects. The question what an author was doing therefore can have a great many answers, and it is even theoretically (though somewhat figuratively) conceivable that the author has not finished doing things yet. We need not, however, inquire whether history can have a present (as Michael Oakeshott seems to deny)[9] to discern that Quentin Skinner did wisely to employ an imperfect continuous tense. In French a future conditional perfect might have done duty, but to speak of "what an author would (turn out to) have done" is to look at a future (to us a past) from the standpoint of what he was doing, and is not quite identical with speaking, from the standpoint of our present, of "what he has done" or (*pace* Oakeshott) "is doing." It is not clear whether an author's action is ever over and done with; but it is clear – and the use of the future conditional underlines it – that we have begun to concern ourselves with the author's indirect action, his posthumous action, his action mediated through a chain of subsequent actors. Such is the necessary consequence of admitting the context to parity with the action, the *langue* to parity with the *parole*.

It has been said in objection to Skinner's position that an author's words are not his own, that the language he uses to effect his intentions may be taken from him and used by others to other effects. To some extent, this is inherent in the nature of language itself. The language he employs is already in use; it has been used and is being used to utter intentions other than his. At this point an author is himself both the expropriator, taking language from others and using it to his purposes, and the innovator, acting upon language so as to induce momentary or lasting change in the ways in which it is used. But as he has done to others and their language, so shall it be done to him and his. The changes he has sought to bring about in the linguistic conventions surrounding him may not prevent language continuing to be used in the conventional ways he has sought to modify, and this may be enough to nullify or distort the effects of his utterance. Furthermore, even when an author has succeeded in innovating, that is, in uttering speech in such a way as to compel others to respond to it in some sense not hitherto conventional, it does not follow that he will succeed in ruling the responses of others. They may – they usually will – impute to his utterance and his innovation consequences, implications, and entailments he may not have intended or wish to acknowledge, and they will respond to him in terms determined by these imputations, maintaining or modifying those conventions of speech

---

[9] Michael Oakeshott, *On History and Other Essays* (Oxford, 1983), and the present writer's review, (London) *Times Literary Supplement*, October 21, 1983, p. 1,155.

they see as directly or indirectly affected by his real or imputed utterance. And so far we are imagining only the actions of respondents contemporary with the author, that is, inhabiting the same linguistic and historical context. Languages display continuity as well as change; even when modified by their use in specific contexts, they outlive the contexts in which they have been modified, and they impose upon actors in subsequent contexts the constraints to which innovation and modification are the necessary but unpredictable responses. The text, furthermore, preserves the utterances of the author in a rigid, literal form and conveys them into subsequent contexts, where they compel from respondents interpretations that, however radical, distorting, and anachronistic, would not have been performed if the text had not performed upon the respondents. What an author "was doing," therefore, includes evoking from others responses the author could not control or predict, some of which would be performed in contexts quite other than those in which he was doing that which he could possibly know he was doing. Skinner's formula defines a moment in the history of the interactions of *parole* with *langue,* but at the same time it defines that moment as open-ended.

II

A review of the state of the art must at this point present an account of its practice. To describe is not to prescribe, and what follows is an account of some practices the historian of political discourse will find himself[10] pursuing, rather than a rigorous injunction to follow them in their order. In the perspective suggested here, however, it seems a prior necessity to establish the language or languages in which some passage of political discourse was being conducted. These "languages" will in strict fact have been sublanguages, idioms, and rhetorics, rather than languages in the ethnic sense, although in early modern history it is not uncommon to encounter polyglot texts that combine vernacular with Latin, Greek, and even Hebrew; we will chiefly be concerned with idioms or modes of speech existing within a given vernacular. Those languages will vary in the degree of their autonomy and stability. From "idioms" they shade off in the direction of "styles" and toward a point where the distinction drawn here between *langue* and *parole* may be lost; but we are typically in search of modes of discourse stable enough to be available for the use of more than one discussant and to present the character of games defined by a structure of rules for more than one player. This will enable us to consider how the players exploited the rules against

---

[10] The English language contains no third-person pronoun without gender. In writing of the authors *in* the history of political discourse, most of whom were men, I am unembarrassed to find myself using the masculine pronoun, but when it comes to the authors *of* that history, a host of distinguished names occurs to remind me that it might just as well have been the feminine.

one another, and in due course how they performed upon the rules with the effect of altering them.

These idioms or language games vary also in origin and hence in content and character. Some will have originated in the institutional practices of the society concerned: as the professional vocabularies of jurists, theologians, philosophers, merchants, and so on that for some reason have become recognized as part of the practice of politics and have entered into political discourse. A great deal may be learned about the political culture of a given society at various moments in its history by observing what languages originating in this way have become accredited, as it were, to take part in its public speech, and what clerisies or professions have acquired authority in the conduct of its discourse. But other languages will be encountered whose character is rhetorical rather than institutional; they will be found to have originated as modes of argument within the ongoing process of political discourse, as new modes invented or old modes transformed by the constant action of speech upon language, of *parole* upon *langue*. There may be less need to look outside the continuum of discourse in search of their origins; equally, there is nothing to prevent languages of the former category, originating outside the mainstream of discourse, from having entered into the process of transformation just described and from having undergone the mutations that engender new idioms and modes of argument. From all this it follows that the generalized language of discourse at any given time – though perhaps this is particularly true of early modern Europe and Britain – may possess a rich and complex texture; a wide variety of idioms may have entered into it and may be interacting with one another to produce a complex history.

Each of these languages, however it originated, will exert the kind of force that has been called paradigmatic (though it has not proved economical to labor the refinements of this term). That is to say, each will present information selectively as relevant to the conduct and character of politics, and it will encourage the definition of political problems and values in certain ways and not in others. Each will therefore favor certain distributions of priority and consequently of authority; should a concept of authority itself be under discussion – as is likely to be the case in political discourse – it will present "authority" as arising in a certain way and possessing a certain character, and not otherwise. However, once we have defined political discourse as drawing on a number of diversely originating "languages" and arguments, we are committed to supposing the presence of a number of these paradigmatic structures, distributing and defining authority in a number of variant ways, at any one time. From this it follows – what is in any case almost self-evident – that political language is by its nature ambivalent; it consists in the utterance of what have been called "essentially contested concepts" and propositions,[11] and in the simultaneous employment of languages

---

[11] For this term, advanced by W. B. Gallie in 1956, see William E. Connolly, *The Terms of Political Discourse*, 2d ed. (Princeton, N.J., 1983).

favoring the utterance of diverse and contrary propositions. But it further follows – what is nearly but not quite the same thing – that any text or simpler utterance in a sophisticated political discourse is by its nature polyvalent; it consists in the employment of a texture of languages capable of saying different things and of favoring different ways of saying things, in the exploitation of these differences in rhetoric and practice, and in their exploration and possibly their resolution in criticism and theory. When a diversity of such languages is to be found in a given text, it may follow that a given utterance is capable of being intended and read, and so of performing, in more than one of them at the same time; nor is it at all impossible that a given pattern of speech may migrate, or be translated, from one language to another found in the same text, bearing implications from the former context and engrafting them among those belonging to the latter. And the author may move among these patterns of polyvalence, employing and recombining them according to the measure of his capacity. What to one investigator looks like the generation of linguistic muddles and misunderstandings may look to another like the generation of rhetoric, literature, and the history of discourse.

It is a large part of our historian's practice to learn to read and recognize the diverse idioms of political discourse as they were available in the culture and at the time he is studying: to identify them as they appear in the linguistic texture of any one text, and to know what they would ordinarily have enabled that text's author to propound or "say." The extent to which the author's employment of them was out of the ordinary comes later. The historian pursues his first goal by reading extensively in the literature of the time and by sensitizing himself to the presence of diverse idioms. To some extent, therefore, his learning process is one of familiarization, but he cannot remain merely passive and receptive to the language (or languages) he reads, and must frequently employ detective procedures that enable him to frame and validate hypotheses asserting that such and such a language was being employed and was capable of being employed in such and such ways. Along this line he must inevitably confront the problems of interpretation, ideological bias, and the hermeneutic circle. What evidence has he for the presence of a language in the texts before him other than his own ingenuity in reading it into them? Is he not programmed by emphases arising from his own culture to detect similar emphases in the literature of the past and devise supposititious "languages" in which these were allegedly expressed? Can he proceed from saying that he has read a certain language in the texts of a past culture to saying that this language existed as a resource available to those performing acts of utterance in that culture?

The historian is characteristically interested in the performances of agents other than himself and does not desire to be the author of his own past so much as to uncover the doings of other authors in and of it. This is probably a reason why his politics are inherently liberal rather than aimed at *praxis*. In the kind of inquiry under examination here, the historian is less interested in the "style," or mode of utterance of a given author, than in the "language," or mode of utterance available to a number of authors for a number of purposes, and his evidence for holding that such and such a "language" existed as a cultural resource for actors in history, and not merely as a gleam in his interpretative eye, tends to be related to the number of actors he can show to have performed in this medium and the number of acts he can show them to have performed. The more he can show (a) that diverse authors employed the same idiom and performed diverse and even contrary utterances in it, (b) that the idiom recurs in texts and contexts varying from those in which it was at first detected, and (c) that authors expressed in words their consciousness that they were employing such an idiom and developed critical and second-order languages to comment on and regulate their employ-ment of it, the more his confidence in his method will increase. Logically, per-haps, he cannot prove that the whole mass of evidence he presents is not the fruit of his ingenuity as an interpreter, but neither can he prove that he is not asleep and dreaming the whole of his apparent existence. The greater the number and diversity of performances he can narrate, the more the hypotheses erected by those who seek to imprison him within the hermeneutic circle must come to resemble a Ptolemaic universe, consisting of more cycles and epicycles than would satisfy the reasonable mind of Alfonso the Wise; in short, the more it will exhibit the disadvantages of nonrefutability.

The problem of interpretation recurs in a more pressing form when we consider that the historian studies languages in order to read them, but not to speak or write them. His own writings will not be constructed in a pastiche of the various idioms they interpret, but rather in language he has devised in order to describe and explicate the workings of these idioms. If in Collingwoodian terminology he has learned to "rethink the thoughts" of others, the language in which he reiter-ates their utterances will not be that used by them, but his own. It will be explicatory in the sense that it aims constantly to render the implicit explicit, to bring to light assumptions on which the language of others has rested, to pursue and verbalize implications and intimations that in the original may have re-mained unspoken, to point out conventions and regularities that indicate what could and could not be spoken in the language, and in what ways the language *qua* paradigm encouraged, obliged, or forbade its users to speak and think. To quite an important extent, the historian's language will be hypothecatory and predictive; it will enable him to state what he expects a conventional user of the language under study to have said in specific circumstances, the better to study what was in fact said under these circumstances. When the prediction is falsified and the speech act performed is not that expected, it may be that the conventions of language need further exploration; that the circumstances in which the lan-guage was used were other than the historian has supposed they were; that the language being employed was not precisely the language he has expected; or, the most interesting possibility of all, that innovation and change were taking place in the language.

It will be at such moments that the historian is most confident that he is not merely the prisoner of his own interpretative ingenuity, but the fact remains that his writings about the language of others will be conducted largely in a paralanguage or metalanguage, designed to explicate the implicit and present the history of a discourse as a kind of dialogue between its intimations and potentialities, in which what was not always spoken will be spoken by him. It does not make the historian an idealist to say that he regularly, though not invariably, presents the language in the form of an ideal type: a model by means of which he carries on explorations and experiments. Since he is ultimately concerned with the performances of agents other than himself, he is constantly alert for occasions on which the explication of language has been carried out by actors in the history he is studying; by the language's own users commenting upon its use critically, reflectively, and by means of second-order languages developed among them for the purpose. These will be occasions on which the actors passed from simple discourse to discourse continued and modified by means including theory, but they will also be occasions that provide the historian with information enabling him to control his former hypotheses and construct new ones. The explication of the languages he has learned to read is his means of pursuing his inquiries simultaneously in two directions: toward the contexts in which language was uttered, and toward the acts of speech and utterance performed in and upon the context furnished by language itself and the further contexts in which it was situated. He will seek next to observe the *parole* performing upon the *langue:* upon the conventions and implications of the language, upon other actors as users of the language, upon actors in any further contexts of whose existence he may become persuaded, and possibly upon those contexts themselves. Language, as we have been using the term, is the historian's key to both speech act and context.

We have seen that the texts he studies may prove to have been compounded of many idioms and languages. The historian is constantly surprised and delighted to discover familiar languages in texts equally familiar, where they have not been noticed before – the language of prophetic exegesis in *Leviathan*,[12] the idiom of denouncing paper credit in *Reflections on the Revolution in France*[13] – though making these discoveries does not always enhance his respect for previous scholarship. But if a proposition derives its validity from the language in which it is performed, and part at least of its historicity from its performance upon the same

---

[12] "Time, History and Eschatology in the Thought of Thomas Hobbes," in *The Diversity of History: Essays in Honour of Sir Herbert Butterfield,* ed. J. H. Elliott and H. G. Konigsberger (London and Ithaca, N.Y., 1970) and reprinted in J. G. A. Pocock, *Politics, Language and Time: Essays in Political Thought and History* (New York, 1971).

[13] See chap. 10, "The Political Economy of Burke's Analysis of the French Revolution."

language, it follows that a text compounded of many languages may not only say many things in as many ways, but also may be a means of action in as many histories; it may be broken down into many acts performed in the history of as many languages as there are in the text. To recognize this will commit the historian to some radical, though not always irreversible, experiments in deconstruction, but before he can pursue these or examine their implications, he needs means of understanding how an act of speech, utterance, or authorship, performed in a certain language, may perform and innovate upon it. His attention now turns from *langue* to *parole,* to the act performed in and on a context; but a knowledge of the context remains necessary to a knowledge of the innovation.

III

Each of the distinguishable idioms of which a text may be compounded is a context in its own right: a way of speaking that seeks to prescribe what things may be said in it and that precedes and may outlast the speech act performed within its prescriptions. We expect it to be complex and sophisticated, to have been formed over time under pressure from a great many conventions and contingencies entering into combination, and to contain at least some elements of a second-order speech that permits its users to reflect on the implications of their use of it. The process of "learning" it, which has just been described, may therefore be thought of as a process of learning its characteristics, resources, and limitations as a mode of utterance which facilitates the performance of some kinds of speech act and inhibits the performance of others; any act performed in it may be viewed as exploiting, exploring, recombining, and challenging the possibilities of utterance of which it consists. But language is referential and has a variety of subjects; it alludes to those elements of experience out of which it has come and with which it offers to deal, and a language current in the public speech of an institutional and political society may be expected to allude to those institutions, authorities, value symbols, and recollected events that it presents as part of that society's politics and from which it derives much of its own character. A "language" in our specialized sense, then, is not only a prescribed way of speaking, but also a prescribed subject matter for political speech. We have reached a point where we can see that each language context betokens a political, social, or historical context within which it is itself situated; we are obliged at the same point, however, to acknowledge that each language to some degree selects and prescribes the context within which it is to be recognized.

Given that any such language has taken time to form, it must display a historical dimension; it must possess and prescribe a past made up of those social arrangements, historical events, recognized values, and ways of thinking of which it has been able to speak; it discourses of a politics from which the character of pastness cannot be altogether separated. The historian therefore cannot easily satisfy the demand, often made of him, that he present acts of political speech as determined (in the terminology criticized by Oakeshott) by the "primordial" demands of a "present of practical action";[14] because language characterizes the present in speech loaded with intimations of a past, the present is difficult to isolate or to state in immediate practical purity. Political speech is of course practical and informed by present necessities, but it is none the less constantly engaged in a struggle to discover what the present necessities of practice are, and the most powerful minds using it are exploring the tension between established linguistic usages and the need to use words in new ways. The historian has his own relation to this tension. He knows what norms the language he is studying usually implied, but he may also possess independent knowledge that these norms and the society they presupposed were changing, in ways and for reasons the language as yet lacked means of recognizing. He will therefore look for indications that words were being used in new ways as the result of new experiences, and were occasioning new problems and possibilities in the discourse of the language under study. It will be a problem for him, however, that nothing in that language denotes changes in its historical context as satisfactorily as does the language available to him as a historian, but not available to the actors whose language and history he is studying. Faced with problems such as how far he may use twentieth-century categories to explain the categories used in the seventeenth century, he may impose on himself the discipline of explaining only how changes in seventeenth-century language indicated changes in the historical context, what changes were indicated, and what changes occurred in the ways of indicating them. Since the language of seventeenth-century actors responded differently to its historical context from the language he himself uses, it may be long before seventeenth-century speech, interpreted in context, gives him occasion to use the categories of historical explanation he would wish to use – and in some cases that occasion may never arise. But the historian of discourse cannot get out of a language that which was never in it.

The present of practical necessity in which past actors found themselves is not immediately accessible, since it must come to us through the mediation of the language they used; but this does not mean that it is not accessible at all. From the texts they wrote, from our knowledge of the language they used, the communities of debate to which they belonged, the programs of action that were put into effect, and the history of the period at large, it is often possible to formulate hypotheses concerning the necessities they were under and the strategies they desired to carry out, and to test these by using them to interpret the intentions and performances of the texts themselves. We are in search, however, less of the

---

[14] See n. 9, this chapter.

text's "practical" than of its discursive performance. No one has tried to identify the thousand gentlemen whose minds Hobbes once claimed[15] to have framed to a conscientious obedience to the government of the Commonwealth, nor would it tell us much about *Leviathan* to know if they existed. We do not much care to know whether the first readers of *Il Principe* (whoever they were) were moved to accept or reject the legitimacy of rule by the restored Medici, especially as the work seems capable of operating either way; what matters to us is to study the differences that *Il Principe* and *Leviathan* made to the premises on which political discourse was conducted. This is to say, of course, that we are historians of discourse, not of behavior, but it is also to read Machiavelli and Hobbes as they were read by everyone whose response to them we possess in written form; these responses are, without exception, concerned not with their practical political consequences, but with the challenges they present to the normal structures of discourse. The history of discourse is not our arbitrary selection; it declares itself in the literature.

The performance of the text is its performance as *parole* in a context of *langue.* It may simply continue the operative conventions of which the language consists; it may serve to indicate to us that the language was continuing to be used in a world that was changing and had begun to change it; or it may perform on as well as in the language that is its medium, innovating in ways that bring about greater or smaller, more or less radical changes in the use of the language or of second-order language about it. (I am writing here, for simplicity's sake, as if each text were written in only one of the available languages of discourse, instead of being compounded of several.) The historian therefore needs a means of understanding how a speech act is performed within a language context, and in particular how it is performed and innovates upon it.

When an author has performed an act of this character, we are accustomed to say that he has "made a move." The phrase implies game playing and tactical maneuver, and our understanding of "what he was doing" when he made his move thus depends in considerable measure on our understanding of the practical situation he was in, of the case he desired to argue, the action or norm he desired to legitimate or delegitimate, and so on; we hope that his text will indicate such a situation, one of which we have some independent knowledge from other sources. The practical situation will include pressures, constraints, and encouragements the author was under or perceived himself as being under, arising from the preferences and antipathies of others and the limitations and opportunities of a political context as he perceived or experienced it; it is obviously possible, but not obviously necessary, that this situation will extend as far as the relations between social classes. But the practical situation also includes the linguistic situation:

[15] Thomas Hobbes, *Six Lessons to the Professors of the Mathematics . . .* (1656); see William Molesworth, ed., *The English Works of Thomas Hobbes,* 11 vols. (London, 1845), vol. 7, pp. 335–6, 343–7.

that arising from the constraints and opportunities imposed on the author by the language or languages available for him to use, and it is often – perhaps predominantly – within this context (or sector of the context) that the historian of discourse sees the author's "move" performed. <u>Languages are the objects as well as the instruments of consciousness, and the public speech of a society commonly includes second-order languages in which the actors comment upon the languages they are otherwise using.</u> To the extent to which this happens, language is objectified as part of the practical situation, and an author "making a move" in response to some practical necessity may not merely be using some language in a new way, but proposing that it be used in a new way and commenting on the language uses of his society, or even on the character of language itself. It is at this point that the historian of discourse must see philosophy and practice as coexisting rather than as separable: Hobbes or Locke as both philosopher and pamphleteer.

Whatever the idiom or language in which the "move" was performed, whatever the level of consciousness it presupposed, whatever the combination of rhetoric and theory, practice and philosophy it seems to have entailed, the historian looks for ways in which it may have rearranged, or sought to rearrange, the possibilities of language open to the author and his co-users of language; any result of this order that the historian can obtain will furnish a large part of his answer to the question of what the author was doing. In order to obtain knowledge of how a speech act may modify or innovate upon the language it is performed in, it is probably best to begin with utterances at a relatively simple practical, rhetorical, or argumentative level; it also seems best, however, to bear in mind that the act may be performed in a context compounded of several languages simultaneously in use (whether these be thought of as first-order languages interacting with each other or second-order languages interacting with those on which they comment). If we wish to imagine a speech act innovating within and upon a single idiom unconnected with others – and it may be necessary to do so – we must imagine it performing or proposing a change in one of the usages in which that idiom consists: a drastic reversal, perhaps, in the meaning of a key term. But a change confined to a single idiom can reverse only the usages already there, and we shall find ourselves imagining such simple but far-reaching moves as a reversal of value signs: a proposal that what was formerly considered bad be now considered good, or vice versa. Of this *adikos logos* there are some notorious examples in our histories, though their shock effect is usually enough to give rise instantly to second-order language, increasing the number of idioms in use.

We may at this stage turn to the context of experience, rather than of language, and suppose some term in a single idiom, familiarly used to denote some component of experience, being used to denote an unfamiliar component, or to associate the familiar with an unfamiliar component, or more generally to speak of the familiar in an unfamiliar way. Once we have introduced the context (and concept) of experience, we must concede that such innovations may be thought of either as "moves" deliberately performed,[16] or as changes in usage coming about in ways of which the author was more or less unconscious and that indeed took an indefinite number of speech acts to perform; there are wide twilight areas to explore here. On the other hand, once we reintroduce the concept of second-order language – which is likely to introduce itself whenever an actor becomes conscious that a move is being performed – we have reentered the realm in which language conveys consciousness of its own existence and comes to consist of a number of concurrent idioms, from which coexisting first-order languages cannot, as we have seen, be excluded. The context of language reasserts itself and interacts with increasing complexity with the context of experience.

The historian now embarks on a search for ways in which a speech act may innovate in and on a context consisting of several languages in interaction – or, more brutally, how it may innovate in several languages at once. "Moves" of this kind will be moves of translation, passing directly or indirectly from one available language to another. A crucial term, topos, or pattern of utterance may be translated from the context of one idiom to that of another; that is, it may be simply removed into a new context and left to undergo modification there. A problem or subject normally considered by applying one idiom may be considered by applying another, and this may carry the implication, subsequently explicated, that it belongs to a context of experience different from that to which it has previously been assigned. The richer the diversity of idioms or languages of which a public discourse is composed, the more various, complex, and subtle the "moves" of this kind that can be performed. These moves may be rhetorical and implicit, performed without advertisement, and left to work their effects, or they may be explicit and theoretical, explained and justified in some critical language designed to vindicate and elaborate their character; and the use of second-order language is known to set off an escalation with few if any upper limits. All the resources of rhetoric, of criticism, of methodology, of epistemology, and of metaphysics are therefore in principle at the disposal of the sophisticated performer in the field of multilingual discourse; if they are not immediately available to him he has means and motivation to set about inventing them for himself. There is an exponential progress toward – though it is a matter of historical contingency whether there is ultimately attained – the appearance of the fully self-conscious linguistic performer, the "epic theorist" depicted by Sheldon Wolin,[17] who seeks to expli-

---

[16] A striking, not to say flagrant, example is James Madison's announcement in the tenth of the *Federalist Papers* that the word "republic" denoted a state governed by representatives of the citizens, whereas one governed by the citizens themselves was a "democracy." The force of Madison's statement was retrospective, not enactive; he declared that this was, not that it should be, normal usage.

[17] Sheldon S. Wolin, "Political Theory as a Vocation," *American Political Science Review* LXIII, 4

cate and justify all his moves and innovations, and to propose a radical reordering of language and philosophy. Such beings appear from time to time in the historical record; Hobbes was one, though Machiavelli probably was not.

This does not mean that the epic theorist's performance is not historically conditioned, only that it is self-elaborating without immediately apparent limit. It now becomes a major problem for the historian to distinguish between what the author might have done and what in fact he did, since even the epic theorist's capability does not in every case imply intent. But we have reached a point where it seems improbable that the historian's understanding will be advanced through constructing a typology of moves that may in principle be performed or innovations that may be effected; the possible variations seem too diverse to be economically classified, though useful theoretical work may still be done in this direction. The historian is likely to proceed through the location of the author's texts in their contexts; through weighing what he might have done against what he did, the historian attempts an exhaustive explication of the moves he performed, the innovations he effected, and the messages about experience and language he can be shown to have transmitted. This will constitute an account of "what he was doing" insofar as these words can be confined to denoting the author's performances in writing his text.

IV

Agents perform upon other agents, who perform acts in response to theirs, and when action and response are performed through the medium of language, we cannot absolutely distinguish the author's performance from the reader's response. It is true that this is not invariably the case in the literature of politics. The author's manuscript may have lain in an archive for hundreds of years before being published – as did Clarke's report of the Putney debates and most of the works of Guicciardini – and with regard to the period before publication, we have to think of the text as less a performance than a document, less an act[18] than an indication that a certain state of consciousness, and of language usage, existed at an ascertainable time. We may indeed always arrest our study of the text at the point where it indicates to us the state of the author's consciousness and capacity to articulate it, and there are kinds of speech acts that are confined to the expression and articulation of consciousness. An author may have been writing merely to and for himself, or writing private memoranda of thoughts he desired to conceal from others; texts so written do not lose the character of historical actions performed by self-conscious agents. But speech is commonly pub-

---

(1969), pp. 1,062–82, and *Hobbes and the Epic Tradition of Political Theory* (Los Angeles, 1970). For comment, see John G. Gunnell, *Political Theory: Tradition and Interpretation* (Cambridge, Mass., 1979), pp. 51–7, 136–59.

[18] "Less . . . than" does not mean "not . . . but."

lic, and authors commonly publish their works, though the act of writing a text and the act of publishing it may be very different because performed in different situations; Locke's *Treatises of Government* currently offer the most notorious instance of this. The history of discourse is concerned with speech acts that become known and evoke response, with illocutions that are modified as they become perlocutions by the ways in which recipients respond to them, and with responses that take the form of further speech acts and countertexts. The reader himself becomes an author, and a complex mode of *Rezeptionsgeschichte* is required of the historian.

We are at a point where the history of discourse diverges from the history of consciousness. We have the author's text, a cultural artifact inscribed with a certain finality, and by setting this in the contexts furnished by his language and experience, we can say what it was that he "did" down to the moment of his completing it (or publishing it if he got so far); we can estimate his intention and performance, his moves and innovations, as they stood at that moment, and state what he "had been doing" to that point. But to ask what he "was doing" is to employ the imperfect tense and ask an open-ended question; there are answers we have not given and cannot give until we know what the author did to others and to the languages in which he and others conducted their discourse. In order to know this, we must have acts of discourse performed by others in response to his, and in particular to the innovations in language that his acts had performed or begun to perform; we must know what changes in their discourse occurred as they responded to his utterances and performed countermoves to his moves. At this point we move from author to reader, but to reader considered as author; for unless they were performed in the medium – written and published speech – that the author himself employed, the reader's responses have nothing to tell us. There are two reasons for this, or rather there are two senses in which this is true. It is true that we are compelled to work only with the evidence that has survived for us to use, so that responses to a text that were never verbalized, or verbalized only in unrecorded spoken words, are virtually impossible to recapture. It is also true that an author who worked in a written medium may be thought of as working on that medium, as intending to modify the things that could be said and done in it; so that changes he induced in the performances of other writers in that medium may indeed be the changes he intended and performed, or (if at variance with his intentions) performed without intending. We need not therefore apologize for the unrepresentative elitism of studying only those readers whose responses were verbalized, recorded, and presented. The *mentalité* of the silent and inarticulate majority should indeed be sought after and if possible recovered; it may have important information for us. But the history of *mentalités* is not identical with the history of discourse.

The historian begins now to focus on other texts, written and published by those who had read the text considered in the first instance and who were responding directly or indirectly to it. His chief need is for an understanding of how the previous author's innovations, singled out from among the rest of his speech acts, may impose themselves on readers in such a way as to force from them responses congruent with the innovation. He begins by presupposing that an utterance acts upon the consciousness of its recipient, that what is read cannot be unread. There is something unilateral about the act of communication,[19] which does not take place wholly between consenting adults. By speaking words in your hearing, by injecting script, print, or image into your field of attention, I impose on you, without your consent, information you cannot ignore. I have demanded your response, and I have also sought to determine it. I have indeed determined that it is to an act of mine and to information introduced by me that you must respond, and the more complex and intelligible the information imposed by this act of verbal rape – this penetration of your consciousness without your consent – the more I have tried to determine what your response shall be. It is true that if we have shared a medium of communication consisting in a structure of shared conventions, you have more of the freedom that comes of prior consent to the form my acts took; but for this very reason, any challenge or innovation posed by me to those conventions will be hard for you to resist recognizing, and you will have to respond to that innovation as you recognize and understand it. Nor is it likely (unless you are a Stalinist bureaucrat) that you will be able to respond simply by reiterating the existing conventions of discourse as if I had never challenged them; such attempts are of course made and sometimes succeed, but they fail in proportion to your awareness that I have said something you wish to answer. You are more likely to respond to my move with a countermove of your own, and even if the countermove is intended to restore the conventions I challenged, it will contain and register your awareness that I have said something unprecedented and will to that extent contain something unprecedented of its own. To my injection of new wine you will respond by presenting old wine in new bottles. What I "was doing" includes obliging you to do something, and partly determining what that shall be.

But language provides you with resources for determining your own response. If there is a master–slave relationship between us, you may respond in language that accepts and perpetuates my language's manipulation of you;[20] but such relationships are neither simple nor stable, and your understanding of the slave's

---

[19] For more on this, see Pocock, "Verbalising a Political Act: towards a Politics of Language," *Political Theory* I, 1 (1973), pp. 27–45, and "Political Ideas as Historical Events: Political Philosophers as Historical Actors," in *Political Theory and Political Education,* ed. Melvin Richter (Princeton, N.J., 1980).

[20] For the language of the literature of absolutism, and comment on its manipulative strategies with reference to the present writer's theories, see Jonathan Goldberg, *James I and the Politics of Literature: Jonson, Shakespeare, Donne and their Contemporaries* (Baltimore, 1983).

role may not coincide with mine, so that even the servility of your response will be troubling to me and will pervert my language (the literature of slavery is largely about this). The more your language, shared with me, permits you to articulate your perception of the world, the more the conventions and paradigms it contains will permit you to assimilate my speech and deflect my innovations − although, paradoxically, these may also be the means of emphasizing and dramatizing my innovations and rendering them nonignorable. And once you begin verbalizing your response to my utterance, you begin to acquire the freedom to maneuver that arises from what Stanley Fish has termed "the infinite capacity of language for being appropriated."[21] The interpreter and counterauthor begins to "read" the text, taking the words and speech acts it contains to himself and reiterating them in ways and in contexts of his own selection, so that they become incorporated into speech acts of his own. In presenting this process, we tend to speak of author and reader as if they were in an adversary relation, but the process is essentially the same when the relation is that of instructor and disciple, to say nothing of master and slave. The reader acquires a capacity to perform "moves" not at all unlike the "moves" we saw being performed by the author, whether or not these are thought of as countermoves to the author's innovations; the resources of rhetoric, argument, and criticism become his as they are those of any other language agent. He can alter the meaning of terms, remove them from one idiomatic context into another, select and rearrange the order of the various idioms out of which the author compounded his text, and alter the elements of the context of experience to which the components of discourse are taken to be referring. In short, any and all of the speech acts the text has been performing can be reperformed by the reader in ways nonidentical with those in which the author intended and performed them; they can also become the occasion for the performance of new speech acts by the reader as he becomes an author in his turn. In this matrix, it is easy to see how innovation by the author can be − as we have already seen why it must be − met with counterinnovation by the respondent. There is even a sense in which the respondent − let us imagine him a disciple − cannot escape treating the text in this way, since not being the author he cannot use the author's language exactly as the author did; and should the respondent be confronted with a text whose author has been dead for centuries, he inevitably acquires the freedom to interpret it in a historical context that the author did not imagine and a language context that includes idioms he never knew.

The history of discourse now becomes visible as one of *traditio* in the sense of transmission and, still more, translation. Texts composed of *langues* and *paroles*, of stable language structures and the speech acts and innovations that modify

---

[21]Stanley Fish, *Is There a Text in This Class? The Authority of Interpretive Communities* (Cambridge, Mass., 1980), p. 305.

them, are transmitted and reiterated, and their components are severally transmitted and reiterated, first by nonidentical actors in shared historical contexts, and then by actors in historically discrete contexts. Their history is, first, that of the constant adaptation, translation, and reperformance of the text in a succession of contexts by a succession of agents, and second, and under closer inspection, that of the innovations and modifications performed in as many distinguishable idioms as originally were compounded to form the text and subsequently formed the succession of language contexts in which the text was interpreted. What the author "is doing," therefore, turns out to have been continuing and modifying – either more or less drastically, radically, and "originally" – the performance of an indefinite diversity of speech acts in an indefinite diversity of contexts, both of language and of historical experience. It is, on the face of it, unlikely that all these histories can be circumscribed in a single history. Italian usage may be wise in calling an author's posthumous history his *fortuna,* French in calling it his *travail.*[22]

V

It now becomes important to decide whether and when we are to close off Skinner's open-ended context: to cease saying that an author "was doing" those things that were performed by translation, modification, and discussion of a text originally his. This apparently verbal question proves to entail the whole problem of authority and interpretation. Stanley Fish has argued that a text can be said to exert no authority over those who interpret it, but rather becomes dissolved in the continuum of interpretation to which it once gave rise. The historian will not challenge this as a normative proposition; interpreters may legitimately behave in the ways it presupposes, and the historian will not be at all surprised to find them so behaving in history. But he will be no more surprised to find – indeed he thinks he knows already – that human communities in history have sometimes ascribed extraordinary and even divine authority to certain texts, have maintained them in stable textual forms for centuries and even millennia, and have discussed the various ways in which they may be established and discussed subject to the premise that they possess the authority ascribed to them.[23] When this has happened, there is a text in the historian's class, in the sense that he observes the

---

[22] Giuliano Procacci, *Studi sulla Fortuna del Machiavelli* (Rome, 1965); Claude Lefort, *Le Travail de l'Oeuvre Machiavel* (Paris, 1972).

[23] Fish will of course argue that the ascription of authority is an interpretative act and that the text can never be disentangled from the acts of those who ascribe authority to it. I agree with this, but I wish to maintain that (a) the text, persisting over time as an authoritative artifact, is among the determinants of those acts, and (b) the text may be, and in history often is, discerned as a complex of former ascriptions of authority, among which the author's own affirmation of authority for his text may possibly be one.

persistence of a literary artifact of a certain authority and *durée,* and he sets out to investigate the historical occurrences that have accompanied its persistence. There is an obvious contextual sense in which no application or interpretation of an authoritative text is exactly like any other, because each is performed by a specific set of actors in (and on) a specific set of contingencies or circumstances; but this will not persuade the historian that the text has disappeared. If it is of the appropriate character, the text may sustain the existence – or it may be enough to say the appearance – of a certain set of formulas or paradigms, which are to be applied each time the authority of the text is invoked. It may be, of course, that the principles require restating each time they are to be applied, and that every statement of principle interacts with the statement of the case to which it is to be applied. But the exegete may be linguistically capable of abstracting the principle and stating it in an ideal form each time he applies it, and it has been claimed for certain texts, over lengthy periods, that they do support principles that can be, and de facto have been, so stated. The historian notes that authoritative texts vary in the extent to which this abstract rigor is claimed for them: The *lex scripta* differs from the *lex non scripta,* the *Posterior Analytics* from the *I Ching* (which appears to be an infinitely flexible operational matrix, for which authority is claimed on no other ground than that of its flexibility). In the light of such facts, he will not be unduly interested in dissolving the principle into its application, or in showing that the claim that it can be repeatedly abstracted and restated is false; it is not his business to convict the actors in his history of false consciousness, until they begin so to convict one another.

The historian is now recognizing the persistence in certain historical sequences of certain paradigms, institutionalized in certain texts. He recognizes that each application of a paradigm is unique, and that no paradigm can be altogether detached from its application; nevertheless, it is part of the character of a paradigm as he is using the word that it can be sufficiently detached from its application to be stated, and to be discussed in second-order language. If this can happen once, it can happen again, and you can step more than once into the same second-order river. To concede that this can happen more than once is to leave open for historical investigation the question of how many times it has happened in certain historical sequences, that is, how long these sequences have maintained a certain kind of continuity. It is certainly the case that the whole thrust and bias of his method, consisting as we have seen in the multiplication of agents, their acts, and the contexts they have acted in, lead him to suppose that any paradigm will be assimilated to contingency in a relatively *moyenne durée;* but should the *moyenne durée* turn out to have been relatively *longue,* he will feel surprised but not refuted. The longevity of paradigms is not predetermined, and the history of literate discourse has lasted nearer two millennia than three in most cultures where it is found.

The text may have had an author, and the paradigms it has conveyed over time may have been established in it by the intended performances of that author. Suppose – what we have seen to be improbable in most cases, but not impossible in all – that (a) it has conveyed relatively stable paradigms over a long period of time, and (b) these can be shown to have been continuous or congruent with – to have given effect to – intentions it can be said were those of the author. Is there not a sense in which it may be claimed that the author's intentions have continued to exert authority over that period; that they have continued to be effected; that the author "was doing" things long after his death? Clearly, the idiom of posthumous action must be partly figurative, but the figure may convey nothing more than that his intentions were being effected through the persistence of his text and the actions of those who kept it in being and authoritative. We might be able to add that his own speech acts and textual performances played a part in inducing others to regard them as authoritative and maintain them in paradigmatic form. The statement that we are still being acted upon (dare one say "influenced"?) by Plato, Confucius, Hegel, or Marx would then acquire something like a verifiable meaning; it could be inquired into, and the outcome of inquiry would not be predetermined.

VI

In enlarging the inquiry in the direction of these possibilities, I am of course working against the grain of a mode of investigation normally focused on the multiplicity of performances by a multiplicity of agents that discourse, including the persistence of texts, makes possible. To many critics this method seems alarmingly deconstructive of texts, of philosophy, of traditions, and even of authors. Once an author has completed his text (and that text has survived), it may be said that we possess it not merely as a matrix for the performance of diverse speech acts, but as a complex series of statements, perhaps extended over hundreds of printed pages, apparently produced by a single powerful mind concerned to argue at a high level of abstraction and organization, and therefore informed by the rhetorical, logical, or methodical unity its author imposed on it. There now appear students of the text whose concern is to discover the postulates or principles – not immediately apparent to the reading eye but calling for techniques of reconstitution – that endow the text with the unity it is presumed to have possessed or pursued.[24] If these students are concerned to recover the author's act or intention in endowing his text, or texts, with unity, they are asking a historical question to which there may be found an answer, though it is also a historical question whether the author had any such intention. It is one thing to be dealing

[24] See Howard Warrender, "Political Theory and Historiography: A Reply to Professor Skinner," *Historical Journal* XXII, 4 (1979), pp. 931–40.

with Thomas Hobbes, who claimed from the outset of his publications to be embarked upon a philosophical enterprise of a specific kind, and another to be dealing with Edmund Burke, who delivered speeches and wrote pamphlets on a variety of occasions in the course of an active political life. The claim that the latter's works are informed by conceptual and philosophical unity requires a different sort of justification from the same claim with respect to the former. Not all the great intelligences who have engaged in political discourse have engaged, directly or indirectly, in systematic political theorizing.

If, on the other hand, students appear who are in search of a principle on which the text may be endowed with unity irrespective of whether the author can be shown to have intended to proceed on any such principle, these students may have ceased to regard the text as a problem in the reconstruction of performance and may be looking at it only as a problem in conceptual resolution. If they say simply that the text can be made sense of in such a way, and that it does not matter to them whether the author or any previous reader has ever made sense of it in such a way, they are informing us that their philosophical enterprise does not oblige them to study the actions of any historical agent; after which they have only to abstain – and it may not be easy – from inadvertently speaking as if they are after all describing the actions of historical agents and writing history with the disengaged hand. To attend meetings of the Hume Society is to encounter many statements made in the preceding mode, and with such clarity that the only problem remaining is that of distinguishing between the word "Hume" used to denote an actor in history and the word "Hume" used to denote an actor in a philosophical scenario.

The historian invited to consider a text, or a corpus of texts, as a unified body of argument will ask by what acts, performed at what moments and in what contexts, the text was informed or endowed with the unity claimed for it; if he hears it asserted that there exists some postulate on which the text can be seen to possess such a unity, he will ask for information regarding the postulate's presence and action in history. He may learn that it was present in the *langue* that the author of the text found himself using, or that it was asserted by the author as he articulated his *parole*. In either case the historian will have returned the postulate to the context furnished by speech act, language, and discourse, but he will find himself asked by his interlocutor to consider the postulate in relation to the various speech acts performed by the author over the period of time and in the various contexts of speech action involved in the completion of the author's text or texts. He is, in other words, being asked to consider the author performing only those acts that were necessary to complete the text and endow it with whatever unity it possesses, that is, the author acting upon the text and upon his own perceptions and performances in effecting it. At this stage the historian will ask for evidence that the author both intended the production of a coherent text and understood what would constitute its coherence. Since the historian is self-trained to think of political speech as multilingual and polyvalent, he will want to be assured that the author had both the will and the means to organize his text as a single coherent *parole;* and since he is also self-trained to think of actions and perceptions as performed at discrete moments in time, he will want to know at what moments the author saw himself as organizing his text on the basis of the postulate alleged. Did the author establish the postulate as defining his intentions at the outset of his work? Did he come to see that there was such a postulate, and that he was giving effect to it, only as his work proceeded? Did he discover that he had organized his work on the basis of such a postulate only when his texts were complete and he viewed them in retrospect?[25] Any of these questions may be answered affirmatively, and they may be answered in various combinations; but the historian wants to be assured not only that they can be answered, but also that they are the right questions to ask about the text before him.

Let us now suppose that all these questions have been satisfactorily answered: that the author has been shown to have intended and effected the production of a body of writing systematically in accord with the postulates on which he intentionally based it. The latest moment at which he could have intended and effected this was the moment of completing the text, but at that moment, and down to it, the author has been considered only as in dialogue with his text and himself. We may have considered his interactions with the "languages" in which he wrote the text, and with other texts and authors to whom he responded in writing it; nevertheless, to ask about an author's performance in investing his text with unity is to ask about his performance in and upon his text and nothing more. What he "intended," what he "was doing," was closed off at the moment when the text was completed, and it is as if – it will help us greatly if it is the case that – the text can be considered a purely solitary act, an articulation of the author's consciousness and nothing more, a dialogue with himself and no one else. Let us suppose this to be the case: that the text lay undiscovered in a drawer and was read by no one for hundreds of years, until it was unearthed and published (such cases are rare but not unknown). We should then study it as a soliloquy or memorandum: a communication with the author's self. In the event, it does not cease to be an act but, in ceasing to be an act of communication with another, it becomes rather the record of a state, an indication that at a particular time the state of language permitted the articulation of particular states of consciousness. We do not simply pass from a private to a public language, because there are highly private writings by intensely solitary men – Guicciardini's works offer some examples – couched in highly public and rhetorical language, and although uncommunicated writings cannot be said to have changed language,

---

[25] If so, "what he was (had been) doing" was a question the historian himself found it necessary to ask.

there is no reason why they should not be said to have indicated that it was changing. Solilocutive writing does not depart from the history of discourse, but occupies a very special place within it; there is indeed a sense in which the more the text performs the function of expression or reflection, the more it enables us to look away from the history of speech and toward the history of thought. Since the study of political literature in history has been based on the paradigm of philosophy rather than of rhetoric, we have been accustomed to treat texts as philosophy: to isolate them as expressions of their authors' consciousness and to explore the states of consciousness they articulate. Since a great many texts are philosophical and were composed with that end in view, and since it is legitimate and valuable to treat almost any text as articulating a state of mind rather than as performing an act of communication, this method has been and will continue to be practiced to the improvement of our understanding. The demand that every text be considered, exclusively or primarily, as contributory to political action is, quite simply, wrong; perhaps it only seems to have been put forward.[26]

Yet authors communicate their articulations of consciousness. Not only has philosophy since its beginnings been as much dialogic as soliloscutive, but philosophers, having completed texts of so great complexity that we can read and analyze them only as self-contained, carry them to the copyist or the printer and let them loose on publics whose size and membership they cannot for long control; and there have been intensely solitary writers, seemingly concerned only with the self's introspection upon the self, who have not only caused their meditations to be printed but have done so with political as well as philosophical intentions. For one Guicciardini we can find a Montaigne, a La Rochefoucauld, a Rousseau;[27] even Guicciardini may have meant to communicate with other Guicciardini. At this point our study of the act of speech must become a study of the act of publication, which is not quite identical with it; for as we have seen, writing not intended for publication may be couched in public language and may even perform moves and make innovations within it. The act of publication ensures that these innovations will become known to others, but may initially attempt to control or limit who these shall be. The author who acts to procure a limited circulation for his writings is trying to delimit his "public"; one who commissions a printer to expose his works for sale on the market is not. Cases have been reported of authors whose works are written in "twofold" language, conveying an exoteric message to an open readership and at the same time an esoteric message to a closed one. We may even examine the case of an author who

---

[26] See Richard Ashcraft, "On the Problem of Methodology and the Nature of Political Theory," *Political Theory* III, 1 (1975), pp. 5–25, esp. 17–20; discussed in Mark Goldie, "Obligations, Utopias, and their Historical Context," *Historical Journal* XXVI, 3 (1983), pp. 727–46.

[27] See Nannerl O. Keohane, *Philosophy and the State in France* (Princeton, N.J., 1980). She characterizes as "individualism" that introspective mode of political thinking that is concerned with the identity and awareness of the self in political society.

withheld part of his works from publication and wonder what he "intended" by this act of noncommunication or disinformation, as David Wootton has lately done with the secret and irreligious jottings of Paolo Sarpi (but how did they come to be copied?).[28]

Closed-circuit publication and "secret writing" notwithstanding, the act of communication exposes one's writings to readers who will interpret them from standpoints not one's own, and the act of publication in the normal sense of "going public" abandons the attempt to determine who these readers shall be, while attempting to maximize the number of those on whom one's writings shall perform. It might be said, therefore, that publication as the attempt to determine the thoughts of posterity is necessarily self-defeating. From the moment of publication the deconstructions of history begin, and we are left to pursue those continua of interpretation, translation, and second-order discussion of interpretation and translation, which we so unsatisfactorily term "traditions" (John G. Gunnell has rightly warned us against supposing a "tradition" wherever we detect a sequence).[29] Here the historian I have described moves in, with his alertness to the selectivities of reading and interpretation, and his propensity to decompose the "history" of a text into the performance of many mutations in many idioms and contexts, for which the text at times appears little more than the matrix or holding pattern. But among the recurrent phenomena of interpretation we have already noted the habit of vesting texts and groups of texts with canonical authority, and we must look out not only for the deconstruction but also for the reconstitution of authoritative texts by readers, some of whom invest them with that coherence and unity which the historian regards with some suspicion, but which, it is not quite inconceivable, may turn out in some cases to have been fed into them by their authors. Dominick La Capra has called for a history of how texts considered as unities operate in history,[30] and we are prepared to regard texts as well as interpretative communities as vehicles of authority. It is because so many things can go on under the heading of "tradition" that we ought to be wary of using the word.

We have now separated, and subsequently recombined, the text as performing

---

[28] David Wootton, *Paolo Sarpi: Between Renaissance and Enlightenment* (Cambridge, 1983). He calls, *inter alia* (p. 4), for a "history of intellectual deception," not unlike the "secret writing" made famous by Leo Strauss. If such phenomena do not precisely have a history, they frequently occur in historical situations. Like Goldberg (n. 20, this chapter), Wootton is interested in the manipulative rather than the discursive possibilities of language; but you cannot manipulate all of a public all of the time.

[29] Gunnell, *Political Theory: Tradition and Interpretation,* pp. 85–90, and generally; see also the exchange of essays between Gunnell and the present author, "Political Theory, Methodology and Myth," *Annals of Scholarship* I, 4 (1981), pp. 3–62.

[30] Dominick La Capra, "Rethinking Intellectual History and Reading Texts," *History and Theory* XIX, 3 (1980), pp. 245–76. Reprinted in La Capra, *Rethinking Intellectual History: Texts, Contexts, Language* (Ithaca, N.Y., 1983).

an articulation of the author's consciousness and the text as performing an act of communication in a continuum of discourse involving other actors. It is these continua (sometimes misnamed "traditions") that the historian must study if he wants to understand the actions and responses, the innovations and events, the changes and processes, that constitute the history of discourse, though this is not to say that the text as isolated artifact will not furnish him with valuable information about what was going on in the history of the languages in which it was written. A great deal of his attention will therefore be focused on texts undergoing interpretation and deconstruction as they are absorbed into the history of discourse; however, this does not entail his denying that a text may have performed at certain moments in history with that unity that is claimed for it as art or philosophy. When the historian encounters a "great" text – as this author does once or twice in the essays that follow – he knows that the adjective indicates, first, that it has been accorded high authority or adversary status by actors in the history he is studying; second, that it has been recognized as possessing exceptional coherence and interest by critics, theorists, philosophers, and (now he become dubious) historians in the community of scholars to which he belongs. He knows further that it will be his business to move between exploring its structure as a synchronously existing artifact to exploring its occurrence and performance as an incident in a diachronously proceeding continuum of discourse. The fact that these two modes of reality are seldom identical constitutes what might be termed *das Second Treatiseproblem*.

VII

The continua of discourse, which exhibit plenty of abrupt discontinuities, occupy the center of the historian's attention and appear to him to be histories of language taking place in contexts furnished by the history of experience. There is a constant and justified demand that the two histories be connected: that the language used by actors in a society be made to yield information regarding what that society was experiencing, and – since we have come to accord something approaching absolute priority to social experience – that language be as far as possible presented as the effect of such experience. Here the historian is seen to concede a measure of autonomy to language, and this troubles those who cannot tell the difference between autonomy and abstraction. Because he perceives languages as being formed over time, in response to many external and internal pressures, he does not suppose that the language of the moment simply denotes, reflects, or is an effect of the experience of the moment. Rather, it interacts with experience; it supplies the categories, grammar, and mentality through which experience has to be recognized and articulated. In studying it the historian learns how the inhabitants of a society were capable of cognizing experience, what experiences they were capable of cognizing, and what responses to experience they were capable of articulating and consequently performing. As a historian of discourse, it is his business to study what happened in discourse (including theory) in the process of experience, and in this way, which is one among others, he learns a good deal about the experience of those he studies.

The historian is of course well aware that things happen to human beings before they are verbalized, though not before the humans possess means of verbalizing them, and that language can be seen changing under pressures that originate outside it. But this process takes time, and it is his business to study the processes by which humans acquire new means of verbalization and new ways of using those they already possess. They do this by engaging in discourse with one another, conducted through the medium of languages loaded with paradigms, conventions, usages, and second-order languages for discussing usages. This is enough to ensure that the process of responding to new experience takes time and must be broken down into many processes occurring in different ways and at different speeds. The old image in which it was stated that language (or consciousness) "reflects" society strikes the historian as paying insufficient attention to time. Language is self-reflective and talks largely about itself; the response to new experience takes the form of discovering and discussing new difficulties in language. Instead of supposing a single mirror reflecting happenings in an exterior world at the moment of their occurrence, it would be better to suppose a system of mirrors facing inward and outward at different angles, so that they reflect occurrences in the mirrored world largely through the diverse ways in which they reflect one another. Discussion between mirror watchers therefore has to do with how the mirrors reflect one another, even before it focuses on the possibility that there is something new in the field of vision. It would be better still to suppose that the mirrors are arranged diachronously as well as synchronously, so that while some of them share the same moment in time, others are located in its past and future. This would allow us to recognize that the perception of the new is carried out over time, and in the form of a debate about time; the historical animal deals with experience by discussing old ways of perceiving it, as a necessary preliminary to erecting new ways, which then serve as means of perceiving both the new experience and the old modes of perception.

The historian therefore expects the relation between language and experience to be diachronous, ambivalent, and problematic. The tension between old and new, between *langue* and *parole*, would be enough to ensure this, were it not for the additional fact that language games exist to be played by nonidentical players, so that even actors using the same words have to stop and inquire what they mean by them. This seems to account for the appearance of second-order languages (though other preconditions, such as literacy, may have to be met before these are socially possible), and it seems to ensure that, in the histories with

[margin annotation: difficult relationship between language & experience]

which he grows acquainted the normal relation of language to experience will be ambivalent, in the sense that words denote and are known to denote different things at the same time, and problematic, in the sense that debate about how they may be used to denote them is continuous. A society sophisticated enough to have second-order languages will normally be found responding to new experience by conducting debates about problems arising in its discourse. The historian of discourse will therefore have to work outward from the capacities for discourse enjoyed by his actors, toward what he sees (and they came to see) as new elements in their experience, and the intimations of their language may, or may never, intersect those of the language he employs to write the history of their experience. To translate the perceptions of Gerrard Winstanley into those of Christopher Hill is a most problematic enterprise, valiantly confronted.

What this reveals is the peculiar importance of that paralanguage described earlier, which the historian employs to explicate the implications of the language whose history, composed of the performances carried out in it, he is seeking to write. We now see that he employs this paralanguage in two concurrent but distinguishable ways. In the first place, he employs it to erect hypotheses; that is, he affirms that the language carried certain implications that both enlarged and defined the ways in which it could be used. He articulates these implications in order to show what the normal possibilities of the language were, so that should we encounter the anomalies and innovations that accompany paradigmatic change, we will be able to recognize them, reiterate them, and begin to see how they came to be performed. This provides the historian with a necessary matrix for dealing with those moments in which he sees being performed the utterances and responses, moves and countermoves, innovations and counterinnovations, of which a history of *paroles* performed in and upon *langues* has been held to consist. The propositions into which the matrix may be resolved are hypotheses in the sense that they state what the historian expects to have happened, and we may compare them with the preserved language of the texts in order to see if we believe it was what did happen. In the short term, the model provided by the paralanguage is quite manageable.

The long term, however, arises when the historian wishes to write diachronically and in the form of narrative: when, that is, he wishes to write a history of discourse in the form of the changing pattern of some language or constellation of languages, and their uses and potentialities, over a long period of time. He cannot stop to offer his hypotheses for testing each time an actor in his narrative makes a move; economy apart, he may wish to offer accounts of changes in language usage so compressed in meaning, yet so far extended over time, that they cannot be ascribed to the moves performed by identifiable actors at specific moments. He will be driven to write in terms that suggest an ongoing dialogue between the implications of the languages rendered explicit in his paralanguage, and to that extent his history will be ideal and will be written as if it had happened in the world the paralanguage delineates.

Examples will be found in the essays that follow. "Virtues, Rights, and Manners: A Model for Historians of Political Thought" supposes a dialogue between the concepts of "virtue" and "right," and between their implied postulates, to have gone on over some centuries in the context of a European political discourse imagined as widely distributed in space and relatively stable over time. The ideal character of this narrative, however, is circumscribed by the second part of its title, where it is clearly stated to be a model, that is, a set of generalized hypotheses forming a matrix in which, it is suggested, the performances of specific actors in the history of discourse may be situated, in order to see how far the model succeeds in explicating their actions. The model will also come the closer to being an account of reality as it becomes accepted that there was a mode of discourse common to Western Europe, in which the key terms and their implications recurred and were discussed; that is to say, it offers hypotheses concerning the being of a continuum as well as the performances of actors. Chapter 5, "Modes of Political and Historical Time in Early Eighteenth-Century England," employs a model procedure of a rather different sort; it supposes that the intellectual predicament of actors at the time prescribed can be characterized in certain terms and as arising from certain conditions, and that their performances can be interpreted as responding to this predicament with certain strategies said to have been available. The same procedure was followed in the opening chapters of the author's *The Machiavellian Moment*,[31] where a model situation was set up and certain empirically traceable histories, or continua of discourse, were said to emerge from it. That was, of course, no more than that common strategy in historical explanation, whereby a situation is selected and the behavior of actors are said to be intelligible in it. All such strategies expose hypotheses to the kind of criticism devised as appropriate to them.

A less easily defensible case is that of "The Varieties of Whiggism from Exclusion to Reform: A History of Ideology and Discourse," which forms Part III of this book. Here the attempt is not to characterize a single model or problem situation – other than the division between contending "Whig" ideologies after 1689 – and to affirm that what follows becomes intelligible in its light. The attempt is rather to characterize as many as possible – or, within the parameters of the essay, as many as is convenient – of the diverse idioms in which British political thought was conducted for the next century and a half, to trace the history of discourse in terms of the possibilities intimated by each idiom, and to use the resultant conversation was a commentary upon – but also by – the political culture in which it was conducted. There is circumscription: I select these

---

[31] *The Machiavellian Moment: Florentine Political Thought and the Atlantic Republican Tradition* (Princeton, N.J., 1975).

and not other idioms as those in which discourse went on; but the "model" is so multiplex that it may not deserve the name, and the reader is bound to feel that the conversation presented is not between individual or even group actors, but between ideal and hypostatized modes of speech. Two points may be made here. In the first place, I will claim that the explanatory and hypothetical matrix is not lost; it is still being affirmed that the performances of specific actors will fit into the patterns of discourse set out here, so that when they diverge we shall understand them better. In the second place, I will reiterate that the more diachronous the history, the more rapidly it moves through time and the succession of performances, the more necessary we find it to abridge and intensify it in this way. The figures[32] of metahistory become harder to avoid, and the narrative becomes more ideal precisely because it is more tentative. A history of Whig political discourse in ten volumes would have room for many more individual performances and would test the hypotheses advanced here as exhaustively as the heart could desire. It would also be just as enjoyable to write. The relation of reconstruction to deconstruction is not that of symphony to goblin.[33]

VIII

I conclude here with a few remarks on the "state of the art" that is British history. In *The Machiavellian Moment* I emphasized the strength of the Old Whig and Tory, Commonwealth and Country reaction against the financial (by extension "commercial"), oligarchic, and imperial regime that came into being after 1688 and 1714, and I contended that the case for this regime and the society that accompanied it had to be built on new modes of argument, hammered out with difficulty in the face of opposing paradigms. Some readers have objected that this case was nevertheless made, though it is hard to see how this can be an objection; one suspects that their real complaint is that *The Machiavellian Moment* presents the rise of a commercial ideology as contingent, whereas they want it to have been primordial – a straight success story, the natural and undistorted accompaniment to the growth of commercial society. I claim in Chapter 3 to have written an account more dialectical and less Whiggish than that. At all events, the essays that follow are concerned mainly with authors of the eighteenth century who expounded the values of Whig commerce and Whig aristocracy, and the rapid modernization of both society and social understanding that the oligarchic regime witnessed and performed. They are concerned to explore, and in some ways dispel, the paradox that oligarchy and modernity were related and not antithetical.

[32] See Hayden White, *The Tropics of Discourse: Essays in Cultural Criticism* (Baltimore, 1978).
[33] I mean, of course, the goblin heard walking over the universe, and emptying it of meaning, during the playing of the symphony in E. M. Forster's *Howard's End*.

Being a study of historical Whiggism, the book is in some respects a Whig history. It accepts that Whig rule is a crucial fact of modern British history; the regime consolidated (at high cost) the parliamentary form of government, and it established that imperial and exterior relation to Europe that Britain is still dazed by having lost. It expresses no nostalgia for the Whig order, which was described in deeply ironic tones by most of its supporters, but it takes that order seriously: not seriously enough for liberal Marxists, but too seriously for Tory Marxists. The Tory mind of the eighteenth century was a strange blend of Jacobite and republican ideas, and much of that ambivalence survives in the anti-Whig historiography of the present day. These essays join most recent interpreters in presenting the oligarchic period as involved in a fermenting and ungovernable debate over itself; "the deep peace of the Augustans" is a vanished historians' dream, and we study the era in which English and Scottish writers for the first time engaged in fully secular discussion of their society and its destinies, from which point British intellectual history can begin to be written. Yet to present an oligarchic regime as a polity of discussion and self-criticism is in some ways paradoxical, and the historian of discourse is always accused of maximizing the importance of his subject. Those who frame this accusation, however, seldom ask what the presence of discourse means.

Historians who stress, with much justice, the extent to which the Whig regime was a dictatorship by its ruling groups and classes are tempted to see the ruled as repressed and silent; deprived of the means of articulating a radical consciousness, they must accept the speech of their rulers or formulate modes of symbolic and semiotic opposition outside it (hence the debate as to how far crime was a mode of social protest).[34] But this oligarchy was notoriously incompetent at thought control; the nobs and the mobs sometimes shouted and sometimes shot at one another, and we do not have to regard elite and popular culture as incapable of intertraffic. It is true that the great antinomian radicals of the Interregnum appear to have been little known in the eighteenth century – though this might well be further investigated – but enough of the Good Old Cause was kept alive by some very unlikely groups in opposition to make the extent of Tory contribution to later political radicalism a very real question. When the elite is debating its own size, composition, and relation to the populace, the populace may very well be listening, and the Whig oligarchy was not a ruling class, but an oligarchy within the ruling classes, which generated such debate.

The last point is relevant also to those historians of the right wing – far to the right of Edmund Burke – who mistrust the assignment of any role to the debate

---

[34] See Douglas Hay, Peter Linebaugh, John G. Rule, E. P. Thompson, and Cal Winslow, *Albion's Fatal Tree: Crime and Society in Eighteenth-Century England* (London, 1975); John Brewer and John Styles, eds., *An Ungovernable People: The English and their Law in the Seventeenth and Eighteenth Centuries* (New Brunswick, N.J., 1980).

over principles. Post-Namierite historiography is in danger of settling into a belief that there is no reality except the reality of high politics, and that the practice of high politics always succeeds in reducing discourse to insignificance: a belief, not far from a religion, currently set out in what has become the Peterhouse manner – stern, nonrefutable, and arcane. But had aristocratic politics in England been so austere and insolent a domination that its practice was really impervious to discourse, there really would have been a revolution against it. Certainly we can examine the practice of high politics with such minuteness that we do not see the articulation of issues playing any part in it. Although this kind of politics was being practiced in Whig Britain, there was constant and intensive debate as to why it was going on, what its social preconditions and effects were, and whether it was necessary to be governed in this way at all; and in this debate, the aristocratic regime was as animatedly defended, and by as powerful minds and arguments, as it was criticized. There was discourse as well as practice, and discourse must sooner or later furnish practice with one of its contexts, which is why eighteenth-century theorists constantly debated the role of opinion in government.[35]

Because Whig Britain was a highly discursive polity, an oligarchy in which the nature of oligarchy was debated in a public space larger than the oligarchy, there can be a history of Whig discourse. There is a further sense in which the history of discourse is by its nature what we know as a "Whig history." It is a history of utterance and response by relatively autonomous agents. The history of discourse is not a modernist history of consciousness organized around such poles as repression and liberation, solitude and community, false consciousness and species being. It looks at a world in which the speaker can frame his own speech and the utterance cannot wholly determine the response. The historian's world is populated by agents responsible even when they are venal or paranoid, and he distances himself from them as his equals, distinguishing the narration of their actions from the performance of his own. To write history in this way is ideologically liberal and he may as well admit it; he is presupposing a society in which one can utter and another utter a reply, made from a standpoint not that of the first performer. There have been and are societies in which this condition is met to varying degrees, and these are the societies in which discourse has a history.

[35] See J. A. W. Gunn, "Public Spirit to Public Opinion," in his *Beyond Liberty and Property: The Process of Self-Recognition in Eighteenth-Century Political Thought* (Kingston and Montreal, 1983).

PART I

2

◁ ═══ ▷

Virtues, rights, and manners
A model for historians of political thought

The history of political thought is traditionally deeply affected by the study of law. In recent years, however, there have been some interesting undulations and oscillations. Modes of talking about politics which were strikingly remote from the language of the law have emerged into historical prominence; and though there are signs that the historiography of political thought is now moving back into what I shall argue is the law-centered paradigm under which it has traditionally been conducted, it is an article of faith with us all that the needle does not return to its starting point, and some modification of the paradigm is therefore to be expected. The title of this article is designed to circumscribe the modification which may have occurred.

Consult any classical work on this subject – Carlyle or Sabine or Wolin – and we shall find that the history of political thought, at any rate from the Stoics to the Historicists, is organized to a very high degree around the notions of God, nature, and law. The individual is looked on as inhabiting a cosmos regulated by rational and moral principles, essential to its being, which are of the nature of *nomos,* and to these philosophically perceived or divinely revealed systems man-made bodies of jurisprudence are assimilated. God Himself is looked on as a *lex loquens,* and even His role as the author of inscrutable grace does not much detract from this image. Philosophy and faith become modes of cognizing and acknowledging law, with the result that jurisprudence gives access to all but the most sublime forms of intellectual experience. All this is familiar to the point of being most jejunely expressed, and it is a paradigm which very effectively organizes a great deal of highly perdurable knowledge. Yet there are elements of relevant historical reality which it does not fit and may distort – to say nothing of the

From J. G. A. Pocock, "Virtues, Rights, and Manners: A Model for Historians of Political Thought," *Political Theory,* vol. 9, no. 3, pp. 353–68, © 1981 Sage Publications, Inc.; reprinted by permission.

fact that there are civilizations like the Chinese which it obliges us simply to ignore.[1] Thinkers appear who, like Machiavelli, bear no relation to the natural-law paradigm and must therefore be presumed to have been negating or subverting it. Changes in the dominant styles of political thought are brought within the paradigm and treated as evidence of its destruction from without or its exhaustion from within, little attention being paid to the possibility that perhaps they did not belong with it in the first place. Normative presumptions make their appearance, and the historian is driven either to celebrate or to deplore the mutation of naturalism into historicism; while at the center of the process appears a tormented yet oddly triumphant entity by the name of liberalism, denounced by the naturalists as insufficiently natural and by the historicists as insufficiently historical, vindicated by some of its defenders on grounds robustly independent of either nature or history, yet accorded by all three – in consequence of their centralizing concern with it – a place in history a good deal more central (I shall argue) than it has in fact occupied.

I have caused a platoon of straw men to countermarch before us, yet I do not think I have done much violence to the organizing presuppositions within which the history of political thought has been conducted. Recently, however – and in pursuit of a now prevalent technique of discovering and recapitulating the vocabularies and idioms in which political thought has been articulated in the course of its history – there have arisen presentations of that history in which the natural-law paradigm occupies only a part of the stage, and we learn to speak in idioms not reducible to the conjoined languages of philosophy and jurisprudence. I propose to recount parts of this newly constructed history, and then to ask some questions about the role of law in forming the political outlook of the Western mind.

The central occurrence in this recent historiography has been the crucial role accorded to what is variously termed civic humanism or classical republicanism.[2] I continue to feel some preference for the former term in spite of the numerous objections made to it; these arise from the confusions occasioned by the circumstance that there are nine-and-sixty ways of using the word humanism and a strong desire to consolidate them, with the result that whenever one scholar employs the term civic humanism, another will object that humanism wasn't

---

[1] See, most recently, Kung-chuan Hsiao, A History of Chinese Political Thought. Volume I: From the Beginnings to the Sixth Century A.D. Trans. F. W. Mote (Princeton, N.J.: Princeton University Press, 1979).

[2] Hans Baron, The Crisis of the Early Italian Renaissance, 2nd edition (Princeton, N.J.: Princeton University Press, 1966); J. G. A. Pocock, The Machiavellian Moment (Princeton, N.J.: Princeton University Press, 1975); "The Machiavellian Moment Revisited: A Study in History and Ideology," Journal of Modern History LIII, 1 (1981), pp. 49–72. Quentin Skinner, The Foundations of Modern Political Thought. Volume I: The Renaissance. Volume II: The Age of Reformation (Cambridge, Eng: Cambridge University Press, 1978).

always civic. Nevertheless, the affirmation of classical republicanism has something which is humanist about it; it entails the affirmation that *homo* is naturally a citizen and most fully himself when living in a *vivere civile,* and humanist techniques of scholarship and reschematizations of history are mobilized around this affirmation whenever it is made.

What concerns me in this essay, however, is to set the civic humanist mode of discoursing about politics alongside the philosophical and juristic, since it is here that recent historiography has been most interestingly problematic. Though I see Baron's book as a crucial beginning, I am not obliged thereby to review the controversies to which it gave rise; however, one objection raised to his thesis, by Riesenberg[3] and others, was that citizenship in the Italian republics was for the most part defined in jurisdictional and jurisprudential terms, rather than in terms arising from a humanist vocabulary of *vita activa* and *vivere civile.* An Italian commune was a juristic entity, inhabited by persons subject to rights and obligations; to define these and to define the authority that protected them was to define the citizen and his city, and the practice as opposed to the principles of citizenship was overwhelmingly conducted in this language.

Those concerned to expound and explore the language of classical republicanism replied that while this was undeniably true, the two vocabularies were outstandingly discontinuous. Francesco Guicciardini, for example, was a doctor of civil law and had practiced as such; yet in his writings the language of republican virtue is regularly if self-destructively employed, while the language of jurisprudence hardly ever appears, least of all as a tool of normative political theory. Something very similar may be said of Machiavelli, though he was not to our knowledge trained to the law. The argument that Guicciardini and Machiavelli were impractical ideologues out of touch with civic reality does not seem to carry conviction, though there is nothing that a systematically anti-intellectual historian may not be expected to argue sooner or later; and though there is an attempt now going forward to interpret Machiavelli in the context of Roman civil law, it will have to avoid the pitfall of arguing that while he never says anything which is either about the law or expressed in its vocabulary, his silence is evidence of an intent to destroy jurisprudence by ignoring it and talking in other terms.

We have, then, two vocabularies in which political thought has been conducted that are markedly discontinuous with one another because they premise different values, encounter different problems, and employ different strategies of speech and argument. Their discontinuity becomes the more striking when we see them used in the same context and to congruent purposes; and indeed Skinner in the first volume of his *Foundations* has shown that from the late thirteenth century the vindication of Italian republican independence was simultaneously

---

[3] Peter N. Riesenberg, "Civism and Roman Law in Fourteenth-Century Italian Society," in *Explorations in Economic History,* VII, 1–2 (1969), pp. 237–254.

conducted in the republican and juristic modes. From Bartolus onwards, means were found of arguing that a republic was *sibi princeps* and had acquired *imperium mixtum* or *merum* over its citizens and territory; from Brunetto Latini onwards, it was argued that a republic might demand *libertas* as the prerequisite of exercising for itself and its citizens that civic independence and virtue which formed the finest earthly life for man. The word *libertas* might be found in both contexts, yet there was a profound distinction between its use in a juristic and in a humanist context, one connected – as has been pointed out by Hexter[4] – with the distinction between liberty in the negative and in the positive sense.

Law, one may generalize, is of the empire rather than the republic. If one argues in the tradition of Bartolus, the city acquires *libertas* in the sense of *imperium;* possibly it reacquires it from a *princeps* or *imperator;* it acquires a freedom to practice its own laws. If the citizen acquires *libertas*, he acquires a "freedom of the city" – the original meaning of the French *bourgeoisie* – freedom to practice his own affairs protected by the rights and immunities which the law affords him, and also by the *imperium* which decrees and enforces the laws. But the *libertas* of this *bourgeois* is not enough to make him a citizen in the Greek sense of one who rules and is ruled. Guicciardini – and here perhaps (though not certainly) he was thinking as a doctor of laws – could point out that the *popolo* could be said to enjoy *libertà* from the oppression of powerful *grandi*, even when they did not enjoy it in the sense of *partecipazione* in the *governo dello stato*.[5] It could be argued of course that they were most sure of it in the former sense when they also had it in the latter, but Guicciardini could think of other ways of constituting a public authority powerful enough to deter private oppression; what mattered about a *repubblica* was that its authority should be *pubblica*. Nevertheless, to lower the level of citizen participation in a republic could end by reconstituting it as a legal monarchy, in which every man's *libertas*, even his *bourgeoisie*, was protected by law which an absolute sovereign administered. In the last moments of his life King Charles I was heard to proclaim from the scaffold that the people's liberty under law had nothing to do with their having a voice in the government. The juristic presentation of liberty was therefore negative; it distinguished between *libertas* and *imperium*, freedom and authority, individuality and sovereignty, private and public. This is its greatest role in the history of political thought, and it performs this role by associating liberty with right or *ius*.

The republican vocabulary employed by *dictatores*, rhetoricians and humanists articulated the positive conception of liberty: it contended that *homo*, the *animale politicum*, was so constituted that his nature was completed only in a *vita activa*

---

[4] J. H. Hexter, review of *The Machiavellian Moment* in *History and Theory*, XVI (1977), pp. 306–37, reprinted as chapter 6 of *On Historians: Reappraisals of Some of the Makers of Modern History* (Cambridge, MA: Harvard University Press, 1979).
[5] Pocock, *The Machiavellian Moment*, pp. 126, 142–3, 146 n. 59, 232, 254.

practiced in a *vivere civile,* and that *libertas* consisted in freedom from restraints upon the practice of such a life. Consequently, the city must have *libertas* in the sense of *imperium,* and the citizen must be participant in the *imperium* in order to rule and be ruled. Only such a political system, said Guicciardini, was an exception to the general rule that government was a form of violent domination over others.[6] But it was not central to this assertion that the citizen should claim rights as against the *imperium* in which he was himself participant; and for this reason Thomas Hobbes in the next century declared that the *libertas* emblazoned on the towers of Lucca did not prevent that city exercising absolute sovereignty over the lives of its citizens.[7]

James Harrington retorted that Hobbes had mistaken the issue, and the *libertas* of the Lucchese citizen consisted in his membership of the republic – he once called it "King People" – which exercised the sovereignty.[8] The two men were talking past one another. Hobbes argued juridically: he held that there were rights, that rights constituted sovereignty, that rights could not thereafter be pleaded against sovereignty. But the vocabulary of the law is almost wholly lacking from Harrington's discourse. He argued as a humanist: he held that there was in the human animal something planted there by God, which required fulfillment in the practice of active self-rule, and to this something – which he was prepared to call sometimes "nature," sometimes "reason" and sometimes "government" – he was also prepared to give the altogether crucial name "virtue." It is central to the argument I am developing that "virtue" cannot be satisfactorily reduced to the status of right or assimilated to the vocabulary of jurisprudence.

"Virtue" is a word with a long history and a great many meanings. It could be used synonymously with "nature," "essence" or "essential characteristic" – as when Molière's doctoral candidate says that opium puts you to sleep because it has a dormitive virtue; it could bear the Roman-Machiavellian meaning of a capacity to act in confrontation with *fortuna;* it could mean little more than a fixed propensity to practice one of several ethical codes, though this propensity was usually said to require enhancement by Socratic philosophy or Christian grace or both. As developed in the republican vocabulary, it seems to have borne several further emphases. It could signify a devotion to the public good; it could signify the practice, or the preconditions of the practice, of relations of equality between citizens engaged in ruling and being ruled; and lastly, since citizenship was above all a mode of action and of practicing the active life, it could signify that active ruling quality – practiced in republics by citizens equal with one another and devoted to the public good – which confronted *fortuna* and was known to Re-

---

[6] Ibid., pp. 124–5 and nn. 21–22.
[7] Thomas Hobbes, *Leviathan* (London, 1651), Book II, ch. 18, in any edition.
[8] James Harrington, *The Commonwealth of Oceana,* 1656. J. G. A. Pocock (ed.), *The Political Works of James Harrington* (Cambridge, Eng.: Cambridge University Press, 1977), pp. 170–1, 229.

naissance Italians as *virtù*, but which, as Machiavelli was to show, entailed practice of a code of values not necessarily identical with the virtues of a Christian. The last-mentioned were not necessarily political at all, which is why Montesquieu, in the preface to the *Esprit des Lois*, found it desirable to distinguish between *vertu morale, vertu chrétienne*, and *vertu politique;* the third of these was formally unlike the others and entailed a devotion to equality before the laws of a republic.[9] But we must now ask in what sense it is that the word "laws" has just been used, which is part of the problem of the sense in which the word *lois* was used by Montesquieu.

Virtue as devotion to the public good approached identification with a concept of justice; if the citizens were to practice a common good, they must distribute its components among themselves, and must even distribute the various modes of participating in its distribution. Aristotelian, Polybian, and Ciceronian analysis had shown that these modes were highly various and capable of being combined in a diversity of complex patterns; political science in the sense of the science of *politeia* took this as its subject matter. Moreover, a particular mode of participation might be seen as appropriate to the specialized social individual: to be proper to him, to be his propriety or property. Ideas of *suum cuique*, of distribution and of justice were therefore inherent in the civic republican tradition. But there were a number of senses in which the republican or political conception of virtue exceeded the limits of jurisprudence and therefore of justice as a jurist conceived it.

The notion of ruling and being ruled entailed a notion of equality to which that of distribution was not altogether adequate. When one had been accorded the share or role in the political-distributive process appropriate to one's social personality and another had been accorded his, it might be said that *cuique* had been accorded *suum;* but the concept of ruling and being ruled demanded that each of them should recognize that though by any standard but one the shares accorded each were commensurate but unequal, there was a criterion of equality (in ruling and being ruled) whereby each remained the other's equal and they shared in the possession of a common, public personality. While this equality presupposed both distribution and justice, there was a sense in which it transcended them and was not distributable.

If *partecipazione* was distributed according to socially specialized needs and nothing else, there would (said the advocates of republican virtue) be no *res publica* – in Aristotle's terms, there would be no *polis* – in which participation, equality, and ruling and being ruled were possible; to distribute public authority as a matter of private right was to them the classic definition of corruption, and under corruption there would in the end be no rights at all. Equality was a moral impera-

[9]Charles Secondat, baron de Montesquieu, *De l'Esprit des Lois*, 1751 *(Oeuvres Complètes*, Paris: Gallimard, 1949), p. 4.

tive, not as a matter of ensuring *quisque*'s right to *suum* – though it did discharge that function among others – but as the only means of ensuring *res publica:* of ensuring that *imperium* should be truly public, and not private masquerading as public.

The republic or *politeia* solved the problem of authority and liberty by making *quisque* participant in the authority by which he was ruled; this entailed relations of equality which made in fact extremely stern demands upon him, but by premising that he was *kata phūsin* formed to participate in such a citizenship it could be said that it was his "nature," "essence," or "virtue" to do so. But nature may be developed, but cannot be distributed; you cannot distribute a *telos,* only the means to it; virtue cannot therefore be reduced to matter of right. The laws of a republic – the *lois* obeyed by Montesquieu's *vertu politique* – were therefore far less *regulae juris* or modes of conflict resolution than they were *ordini* or "orders"; they were the formal structure within which political nature developed to its inherent end. This is the meaning of Harrington's dictum: "Good orders make evil men good and bad orders make good men evil."[10] He said this not because he did not believe that men were by nature good and political, but because he did.

It begins to look, however, as if the characteristic tendency of jurisprudence was to lower the level of participation and deny the premise that man is by nature political. One might argue that this is because the overwhelming preoccupation of the jurist is with that which can be distributed, with things and rights; if in *suum cuique* we read *suum* as an adjective, the unstated nouns are *res* and *ius.* There is much to be said regarding the meanings which *res* can assume in the juristic vocabulary and the history of those meanings; but for the moment we may develop the contention that since law is of the empire rather than the republic, its attention is fixed on *commercium* rather than *politicum.* As the *polis* and *res publica* declined toward the level of municipality, two things happened: the universe became pervaded by law, the locus of whose sovereignty was extra-civic, and the citizen came to be defined not by his actions and virtues, but by his rights to and in things. We must resist the temptation to overdefine *res* as material objects; but one major value of jurisprudence in the history of mental culture has been its insistence upon, and enrichment of our understanding of, the thick layers of social and material reality by which the *animale politicum* is surrounded and the complex normative life which he must lead in distributing and otherwise managing the things composing these many layers.

Jurisprudence reinforced by rhetoric – it was in the republic that the two tended to become enemies – was the Renaissance mind's main key to understanding the world of socialized things. In a recent essay, Donald Kelley has suggested

[10] Harrington, *Oceana; Works,* p. 838.

that it was the legal humanists of that era who inaugurated a modern understanding of history, and that the role of civic humanists has been overstated.[11] It is not exactly news, but of course it is true, that the lawyers and not the republicans were the first social historians.[12] It has always been the case against the classical citizen that he is at heart a tragic hero, unsafe to associate with, who insists that he is living in the realm of freedom and not that of necessity. This is why he is concerned with nondistributable goods like equality and virtue, and it is also why he is constantly confronted with *fortuna*. In *The Machiavellian Moment*, I was concerned to study the material foundations – arms first and property after – which he found it necessary that virtue should have in the realm of necessity.

I am allowing my language to become Arendtian because I am interested in the possibility that jurisprudence can be said to be predominantly social, concerned with the administration of things and with human relations conducted through the mediation of things, as opposed to a civic vocabulary of the purely political, concerned with the unmediated personal relations entailed by equality and by ruling and being ruled. I am also a non-Marxist interested in finding circumstances under which Marxist language can be employed with validity, and I am intrigued by the connection we seem to be uncovering between law, liberalism, and *bourgeoisie*. "With a great price bought I this freedom," says the Roman officer in *Acts* 21 according to the Authorized Version;[13] but in the French translation published at Geneva in 1588 he says: *"j'ay acquis ceste bourgeoisie avec une grande somme d'argent."* He is talking about citizenship in the limited sense of a negative liberty to enjoy one's life and goods in immunity from arbitrary action by servants of the prince (he has just discovered that he cannot flog St. Paul because the latter enjoys *bourgeoisie romaine* too). We are discovering (1) that liberty defined by law invests the citizen with rights but no part in *imperium*; (2) that law discriminates between the *libertas* which it guarantees to the citizen and the *imperium* or *auctoritas* of the prince or magistrate who administers the law; (3) that the law defines the citizen in terms of the *ius ad rem* and *ius in re* which he acquires through his role in the possession, conveyance, and administration of things. Civil law, then, presents us with possessive individualism in a form long predating early modern capitalism, and it presents us with an ancient form of that separation and recombination of authority and liberty which political theorists term liberalism. It is of no small interest to find the word *bourgeoisie* employed to denote a negative citizenship, consisting of the possession and transference of things subject to law and sovereign authority; for this casts light upon

---

[11] Donald R. Kelley, "Civil Science in the Renaissance; Jurisprudence Italian Style," *The Historical Journal* XXII, 4 (1979), pp. 777–794.

[12] J. G. A. Pocock, *The Ancient Constitution and the Feudal Law* (Cambridge, Eng.: Cambridge University Press, 1957); Donald R. Kelley, *The Foundations of Modern Historical Scholarship: Language, Law and History in the French Renaissance* (New York: Columbia University Press, 1970).

[13] Hexter, *On Historians*, pp. 295–296.

that little-studied subject, the history of the noun and concept *bourgeoisie* before
it acquired its Marxist meaning.

Social first and political after, the civil and common law define individuals as
possessors by investing them with right and property in things, and ultimately
(as in Locke) in themselves. They define law itself as Janus-faced, because it is at
one and the same time the right of the subject and the command of the prince.
In a recent remarkable study of *Natural Rights Theories: Their Origin and Development,* Richard Tuck has emphasized the extent to which individuals were invested
with rights that they might surrender them absolutely to the sovereign.[14] He is
still playing one pole of the juristic magnet against the other, and is recounting
with renewed sophistication the classical history of what we have come to term
liberalism: the story of how rights became the precondition, the occasion, and
the effective cause of sovereignty, so that sovereignty appeared to be the creature
of the rights it existed to protect. It is impossible to deny that this is the principal
theme of the history of early modern political thought. But it has long been the
principal criticism of the liberal synthesis that because it defined the individual
as right-bearer and proprietor, it did not define him as possessing a personality
adequate to participation in self-rule, with the result that the attempt to ground
sovereignty in personality was not thoroughly carried out. I do not intend to use
history as a means of exploring this normative criticism; but I shall investigate
some historiographic consequences of the discovery that alongside the history of
liberalism, which is a matter of law and right, there existed throughout the early
modern period a history of republican humanism, in which personality was considered in terms of virtue.

In *The Foundations of Modern Political Thought,* Skinner opened up a thirteenth-
and fourteenth-century scene in which the jurist and humanist vindications of
republican liberty were conducted side by side, as far as we can see without
overlapping and apparently without colliding. He carried his exploration of civic
humanist politics as far as 1530, when this form of thought is held to have been
eclipsed with the last Florentine republic; and after a study of the more Ciceronian humanism of England and the more juristic humanism of France, he trans-
posed the second volume of his history into the key prescribed by the law-centered paradigm. That is, it became his business to deal with the themes of relations
between the ecclesiastical and civil authorities, the revolt against the Catholic
view of the divine order, and the problem of resistance within the civil order.
These questions were predominantly discussed in the vocabularies of law; and
even their philosophical matrix was one which presupposed that the truths of the
divine order were to be described as laws, and proceeded to ask whether these
laws were known to us as aspects of the divine nature or as commands of the

---

[14] Richard Tuck, *Natural Rights Theories: Their Origins and Development* (Cambridge, Eng.: Cambridge
University Press, 1980).

divine will. Skinner emphasized the historical role of the Ockhamist and Sorbonnist adoption of the latter position, and showed the ways in which it was conducive to proto-Protestant theses concerning man's relation to God, to Stoic rather than Aristotelian views of the origin of the civil order, and to theories of the locus of political authority in which choices between absolutist, populist, and individualist alternatives tended to become starker.[15] He was thus able to conclude his book at a point where theories of the state, of resistance to the state, and of civil society as the ground of such resistance, had become consolidated in their early modern forms.

This enterprise could be conducted within the requirements of the law-centered paradigm, and did not require much allusion to the vocabulary of republican virtue. It is true that when Machiavelli was read by jurists and scholastics, he tended to emerge in the company of Ockham, Marsilius, and Luther, and there are Spanish Thomists who sought to refute him and them in a single package. But to do this it was necessary to translate Machiavelli into a language he had altogether ignored; whether he intended anything by ignoring it is a question past solution. The point here is that, if there is an independently evolving vocabulary of republican virtue, it is not necessary to trace its history in order to deal with that of the controversies pursued in Skinner's second volume; and because his history of republican thought effectively concludes about 1530, and his book as a whole comes to an end about 1590, he does not reach the point where republican virtue somewhat unexpectedly resurfaced in the otherwise law-centered, king-centered, and God-centered thinking of the Anglophone north. There are good reasons for this hiatus, yet I continue to lament it; for we need some answers to the question which Hexter has characteristically phrased as "how the devil" did this happen?[16]

To write the history of political thought in law-centered terms – which is largely equivalent to writing it as the history of liberalism – is, as we have seen, paradigmatically enjoined; and to contend, as is done here, that the languages of right and virtue are not readily interchangeable is to make the latter appear an intruder and anomaly in a field defined by the former. There are signs – not, however, to be found in Skinner – of an impulse to ignore the civic humanist paradigm or to assimilate it to the juristic. Kelley's essay suggests that civic humanism has had its fair share of attention, and we should now get back to the serious business of studying jurisprudence; Tuck, too, strives to bring the republican image within the rubric of civil and natural law. He seizes on the construction, by the Dutch theorists Pieter de la Court and Baruch Spinoza, of a classical republic out of a jurist's state of nature, and suggests that I would have had to

[15] J. G. A. Pocock, "Reconstructing the Traditions: Quentin Skinner's Historians' History of Political Thought," *The Canadian Journal of Political and Social Theory* III, 3 (1979), pp. 95–113.
[16] Hexter, *On Historians*, p. 288.

modify my conclusions if I had taken account of these writers.[17] It has been shown, however, by Haitsma Mulier that they were polemicists of the States party, anxious to invest the republic – i.e., the city or province – with sovereignty, and therefore going back to the creation of *jus* in a state of nature as a means of establishing its *majestas* rather than its *virtus*.[18]

Prior at any rate to the Scottish jurisprudence of the eighteenth century – on which we await forthcoming work by James Moore,[19] Nicholas Phillipson and others – and to comparable developments in France and in the thought of Rousseau, it seems highly important to stress that the two modes remained incommensurate. Virtue was not reducible to right, and if a full-bodied republic should be found emerging from the jurist's state of nature, it was for the less than republican purpose of creating and transferring the rights which were all that a state of nature could generate. Populism, therefore, which arose from investing a *populus* with *dominium, jus,* and *imperium,* was linguistically and politically distinct from republicanism, which arose from investing them with *virtus.* The former was in principle likely to generate *bourgeoisie,* the latter the *vivere civile;* and much confusion exists because the German language uses the same word to denote "bourgeois" and "citizen."

Viewing the historiographical field in North American perspective, I am further aware that to reassert the law-centered paradigm may have the effect of maintaining the liberal paradigm in a form which I have come to find misleading. There is a conventional wisdom, now taught to students, to the effect that political theory became "liberal" – whatever that means, and whether or not for more or less Marxist reasons – about the time of Hobbes and Locke, and has in America remained so ever since. I find this a serious distortion of history,[20] not because Hobbes and Locke did not take part in a great remodeling of the relation of right to sovereignty, conducted within the premises of the law-centered paradigm, but because to study that paradigm and nothing else leads to a radical misunderstanding of the roles in history played by both liberalism and jurisprudence, as well as of the relations between right and virtue with which this article has been concerned. I propose in conclusion to offer what I consider a better historical interpretation, which will permit me to deal with the third term of the triad composing my title: the concept of "manners."

[17] Tuck, *Natural Rights Theories,* p. 141, n. 58.

[18] E. O. G. Haitsma Mulier, *The Myth of Venice and Dutch Republican Thought in the Seventeenth Century* (Assen: Van Gorcum, 1980).

[19] James Moore, "Locke and the Scottish Jurists," distributed by the Conference for the Study of Political Thought in "John Locke and the Political Thought of the 1680s; papers presented at a symposium sponsored by the Conference for the Study of Political Thought and the Folger Institute for Renaissance and Eighteenth-Century Studies," 1980.

[20] J. G. A. Pocock, "The Myth of John Locke and the Obsession with Liberalism," in J. G. A. Pocock and Richard Ashcraft, *John Locke* (Los Angeles: Clark Memorial Library, 1980); and ch. 3, this volume.

Hobbes's work coincides in point of time with Harrington's, which played a leading role in introducing concepts of republican virtue into England; and Locke's *Treatises* are closely associated, and yet cannot be connected, with the establishment of the eighteenth-century Whig commercial regime and the reaction against it in the name of virtue. We may endorse the judgment of Skinner and Dunn that Locke's work is "the classic text of radical Calvinist politics"[21] – which were certainly constructed within the law-centered paradigm – and yet add the suggestion that this was a seventeenth-century enterprise, and that Locke's politics mark the close of one age rather than the beginning of another. From 1688 to 1776 (and after), the central question in Anglophone political theory was not whether a ruler might be resisted for misconduct, but whether a regime founded on patronage, public debt, and professionalization of the armed forces did not corrupt both governors and governed; and corruption was a problem in virtue, not in right, which could never be solved by asserting a right of resistance. Political thought therefore moves decisively, though never irrevocably, out of the law-centered paradigm and into the paradigm of virtue and corruption.

The appearance of a new ruling elite (or "monied interest") of stockholders and officeholders, whose relations with government were those of mutual dependence, was countered by a renewed (or "neo-Harringtonian") assertion of the ideal of the citizen, virtuous in his devotion to the public good and his engagement in relations of equality and ruling-and-being-ruled, but virtuous also in his independence of any relation which might render him corrupt. For this, the citizen required the autonomy of real property, and many rights (including the right to keep and bear arms) were necessary in order to assure it to him; but the function of property remained the assurance of virtue. It was hard to see how he could become involved in exchange relationships, or in relationships governed by the media of exchange (especially when these took the form of paper tokens of public credit) without becoming involved in dependence and corruption. The ideals of virtue and commerce could not therefore be reconciled to one another, so long as "virtue" was employed in the austerely civic, Roman, and Arendtian sense selected at the outset of this essay and highly active in the eighteenth-century debate; but now it was perceived that such a virtuous citizen was so much of a political and so little of a social animal as to be ancient and not modern, ancient to the point of being archaic.

Virtue was redefined – though there are signs of an inclination to abandon the word – with the aid of a concept of "manners." As the individual moved from the farmer-warrior world of ancient citizenship or Gothic *libertas*, he entered an increasingly transactional universe of "commerce and the arts" – the latter term

[21] Skinner, *The Foundations of Modern Political Thought*, II, p. 239; John Dunn, *The Political Thought of John Locke: An Historical Account of the Argument of the Two Treatises of Government* (Cambridge, Eng.: Cambridge University Press, 1969).

signifying both the productive and audio-visual skills – in which his relationships and interactions with other social beings, and with their products, became
increasingly complex and various, modifying and developing more and more aspects of his personality.[22] Commerce, leisure, cultivation, and – it was soon
perceived with momentous consequences – the division and diversification of labor combined to bring this about; and if he could no longer engage directly in
the activity and equality of ruling and being ruled, but had to depute his government and defense to specialized and professional representatives, he was more
than compensated for his loss of antique virtue by an indefinite and perhaps
infinite enrichment of his personality, the product of the multiplying relationships, with both things and persons, in which he became progressively involved.
Since these new relationships were social and not political in character, the capacities which they led the individual to develop were called not "virtues" but
"manners," a term in which the ethical *mores* and the juristic *consuetudines* were
combined, with the former predominating. The social psychology of the age
declared that encounters with things and persons evoked passions and refined
them into manners; it was preeminently the function of commerce to refine the
passions and polish the manners; and the social ethos of the age of enlightenment
was built upon the concept of close encounters of the third kind.

"Manners," declared Burke, "are of more importance than laws . . . they aid
morals, they supply them, or they totally destroy them."[23] I would like to suggest that he had in mind *ordini* rather than statutes: the "laws" made by legislators framing a classical order; for the concept of "manners," though it does not
belong to the operational vocabulary of jurisprudence, was in fact enormously
advanced by and through the study of natural and civil law, particularly *jus
gentium*. We are now in the era of a revived and modernized natural jurisprudence, based on the notion that an intensive study of the variations of social behavior throughout space and time would reveal the underlying principles of human nature on which the diversities of conduct were based and from which *lois*
took their *esprit*. Jurisprudence, whatever it was like as the formal study of law,
was the social science of the eighteenth century, the matrix of both the study and
the ideology of manners. Once again law was pitted against virtue, things against
persons, the empire against the republic. The tensions between virtue and commerce, ancient and modern, helped endow eighteenth-century jurisprudence with
the complex historical schemes and the nascent historicism which make Adam
Smith's *Lectures on Jurisprudence* a theory of the progress of society through the
four stages of production. It has even been possible for Forbes and Stein to trace
this development of jurisprudence without ascribing it to the ideological need to

---

[22] See ch. 6, this volume.
[23] Edmund Burke, *Letters on a Regicide Peace*, 1796 (*The Works of the Right Honorable Edmund Burke*,
London, 1826, vol. VIII, p. 172). See below, p. 209.

defend commerce against ancient virtue;[24] but there is no question but that this need was being met and an ideological defense waged.

But the defense of commercial society, no less than the vindication of classical virtue, was carried out with the weapons of humanism. The eighteenth century presents us with a legal humanism, or humanist jurisprudence, whose roots were in Kelley's "civil science of the Renaissance," being employed against the civic humanism of the classical republicans in a way hard to parallel in the sixteenth century. The effect was to construct a liberalism which made the state's authority guarantee the liberty of the individual's social behavior, but had no intention whatever of impoverishing that behavior by confining it to the rigorous assertion of ego-centered individual rights. On the contrary, down at least to the end of the 1780s, it was the world of ancient politics which could be made to seem rigid and austere, impoverished because underspecialized; and the new world of the social and sentimental, the commercial and cultural, was made to proliferate with alternatives to ancient *virtus* and *libertas,* largely in consequence of the jurists' fascination with the universe of *res.* Now, at last, a right to things became a way to the practice of virtue, so long as virtue could be defined as the practice and refinement of manners. A commercial humanism had been not unsuccessfully constructed.

About 1789, a wedge was driven through this burgeoning universe, and rather suddenly we begin to hear denunciations of commerce as founded upon soullessly rational calculation and the cold, mechanical philosophy of Bacon, Hobbes, Locke, and Newton. How this reversal of strategies came about is not at present well understood. It may have had to do with the rise of an administrative ideology, in which Condorcet, Hartley, and Bentham tried to erect a science of legislation on a foundation of highly reductionist assumptions. But that is another chapter in the history of both jurisprudence and humanism: one lying outside the confines of the present model.

[24] Duncan Forbes, *Hume's Philosophical Politics* (Cambridge, Eng.: Cambridge University Press, 1976); Peter Stein, *Legal Evolution: The Story of an Idea* (Cambridge, Eng.: Cambridge University Press, 1980). See also Pocock, "Cambridge Paradigms and Scotch Philosophers: A Study of the Relations between the Civic Humanist and the Civil Jurisprudential Interpretations of Eighteenth-Century Social Thought," in *Wealth and Virtue: The Shaping of Political Economy in the Scottish Enlightenment,* ed. Istvan Hont and Michael Ignatieff (Cambridge, Eng.: Cambridge University Press, 1983).

3

◁══▷

Authority and property
The question of liberal origins

If one sought to characterize the drift of recent historical thinking about the crises of seventeenth-century England, one might well say that it has been in the direction of a heightened awareness of the dialectic between authority and liberty in both the politics and the political thinking of the period. In the field of general history, J. H. Plumb's very important theses of the "growth of stability" and the "growth of oligarchy" have shifted some of our attention away from the first crisis period of 1640–60 and toward the second crisis period of 1680–1720.[1] We now see the latter as culminating in the establishment of that oligarchical, commercial, and imperial Britain against which the American Revolution was directed, but whose problems America in some respects inherited;[2] and the search for the origins of this regime has obliged us to go back to the first crisis period and examine it in terms of restoration as well as of revolution. It does not diminish the radical or the revolutionary character of the things which happened at the beginning and end of the 1640s to say that we cannot understand the revolutionary impulse without also understanding its exhaustion; the study of how revolutions die is a little-known branch of political science.[3] Perhaps the revival of emphasis on this problem reflects the mood of our own society since 1970; whether this is so or not, it is a problem we do well to study. We shall not understand the way in which the traditional constitution and the rule of the established elites were challenged and changed during the 1640s until we understand how and why they were apparently restored in 1660, and how far that restoration was apparent and how far real. We still lack a good conceptual vocabulary for dealing

---

From *After the Reformation: Essays in Honor of J. H. Hexter,* edited by Barbara C. Malament, pp. 331–54. © 1980 University of Pennsylvania Press; reprinted by permission.

[1] J. H. Plumb, *The Growth of Political Stability in England, 1675–1725* (London, 1967).
[2] See chap. 4, this volume. Both chaps. 3 and 4 were first written in 1976.
[3] Cf. James H. Meisel, *Counter-revolutions: How Revolutions Die* (New York, 1966).

51

with this problem; the various attempts which have been made to determine how far the restored order was more commercially oriented than the prerevolutionary are useful but by no means sufficient.

However, these are problems for historians; political theorists, on the other hand, continue (rightly) to make assumptions in their own work which they base on an understanding of what occurred in seventeenth-century political thought. What Hobbes said and what Locke said is still supposed to be important to our understanding of our own political culture; what have the historians been doing to that? One must still begin by emphasizing that we cannot study the first crisis period solely in terms of Hobbes, or the second in terms of Locke; each period furnishes a complex texture of thought which both provides the context for Hobbes (or Locke) and proves to have functioned autonomously, in ways which are important to us without necessarily including Hobbes (or Locke) at all. Thus, our understanding of the thought of the first crisis period must continue to focus very largely on the enormously significant topic of that great explosion of quasi-democratic antinomianism which we call Puritan radicalism for short; and this is a subject which seems to have grown more problematical as our understanding of it has deepened. We know much more than we did twenty years ago about the workings and inner logic of millennialism and antinomianism; one need only mention the names of Norman Cohn, William M. Lamont, Sacvan Bercovitch, and Christopher Hill in this connection;[4] and we have moved away from the problem, much debated a generation ago, of how far religious perception was a mask for perception of material and social change, to the extent that we can now see that, for the Puritan radical, spirit and matter were virtually interchangeable terms, so that arguing for the primacy of the one mode of thought over the other is like arguing about the chicken and the egg. There is even a tendency to see this hylozoistic spiritual materialism as the mainstream of radical thought, and the scientific revolution of the Restoration period as, in ideological terms, a conservative reaction aiming at the separation of spirit and matter in the name of authority and rational order.[5]

But there are problems here for those who wish to interpret Puritan radicalism as part of the consciousness of a revolutionary bourgeoisie: a radical antinomianism which is essentially part of the continuing protest of the Brethren of the Free Spirit seems to cut too deep into social and spiritual experience to be dismissible (even though it is partly explicable) as the ideology of discontented small tradesmen and craft-masters, and when one compares the earlier with the later writings of Christopher Hill — a major student of this subject — one seems to detect

[4] Norman Cohn, *The Pursuit of the Millennium*, rev. ed. (New York, 1967); William M. Lamont, *Marginal Prynne, 1660–1669* (London, 1963) and *Godly Rule: Politics and Religion, 1603–1660* (London, 1969); Sacvan Bercovitch, *Typology and Early American Literature* (Amherst, 1972). For Hill, see n. 6 below.

[5] M. C. Jacob, *The Newtonians and the English Revolution, 1689–1720* (Ithaca, 1976); Charles Webster, *The Great Instauration* (New York, 1976).

something like a shift from an Old Left to a New Left perspective. In his earlier works, Independents and Levellers appear as pioneers of an entrepreneurial and market society, much as they do in the interpretations of C. B. Macpherson; but as Hill continues his investigations of chiliasm and antinomianism,[6] we move left even of the Diggers, into the society of Seekers, Ranters, Familists, and Muggletonians, and the social setting is less that of a nascent bourgeoisie than that of the roving masterless men from the margins of craft and cultivation in a preindustrial society – social types who might appear at any time from the thirteenth to the seventeenth century, and who look more like intellectual equivalents of Eric Hobsbawm's *Primitive Rebels*,[7] or the "wandering braves" of early Mao, than the "industrious sort of people" about whom Hill has often told us. I do not doubt – knowing my Marxists – that a diligent attempt will be made to sort out the protobourgeois from the prebourgeois among the English radicals; and I do not doubt – knowing my seventeenth century – that this classification will not turn out to be very satisfactory. Writing as one no more committed than Hexter to a sequential class interpretation of history, I suspect that what we have found is the radical consciousness of Laslett's *World We Have Lost*[8] – that of a society of masters and servants.

A further set of problems in the interpretation of Puritan radicalism is created by that shift of emphasis from revolution toward restoration which furnishes the general background of this survey. If we are to organize our thinking around the fact that the first crisis period culminated in the apparent re-establishment of the traditional elites and the second in the confirmation of Whig oligarchy, we must look back at that marvelous explosion of radical consciousness which occurred around 1649 and ask where it all went to. It is very tempting to reply – we would all like to believe – that it went somehow underground in Restoration London, or in the English villages under the game laws, and resurfaced a century and a half later, in the era of Tom Paine and William Blake. There is a romanticism of the English Left which feels that this must have happened, and it is perfectly possible that it did; but neither the school of Christopher Hill, with their emphasis on the middle seventeenth century, nor the schools of George Rudé and E. P. Thompson,[9] with their emphasis on the late eighteenth, have

---

[6] Christopher Hill, *Puritanism and Revolution: Studies in Interpretation of the English Revolution of the Seventeenth Century* (London, 1958; New York 1964); *Intellectual Origins of the English Revolution* (Oxford, 1965); *Society and Puritanism in Pre-Revolutionary England,* 2d ed. (New York, 1967); *God's Englishman: Oliver Cromwell and the English Revolution* (New York, 1970); *Antichrist in Seventeenth-Century England* (London and New York, 1971); *The World Turned Upside Down: Radical Ideas During the English Revolution* (New York, 1972).

[7] Eric Hobsbawm, *Primitive Rebels* (New York, 1965).

[8] Peter Laslett, *The World We Have Lost: English Society Before and After the Coming of Industry* (London, 1965).

[9] George Rudé, *The Crowd in History: A Study of Popular Disturbances in France and England, 1730–1848* (New York, 1964); *The Crowd in the French Revolution* (Oxford, 1959); *Wilkes and Liberty: A Social Study of 1763 to 1774* (Oxford, 1962); E. P. Thompson, *The Making of the English Working*

yet brought to light evidence which enables us to speak very confidently about what happened to underground radicalism in the intervening period. What, after all, do we mean by "underground"? Where does popular or populist radicalism go in an era of repression? Is it kept going as an underground tradition by obscure articulate groups, or does it retreat into silence, to a level of subconscious or subarticulate potentiality, waiting to become actual again? If we are unsure which of these to look for, it is for lack of evidence rather than lack of theory.

But in a restorationist perspective – one in which the recovery of authority looks as important (if not as attractive) as the assertion of liberty – we find ourselves re-examining the radical tradition itself and asking what elements of authority may be found even there.[10] The reality of antinomian libertarianism is not to be denied; all the same, the origins of all Puritan political thought are largely to be found in the search for the godly magistrate, and there is a sense in which the true meaning of antinomianism was that the individual must be prepared to act as his own magistrate – which imparted a peculiar tension to the definition of the individual as male family head, and to what the prophetic women of the Puritan sects thought about that.[11] The point is, however, that we must be prepared to find magisterial as well as radical elements at the heart of the antinomian tradition itself; even Gerrard Winstanley has been shown to be involved in the search for magistracy, and William Sedgwick – a friend but not an ally of Reeve and Muggleton – can be shown to have employed the antinomian scepticism of all claims to authority as a paradoxical justification of submission to whatever authority exists.[12] And this was Sedgwick's central and permanent position; we should not think that every antinomian retreated into quietism only after his radical and revolutionary impulses had been defeated. In a world of magistracy, the antinomian effect could start at several points and move in several directions, and this is to say nothing of the broader theoretical contention – one not limited to the seventeenth century – that it is impossible to assert even the most radical liberty without asserting some conception of authority at the same time. Even the Putney debaters, even George Fox, even Lawrence Clarkson, would have agreed unhesitatingly with this thesis.

Class (New York, 1964); *Whigs and Hunters: The Origin of the Black Act* (London, 1975); "The Moral Economy of the English Crowd in the Eighteenth Century," *Past and Present,* 50 (February 1971): 76–136.

[10] J. H. Hexter, "A New Framework for Social History," in *Reappraisals in History* (Evanston, 1961), was the first to propose this restorationist perspective.

[11] Keith Thomas, "Women in the Civil War Sects," in *Crisis in Europe, 1560–1660,* ed. Trevor Aston (New York, 1965).

[12] The distinction between the "magisterial" and "radical" Reformations may be studied in S. H. Williams, *The Radical Reformation* (Philadelphia, 1962). On Winstanley, see G. E. Aylmer, ed., *"England's Spirit Unfoulded,"* *Past and Present* 40 (July 1968):3–15; J. C. Davis, "Gerrard Winstanley and the Restoration of True Magistracy," *Past and Present* 70 (February 1976): 76–93. On William Sedgwick, see article in *Dictionary of National Biography;* works in Donald Wing ed., *Short Title Catalogue . . . ,* (3:224–25); and in particular *Animadversions upon a Letter and Paper, first sent to His Highness by certain gentlemen and others in Wales* (London, 1656).

The shift which I am trying to describe in our understanding of the first critical period can now be stated in another way. From William Haller to Christopher Hill, the emphasis has rested upon the idea of liberation, upon the rediscovery by the saint of his own radical liberty, in salvation, in society, or in both.[13] There is no need to abandon that emphasis; it retains validity; but we have been obliged to set beside it the perception that seventeenth-century men were still pre-modern creatures for whom authority and magistracy were part of a natural and cosmic order, and that the starting point of much of their most radical thinking was the unimaginable fact that, between 1642 and 1649, authority in England had simply collapsed.[14] In this reading, the central polemic of the English Revolution is not the Putney Debates, but the Engagement Controversy; and to say this is not to be describing an ideological reaction by conservative scholars to the events of 1968 or 1970. The line of research in question is some years older, and it presents English thinkers as responding with the greatest radicalism to the proposition that since authority had disintegrated, and God had withheld his word as to where it was now lodged, the individual must rediscover in the depths of his own being the means of reconstituting and obeying it. The pessimism of Anthony Ascham was a protest against the individual's being placed in this dilemma;[15] the patriarchalism of Sir Robert Filmer now became a demonstration that he did not possess the natural freedom which would otherwise place him in it;[16] but we can tabulate a list of singularly tough-minded responses to the challenge. Antinomianism itself was one: if the law had been withdrawn from men, it was that the spirit might take its place, and we can think of antinomianism as egg as well as chicken, as effect as well as cause of the English dilemma. But it is only one such response, and both Hobbes and Harrington can be depicted as answering the question what it was in men that ultimately made authority possible. To say that the individual sought to preserve himself, drew the sword to do so, but gave up his sword to Nimrod or Leviathan when he discovered the futility of the method, was one way of defining the roots of political capacity;[17]

---

[13] William Haller, *Liberty and Reformation in the Puritan Revolution* (New York, 1955, 1963).

[14] J. G. A. Pocock, *Order and Authority in Two English Revolutions* (Wellington, 1973).

[15] Perez Zagorin, *A History of Political Thought in the English Revolution* (London, 1954); Irene Coltman, *Private Men and Public Causes* (London, 1962); and above all, John M. Wallace, *Destiny His Choice: the Loyalism of Andrew Marvell* (Cambridge, 1968).

[16] For Filmer's role in the Engagement Controversy see Wallace, *Destiny His Choice*, and for a full and serious study of his thought, Gordon J. Schochet, *Patriarchalism in Political Thought* (Oxford, 1975). Also James W. Daly, *Sir Robert Filmer and English Political Thought* (Toronto, 1978). Wallace has since argued that *Patriarcha* itself was written about 1648.

[17] Wallace, *Destiny His Choice;* and Quentin Skinner, "Hobbes's *Leviathan*," *Historical Journal* 7 (1964): 321–33; "History and Ideology in the English Revolution," *Historical Journal* 8 (1965): 151–78; "The Ideological Context of Hobbes's Political Thought," *Historical Journal* 9 (1966): 286–317; "The Context of Hobbes's Theory of Political Obligation," in *Hobbes and Rousseau: A Collection of Critical Essays*, ed. Maurice Cranston and Richard S. Peters (New York, 1972); "Conquest and Consent: Thomas Hobbes and the Engagement Controversy," in *The Interregnum: The Quest for Settlement*, ed. G. E. Aylmer (Hamden, Conn., 1972).

to say that the individual whose sword was rooted in property was free from fortune to pursue the goods of the mind, and could now join with others to form a political body whose soul was collective intelligence, was another and a very different way;[18] but both were answers to the question how men left with nothing but the sword could restore the rule of reason and authority. It is important to add that for both Hobbes and Harrington – and forming the closest link between their respective systems – a principal motive in reconstituting a natural politics was to deny separate authority to the clergy;[19] but nearly all the threads in the inconceivably complex texture of English thought in the first critical period can be attached to and often deduced from the radical need to reconstruct authority, and though this is not the only valid mode of approach, it was quite certainly the one uppermost in the minds of most people then engaged in systematic thought. There can be no question of diminishing the radical libertarianism of the period when one points out the significance of the conservative impulse; the two were inherent in one another.

I want next to apply aspects of this analysis to the question of authority and property, which furnishes the first part of this paper's title. Debaters during the Puritan revolution had much to say about property, and began, as we know, to distinguish between the various historical modes in which it operated in society; and it is one of the most difficult, and valuable, questions before us to determine how far these discussions were based upon actual, if mediated, perceptions of the changing forms of property in contemporary reality. To begin with, it does us no harm to recall that the word is spelt in seventeenth-century printings both as *property* and as *propriety;* there is no consistent change in meaning between the two spellings, and had there been a tape recorder as well as a shorthand writer in the church at Putney, we might have learned something by hearing how Ireton and Rainborough pronounced the word. The point is that *property* was a juridical term before it was an economic one; it meant that which was properly one's own, that to which one properly had a claim, and words such as *proprium* and *proprietas* were applied as much to the right as to the thing, and to many things as well as the means of sustenance or production. Clearly, the word was often used in its crudely obvious sense; when a speaker in Richard Cromwell's Parliament says, "All government is founded in property, else the poor must rule it,"[20] there is not much point in being sophisticated about him; and it is often valuable to search behind

---

[18] J. G. A. Pocock, *The Political Works of James Harrington* (Cambridge, 1977), particularly book I of *The Prerogative of Popular Government* (1658).

[19] J. G. A. Pocock, *The Machiavellian Moment* (Princeton, 1975), pp. 396–400; "Time, History and Eschatology in the Thought of Thomas Hobbes," in *Politics, Language and Time* (New York 1971); introduction to *The Political Works of James Harrington;* "Contexts for the Study of James Harrington," *Il Pensiero Politico* XI, 1 (1978): 20–35.

[20] Adam Baynes; see J. T. Rutt, ed., *The Diary of Thomas Burton . . . ,* 4 vols. (London, 1828), 3:147–48.

the word in its juridical uses for perceptions of what we mean when we employ it in its economic-productive sense. This is what some important seventeenth-century analysts were doing. It is now naive to become excited whenever we espy the word "property" in seventeenth-century debate, and to suppose that masks are being cast aside and we now see what the debate was really about. Sometimes they are not being cast aside, and sometimes we cannot be sure that they were masks at all. We have to know a good deal about the strategies of contemporary debate and the structures of contemporary language before we start peeling these down to assumptions about or perceptions of productive relations; and if this is going to be possible on some occasions, there are going to be other occasions on which analysis can only take us in other directions. This will have to be kept in mind even when we are dealing with seventeenth-century people who specifically talked about changes in social relations consequent upon changes in the modes of holding or exploiting land or movable goods.

Thus, when Ireton at Putney says that all he is arguing for "is because I would have an eye to property,"[21] and proceeds to affirm that the property that confers the franchise must be an inheritable freehold, he is not so much defending a particular form of property as seizing the high ground in debate. The Levellers are visibly uncertain whether they are trying to extend the franchise to people who hold property in other legally determined ways, or querying the necessity of the association between property and franchise altogether, and Ireton is exploiting their uncertainty. Had the Levellers seen themselves as playing the former role, the debate at Putney could have resolved itself — as it never did — into specific discussion and negotiation about the legally or economically defined categories of proprietor to whom the franchise might be extended; and there might, when all is said and done, have been an agreed compromise about that. Ireton had no commitment to freehold or to historic right as such; we know this from other proposals which he was prepared to entertain. But once the Levellers got upon the ground of manhood suffrage, or anything near enough to it to suggest that the right to suffrage might be established on grounds to which property was only marginally related, they were raising the question of what the political personality and its freedom really were and on what grounds they could be established and talked about. This was the question quite consciously before the minds of the variously sophisticated debaters at Putney; it returns us to a known seventeenth-century mental universe, one for which people at that time had a wide range of words and ideas; and it reopens for us the question of the authority by which people claim and exercise their liberty. Again and again in the Putney transcript, we encounter moments at which the debaters get off the unfamiliar ground of trying to clarify their feelings about property and pursue instead what

[21] A. S. P. Woodhouse, ed., *Puritanism and Liberty* (London, 1949), p. 57.

really concerns them and they really know how to argue about: the problem of establishing the title by which they are acting as they are; the real center of debate in the first critical period—the basis in right of the *de facto*.

Right and principle, it can be no surprise to anyone to hear, were more real in the minds of these debaters than social structure and change. Different assumptions concerning the basis for action in right would have different consequences in action undertaken, and of course they knew that; but Ireton was not simply aligning himself with those whose property was freehold and defending their monopoly of the franchise – there is nothing to suggest he would have objected to going some way outside that group – so much as anchoring in social and historical reality his authority for being and acting as he was, and insisting that rights must be confined to those whose authority could be similarly anchored. And he did not see in the Levellers the spokesmen of a different group of proprietors with alternative claims to the franchise – a description they would not have recognized themselves – so much as people with no understanding of how to anchor authority in society at all, and no theory of property to be pitted against his. The fear that the poor will use an authority not rooted in property to redistribute property is, of course, present at Putney; but it is rather a stick to beat the Levellers with than a fear of anything specific. It is crude and unelaborated by those who express it, and rather ignored than answered by those who defend themselves against it; whereas the problem of authority at large can be and is discussed at great length by debaters on both sides, and by all contributors to the mid-century polemic, in language whose complexity defies reduction to the single issue of property.

On the assumption, then, that people think about what they have the means of verbalizing, and that relations between the center and the margins of a linguistically structured world must be problematical, we must often say that property in the midseventeenth-century crisis was discussed as part of the problem of authority, and rather less often that this order was reversed. This does not mean that minds of the period were unaware that the ways in which men held and exploited property, and behaved as social and political beings in consequence, were changing; on the contrary, a few contemporary theorists grounded their explanations of the whole crisis on precisely this perception, and it is of enormous importance in the history of social thought that this should have happened. But it is clearly not a sufficient explanation of its happening to say (1) that changes in property relationships were happening; (2) that a few people noticed; and (3) that everybody who did not notice nevertheless reflected the changes without noticing them. The patterns of human thinking at any period are more complex than that; and, especially when this order of change has never been noticed before, there must have been reasons inherent in the patterns of thought which led some people to notice – reasons which may or may not have been immediately connected with the changes that were noticed. On the assumption that ideas about authority and ideas about property were independent variables, I would like next to look into the seventeenth-century perception that property itself was changing.

C. B. Macpherson, as we all know, put forward some years ago, in *The Political Theory of Possessive Individualism,* the hypothesis that seventeenth-century political thought was importantly affected by the growth of a perception of property as marketable.[22] He constructed a model – an excellent one – of the social and political consequences of a set of market assumptions, and then tested for the presence of his model, or elements of it, in various seventeenth-century thinkers. As a result he was led to award middling high points to the Levellers and Harrington, much higher points to Hobbes and Locke, in proportion as he was able to find elements of the model in their thinking; and he concluded that the median score, so to speak, was high enough to justify the hypothesis that market assumptions were a constant determinant of thought in this period. Some of us were never altogether happy with this, because it never seemed quite dialectical enough; it all sounds rather as if something is known to have been going on, and various more or less sensitive instruments have recorded it with greater or less precision; and our notion of the behavior of consciousness in history has always been rather less barometric than that. We also thought that Macpherson's model tested for the presence of one thing at a time, and that if one started from the assumption that there were several kinds of possessive individual, and so of possessive individualism, and that there was argument going on as between several modes of property and individuality, a more dialectical and less barometric picture might result. In particular, there was doubt concerning his interpretation of Harrington, because Harrington had two models of property relationships, one defined by the presence of dependent military tenures and the other by their absence, and there was little need to involve the market in stating the difference between them. Everything relating to that debate is now in print elsewhere;[23] but it is possible to push the issue a little further, in a direction which takes us to the second part of my title: the question of liberal origins.

There is now a paradigm of liberalism, though one set up more by those who would attack than by those who would practice it. It is interesting to observe how the notion of liberalism is defined in much the same way, and attacked for

[22] C. B. Macpherson, *The Political Theory of Possessive Individualism: Hobbes to Locke* (Oxford, 1962). Cf. Joyce O. Appleby, *Economic Thought and Ideology in Seventeenth-Century England* (Princeton, 1978).
[23] J. G. A. Pocock, *The Ancient Constitution and the Feudal Law* (Cambridge, 1957), chap. 6; Macpherson, *Possessive Individualism,* chap. 4; Pocock, *Politics, Language and Time,* chap. 4; *The Machiavellian Moment,* chap. 11; Macpherson, chap. 5, and Pocock, chap. 3, of *Feudalism, Capitalism and Beyond,* ed. Eugene Kamenka and R. S. Neale (Canberra, 1975). See also the debate between Macpherson and John F. H. New, reprinted in *The Intellectual Revolution of the Seventeenth Century,* ed. Charles Webster (London, 1974), I–V.

much the same reasons, among political theorists and ideologues: on the one hand by socialist humanists – followers of Macpherson or Wolin or McWilliams or Lowi – and on the other hand by the classical conservative followers of Strauss or Arendt or Oakeshott.[24] Liberalism, as they all define it, is a view of politics founded on the conception of the individual as a private being, pursuing goals and safeguarding freedoms which are his own and looking to government mainly to preserve and protect his individual activity; and it is suggested that because this individual withholds from government so much of his personality – which he says is not the government's business but his own – government tends to become highly impersonal, and therefore paradoxically authoritarian in those areas from which it does not altogether abstain. The paradox of liberty and authority, on which I am basing my interpretations of seventeenth-century thought, was stated in these terms by Hume, and it is highly arguable that his formulation was prophesied by Hobbes; but through the nineteenth and twentieth centuries there has grown up a long tradition of attacking it. The attack is always, at least in form, humanist, and entails the charge that the liberal concept of individuality omits too much in the interactions of personality with politics and society which is essential to personality, and so tends to dehumanize both government and the governed. On the left the charge is one of failure in social humanism: the liberal individual is said to be engrossed in acquisitive activity, and so to detach himself from a politics which he pays to repress those whom acquisitiveness excludes. On the right the charge is one of failure in civic and intellectual humanism: both the acquisitive individual and the wage-earning individual who looks to the state for protection against him are charged with abandonment of politics – by which is meant the heroic moralism of political and philosophical decision, practice, and contemplation. It is perhaps because the socialist concept of individuality has been heroic since its beginnings that the socialist and nonsocialist versions of antiliberalism so often look like mirror-images of one another. One has to have been attacked, from right and left simultaneously, for depoliticizing thought and dehumanizing history,[25] to realize just how far this brand of humanist heresy-hunt has been allowed to go.

Both versions of antiliberalism are intelligible and to that extent convincing, and there is a wide range of historical phenomena to which both are in various ways applicable. But the accusations which they level are becoming routinized – which is what one means by a heresy-hunt – and this gives one reason to believe that the range of phenomena to which they apply may have been exaggerated.

[24] Macpherson, *Possessive Individualism;* Sheldon Wolin, *Politics and Vision* (Boston, 1960); Wilson Carey McWilliams, *The Idea of Fraternity in America* (Berkeley, 1973); Theodore Lowi, *The End of Liberalism* (New York, 1969). For Oakeshott, see *Of Human Conduct* (Oxford, 1975).

[25] Richard Ashcraft, *Political Theory* 3 (1975): 13, 15, 22–23; Dante Germino, *Virginia Quarterly Review* 51 (1975): 628–32; Neal Wood, *Political Theory* 4 (1976): 104. Compare Hexter's review of *The Machiavellian Moment* in *On Historians*.

The antiliberals of both camps tend to write as if the liberalism which they define had held the field – or had expanded its control of the field without effective opposition – from the days of Hobbes and Locke even to the days of Marx; and it is this supposition which recent historical research has tended to modify. If one expresses scepticism of the historic reality of such concepts as "liberal," or for that matter "bourgeois," the heresy-hunter will of course interpret that as meaning that one is a "liberal" or "bourgeois" in disguise; but among reasonable beings, there is a useful purpose to be served by going back to some doubts concerning Macpherson's "possessive individualism." We shall be engaged in the exercise of trying to get a paradigm into perspective, though readers of Kuhn will know that a covert attack on the paradigm may be entailed.

There is one English thinker of the first critical period who fits the Macpherson model very well indeed – so much so that his possessive individualism does not need to be brought to light by a complicated exegesis, but is expressly rendered in his own words. He depicted men in society as creatures who drove hard bargains with one another, the stronger party always dictating the terms of the bargain to the weaker; he said that this was peculiarly the characteristic of a society where property consisted in movable goods and wealth; he proposed that what was needed in so individualist a society was a sovereign and indeed absolute central authority to regulate the bargaining process; and he pointed out that in a commercial society such a sovereign could govern with the aid of salaried professional soldiers. So here we have one full-blooded possessive individualist in the middle of the seventeenth century, and where there was one there were doubtless more; we must not play the trick of isolating this man by seeming to emphasize him. But his name was Matthew Wren; his father was a Laudian bishop currently a prisoner in the Tower; and the circumstance that his grandfather had been a mercer will not really make a business spokesman out of him. Furthermore, he expressed these views in the form of a critique of James Harrington's *Oceana,* of which he was the leading contemporary opponent;[26] and he was attacking Harrington's doctrine that the form of property determining politics was land, whose stability – as opposed to the mobility of goods and money – set men free to be the rational political creatures which they were by nature. Harrington was, to some degree, an agrarian utopian, and he had affirmed that two girls left to share a cake would construct the choice rationally, by having one girl cut the cake and the other choose her piece. It was Wren who replied that the stronger girl would offer the other a small piece of cake to fetch her some water to drink

---

[26] [Matthew Wren], *Considerations upon Mr. Harrington's Commonwealth of Oceana, restricted to the First Part of the Preliminaries* (London, 1657); Matthew Wren, *Monarchy Asserted, or the State of Monarchicall and Popular Government, in Vindication of the Considerations upon Mr. Harrington's Oceana* (Oxford, 1659). Harrington's replies are *The Prerogative of Popular Government,* book 1; *The Art of Law-Giving,* book 3, and *Politicaster* (1659); see *Works* (1977).

with her larger share; as succinct a statement of the possessive individualist position as could be found.[27]

In the parable of the cake Harrington saw the image of the aristocracy proposing a range of choices and the democracy exercising the actual decision between them, which was not only his basic conception of the political process, but — he insisted — the essential means of infusing into the body politic a rational and political soul. This was the true target of Wren's attack: he was specific in denying that the body politic could possess a soul, and went so far as to remark that before we could even discuss such an idea we should have to know what the soul was and what the philosophy pertaining to it[28] — a rather startling remark from the son of a bishop and one who was much admired by other bishops. Harrington's ideas about the soul-body relationship in politics are rooted in ancient and medieval physics and medicine — "the contemplation of form," he once wrote, "is astonishing to man, and hath a kind of trouble or impulse accompanying it, that exalts his soul to God"[29] — and his agrarianism links him (though not directly) with the tradition of radical hylozoism, which I mentioned earlier: he is not immeasurably remote from Gerrard Winstanley, who conflated the relations of reason with matter, soul with body, Christ with mankind, and men with the earth in a system of social justice. It was Wren who was the modern, and only in the next century was Harrington seen as a pioneer of experimental science.[30] If we relate him in any degree to radical Puritanism, we commit ourselves to emphasizing the extent to which Puritan thought was rooted in antiquity.

The alliance with which Harrington felt himself confronted was that of mathematicians with clerics. From the time he read Wren's *Observations,* he began denouncing "mathematicians" as people who would reduce political society to a calculus of interested forces in order to deprive it of its rational soul. We might expect, given everything we have read or been given to understand concerning Hobbes, that Harrington would rank him among enemies of this stripe, and it is of course possible to argue that he should have. But the significant fact is that Wren attacked Hobbes as well as Harrington, and that Harrington defended Hobbes against both Wren and the Laudian doctor Henry Hammond,[31] the reason being that Harrington and Hobbes both desired to assert that Israel, from Moses to Samuel, had been a pure theocracy, and that consequently no order of clergy could claim a divine right to political authority.[32] We might suppose that this adventitiously deflected Harrington's attention from the fact that Hobbes

[27] Wren, *Considerations,* p. 36.   [28] Ibid., p. 20.

[29] Harrington, *A System of Politics,* the last political work he wrote.

[30] Duncan Forbes, *Hume's Philosophical Politics* (Cambridge, 1975), chap. 1, contains interesting evidence on this.

[31] Harrington, *The Prerogative of Popular Government,* book 2.

[32] *The Machiavellian Moment,* pp. 397–98.

also was among the mathematicians, were it not that Wren belonged to a largely clerical circle who repudiated Hobbes's mathematics as energetically as they repudiated everything else about him. Wren was a layman, but he was a protégé of John Wilkins, warden of Wadham College and founding father of the Royal Society, who serenely made the transition from being Cromwell's brother-in-law under the Protectorate to being bishop of Chester under the Restoration. It was Wilkins who had urged him to undertake the criticism of Harrington;[33] and the Oxford professors of mathematics, whom Hobbes had attacked in 1656, were all of the same kidney as Wilkins.[34] Harrington could see as little difference between protectoralists and royalists as he could between Presbyterians and Anglicans, and he was justified by his own perspective. Wren's commercially based theory of politics is the foundation of an antihylozoism which enables him both to undermine Harrington's republicanism and to restore the position of the clergy against the attacks of Harrington and Hobbes. It would be delightful to conclude by finding an ideological aspect to the differences between Hobbes's mathematics and those of the Oxford circle, but I do not know if this can be done.

At all events, here is the ideological context for the most specific piece of possessive individualism known so far. It was the bishops who promoted the "bourgeois ideology," the Latitudinarians who were the liberals. We have fallen in with that tradition which sees Restoration Arminianism, rather than Puritanism, as the ideological reinforcement of the scientific revolution and particularly with the important work of Margaret C. Jacob, who has argued that Newtonian science was promoted by a Latitudinarian clergy, many of whom had made some sort of transition from the Laudian ranks, as an antidote to a lingering and potentially radical hylozoism, which had survived from the Puritan revolution and forms a kind of underground or dark underbelly to Restoration philosophy.[35] One can see how both a physics based on laws of motion, and a politics based on interest and acquisition, would serve their purpose, and there is much to be done with the notion of a hylozoistic and in some respects occultist underground, running through the Restoration and the clandestine aspects of the early Enlightenment, to surface again in the late eighteenth century. The immediate point I should like to make, however, is that the thesis that individualism points toward authoritarianism seems to be holding up well, but that we are obliged to leave a good deal of room for the possibility that the authoritarians promoted individualism for their own ends. I have been suggesting in this paper the usefulness of remembering that the notion of property might subserve that of au-

[33] Wren, *Considerations*, unpaginated introduction; Barbara Shapiro, *John Wilkins, 1614–1672: An Intellectual Biography* (Berkeley and Los Angeles, 1969), pp. 116–17.
[34] Hobbes, *Six Lessons to the Savilian Professors of the Mathematics* (1656), in *The English Works of Thomas Hobbes*, ed. William Molesworth, 11 vols. (London, 1845), vol. 7.
[35] Webster, *Intellectual Revolution*, pp. xiv–xxv, is a useful anthology of writings on this question; Jacob; *The Newtonians and the English Revolution*.

thority, rather than the other way about; and we seem to have been looking at cases where a possessive-individualist view of society was promoted by members of a recovering ruling class, rather than by members of any new class which was replacing it. That the ruling classes of England became significantly more commercial in their membership and behavior during the first critical period seems much harder to maintain than that, during the same period, some of them discovered the utility from their point of view of a commercially based ideology. The clergy and other administrative elites may have invented a bourgeois ideology without belonging to, or recognizing the predominance of, any bourgeoisie that practised the ethic they described. This does not tell us, of course, how it became possible to invent such an ideology; but there has to be a non-Marxist reading of English history in which the ruling elites use the commercial classes without surrendering to them. This suggests an answer to the only problem that arises from Jacob's excellent study: if – as she insists – Hobbes was the apologist of market society, and the Latitudinarians and Newtonians were the apologists of market society, why was Hobbes the principal enemy whom the latter desired to overthrow?

But the Restoration of 1660 was the restoration of the established landholders as well as of the clerical and bureaucratic elites;[36] and therefore a view of political power based on the acquisition of movable goods is only one of the ideologies of property and authority possible in the era of history that then began, though it would be fair to say that the individual as magistrate was very rapidly replaced by the individual as proprietor. The second critical period, which we date from about 1675 to 1720, marks the beginnings of the *verità effettuale* of that tension between real and movable property which Harrington and Wren had prefigured, and our use and understanding of the liberal paradigm has to be re-examined in this light. Our histories of political thought in this second period have traditionally been dominated by the figure of Locke, and it has been established practice to interpret all contemporary and subsequent thought about politics with reference to his theories of consent, trust, and dissolution, and all thought about property with reference to his theories of labor and acquisition. But for about twenty years the received image of Locke has been subjected to some powerful solvents, as a result of which his role has been not so much diminished as rendered problematical. Peter Laslett demonstrated that the *Two Treatises* were written well before the Revolution of 1688, as a by-product of the Filmerian controversy of 1679–81; work carried out by myself on the ideological climate of the years beginning about 1675 seemed to uncover whole universes of discourse – the controversy over parliamentary history, the neo-Harringtonian revival – which were of great importance to Locke's closest associates, but which Locke himself

---

[36] For the last mentioned, see G. E. Aylmer, *The State's Servants* (London, 1973).

ignored while doing nothing to terminate; Philip Abrams and John Dunn brought to light readings of the theory of consent, and of Locke's politics in general, a good deal more angled toward the problem of authority than we used to think, and of such a character that it was doubtful how usefully the concept of liberalism could be employed in speaking of him.[37] There is now going forward a revision of the ideology of 1688, both in the months of revolution itself and in the ensuing twenty-five years, which indicates that Locke's position – his insistence that a dissolution of government was not a dissolution of society – while seemingly moderate, was in fact too radical to represent the emerging political reality. Some Whigs in the Convention not only insisted that there had been a dissolution of government, but were prepared to fill the vacuum with structures that recall the 1650s as much as anything in the *Two Treatises;*[38] but those Tories who had reluctantly accepted the revolution – and whose ideas dominate the thinking of the next quarter-century[39] – not only successfully maintained (and obliged the Whigs to agree) that there had not been a dissolution of government, but forced a general revival, reconsideration, and even reprinting[40] of the debate of 1649–51 concerning obedience to a *de facto* regime, which was to be of great importance to Edmund Burke a full hundred years later.[41] This was why the Whigs had to settle for a constitutionalist rather than a contractualist legitimation of the Revolution.

The effect of all this has been to create problems in the historical if not the philosophical understanding of Locke's political thought; our perception of the context in which he operated has been so greatly enlarged and complicated that we now have great difficulty in seeing how he should be connected with it, and this is rendered no easier by Locke's own secrecy regarding his authorship and denials of concern in aspects of debate which almost certainly did concern him.[42]

[37] Peter Laslett, ed., *John Locke: Two Treatises of Government* (Cambridge, 1960, 1963); Pocock, *The Ancient Constitution and the Feudal Law,* chaps. 8–9; *Politics, Language and Time,* chaps. 3–4; *The Machiavellian Moment,* pp. 423–24, 435–36; Philip Abrams, ed., *John Locke: Two Tracts on Government* (Cambridge, 1967); John Dunn, *The Political Thought of John Locke: An Historical Account of the Argument of the Two Treatises of Government* (Cambridge, 1969). On Locke and liberalism, cf. M. Seliger, *The Liberal Politics of John Locke* (London, 1969), for whom the elements of authoritarianism in Locke are inherent in the liberal tradition. Dunn argues that they are anterior to it.

[38] Julian H. Franklin, *John Locke and the Theory of Sovereignty* (Cambridge, 1978); Mark Goldie, "The Origins of True Whiggism," *History of Political Thought,* I, 2 (1980), pp. 195–236.

[39] See J. P. Kenyon, *Revolution Principles: The Politics of Party, 1689–1720* (Cambridge, 1977); Martyn P. Thompson, "The Reception of Locke's *Two Treatises of Government,"* *Political Studies* 24 (1976).

[40] See Skinner, "History and Ideology in the English Revolution."

[41] See Burke's *Reflections on the Revolution in France* (1790) and *An Appeal from the New to the Old Whigs* (1794). H. T. Dickinson, *Liberty and Property: Political Ideology in Eighteenth-Century Britain* (London, 1978).

[42] Thus, it is not possible to discover Locke's connection with the neo-Harringtonian writings sponsored by Shaftesbury in 1675–77, though he must have been very close by; K. H. D. Haley, *The First Earl of Shaftesbury* (Oxford, 1968), pp. 391–93. For other instances see Laslett, passim, and Maurice Cranston, *John Locke: A Biography* (London, 1957).

It is not possible any longer to regard him as, in isolation, the philosopher of the Revolution, and it will be some time before this reconstruction of the context restores us to having the means of assessing his real importance in the history of ideas and ideology. That importance was probably great, but we have at present no very satisfactory way of evaluating it.

It is clear – to begin moving from an emphasis upon government toward an emphasis upon property – that Locke played no predominant role in the formation of what Caroline Robbins has called "the Whig canon" in the tradition of "the eighteenth-century commonwealthmen."[43] That group of middle and late seventeenth-century writers, and the Tories as well as Whigs of the second critical period who singled them out for canonization, are defined by their relation to the classical republican tradition, with which Locke had little if anything to do. They took a "country" as opposed to a "court" view of the ideal of the balanced constitution, which, following Corinne C. Weston,[44] we now date back to Charles I's *Answer to the Nineteen Propositions of Parliament*, published in 1642; and they saw this balance as threatened by the renewal of the crown's command of parliamentary patronage, which had first surfaced about 1675. For a century and a half, from the Bill of Exclusion through the American Revolution to the First Reform Act, the secret of English government, and the matter of English political debate, was to be the role of patronage, or, as its enemies termed it, "corruption"; and what still requires emphasis is that this was to be discussed in terms of the relation of property to personality. What troubled the "country party" or "commonwealth" thinkers – among whom, we now know, nearly all articulate Americans of the Revolutionary generation are to be included[45] – was less the encroachment of the executive's constitutional powers on those of the legislature, than the growth of the executive's capacity to bring the members of the legislature, and of society in general, into personal, political, and economic dependence upon it. This destroyed the balance of the constitution by destroying that personal independence which could only belong to men whose property was their own and did not consist in expectations from the men in government; and the moral quality which only propertied independence could confer, and which became almost indistinguishable from property itself, was known as "virtue." What we used to think of as the Age of Reason may just as well be called the Age of Virtue; or rather, what used to appear an age of Augustan serenity now appears an age of bitter and confused debate over the relations between reason, virtue,

---

[43] Caroline Robbins, *The Eighteenth-Century Commonwealthman: Studies in the Transmission, Development and Circumstances of English Liberal Thought from the Restoration of Charles II until the War with the Thirteen Colonies* (Cambridge, Mass., 1959).

[44] Corinne C. Weston, *English Constitutional Theory and the House of Lords* (New York, 1965).

[45] There is now an extensive literature on this subject; see Robert E. Shalhope, "Toward a Republican Synthesis: The Emergence of an Understanding of Republicanism in American Historiography," *William and Mary Quarterly*, 3d ser., 29 (1972): 49–80.

and passion.[46] I am looking ahead from a "second critical period" ending about 1720 to an "eighteenth century" which ended about a hundred years later because it is important to emphasize that the polemic against Alexander Hamilton which Jefferson and Madison conducted in the 1790s was to a remarkable degree a replay of an English polemic which had begun in the 1670s[47] – but which could not have been conducted in the sixteen-fifties because the relation of patronage to property was not then in question.

What revisions may all this suggest in our thinking about possessive individualism, about the paradigm of liberalism and that antiliberal interpretation of modern political history whose different versions we looked at earlier? In the first place, it must be observed that our emphasis has moved forward in time. We no longer see the essential shifts in either the structure or the ideology of English property as taking place in the middle seventeenth century, still less in the so-called Tawney's century preceding it,[48] but in the quarter-century following the Revolution of 1688. It was then that what had been a highly theoretical debate between Harrington and Wren exploded and became a public issue, and a commonplace of debate came to be that major changes had occurred in the character of property itself, and consequently in the structure, the morality, and even the psychology of politics. All these things began, with spectacular abruptness, to be discussed in the middle 1690s; and compared with this great breakthrough in the secular consciousness of political society, the attempt to discover market connotations in Hobbes, or even Locke, sometimes looks rather like shadow play. There are some reasons for thinking that the great debate over property and virtue was conducted on premises not apparent to Hobbes or even Wren; as for Locke, the point to be made is that the debate seems to have been conducted with very little reference to anything he had said. An analysis of his writings will certainly define for him a position in relation to it, and we will some day find out when this analysis and definition were first conducted; but if one desires to study the first great ideologist of the Whig system of propertied control, one may study not Locke, but Defoe.[49] The articulation of political thought in the second critical period was moving from the control of philosophers into that of men of letters and semiprofessional journalists. Again, let me say that Locke will return to us, but he is at present moving along a remote orbit.

In the second place, the great debate over property was conducted in terms to which the Macpherson market model does not seem altogether crucial. Harring-

---

[46] See chaps. 13–15 of *The Machiavellian Moment*. Such a synthesis, still necessary in histories of political thought, would be redundant to a historian of literature or philosophy.

[47] See Lance Banning, *The Jeffersonian Persuasion* (Ithaca, 1977).

[48] For a study of the historiography of the period from 1540–1640, see Lawrence Stone, *Social Change and Revolution in England, 1540–1640* (London, 1965), pp. xi–xxvi.

[49] *The Machiavellian Moment*, chap. 13. The history of political thought—as distinct from that of social awareness in literature—seems to be without a full-length study of him.

ton – who remained a significant figure in the next century – had operated with a simple distinction between feudal and freehold tenure; Wren and others had pointed to the possible importance of commercial wealth; but there had really been, and was to be, very little attention paid to the thought that freehold land was liable to become a marketable commodity. What Harrington and Wren both desired to say, from opposite value positions, was that land, or real property, tended to make men independent citizens, who actualized their natural political capacity, whereas mobile property tended to make them artificial beings, whose appetites and powers could and must be regulated by a sovereign. If we are to move Hobbes into the latter camp – as is certainly possible – it was not apparent to the debaters in the 1650s that he belonged there, or that he was an advocate of a mobile-property society in the way that Wren was. But Harrington and Wren lived on the eve of a great reassertion of control by the landed elites in society, fully as important as the expansion of commerce and finance which was to accompany it; and the debate they had begun was to be continued in the context of a dialogue between real and mobile property within the post-1660 and post-1688 political order.

If we look at the history of events in the growth of political consciousness, we find that there was a confrontation between real property and government patronage before there was a confrontation between real and mobile property, and that when the latter occurred it was because mobile property presented itself in the guise not of a marketable commodity, so much as of a new and enlarged mode of dependence upon government patronage. The ideal of property as the basis of independence and virtue was first stated as against the revival of patronage by the court politicians in the 1670s. No conflict with mobile property was entailed or implied, and the critique of patronage was as acceptable in London as in the shires. What escalated the great debate was not the political revolution of 1688, but its largely unanticipated consequence, the so-called financial revolution of the 1690s;[50] and this confronted the ideology of real property with a threat from the operations not of a trading market, but of a system of public credit. At very high speed there was created a new class of investors great and small – Locke was one of them – who had lent government capital that vastly stabilized and enlarged it, and henceforth lived off their expectations of a return (sometimes a marketable one) on their investments. The landed classes, and still more their ideologues to the right and left, saw in this process a revolutionary expansion less of a trading and manufacturing market, than of a system of parliamentary patronage. The mode of property which they now began to attack, and to denounce as a new force in history, transforming and corrupting society, was not property in exchangeable commodities – they called this "trade" and greeted it as a means

[50] P. G. M. Dickson, *The Financial Revolution in England: A Study in the Development of Public Credit* (London, 1967).

to independence and virtue – but property in government office, government stock, and government expectations to which the National Debt had mortgaged futurity: there is a real sense in which the sense of a secular future is the child of capitalist investment.[51] They called this "public credit," a mode of property which rendered government dependent on its creditors and creditors dependent on government, in a relation incompatible with classical or agrarian virtue. It was a property not in the means of production, but in the relationships between government and the otherwise property-owning individual; these relationships could themselves be owned, and could be means of owning people. The perception of credit in many ways preceded and controlled the perception of the market; it can be traced in the literature how the Tory and Old Whig ideologues came to perceive "commerce" as a new and ambivalent force in history mainly in proportion as they came to perceive it as the precondition of "credit." It was the latter concept that was and remained crucial.

Once we are prepared to admit that the first widespread ideological perception of a capitalist form of political relations came into being, rapidly and abruptly, in the last years of the seventeenth century and the two decades following, a number of consequences follow. I have tried to show elsewhere that since capitalism in this form was perceived in terms of speculation rather than calculation, its epistemological foundation appeared as fantasy rather than rationality – with some interesting sexist implications – and that goods had to be reified, and the laws of the market discovered or invented, in order to restore reality and rationality to an otherwise purely speculative universe.[52] The interests succeeded the passions – as is beginning to emerge from the researches of scholars[53] – as a means of disciplining and rendering them manageable and intelligible. But it was the individual as classical political being whose capacities for self-knowledge and self-command – expressed in the ideal of virtue – were rendered uncertain and dissolved into fantasy, other-directedness, and anomie by the corruptions of the new commercial politics. The social thought of the eighteenth century has begun to look like a single gigantic *querelle* between the individual as Roman patriot, self-defined in his sphere of civic action, and the individual in the society of private investors and professional rulers, progressive in the march of history, yet hesitant between action, philosophy, and passion. It seems perfectly possible that both classical economic man and classical socialist man were attempts to rescue the individual from this Faustian dissociation of sensibility.

This suggests that we might keep intact that important element of the antiliberal paradigm which presents classical political man as somehow destroyed by the advent of eighteenth-century capitalism; and we should indeed keep this

[51] See chap. 5, this volume.   [52] See chap. 6, this volume.
[53] Albert Hirschman, *The Passions and the Interests: Arguments for Capitalism before Its Triumph* (Princeton, 1976).

generalization in view and try to state it correctly. But the juxtaposition of polity and economy – to borrow the language of Joseph Cropsey[54] – ought not to be stated as a simple antithesis; I want to argue that it was an unending and unfinished debate. The main historical weakness in the antiliberal position is that all its practitioners, right and left, are so anxious to find, that they antedate and exaggerate, some moment at which economy became emancipated from polity and market man, productive man, or distributive man declared that he no longer needed the *paideia* of politics to make him a self-satisfactory being. I cannot find such a moment (not even a Mandevillean moment)[55] in the eighteenth century, because the dialogue between polity and economy remained a dialogue, and because both political man and commercial man were equipped with theories of property as the foundation of political personality which could not be separated from each other. Once political virtue was declared to have an agrarian base, it was located in the past; and the movement of history toward credit, commerce, and the market was defined as a movement toward culture but away from virtue. Subject to these definitions, the formulation of a "bourgeois ideology," in the naive sense of a declaration that market behavior was all that was needed to make a human being a human being, was an extraordinarily difficult task, and we should doubt if it was ever naively accomplished. If we find someone who seems to us to have formulated such an ideology, we have to remember that he emerged from a context in which it was openly problematic whether such a thing could be done, and we should not be surprised to find in his ideology unresolved contradictions of which he was well aware. It might even be that the ideology of market society was perfected as an antithesis by those who desired to destroy it.

I return in conclusion to the suggestion that Macpherson's market model explained only one group of phenomena and did not account for their opposites. I think that both socialist and classical antiliberals have been so intent on the location of economic man that they have taken account only of those phenomena which indicate his presence, and have suggested that one set of chromosomes always drove out another, with the result that somewhere in the eighteenth century or the nineteenth must be found the moment when political man died and economic man reigned in his stead. It is now in doubt if such a moment ever occurred at all. It seems that the classical ideal quite simply did not die; that it was reborn with the great recovery of aristocracy which marks the later seventeenth and early eighteenth centuries, with the result that property was always discussed in the political context of authority and liberty.[56] Property was the foundation of personality; but the acid test of personality was whether it required

---

[54] Joseph Cropsey, *Polity and Economy: An Interpretation of the Principles of Adam Smith* (Chicago, 1957).
[55] Thomas Horne, *The Social and Political Thought of Bernard Mandeville* (New York, 1977).
[56] For a study of Adam Smith contrary to the liberal paradigm, see Donald Winch, *Adam Smith's Politics: An Essay in Historiographical Revision* (Cambridge, 1978).

most to be affirmed in liberty or governed by authority. When modes of property arose that did not favor political virtue, they suggested private freedom and political sovereignty, and to that extent the antiliberal paradigm holds good; but – the strength of the classical ideal remaining – the apparition of an individual rendered nonpolitical and nonvirtuous by his property occasioned terrible conceptual problems. By the middle of the eighteenth century, the historically problematic individual, who could neither return to ancient virtue nor find means of completely replacing it, had made his appearance; and he was present, uneasily but effectively occupying the stage of history, before classical economic man, American democratic man – a close relative – or German dialectical and in due course socialist man, had arisen to suggest ways of escaping or resolving his problems. In this scenario, we can, of course, find highly systematic liberal philosophies occurring from time to time; but they always appeared in response to problems which they did not persuade everybody they had succeeded in solving, and they can be made to look as much like incidents as like turning points in the history of social consciousness. I am not calling in question the historical reality of "liberalism" or "possessive individualism," so much as those "liberal," or rather antiliberal, interpretations of history, in which everything leads up to and away from a monolithic domination of "liberal" ideas somewhere in the nineteenth century. I see the formulation of these ideas as always problematic and precarious, and I am even prepared to entertain the notion that "liberal" or "bourgeois" ideology was perfected less by its proponents than by its opponents, who did so with the intention of destroying it. What went on in the eighteenth century was not a unidirectional transformation of thought in favor of the acceptance of "liberal" or "market" man, but a bitter, conscious, and ambivalent dialogue. In contemporary scholarship, it is the Marxists who are the Whigs,[57] their critics who command a dialectic.

[57] Professor Macpherson was heard, at this point in the original reading of this essay, to remark that he had been called many things in his time, but never that before. I remain impenitent.

4

◁═══════════════════════════════════════▷

1776
The revolution against Parliament

I

We come at last to consider a truly British revolution;[1] one which even involves
a revolt against being British. In 1641 and 1688 the kingdom of Great Britain
did not exist, and the events in Scotland which preceded one English Revolution
in 1637 and followed another in 1689 took place in what was still, though it was
ceasing to be, an autonomous political culture; while the unsuccessful last stands
of the Old Irish and Old English aristocracies in 1641 and 1689 occurred in an
Ireland whose political development had not yet reached the point where so sophisticated a term as "revolution" in its modern sense would be appropriate. John
Pym and John Adams may have been revolutionaries; Sir Phelim O'Neill and
Swearing Dick Talbot were not. But in the high eighteenth century provincial
variants of Whig political culture had established themselves in Lowland Scotland, among the Anglo-Irish, in New England, in Pennsylvania, and in Virginia;
there was a kingdom of Great Britain and, briefly, there was an Atlantic British
political world — rather vaguely termed an empire — which reached from the
North Sea to the headwaters of the Ohio. But within this greater Britain there
occurred a revolution which must be thought of as the outcome of its common
development, but which resulted in the detachment of its English-speaking sector on the mainland of North America, to become a distinct nation and a highly
distinctive political culture. The first revolution to occur within a "British" political system resulted in its partial disruption and the pursuit by one of its

From *Three British Revolutions: 1641, 1688, 1776*, edited by J. G. A. Pocock for the Folger Shakespeare Library, pp. 265–88. © 1980 Princeton University Press; reprinted by permission of Princeton
University Press.

[1] This essay was read to a symposium on "Three British Revolutions: 1641, 1688, 1776," held at
the Folger Shakespeare Library in 1976.

components of an independent history; and the same is true of the second, otherwise known as the Irish Revolution of 1912–22.

Since, when we talk of "Britain," we mean an English domination of associated insular and Atlantic cultures, there is a profoundly important sense in which the American Revolution can only be understood by placing it in a series of crises occasioned by the growth and change of English political institutions. To Americans, its significance must be national; an American personality had taken shape in an American environment, and the Revolution is the crisis of its independence. This, obviously, is beyond refutation. But in the "British" context, we have to see it, first as a crisis in the history of the Anglo-Scottish consortium set up in 1707, second as a crisis in the history of that central and most English of its governing institutions, the King-in-Parliament. In 1641–60 and in 1688–89, crises occurred in the relations between the English Crown and English propertied society, from which the King-in-Parliament emerged reinforced, if profoundly transformed; the ability of England to create and consolidate "Britain" and to pursue an Atlantic empire was one of the byproducts of 1688. But in 1776, or rather between 1764 and 1801, the capacity of Parliament for provincial government – and in lesser degree, the way in which it currently governed English society – were severely challenged. In the American colonies there occurred the revolution against Parliament which I have chosen for my title; the authority of Parliament was successfully overthrown, its appropriateness as a form of government was denied to the satisfaction of Americans, and there emerged a new political society, a transformed version of a quasi-republican alternative to parliamentary monarchy which had been latent in the English tradition since the revolutions of the seventeenth century. In Britain proper, however, the authority of Parliament was shown to be so deeply rooted in the conditions of society that its overthrow was unthinkable anywhere to the right of Thomas Paine; the revolt of America did very little to shake it, and after fifty harsh years of industrialization and war it proved capable of enlarging and later democratizing its own electoral base. To complete the post-American picture of the now sundered North Atlantic, we must add the Anglo-Irish relationship as a case intermediate between independence and parliamentary union; the former was only marginally attempted during 1780–1801, but the latter did not take root.

In a context of British history, therefore, the origins of the American Revolution present two characteristics: the inability of Whig parliamentary government to extend itself to colonies of settlement, and the existence within the parliamentary tradition of a republican alternative which could be used to deny Parliament its legitimacy and to suggest that other modes of government were possible. It is not hard to see why the colonial élites could not develop into parliamentary county gentries, but I must leave to others the description of what manner of political beings they did become; it should be emphasized, however, that for a long time they imagined themselves as parliamentary gentries, and only in revolutionary trauma admitted that they must be something else. The importance of the alternative ideology – the republican, commonwealth, or country tradition – is that it provided Americans with a radical but rather shallow explanation of why they could no longer be parliamentary Englishmen, and a rather profound understanding of what else they might become. But in tracing history in terms of contemporary self-understanding – which is what the history of ideology really amounts to – one is not playing a barren game of pitting one cause against another cause, or one factor against another factor; one is exploring the contemporary perception of possibilities and impossibilities, and the limitations of that perception. It can also be shown, I believe, that ideology offers a commentary on the growth and change of the parliamentary institution, which assists us in understanding the limitations of parliamentary reality: the reasons why governing America, but not governing Ireland, confronted Parliament with challenges it preferred not to meet.

II

When James Harrington – who insisted that domestic and provincial government were different in kind – surveyed in the late 1650s the imminent failure of the first English revolution, he felt quite sure of two things. The first was that the government of Charles I had collapsed because there was no longer a feudal aristocracy to support it; the second was that the government of Charles II – if restored, as seemed increasingly likely – would not have the support of any viable hereditary or entrenched aristocracy, because such could exist only in a feudal form. There was a good deal to be said for the first of these perceptions, but a good deal less for the second; Harrington had failed altogether to predict that spectacular reconstitution of a governing aristocracy which followed the decline of the Tudor magnate class whose crisis has been charted by Professor Stone. In 1642 the House of Lords could do little to arrest the drift toward civil war; in 1688 those peers who happened to be in London could come together of themselves to exert a measurable influence on the situation precipitated by the flight of James II.[2] The Restoration of 1660 – which may be said to have begun with the solid determination in Richard Cromwell's Parliament to bring back the House of Lords[3] – had marked the recovery of parliamentary and political aristocracy. The creation of peers by Charles II had furthered, though it had not caused, the growth of a class of habitual politicians who frequented the Court,

[2] David Ogg, *England in the Reigns of James II and William III* (Oxford, 1955), pp. 217, 219–20. See also David H. Hosford, *Nottingham, Nobles and the North: Aspects of the Revolution of 1688* (Hamden, Conn, 1976).

[3] J. T. Rutt, *The Diary of Thomas Burton* . . . (London, 1828), III and IV; Harrington, *Works*, Pocock, ed., Introduction, pp. 102–4.

the Town, and to some extent the City, knew each other well if they hated each other heartily, and maintained that inner world of high politics whose existence continues to fascinate English neo-conservative historians to the point where they are reluctant to acknowledge the political reality of anything else. It is the presence and efficacy of this coterie which marks the real difference between 1641 and 1688; but though the word "Court" was in use in both eras, the decline of the old palace-centered political world of courtiers and councillors was irremediable. The new Court was attendant upon Parliament as much as upon the King; and it was made up of men who understood the simpler arts of parliamentary management, of acting as a "screen or bank" between King and Commons, at any rate better than their predecessors had done, and who found in the House of Lords a very tolerable political club.

In the reign of Charles II it was already understood that there existed a class of parliamentary managers and magnates – moving steadily into the hereditary peerage but never identical with it – whose strength consisted in their closeness to executive authority and in (what was not quite the same thing) their command of political patronage, influence, and what its enemies termed corruption. One need not deny the importance of economic change – of the strict settlement, the mortgage, and improved techniques of estate management – in permitting a class of great landowners to survive and engross its estates,[4] if one emphasizes that the governing aristocracy of late Stuart and Hanoverian England was a parliamentary aristocracy; and though we may debate the control and efficacy of patronage as a technique of government, we need not doubt its reality as an issue and a value. Whig England, it may be said, held as a self-evident truth that every political man was entitled to life, liberty, and the pursuit of influence. One might even question, in tracing the growth of this governing order, the importance of 1688 itself, considered as an isolated episode. Too many reluctant Tories, cursing their King and themselves with equal fervor, went along with that amazing and undesired upheaval to give it the immediate character of a shift in social power. The stress might fall rather upon two of the Revolution's admitted consequences: the "financial revolution" of the mid-1690s and, twenty years later, the Septennial Act, which formed the keystone of what J. H. Plumb has termed "the growth of oligarchy."[5] In the first of these were created the great institutions of public credit – the Bank of England, the National Debt, and, less auspiciously, the South Sea Company – which brought the postrevolutionary regime the political

[4] The classic views are those of Sir John Habakkuk; see most recently, "The Rise and Fall of English Landed Families," *Transactions of the Royal Historical Society*, 5th ser., 29 (1979), pp. 187–208, and 30 (1980), pp. 199–221. For a criticism, see Eileen Spring, "The Family, Strict Settlement, and Historians," *Canadian Journal of History* XVII, 4 (1983), pp. 379–398.

[5] P. G. M. Dickson, *The Financial Revolution in England: A Study in the Development of Public Credit* (London, 1967); J. H. Plumb, *The Growth of Political Stability in England, 1660–1730* (London, 1967).

stability, founded on a large class of investors, and the financial resources necessary to wage war in Europe, to absorb a Scotland ardently desirous of commercial opportunity, and to pursue empire in the Atlantic, the Mediterranean, and India. In the second – after two decades of Country and Tory rebellion against war, high taxes, and government by patronage and finance – the parliamentary aristocracy and gentry deliberately moved to reduce the competitiveness of politics even if this meant confirming the supremacy of influence and patronage. Long parliamentary terms and uncontested elections opened the way to the England of Walpole and Newcastle, the Scotland of the Dukes of Argyll.

This was the Britain, at once oligarchic and imperial, against which the American Revolution was directed; and it is important for us to realize that its personality was a deeply divided one. The function of parliamentary oligarchy was to maintain unity between government and landed society, that unity of the political nation without which there could be no government; but among the necessary means of doing this was the maintenance of a unity between government, commerce, and finance which was dynamic in its pursuit of mercantile, naval, and military empire and a specific role in the European power system. Every perceptive observer of eighteenth-century reality recognized this harnessing of the static and the dynamic; the political nation desired stability more than empire, but pursued empire as a byproduct of its means of maintaining stability. Out of this there was in due time to emerge a kind of fixed law of modern British politics, that empire is to be yielded when it threatens the normal conduct of political competition – an experience unknown to Americans until very recently. But to eighteenth-century minds there was another and more immediate necessary consequence: the necessity of a sovereign Parliament. Whether one looked at the need to maintain the unity of government and society, or at the need to pursue the policies of war and empire, it was clear that executive and legislature must be linked by the same ties as those that bound the governing oligarchy to the nation which it both ruled and represented; and, whether symbolically or practically, the two most obviously necessary modes of this unity were legislative supremacy and a politics of influence. The latter did as much as the former to root executive in legislature and government in society.

This was the system to which the not altogether narrow political nation of the age of oligarchy was to find itself committed; but it was at once the strength and the weakness of opposition ideology that it altogether denied this system's validity. Here we encounter that quasi-republican alternative which I mentioned earlier, and to understand its origins and character we must return to the first English Revolution. As early as 1642 it had been argued on behalf of the traditional constitution that King, Lords, and Commons corresponded to the monarchy, aristocracy, and democracy of a theoretical republican balance, and more vaguely to the executive, judicial, and legislative powers; and that between them there existed an equilibrium in which each was restrained by the other two from the excess which led to degeneration.[6] After 1649 it was contended that a hereditary King and Lords had proved harmful to the balance, and Harrington's *Oceana* is a blueprint for a balanced republic with no hereditary element; but the theory had originally been advanced on behalf of the traditional constitution, and continued to figure in its justification in 1660 and in 1688. Balance presupposed the independence of each of the three constituent parts, and it could be asserted that hereditary tenure effectively guaranteed the independence of a nonelected aristocracy, so long as these did not hold the Commons in dependence, which in a post-feudal society they no longer did. There were only two features of the eighteenth-century constitution which were really incompatible with the paradigm of balance, and of these one was generally recognized, but the other hardly at all. What was not well understood was that the independence of executive and legislature from one another would not ultimately mesh with the indisputable fact that the legislative authority was that of King-in-Parliament, executive in legislature, and must ultimately collide with the principle of the sovereignty of Parliament. The King's ministers were not attacked for sitting in Parliament, but they were attacked for allegedly filling Parliament with the recipients of government patronage. For what was universally acknowledged was that if the members of the legislature became dependent upon patronage, the legislature would cease to be independent and the balance of the constitution would become corrupt. Corruption on an eighteenth-century tongue—where it was an exceedingly common term—meant not only venality, but disturbance of the political conditions necessary to human virtue and freedom.[7] The only self-evident truth mentioned in Paine's *Common Sense* is that the King exercises despotic authority because he has monopolized parliamentary patronage.[8] To us it may seem that this would not have been self-evident even if it had been true, but to Paine's contemporaries it was a necessary and inescapable consequence.[9]

The remarkable fact here—another of the profound cleavages in the Whig mind—is that though the conscious practice of the age was founded upon the necessity of influence no less than upon the independence of property, its moral theory was almost unanimous in declaring that the two were incompatible and that corruption was fatal to virtue. The most sophisticated thinkers of the century—Montesquieu, Hume, Adam Smith, Alexander Hamilton—were those who conceded that though patronage and the commercial society on which it rested

---

[6] In *His Majesty's Answer to the Nineteen Propositions of Parliament* (London, 1642); see Corinne C. Weston, *English Constitutional Theory and the House of Lords* (New York, 1965).

[7] J. G. A. Pocock, *Politics, Language and Time* (New York, 1971), ch. 4.

[8] Philip S. Foner, *The Life and Major Writings of Thomas Paine* (Secaucus, N.J., 1974), pp. 8, 116.

[9] The revolutionary Paine was here only stating as a fact what the conservative Hume had predicted as a probability; see his essay, "Whether the British Government inclines more to Absolute Monarchy or to a Republic" (*Essays Moral, Political and Literary*, 1741).

must destroy virtue, the conditions of human life were such that virtue could never be fully realized, that it was dangerous to pretend otherwise, and that alternative social values must be found. This was perhaps the most fundamental problem in eighteenth-century political and moral philosophy, but here is not the place to pursue it;[10] what matters more immediately is that we have found the ideological fault-line along which British and American political beliefs and practices were to break apart.

There was a quasi-republican critique of parliamentary government which declared that corruption must be ended and the independence of the component parts of the balance restored. This commonwealth or Country ideology[11]—there are various names for it—was on both shores of the Atlantic considerably better articulated than was the defense of existing practice, but in the American colonies it came to have an importance far greater than it ever possessed in Britain where it originated. In England, and to a far lesser extent in Scotland, two groups normally excluded from the citadels of power—Tory gentlemen and Old Whig urban radicals, Bolingbroke at one extreme and Catherine Macaulay at another—perfected the critique of Whig oligarchy and patronage in the hope of mobilizing independent country members against whatever ministry they were attacking. But such attempts almost invariably failed, with the last years of Queen Anne as the only serious exception; and they failed not just because the country gentry were as keen in the pursuit of influence as the next man, but because they had an understanding of their role in the parliamentary system a good deal more satisfying than any they found in the commonwealth and Country ideology. The front benches were there to provide the King with ministers, the back benches to act as the grand jury of the nation; and there they sat, far better Tories than Bolingbroke could ever be, stolidly supporting the ministry of the day because in the last analysis it was the King's ministry, until there arose one of those very rare occasions on which they could support it no more. The commonwealth or Country ideology,[12] of vast importance in the history of thought, was therefore of very little importance in the history of English practice; and I say that as one who considers the life of the mind quite as important as the life of politics. But in the American colonies, where political experience and practice were of a different kind—where the intimate union of executive with legislature, of monarchy with aristocracy and gentry, of government with society, could not be duplicated in microcosm—it was another matter. The balance provincial, as Harrington had

[10] Pocock, *The Machiavellian Moment* (Princeton, 1975), chs. 13–15.

[11] Caroline Robbins, *The Eighteenth-Century Commonwealthman* (Cambridge, Mass., 1959); Isaac F. Krammick, *Bolingbroke and his Circle: The Politics of Nostalgia in the Age of Walpole* (Cambridge, Mass., 1968); Bernard Bailyn, *The Ideological Origins of the American Revolution* (Cambridge, Mass., 1967).

[12] The term "Commonwealth" suggests urban Old Whigs, the term "Country" Tory landowners; the ideology is much the same whoever expresses it.

said, was not the balance domestic; and an ideology that presented parliamentary practice as normally corrupt looked very different when it was a question first of fearing, then of repudiating, the authority of Parliament itself.

III

There is no need to retell here the story of the 1760s and 1770s from the American point of view. A galaxy of distinguished historians have explained how the colonists found Parliament claiming to legislate for them in ways which they found unacceptable, and came as a result, after many crises and reversals of feeling, to discover and proclaim that they were no longer subjects of the King, even in Parliament; and these historians have rightly moved on to consider the social structure and historical experience of the peoples who made this claim, and how it was that they came — as Edmund Burke, an Irishman, was one of the first to observe[13] — to constitute a distinctive nation which must be governed in its own way. History is normally written in terms of national development, and a history of divergence is written in terms of the development of divergent nationalities. But the value of considering the American Revolution as a British revolution is that it obliges us to consider it in terms of a divergence of political styles within what had been a common tradition, and so to ask how it happened that the divergent nationalities acquired the political styles that they did. When Burke spoke in 1775 no one knew that there would be an independent America or how it would be governed, and the form of government it ultimately acquired was certainly not the simple product of its autonomous experience. I have suggested so far that the parliamentary institution could not take root under colonial conditions, and that the ideology of parliamentary opposition was sufficiently radical in its criticism of the way in which the institution had developed to provide conceptual means of first repudiating and then replacing it. But the implication seems plain that we must return to the history of the parliamentary institution itself and reexamine its failure to deal with provincial government; a possible question is whether this failure may have arisen from the circumstance that the institution itself was in a state of crisis.

The early part of the reign of George III was certainly one of confusion and abnormality in the politics of oligarchy. There had been, before the King's accession, the wartime ministry of the elder Pitt, himself a figure dynamic and demagogic enough to cause discomfort to the Old Corps of Whigs, which had brought unexpected global victories and an unlimited prospect of empire on the North American continent. From the Stamp Act to the Quebec Act, the legislation to which the colonies objected was designed to rationalize this empire and make it governable; and both the great contemporary historian David Hume[14] and the

---

[13] In the *Speech on Conciliation with America* (1775).
[14] J. Y. T. Greig (ed.), *The Letters of David Hume* (Oxford, 1932), II, 301.

great modern historian Sir Lewis Namier[15] – neither of them English – made it their charge against Pitt, later Earl of Chatham, that he had saddled Britain with unlimited empire and then collapsed into irresponsibility at the height of the crisis generated by its acquisition. Hume indeed thought that the empire should never have been acquired at all, and I have no idea what Namier thought on that subject. But the implication is plain at least that empire was contingent and not necessary to the purposes of British government. Pitt had not conquered the St. Lawrence and the Ohio to open the way to Daniel Boone and George Rogers Clark; an empire of settlement was of less interest than controlling the riverine aspects of a system of Atlantic commerce. Americans were indeed beginning to say that the empire of settlement would be theirs and would some day transfer the seat of government from Britain across the Atlantic; and deep in such expressions of manifest destiny, the dim outlines of what might have become a struggle for *British* independence can be sighted. Chatham once declared that the day Parliament ceased to be supreme over America, he would advise every gentleman to sell his lands and emigrate to that country; the greater partner, he said, must ever control the less.[16] More immediately, England was the ruling partner and the roots of Parliament were in English landed and commercial society. It was this which was to render conciliation with the colonies ultimately impossible.

A further cause of disruption in the normal conduct of parliamentary politics had been the ministerial initiative taken, soon after his accession, by the young George III and his friend Lord Bute. The meaning of this has been intensively debated, but it seems clear that the King had no intention of overthrowing the oligarchical order and no means of doing so; and though his private as well as his public rhetoric is somewhat flavored by the language of Tory opposition, it was to prove important that he had certainly no intention of coming forward as that "patriot king" which was Bolingbroke's final contribution to the ideology of separated powers. But in driving Pitt and then Newcastle from office, the King and Lord Bute overplayed their hand sufficiently to provoke both Whig and radical – not to mention Tory – opposition. Radical displeasure erupted in London and took the form of the Wilkite movement; and the circumstance that George's chief adviser for a year or two was a Scot, and a Stuart into the bargain, produced a wave of venomous anti-Scottish chauvinism, such as lay always at the roots of eighteenth-century opposition, and regrettably reappears in the writings of both Adams[17] and Jefferson[18] years later. Radical opposition – which was

---

[15] Namier, *England in the Age of the American Revolution,* 2nd ed. (London, 1961), pp. 159–60.

[16] Max Beloff (ed.), *The Debate on the American Revolution* (London, 1949), p. 102 (from *Chatham Correspondence,* II, 369–72). See also "Josiah Tucker," Chap. 9, this volume.

[17] John Adams, *Autobiography (The Adams Papers,* ed. L. H. Butterfield [Cambridge, Mass., 1961], III, 352): "an insolent, arbitrary Scotch faction, with a Bute and a Mansfield at their head for a ministry . . . ."

[18] See Jefferson's drafts for the Declaration of Independence: "Not only soldiers of our common blood, but Scotch and foreign mercenaries to invade and destroy us . . ." Carl Becker, *The Declaration of Independence* (New York, 1933), pp. 169, 172.

necessarily popular in the sense that it was outside the intimate proceedings of oligarchical politics – automatically took the form of an outcry against corruption, and the King, who had set out with some vague idea of reducing the aristocracy's control over patronage, found himself tagged as its chief upholder. It was much easier to denounce the influence of the Crown when the Crown proposed to exert that influence with the aid of advisers whom neither radicals nor aristocrats liked.

When Bute left the scene, George III punctiliously sought his ministers within the established world of English politics; but his own activities, coupled with those of the opposition in the streets of London, Boston, and Philadelphia, were bringing the oligarchy into a state of disarray from which it did not fully recover. Chatham's retreat into psychic instability was an accident of personality; but Sir Lewis Namier's detestation of Edmund Burke – which ran very deep indeed – was in part the effect of his belief that Burke's rhetoric escalated into a moral and constitutional issue the perfectly natural desire of a Whig faction to return to power. The point, however, about the Rockingham Whigs – a rather inarticulate group whom Burke served in the role of hyperarticulate genius – is that they simply did not know what to do with power when they had it; and when in due course the King found in Lord North a minister who could hold Parliament together, he was merely filling a vacuum left by the inefficacy of Whig politicians. Though it may not show up in their day-to-day maneuverings within the world of high politics, these were caught between two fires. They could not run with the London, country, and American radicals whose denunciations of corruption were increasingly turned against aristocracy as well as Crown; and this deprived them of one of their normal rhetorical means of attacking a ministry they did not like. They would never have made very good leaders of a Country movement, and in the era of Jack Wilkes and Sam Adams – insofar as they knew about the latter – they did not even want to try. The case for Burke's *Thoughts on the Present Discontents,* if there is one, is that he was looking for an alternative rhetoric to that of the commonwealth ideology; to his formidable critic Catherine Macaulay, however, it seemed that he was merely watering down the language of the radical tradition.

A simple dialectic would suggest as the outcome of this situation a wave of reform originating with leaders out of doors;[19] but in Britain this did not happen, whereas in the American colonies it did. The two phenomena are of course discontinuous: only externally and rhetorically were the American radicals a Country movement originating in the context of British politics, and they made it their aim not to reform Parliament, but to repudiate its authority. But it is of vast importance in the setting of American history that they found the only ideological means of doing this to entail the assertion that the parliamentary institution

[19] John Brewer, *Party Ideology and Popular Politics at the Accession of George III* (Cambridge, 1976).

itself was corrupt—not just accidentally, but inherently – and must be replaced
by drawing upon the quasi-republican alternatives supplied by the opposition
tradition. And one cannot consider the political culture of the Founding Fathers
without discovering that the language of commonwealth ideology, however inadequate as a rhetorical tool in parliamentary Britain, offered superlative intellectual equipment for debating the problems of eighteenth-century politics and
society, and for founding institutions which have endured. The Nixon Administration was immolated on altars originally built by the Old Whigs; and the
knives were still sharp.

In the context of British history, however, to which the view of 1776 as a
British revolution commits us, we have to ask not only why there was a revolution against Parliament in the American colonies, but what this means in terms
of the history of Parliament itself. Is there, for instance, any deep relationship
beween the attempts to legislate for the colonies in the 1760s and the ministerial
upheavals which followed the intervention of Bute and George III? It seems plausible to suggest that there was not – that more or less any ministry might have
started legislating for America with no sense of doing anything out of the ordinary – but we continue to find the thought enticing that more stable ministries
might have proved less stubborn and might have desisted before the crisis became
irremediable. There persist, both in American and in British thinking, various
forms of nostalgia (the reasons for their existence are themselves historically interesting) which continue to suggest that the severance of America from Britain
might, and almost should, have been avoided. I cannot imagine that these feelings run very deep, and my main reason here is a firm conviction that parliamentary institutions and a continental empire of settlement were, in no long run,
incompatible. But a subsidiary theme of this nostalgia on the American side is
the will to believe that the loss of America was a terrible shock to the British
nations and marked a profound crisis in the stability of their governing institutions. It seems important to explain, in conclusion, some reasons for thinking
that this was not the case at all; that the loss of America was an effect of the
stability of eighteenth-century politics, much more than of their instability or of
the fact that they were beginning to change, and was accepted in a way which
did their stability no harm at all.

IV

If there was a moment at which an American Revolution became inevitable, it
was the moment at which it became unalterable that the colonies thought of
themselves as (to use a phrase of the time) "perfect states," which must – demo-
cratically or otherwise – generate legislative governments with all the attributes
of sovereignty. Perhaps this did not happen until 1776, when they declared

themselves "states" and set about just such a pursuit of sovereignty in formally revolutionary terms; but a powerful cause in precipitating this Revolution was the discovery that sovereignty was indeed legislative and was therefore unsharable. The British had always been perfectly clear that this was the case, and that Parliament must legislate for the colonies if it had any claim to govern them at all; but we all know that the ideological history of the Revolution consists largely of the extraordinary difficulty with which Americans brought themselves to acknowledge this self-evident truth. Because they began with believing themselves to be British, living under a free constitution, they supposed themselves to enjoy the civil rights, the constitutional liberties, the political virtues, and the natural freedoms that went with it; and so indeed they did, until they began trying to plead these things against the supremacy of Parliament. Then they discovered how far away Parliament really was and how little they understood that institution or those whose lives were intimately bound up with it. The British, except insofar — and it was to a considerable extent — as their thinking was confused by the commonwealth ideology of separated powers, had a very clear understanding that liberty depended upon the supremacy of Parliament, upon its legislative sovereignty (perhaps symbolic rather than active), and upon the continuation of a government of influence and patronage. The great American discovery was to be that the commonwealth ideology provided many of the conceptual bases for a new and successful form of government, but this came about only after it had helped render a revolution inevitable by delaying their recognition of the revolutionary nature of what they were asking. Perhaps this is why one of the first to call for revolutionary independence was Thomas Paine — an Englishman in some ways closer to Puritan and Cromwellian than to Whig or even Old Whig ways of thought.

When the Americans and some of their supporters argued that the King should offer his protection to a number of legislatures virtually equal with one another, Lord North observed that the argument was that of a Tory.[20] When Jefferson, in *A Summary View of the Rights of British America,* virtually invited George III to assume the role of Bolingbroke's "patriot king," who dealt with Parliament independently of the channels provided by ministers, their connections, and their influences, he invited him to deal in this way with an indefinite number of parliaments at the same time. We know that George never had the intention of acting as a patriot king, and it seems in the highest degree unlikely that Jefferson thought he was going to; the strategy of the *Summary View* is surely to offer the King a role in order to denounce him for refusing it. But the reason why George could never be a patriot king is also the reason why a plurality of legislatures was an impossibility under eighteenth-century conditions. He never thought of moving outside the established patterns of oligarchical politics because he knew,

---

[20] G. H. Gutteridge, *English Whiggism and the American Revolution* (Berkeley and Los Angeles, 1963), p. 62.

without having to think about it, that the only way to govern Britain was for
him to find ministers who could sustain his government in Parliament (his errors,
which were many, did no more than raise a few questions about the monarch's
personal role in finding and maintaining ministries) and that this could not be
done unless there was a consistent and exacting symbiosis between King, ministers, and the two houses; one in which influence, patronage, and touchy personal
relationships required constant attention; one which certainly could not be sustained with more than one truly sovereign legislature at a time. This was why
the Parliament of Scotland had been absorbed in 1707; and Josiah Tucker, the
most astute of conservative English observers of the American crisis, drew the
conclusion that a separate Irish Parliament had become intolerable.[21] There was
no middle way between legislative union and legislative independence; Ireland
must be drawn into union, America must become independent. Tucker's advice
for Ireland was not taken till twenty years and a bloodbath later; but that is about
the norm for Irish history.

There were conservative as well as radical reasons why Englishmen should
welcome American independence, and the former of these were very like the
reasons for supporting American subjugation. Our thinking on these matters is
often confused by the memory of the late nineteenth- and early twentieth-century
British Commonwealth, in which independent legislatures under the same Crown
proved to be perfectly feasible; but what needs stressing about that by now somewhat unreal association is that it came into being at a time when electoral politics, both British and colonial, had become more democratic and less dependent
on the exercise of influence by the Crown. Under the conditions of the age of
oligarchy nothing of the kind was feasible. Since we know that English radicals
in the age of the American Revolution were demanding a wider franchise and a
reduction of influence, we vaguely feel that they were demanding both what
might have rendered the Revolution unnecessary and what Americans were demanding for themselves. But such thinking is not very exact. In April 1777,
Edmund Burke wrote to his constituents at Bristol:

> But if the colonies (to bring the general matter home to us) could see that in Great Britain
> the mass of the people are melted into its government, and that every dispute with the
> ministry must of necessity be always a quarrel with the nation, they can stand no longer
> in the equal and friendly relations of fellow-citizens to the subjects of this kingdom.[22]

Burke was talking about what he hoped would not happen; he was attempting
both a tortuous justification of the Rockinghams' withdrawal from Parliament
and a protest against the wartime state of mind. But there is a deeper meaning

[21] *A Series of Answers to Certain Popular Objections against Separating from the Rebellious Colonies and Dis-
carding them Entirely* (Gloucester, 1776), pp. 57–58. The point is repeatedly made in Tucker's
works; he insists that a plurality of independent legislatures can lead only to Tory consequences.
[22] "A Letter to the Sheriffs of Bristol," in A. J. George, ed., *Edmund Burke: Speeches on the American
War* (Boston, 1891), p. 194.

to his words. Since the summer of the preceding year the Americans had in fact been engaged in a quarrel with the British nation – they had declared as much in a public document now dated July 4, 1776 – and a reason for this state of affairs was that, even in the age of oligarchy, there was a real sense in which the mass of the people was melted into its government. Those out of office might have a quarrel with the ministry, but they must support the sovereignty of its Parliament; those excluded from the franchise might have a quarrel with the oligarchy, but it was in Parliament that they must seek representation. The parliamentary institution had taken root in the nation, and influence was for the present among the means implanting it there. These conditions had not been established in America, and nobody had ever thought of ways of implanting them.

This was why no British politician – certainly not Burke – had ever envisaged a solution of the colonial problem which did not involve the ultimate sovereignty of Parliament; Burke had only said that Parliament should refrain from exercising it. This was why Burke and his friends found themselves totally powerless in politics; the political nation was supporting its Parliament as usual. And this was why neither the war against the Americans, nor the peace which consented to their independence, was so overwhelmingly unpopular as to threaten the stability of institutions; you might almost say that the sovereignty of Parliament was the end to be sustained, and that subjecting an empire or letting it go were but two ways of doing it. If – to borrow language from leaders of the historical profession – Plumb's "growth of oligarchy" was the remedy found in the eighteenth century for the problems occasioned by Stone's "crisis of the aristocracy" in the seventeenth, it might seem that the loss of an empire was a high price to pay for institutional stability. But the empire was surrendered, and the stability of institutions maintained. There is this to be said for the old and misleading adage about the British empire being "acquired in a fit of absence of mind": the British are more interested in maintaining than in expanding themselves (and will always let their overseas loyalists go when it suits them). By way of contrast, let us think for one moment about the Northwest Ordinance, about Jefferson's "empire of liberty," about Clay and Monroe, Jackson and Polk; and we shall realize the paradox that the new republic, born of the revolt against empire, had a commitment to empire – and to empire of settlement – built into its structure in a way that the parent system never had. The American Revolution was, among other things, the greatest revolt of white settlers since the Decline and Fall of the Roman Empire, which it did not otherwise resemble; for the Romans allowed themselves to become absorbed by their own empire, and the British never made that mistake.

It may seem that I am giving somewhat too conservative an interpretation of the radical tensions of mid-Georgian England; but the immediate future lay with conservatism. The attempts at parliamentary reform made in the 1780s had essentially failed before the French Revolution and the great reaction against it; and it can be argued that one reason for their failure was that the commonwealth ideology, on which their rhetoric was still founded, was by now visibly out of touch wih reality. According to conventional reforming wisdom, corruption had destroyed the balance of the constitution, and its principles must be restored by a return to its uncorrupt democratic component. But the nation had just passed through a painful and inglorious war to maintain its parliamentary institutions as it understood them, and neither radical, nor Tory, nor American arguments could stand against that. The election of 1784 marked the end of the old style of opposition, as the political system turned decisively toward a minister – the younger Pitt – who could hold power, and who looked as if he could conduct reforms, on terms which held the parliamentary institution together. Burke managed to be on the losing side as usual, but his ideology had the future before it. There could be no return to first principles, he said, within a prescriptive system. It is not without significance that he had first enunciated his hatred of doctrinaire politics in order to castigate ministers for opening up the problem of colonial legislation when there existed no answer to it.

But across the Atlantic, the republic born of the great revolution against Parliament was engaged in the return to first principles because there was nowhere else to go. On discovering that parliamentary government had never included them, they had turned to the quasi-republican alternative which the parliamentary tradition had brought them, and were now studying the commonwealth ideology in all its intellectual richness in the attempt to get themselves a form of government. This is not the place to speak of the extraordinary ingenuity with which they transformed their intellectual legacy as they thought suited them best. But we can understand the depth and bitterness with which Hamilton was accused of wanting to restore the British form of government,[23] if we reflect that the repudiation of Parliament entailed the idea that it was founded upon executive corruption. Since Hamilton wanted a strong executive, with a base in public credit and a supply of political patronage, he must be plotting to restore the monarchy and hereditary aristocracy; these truths were, very nearly, self-evident. But Hamilton's spirit went marching on, past this particular misunderstanding, and the final paradox of this episode in British history remains to be noted. In the course of the nineteenth century, parliamentary monarchy democratized and reformed itself, in ways which may well have entailed a restatement of the principle of oligarchy but did involve the elimination of most of the classic and familiar forms of patronage, influence, and corruption. Democratic federalism grew into the greatest empire of patronage and influence the world has known,

[23] Gerald Stourzh, *Alexander Hamilton and the Idea of Republican Government* (Stanford, 1970); Lance Banning, *The Jeffersonian Persuasion* (Ithaca, N.Y., 1978).

and remains to this day dedicated to the principle that politics cannot work unless politicians do things for their friends and their friends know where to find them. New democrat is but old Whig writ large; and the Federal Constitution, that great triumph of the eighteenth-century political art, seems to have perpetuated the eighteenth-century world it was designed to deal with. Far more than Trollope's Duke of Omnium, Richard Nixon was a figure of the Old Whig political imagination. Far from his being an anomaly within the American political tradition, the only aspect of his downfall that would have surprised a Founding Father is that his was the only presidency to end in removal for causes shown in the space of two hundred years. But do not our governing assumptions determine realities? America may have guaranteed the survival of the forms of corruption it was created to resist.

PART II

5

◁══════════════════════════════════════▷

Modes of political and historical time in early eighteenth-century England

History — in all but a few, rather esoteric, senses of the term — is public time. That is, it is time experienced by the individual as public being, conscious of a framework of public institutions in and through which events, processes and changes happened to the society of which he perceives himself to be part.

The public realm, unlike the social realm, must be conceived as institution-alized and formalized, since otherwise the distinction between public and private cannot be maintained; and the institutionalization of the public realm leads to the institutionalization of social experience and of modes of apprehending it, and consequently to the institutionalization and differentiation of apprehended time. To say that "history is public time," therefore, is to say that individuals who see themselves as public beings see society as organized into and by a number of frameworks, both institutional and conceptual, in and through which they apprehend things as happening to society and themselves, and which provide them with means of differentiating and organizing the things they apprehend as happening. This is why the archaic dictum that "history is past politics" has more to be said for it than we are disposed to recognize, and why the history of historiography is to so large an extent part of the history of political discourse.

There are a number of ways of classifying the conceptual frameworks by which people order their consciousness of public time. One may classify them profes-sionally and institutionally, in such a way as to suggest that the law provides one ordering of time, the church another, parliament a third and so on; but in eighteenth-century England such orderings and their languages had drawn to-gether to a point where it seems truer to say that time and history were ordered by consciousness of a public realm or political nation, which could itself be or-

From *Studies in Eighteenth-Century Culture*, vol. 5, edited by Ronald C. Rosbottom for the American Society for Eighteenth-Century Studies, pp. 87–102. © 1976 University of Wisconsin Press; re-printed by permission.

dered and conceptualized in a number of different ways. A preferable mode of classification, therefore, may be one which enumerates different ways in which a political society may order consciousness of its existence in time and of time as the dimension of its existence. This classification can be arranged around two dominant notions, that of continuity and that of contingency. Under continuity we may see society describing itself as perpetuating its usages and practices, transmitting its different forms of authority and, in these and other ways, maintaining its legitimacy.[1] Society will be seen as a complex of institutions and as an institutionalized whole; and its continuity as a whole will be predominantly defined in terms of the modes of continuity characteristic of those institutions held to be peculiarly important to its structure. Under the heading of contingency, however, we become aware of other and less institutionalized phenomena. We are in the domain of fortune, as it used to be called: of the unpredictable contingencies and emergencies which challenge the human capacity to apprehend and to act, and which may appear either exterior or interior to the institutional structure of society.[2] In either case, however, what is institutionalized is now the capacity to act in response to contingency, and the institutional structure is now a continuous capacity for action rather than a continuous transmission of legitimacy — a change of emphasis which cannot but operate to diminish institutionality and render the institutional more of a short-term response to contingency than it was before.

When time is the dimension of continuity, the institutional structure is seen as successfully creating its own time — though if it is fully successful in doing so, this will by no means be the same as creating its own future, but rather ensuring that no future ever comes into existence. When time is the dimension of contingency, the structure is seen as striving to maintain itself in a time not created by it, but rather given to it by some agency, purposive or purposeless, not yet defined. It may succeed or fail in maintaining itself; and if it succeeds, this may mean that it succeeds in preserving its own existence in the midst of a history it does not otherwise modify, or that it succeeds in imposing itself on exterior time and re-creating the latter in the image of its own continuity — thus absorbing history into itself — or that it succeeds in adapting itself, together with its own continuities and their time-dimensions, to exterior contingencies and their histories, while at the same time imposing its changing continuities on exterior contingencies in such a way as to bring about a dialectical relationship between

---

[1] J. G. A. Pocock, *The Ancient Constitution and the Feudal Law* (Cambridge: Cambridge University Press, 1957); "Time, Institutions and Action: An Essay on Traditions and their Understanding," in *Politics, Language and Time* (New York: Atheneum, 1971); "Modes of Action and their Pasts in Tudor and Stuart England," in Orest Ranum, ed., *National Consciousness, History and Political Culture in Early Modern Europe* (Baltimore: Johns Hopkins University Press, 1975).

[2] J. G. A. Pocock, *The Machiavellian Moment* (Princeton: Princeton University Press, 1975).

continuity and contingency, the political society and history. To the student of the patterns of historical consciousness that arise in these ways, the important question to determine is that of what the time-creating agencies are — institutional or extra-institutional, human or extra-human — and whether they act to perpetuate simple continuities, to perpetuate simple domains of contingency, or to create new futures.

As English political and historical thought — to which I shall here confine myself — passes from the seventeenth into the eighteenth century, we encounter some interesting and important case studies of this order. We seem — though it is possible to overstate this point — to be passing out of a period in which it was generally supposed that contingent time and its events were the creation of God, and that the history thus created was more than merely contingent, in the sense not only that faith in the goodness of providence entailed our believing that it had a pattern we did not know, but also that belief in the content of revealed prophecy gave us certain keys to the pattern of its eschatological climax. To seventeenth-century intellects, the fulfillment of types by antitypes, or the literal or symbolic fulfillment of specific prophecies, could be utilized, in expectation, to build up scenarios for sacred futures, in the movement towards which favored secular societies might realize their history as latter-day Israels. But in the wake of the Puritan failure England — if not New England — had opted for a less prophetic form of religion which made less demand for an Elect Nation;[3] and the millennial and messianic projections of the sacred future, which had formed so important a constituent of secular historical consciousness, seem to have survived mainly in the form described by Tuveson in *Millennium and Utopia,* where the long-standing tendency to see the millennium as the resurrection of mankind's Adamic potential had led to its being described as the rational and even scientific perfection of human society in a future no less secular for being providential. This kind of religiose progressivism figures in eighteenth-century thought, but not as one of its major political rhetorics; one is tempted to call it the opium of the Unitarians, though the idea of a providentially ordained increase of rationality was not without its contribution to the formation of associationist utopias.[4]

At the other end of the cosmic scale from that at which God created the phenomena of time from the standpoint of a *nunc-stans* which knew no future, traditional thought had located the humblest and least rational or sacred — though

---

[3] William Haller, *Foxe's Book of Martyrs and the Elect Nation* (New York: Columbia University Press, 1963); William M. Lamont, *Godly Rule: Politics and Religion, 1603–1660* (London: Macmillan and Co., 1969).

[4] Ernest Tuveson, *Millennium and Utopia* (Berkeley and Los Angeles: University of California Press, 1949); Jack Fruchtman, Jr., *The Apocalyptic Politics of Richard Price and Joseph Priestley: A Study in Late Eighteenth-Century English Republican Millennialism.* Transactions of the American Philosophical Society, vol. 73, pt. 4 (Philadelphia: 1983).

far from the least important − of the time-creating agencies: that "custom" which
was "recorded and registered nowhere but in the memory of the people."[5] Founded
upon the individual's ability to recall and summarize his own experience and to
presume its continuity with the experience transmitted to him as that of his
ancestors, this conception had generated two distinct but closely-linked ideological patterns. The first of these was the ideology of the Ancient Constitution,
properly so called: the elaborate set of historical arguments by which it was sought
to show that the common law, and the constitution as it now stood, had been
essentially the same since pre-Conquest times and − if the argument were pressed
home − since time immemorial, or at least since an unrecorded beginning in the
woods of Germany. The second, which could, though with difficulty, be expressed without reference to the first, was the more highly sophisticated philosophy of prescriptive conservatism outlined by Sir Matthew Hale after the Restoration and perfected by Burke a century and a quarter later. This emphasized that
in a purely traditional system, where everything was known simply by the fact
of its transmission, there was no more to be known concerning any institutional
fact than that it must be presumed continuous with some antecedent fact or set
of circumstances. Consequently, we could never locate a customary institution in
any context, whether of universal laws or contingent circumstances, which might
permit of its being evaluated or compared with what had been done under other
circumstances − we might only accept it, on grounds which entailed acceptance
of the whole complex of traditions or transmitting institutions from which it
came.

These two ideological constructs, it should be noticed, entailed two images of
public time, sharply opposed yet as intimately connected as the two faces of
Janus. In the one, time appeared as pure transmission, the image and perpetuation of a past in which was contained, yet contained without a beginning, everything which was needed by way of an institutional complex − somewhat as Cru-
soe finds on the wreck everything he can want, without knowing how it got
there. In the other, each moment in the creation and transmission of a custom
could be depicted in such a way that the stress on the absence of beginnings made
it possible to speak of each act as at once uniquely itself and perfectly continuous
with all that had gone before it. The custom-creating people were now housed
wholly within the continuity of their own transmission, and it became possible
to speak of each act as uniquely theirs, performed in and out of their own historic
individuality "as the silkworm spinneth all her web out of herself only."[6] It is
the paradox of custom in Old Western thought that it deals with the wholly

---

[5] Sir John Davies, *Irish Reports* (London, 1674), preface dedicatory, unpaginated. See *The Ancient
Constitution and the Feudal Law*, pp. 33−34, and for the antithesis between custom and the *nunc-
stans*, *The Machiavellian Moment*, chs. 1−2.
[6] Davies, *Irish Reports; Ancient Constitution*, pp. 33−34.

particular by making it appear wholly continuous, immemorial and self-creating; and part of the paradox is that the philosophy of custom has helped to generate the philosophy of historicism.

This way of thinking, however, while far from extinct at the beginning of the eighteenth century – and massively revived in a changed form by Edmund Burke at the end of it – had during the second half of the seventeenth undergone severe and damaging challenge from the resurgence of feudal studies, which had produced an image of the Norman-through-Plantagenet past as historically autonomous in the sense that it was founded upon a web of social relations which could be studied in detail and shown to be structurally unlike anything prevailing in either the antiquity which had preceded it or the modernity which had taken its place. The feudalization of the middle period of English and Western history – as it may be called – had produced two sharply differing ideological polemics, in the debate between which much of the significant historiographical activity of the eighteenth century goes on, and which may be compared in respect of the structures of institutionalized time to which each gave rise.

The first polemic – Tory at the time of its inception in the 1680s, but successfully taken over by the Whigs some twenty years later – was authoritarian in its implications and in due course gave rise to a kind of presentistic conservatism. (The ugliness of this adjective is the result of our having no familiar or elegant term for thought which uses the uniqueness of the present as a source for political authority; "modernist," while slightly less abrasive, probably carries too many irrelevant connotations.) This line of argument emphasized that neither law nor parliament nor constitution was immemorial, and consequently that none could make claims against the sovereign authority on grounds of its supposed prior antiquity. Filmerian advocates of divinely appointed hereditary monarchy could of course go on to argue that if the constitution was not immemorial the kingship itself was, being rooted not in mere custom but in patriarchal and even Adamic antiquity and an original divine sanction. But after 1688 this argument—which had been widely but not monolithically adopted by Tories – became harder to maintain and the appeal to a feudal past was seen as carrying conservative implications of another and a less antiquarian kind. If the constitution constantly underwent historical change – from pre-feudal to feudal to post-feudal – it would follow that it contained no principles of antiquity on which claims either to or against authority might be based; and consequently the case for sovereignty became the case for some final, uncontrollable and in this sense absolute authority to which appeal might be made in fluctuating and lawless circumstances, and which was above the law for the simple reason that no law which might limit it could otherwise be found.[7] This was rather the case for sovereignty than the case

---

[7] *The Machiavellian Moment*, chs. 13–14. This interpretation replaces that stated in the concluding chapter of *The Ancient Constitution and the Feudal Law*, where it was suggested that belief in the

for divine right; on grounds which were in their own way historicist it looked back to the *de facto* controversy of 1649 and after, to Hobbes, who was in some measure a participant in that debate,[8] and to those pioneer "bourgeois" and "liberal" theorists – these are not adjectives which I find specially illuminating – who had begun to argue that a sovereign was necessary because men in the pursuit of their natural freedom imposed bargains on one another to the limit of their power. This argument was presentist to the extent that it denied that any morally regulating principle was immanent in time, and saw nothing but the moment and its strategies as providing the context in which the effort to moralize and regulate must be made. There also seems to have been a fairly clear ideological association between the use of this argument and the tendency to see the economy as consisting in exchange rather than inheritance; the early economic individualists were all theorists of sovereignty, whether they believed that the sovereign should regulate the actors in the economy or should *laisser les aller*. It was in part on the question of commerce that presentist sovereignty, in its Whig phase, was to become the opponent of the second polemic, to which I now turn.

This second polemic founded on the feudalization of the past had a career even more complicated than the first. In party terms, it moved from Whig to a combination of Old Whig and Tory; in terms of content, it originated with the specialized brand of anti-Normanism – or more precisely anti-Gothicism – employed by James Harrington, under the Protectorate, to suggest that the Ancient Constitution was feudal and outmoded, and therefore ripe for revolutionary transformation. For Harrington, there were no organizing principles immanent in the English past; what he called "ancient prudence" was Spartan and Roman, a commonwealth of armed freeholders which had been corrupted and feudalized by emperors and their Gothic mercenaries, but might now be restored to its true principle in England in consequence of the decay of military tenures.[9] This was to place England at a crucial point on an agrarian version of the Polybian cycle of constitutions, a vision of time more Hellenic than Christian, but to make that point a Machiavellian *occasione* at which there was opportunity to escape from history into the timeless stability of a true republic. By invoking cyclical imagery, Harrington invoked also the idea of a set of organizing principles, from which there could be only degeneration and to which there must be return; but he integrated English history into the classic cycle, and by insisting that freedom must be rooted in individual autonomy, itself rooted in the individual's posses-

antiquity of the constitution reigned supreme after 1688. See also Isaac F. Kramnick, *Bolingbroke and His Circle: The Politics of Nostalgia in the Age of Walpole* (Cambridge, Mass.: Harvard University Press, 1968).

[8] Quentin Skinner, "Conquest and Consent: Thomas Hobbes and the Engagement Controversy," in G. E. Aylmer, ed., *The Interregnum: The Quest for a Settlement, 1646–1660* (Hamden, Conn.: Archon Books, 1972).

[9] *Ancient Constitution*, ch. 6; *Politics, Language and Time*, ch. 4; *The Machiavellian Moment*, ch. 11.

sion of land, he further kept alive the time-structure of the natural economy, in which property was better if inherited than if exchanged. His successors, the so-called neo-Harringtonians,[10] retained the essentials of his time-scheme, but reversed the pattern of his history; re-affirming in the conditions of the Restoration the orthodox ideology of the Ancient Constitution, they located the stable commonwealth of armed freeholders in a Gothic and parliamentary past, and imposed upon the present the burden of escaping corruption. The principles which must be preserved if corruption were to be avoided – the principles of republican balance – were now imputed to the English past, and the Ancient Constitution depicted as an equilibrium of king, lords and commons. To maintain the inheritance of immemorial custom now became the necessary means of escaping the *anakuklosis*.

We might term this a process of classicization. The principles – balance in the constitution, virtue and independence in the individual – on which the polity must rest were now represented as a stable and stabilizing structure, located in the past as a source of legitimacy, and any movement from them was represented as degeneration. The classical politics in Western thought included by this time the disturbing suggestion, made by Machiavelli, that since virtue was action, it must sooner or later alter the conditions on which it rested and so render itself impossible; but eighteenth-century classicism seldom conveyed Machiavellian ideas in their full dynamism and rigor, and intimations of political mortality usually took the form, first of hints that no system of virtue could hope to endure forever, and second of warnings that the process of corruption, once begun, was almost impossible to check, even by the one known cure of drastic return to the constitution's original principles. The stakes were high when the individual was engaged in the practice of civic virtue, for he must commit his entire moral personality to the preservation of a classic ideal amidst a history not inherently friendly to it. If the individual was to be virtuous, he must live in a virtuous city; in a corrupt city, the individual himself must be corrupted.

The historical scene was rendered far more precarious by the late seventeenth century's realization that the personal autonomy, necessary if the individual was to practice virtue in a republic, needed a material foundation in the form of property. If the function of property was to confer independence on the individual, it must involve him in as few as possible contingent relations with other individuals; and the ideal form of property thus came to appear the inheritable freehold or fee simple in land, on which the Roman or Gothic citizen warrior had based his capacity for self-defense and self-government. But this ideal existed in the past. By the closing decade of the seventeenth century English and Scottish social critics were increasingly disturbed by the rise of professional armies, in

---

[10] *Politics, Language and Time*, chs. 3–4; *The Machiavellian Moment*, ch. 12.

which the citizen alienated the vital function of self-defense to a hired and banausic specialist, and thus became in some measure corrupt; and it had already been perceived that what enabled him to take this fatal step was the increased circulation of goods and money, which enabled him to pay a substitute to defend him while he both enjoyed the benefits of an expanding culture and accumulated further riches as the means to further enjoyment. But what soon became known as "the progress of the arts" was an irreversible process, whether one thought of it as the expansion of culture or as the corruption of virtue; the uncomplicated Roman or Gothic world lay far in the past; and profound changes were beginning to occur in Western man's understanding of history, as a result of the perception that economic and cultural growth must be thought of as both progress and corruption. Culture and liberty, it began to appear, were ultimately incompatible; the Goths were both despicable as artists and admirable as freemen; and what raised man above the condition of the savage must ultimately sink him below the level of the citizen. Man's quarrel with his own history, that most characteristic feature of the modern mind, may be dated in England from about the foundation of the National Debt. And should anyone wish to challenge my use of the masculine gender, I will point out that the classical ideal in politics and history was still a profoundly masculine way of thinking, and that its perception of the feminine was part of the crisis in awareness which I am seeking to explore.

The National Debt was a device permitting English society to maintain and expand its government, army and trade by mortgaging its revenues in the future. This was sufficient to make it the paradigm of a society now living to an increasing degree by speculation and by credit: that is to say, by men's expectations of one another's capacity for future action and performance. Since a credit mechanism was an expansive and dynamic social device, the beliefs men had to form and maintain concerning one another were more than simple expectations of another's capacity to pay what he had borrowed, to perform what he had promised; they were boomtime beliefs, obliging men to credit one another with capacity to expand and grow and become what they were not. Far more than the practice of trade and profit, even at their most speculative, the growth of public credit obliged capitalist society to develop as an ideology something society had never possessed before, the image of a secular and historical future. Without belief in the progress of the arts, the investing mercantile society literally could not maintain itself.

But in what was belief in such a future to be rooted? Not in experience, since there is no way of experiencing a future; not in reason, since reason based on the perception of nature cannot well predict the exercise of capacities that have not yet been developed; not in Christian faith, since the most apocalyptic of prophecies is not concerned to reveal the future state of the market. There remained imagination, fantasy or passion; and Augustan social thought is visibly obsessed at times by the spectacle of a society advancing at high speed into a world it can only imagine as existing in the forms which it may desire. Not only must the speculative society maintain and govern itself by perpetually gambling on its own wish-fulfillments; a new dimension was added to that dependence of all men upon all men which thinkers in the classical tradition wished desperately to avoid – though Christian and Hobbesian thinkers alike rather welcomed it – by the imminence of a state of affairs in which not only was every man in debt to every other man, but every man was judged and governed, at every moment, by other men's opinion of the probability that not he alone, but generations yet unborn, would be able and willing to repay their debts at some future date which might never even arrive. Men, it seemed, were governed by opinion, and by opinion as to whether certain governing fantasies would ever become realized.[11]

If the speculative society constantly gave itself credit for attaining levels of wealth, power and satisfaction which it had not yet achieved, and so sought to advance towards them, it constantly sought to transform itself by actualizing the imaginable but not predictable. Now it is an evident fact in the history and sociology of inter-sexual perception that masculine minds constantly symbolize the changeable, the unpredictable and the imaginative as feminine, though why they do so I would rather be excused from explaining. The random and the recurrent, the lunar and the cyclical, were summarized by Roman and Renaissance minds in the figure of *Fortuna,* who symbolizes both the history in which the republic endeavors to maintain itself, and the contingent with which virtue – that obviously virile quality – contends. It frequently occurs, in that Augustan journalism concerned with evaluating the impact of public credit upon society, that Credit is symbolized as a goddess having the attributes of the Renaissance goddess Fortune, and even more than she equated with fantasy, passion and dynamic change.[12] She stands for that future which can only be sought passionately and inconstantly, and for the hysterical fluctuations of the urge towards it. There seems to be an important link between capitalism and romanticism in this renewed feminization of time and of the process of actualization of fantasies on which – though never quite completed – the speculative society depends.

The Augustan political journalists – Defoe, Steele, Addison, Mandeville – display an uneasy concern with the increasingly visible public role of women, and it would appear that this is connected with their increasing perception of the growth of credit finance. Defoe and Addison both employ a female figure to denote the idea that the credit mechanism has endowed society with an excessively hysterical nervous system, and both suggest solutions in terms of what Montesquieu was later to describe as the conversion of *crédit* into *confiance*.[13] That is, credit was no longer to fluctuate wildly with the hopes and fears of the invest-

---

[11] For detail see *The Machiavellian Moment,* ch. 13. I would not now use the word "Augustan" so confidently; see pp. 248–9.

[12] Defoe, *Review,* III, nos. 5–7, 92, VII, nos. 55, 57–9, 116; Addison, *Spectator,* no. 3.

[13] *De l'Esprit des lois,* book XIX, ch. 27.

ing public, but to acquire a stability based on continued experience of the real if mobile goods of society. Addison's famous parable of how the vaporish virgin Public Credit is cast into the depths of despair by one set of phantoms and raised to manic heights by another depicts only the beginnings of the process. Clearly, the lady was Danaë; she needed to be fertilized by a shower of gold; but was it continued experience that gave the gold its value, or only fantasy in another form? The conversion of paper into bullion, of *crédit* into *confiance,* was at best no more than the conversion of fantasy into opinion, and it did not appear that even that conversion could ever be quite completed. In the world of credit finance, government was founded on opinion and reason was the servant of the passions; and though Montesquieu had depicted a society which converted *crédit* into *confiance* by borrowing to expand its commercial and military power, even this mode of controlling and determining the future must remain dependent on the fears and fantasies of those who must continue to invest. If Credit was like Machiavelli's prophet in needing a sword in reserve in case the people should cease to believe, she needed it for the further reason that having once begun to prophesy, she could not stop. The secular future was open and indefinite, and society must go on advancing into it.

The frugal merchant appears at this point, as one whose willingness to invest in the future was the product of his confidence in the present. In a sense he was engaged in the process of reifying the exchange of fantasies, and thus creating an actual future; but what we earlier called presentist conservatism makes its return with him, because a present, no matter how solid in appearance, which consists in a series of steps towards an imagined future, can never be purged of fantasy and passion, or endowed with any set of principles more morally stable than the laws of the market. Bating an invisible hand – a concept whose presence even in Adam Smith can be overstated – there could be no moment in such a present at which human fantasies and passions were not less than perfectly self-disciplined, and the intervention of a sovereign, ultimate and uncontrollable power might not be called for. But the actions of sovereign and subject alike in such a scenario must remain imperfectly rational or moral, and the Machiavellian divorce between politics and morality retained its status as a decree *nisi.* But there was the other side of the Machiavellian formulation: if virtue was not absolute it was corrupt, and if it was corrupt must it not degenerate further? Neither David Hume nor Adam Smith denied that a society might be so heavily in debt to itself as to collapse altogether.[14]

There were in all this the makings of a historical dialectic, an ideology of self-transformation. But it is notorious that English culture, though it may produce great historians, does not produce philosophers of history; though there was a generation when Scotland produced the latter in some abundance, and the need

[14] Hume, *Essays Moral, Political and Literary,* "Of Public Credit"; Smith, *The Wealth of Nations,* book V, ch. 3, "Of Public Debts."

to discover reliable laws of the market, inherent in the situation I have described, was among their motivations. But in England proper the dialectic between virtue and commerce did not reach a crisis. The Whig constitution, alleging its peculiar blend of classical balance and customary antiquity, worked too well. The American colonies broke away, proclaiming incorrectly the irredeemable corruption of the mother country,[15] and set up a republic of their own, on new principles which, as Gordon Wood has shown,[16] blended a new form of dynamism with the classical struggle to preserve virtue against change. But to Britons it seemed that either the repression or the surrender of the colonies would be worth while if it preserved the sovereign authority of parliament; and the writings of Josiah Tucker, perhaps the most authoritative presentation of the British theoretical response to the American crisis, form a classic of presentist conservatism.[17] They are overlaid, in our vision of the history of political thought about this time, by the fact that a few years later Edmund Burke, responding to Yorkshire radicals before he responded to French revolutionaries, began a re-statement of English conservatism along lines which display, as well as the realistic modernism of the commercial Whigs, dominant elements of the customary and traditional vision inherited from the seventeenth century. There were no original principles of the constitution, he declared, from which degeneration might occur or to which a return could be made; but this was not because a new world of commerce had come to replace that of Gothic agrarianism, but because, in a constitution whose every part was presumed to be immemorial, no such principles could be located.[18] Burke was effecting a return from presentist to traditionalist conservatism, though it should be remembered that in a properly articulated tradition, every moment is its own present; and he might well have assented to the interpretation, put forward by Hume before him and by Coleridge after him, of English history as an ongoing dialogue beween conservators based on the land and innovators based upon commerce. The complexity of the institutions through which the dialogue was conducted helped guarantee its continuation.

A liberal interpretation of the constitution, of the relations between virtue and commerce, and of the relations between personality, polity and economy, ensured that England did not develop a dialectical historicism based on the need to maintain consciousness of a self being constantly transformed into its antithesis.[19] Nor

---

[15] Bernard Bailyn, *The Ideological Origins of the American Revolution* (Cambridge, Mass.: The Belknap Press, 1967); *The Origins of American Politics* (New York: Knopf, 1968); Pocock, "Virtue and Commerce in the Eighteenth Century," *Journal of Interdisciplinary History*, 3 (1972).

[16] Gordon S. Wood, *The Creation of the American Republic* (Chapel Hill: University of North Carolina Press, 1969).

[17] See ch. 9, this volume.

[18] See Politics, *Language and Time,* ch. 7, "Burke and the Ancient Constitution: A Problem in the History of Ideas."

[19] See Mollyanne Marks, "Renovation of Form: Time as Hero in Blake's Major Prophecies," in Ronald C. Rosbottom, ed., *Studies in Eighteenth-Century Culture,* vol. 5 (Madison: University of Wisconsin Press, 1976).

did the younger Pitt's war finance produce, in the third cycle of major French wars, the sort of reaction against the alliance between the military and monied interests which Swift had launched against Marlborough and Godolphin. In 1776 – a year whose significance in the history of political thought has been celebrated elsewhere – there appeared, among other notable documents, Adam Smith's *Wealth of Nations* and Jeremy Bentham's *Fragment on Government,* each signifying in its own way that the interaction between the ideas of balance and corruption, virtue and commerce, which had marked what I am tempted to call the first eighteenth century, was beginning to be played out. In the second eighteenth century, that of the democratic revolutions and the struggle against Napoleon, new perceptions of institutionalized time were to be generated by political discourse, at once less classical and – for all the convergence of Coleridgean and German thought – less dialectical. England, having done much to transform the historical self-perception of Europe, was now moving away from France and Germany along paths of her own, while at the same time English and American thought were to develop along sharply divergent lines.

6

◁══════════════════════════════════════▷

The mobility of property and the rise of eighteenth-century sociology

Property appears in the Western tradition of political discussion under a number of heads, which might be summarised as follows: First and foremost, there is the tradition begun by Aristotle and continued by Aquinas, in which property appears as a moral and political phenomenon, a prerequisite to the leading of a "good life," which is essentially civic. In the form of the Greek *oikos,* a household productive unit inhabited by women, minors and slaves, it provided the individual with power, leisure and independence, and the opportunity to lead a life in which he (not until Mary Wollstonecraft do we encounter a thinker systematically interested in adding "she" to this context) could become what he ought to be. Property was both an extension and a prerequisite of personality (and we should be aware of the possibility that different modes of property may be seen as generating or encouraging different modes of personality). The citizen possessed property in order to be autonomous and autonomy was necessary for him to develop virtue or goodness as an actor within the political, social and natural realm or order. He did not possess it in order to engage in trade, exchange or profit; indeed, these activities were hardly compatible with the activity of citizenship. Greek politics were not based on bourgeois concepts, which seems odd when you consider that "politics" and "bourgeois" have the same root meaning of "living in a city." The *polis* and the *bourg, Burg* or borough were profoundly different places, and it is hard to estimate the amount of confusion caused by the circumstance that the German word for "citizen" is *Bürger.* But we are constantly reminded not merely that Karl Marx can be considered a thinker among the classical Western moralists, but that the Western moral tradition displays an astonishing unity and solidarity in the uneasiness and mistrust it evinces towards

From *Theories of Property: Aristotle to the Present,* edited by Anthony Parel and Thomas C. Flanagan for the Calgary Institute for the Humanities and the Wilfred Laurier University Press, pp. 141–66. © 1978 Wilfred Laurier University Press; reprinted by permission. Some revisions to this text.

money as the medium of exchange. Because so many of the components of the good life can be had for money, we are under a constant temptation to mistake money for the *summum bonum,* and an individual drawn wholly into the life of monetarised exchange relationships would be living in a commodified parody of the natural and divine order, tempted to regard himself and his wealth idolatrously. In every phase of Western tradition, there is a conception of virtue – Aristotelian, Thomist, neo-Machiavellian or Marxian – to which the spread of exchange relations is seen as presenting a threat. In this perspective those thinkers of the seventeenth through nineteenth centuries who argued on individualist, capitalist or liberal premises that the market economy might benefit and transform human existence appear to be the great creative heretics and dissenters.

In the form of *oikos* within *polis,* property appears as an item within a scheme of relationships which are essentially political and obtain between citizens set free by their property to engage in them. But there is another face of the Western tradition of no less importance to the understanding of property: the language of jurisprudence, inaugurated by the Roman civilians, strongly present in Aquinas, and carried on by a succession of jurists and natural-law theorists into the age of Locke. In this tradition property, without losing any of its significance to personality, was defined less as that which makes you what you are than as that to which you have a right. With this interpretation we enter upon that fascinating and elusive relationship between the notions of right and ownership, and upon that world of language in which "property" – that which you owned – and "propriety" – that which pertained or was proper to a person or situation – were interchangeable terms. The distinction between persons and things gained in prominence; and instead of being the mere prerequisite to political relations between persons, property became a system of legally defined relations between persons and things, or between persons through things. Since the law defined justice in terms of *suum cuique,* it was possible to define the good life in terms of property relations, or of human relations as the notion of property served to define them, though the thought which stemmed from the *polis* constantly asked whether this definition of justice was adequate. The social relations which law and property defined included many which obtained between men engaged in transferring, exchanging and conveying possessions and even rights; and the vision of the law was therefore less hostile than that of the *polis* towards trade, profit and accumulation. Because jurisprudence and the jurist's conception of justice were concerned with men and things, they were less concerned with the immediate relations between men as political actors or with the individual's consciousness of himself as living the good life. Consequently, under jurisprudence, the notion of the political itself changed and became less the system of relations between citizens and more the system of relations between authorities and subjects necessary to a life lived under law.

Both views, however, incorporate the notion of property in, and subject it to, a complex moral universe; and in both contexts we have learned to talk about an "ancient" view of property as opposed to a "modern" view. We associate "modern" ideas of property with both capitalism and socialism, which entail those very complex schemes of production and exchange that we call "economics," a word derived from the ancient *oikos* and *oikonomike*, which it supplants; and we see reason to believe that the transition from ancient to modern was bound up with the advent of capitalism. We also incline to think that as this transition took place, two other things happened: the notion of unlimited acquisition escaped from many if not all traditional moral restraints – an escape which was itself legitimised – and the increasingly complex and dynamic relationships and processes which we call "economics" began to surpass in importance the political relations among people, swallowing up the ancient *polis* as they swallowed up the *oikos*. It is reasonable to inquire after the actual or perceived effects of this upon personality.

I dwell on all this because I want to establish a setting in which to pursue the next phase of the transition from ancient to modern notions of property: the problem posed by Professor Macpherson in his writings since he coined the notion of "possessive individualism" in 1962. He laid down the paradigm of an unrestricted right of acquisition emerging from legal and moral constraints, which were those of the scholastic jurisprudence elaborated by Aquinas and Suarez. The recent book by James Tully has explored the relation of Locke to Suarez and Grotius.[1] I am going to put forward an alternative thesis, in which I shall lay emphasis on the revival in the period defined of ideas about classical politics and the view of property that went with it. I shall suggest that it was against these civic, rather than juristic, conceptions of property that new economic forces were recognized and defined as asserting themselves, in such a way that capitalist property was recognized as historically new because it was post-classical and modern, and man as proprietor and political animal was seen as existing in the historical dynamic that economic and moral forces created. But if one employs the paradigm of classical politics, rather than that of natural jurisprudence in interpreting this great revolution in the concept of property – this transformation of the relations between *polis* and *oikos,* and between polity and economy, in the words of Joseph Cropsey[2] – one is not discounting the importance of ideas about property derived from natural jurisprudence. Tully shows us that these ideas were operative in the case of Locke; Duncan Forbes and others have insisted on their importance in the case of Hume.[3] We shall have to return to them, but for the

[1] James Tully, *A Discourse Concerning Property: John Locke and his Adversaries* (Cambridge University Press, 1980).
[2] Joseph Cropsey, *Polity and Economy: An Interpretation of the Principles of Adam Smith* (The Hague, 1957).
[3] Duncan Forbes, *Hume's Philosophical Politics* (Cambridge, 1975).

present it will be contended that the story can be better understood by operating
with the ideas of classical politics.

In England after 1649, a shattering collapse of civil authority faced theorists
with the necessity of re-conceptualising it from its foundations. In this enterprise
both ways of thinking about property played a role. Thomas Hobbes operated
within the paradigm of natural jurisprudence; he showed individuals acting in
and from a state of nature, extending their power over things and in so doing
coming to interact with one another, acquiring possession and right over things
against one another, and even acquiring possession over rights in such a way that
they could transfer them to a sovereign whom they instituted by the act of transfer.[4] His individuals move from the pre-possessive to the possessive, the pre-
political to the political, the pre-human to the human.

James Harrington operated within the paradigm of classical politics so completely that the concepts of right and obligation make no appearance in his works
at all.[5] His individuals never occupy a state of nature; they are naturally political,
having been created by God in His image as capable of intelligent self-rule. But
because they live between heaven and earth, they occupy a dimension of secular
history, which is partly governed by fortune. This agency redistributes property,
which is to redistribute the capacity to act as fully political beings. Property
brings power: the power of masters over servants, the power of masters over
themselves; but whenever fortune has brought about the existence of a sufficient
number of masters, these may leave the domain of power and enter that of authority. Authority is not distributed by property, but by the free masters' recognition of one another's political capacity; in instituting it among themselves,
they enter upon the world of political relations and begin to act as the images of
God which they are.

Property and power are the prerequisites of authority and virtue. They discharge no other function than that of the *oikos* in Aristotle and need not (though
they do) possess any other social or economic characteristics than those which
distinguish masters from servants. Because they are liable to redistribution by
fortune, they bring to Harrington's politics an historical dimension, and he was
able to organise history around the distributions of property; but at bottom his
theory of history is simple, binary and cyclical. The *oikos* exists in sufficient
numbers, or it does not. In the ancient republics it existed in the form of the
yeoman smallholding of the citizen warriors; then it was overcome by the *feudum;*
now it is restored in the shape of the yeoman or gentleman freehold, and military

[4] See Quentin Skinner, "The Context of Hobbes's Theory of Political Obligation," in *Hobbes and
Rousseau,* ed. Maurice Cranston and R. S. Peters, (New York, 1972), and "Conquest and Consent:
Thomas Hobbes and the Engagement Controversy," in *The Interregnum: The Quest for Settlement,
1646–1660,* ed. G. E. Aylmer (Hamden, Conn., 1972).
[5] See also chap. 2, this volume.

and political capacity are restored with it. One should note, however, that Harrington's first readers early assumed what he had never said, that the breakup of feudal tenures had had something to do with trade. There was a perception of such a thing, though it had small enough place in the vocabulary of classical politics.

Since Harrington thought it the function of property to provide a large but limited number of people with the basis of independence from which they could practise the equal relations existing among republican citizens, he found that this could be best performed by the relative stability of landed realty. But there were others (of whom, *pace* Macpherson, Hobbes is not necessarily the best example) who aimed to present men as acquisitive and competitive beings whose activities required regulating by a powerful and independent sovereign. Some of these theorists found that a commercial society best illustrated both the subject's competitiveness and the sovereign's independence. In their hands mobility, exchange and acquisition furnished so many arguments for absolute monarchy; and some latter-day criticisms of the liberal order were in this sense anticipated and acknowledged.

A generation later, Sir William Temple produced a carefully constructed anti-Harringtonian statement when he declared that "power," which he called "strength" and "riches," was always on the side of the governed, and nothing but what he called opinion (a crucial term in this story) could prevail on them to submit to the "authority" of government.[6] The next century was to be passed in elaborating the theme that it was in the multiple activities of commercial, cultivated and specialised societies that opinion in Temple's sense could best develop. The commercial, which Marxists call the bourgeois, order was from its first appearance in theory geared to the stabilisation of authority.

But the 1670s saw the revival of Harringtonian theory. Neo-Harringtonianism supplied an idealisation of propertied independence with which it was hoped to mobilise the country gentry in parliament against the crown's revived power of parliamentary patronage, known as corruption. Here classical politics became for the first time a staple of English political rhetoric; and its persistence for more than a hundred years in the face of every discouragement and defeat suggests that it answered some fairly profound ideological needs. From then on there were to exist two parallel and competing doctrines of propertied individualism: one which praised the gentleman's or yeoman's independence in land and arms as performing the functions of the *oikos* in an English or Virginian *polis,* and one which praised the mobility of the individual in an increasingly commercial society as teaching him the need for free deference to authority.

In pursuit of the dialectic between these two modes of individualism, these

[6] *The Works of Sir William Temple* (London, 1770), vol. I, pp. 29–57; "An Essay on the Origin and Nature of Government," written in or after 1672.

two definitions of the political function of property, we shall not linger upon that remarkable episode in the history of property theory associated with the names of Filmer and Locke. If we fully analysed the debate of the 1680s, we should doubtless learn a great deal; but in a history of property theory organised around the duality of classical and commercial politics, it is difficult to retain the image of Locke as the hinge on which history turned. As Tully has shown, he stands in the lineage of those thinkers who approached the politics of property through the language of natural jurisprudence. He was, as far as can be told, utterly indifferent (though at the same time very close) to that revival of classical politics taking place in the neo-Harringtonian ideology of the country opposition. He cared nothing for the virtue of independence threatened by corruption, and it is tempting to try and place him among the philosophers of the commercial order. But neither the refutation of Filmer in 1680 nor the justification of revolution nine or ten years later necessitated the assertion of the commercial order; it was not yet a crucial issue in English ideological debate. Within a very few years it was to become so, and Locke was to be personally involved; but its presence is not to be detected in his *Treatises on Government,* and when the great debate began it is hard to detect Locke's presence in it.

I am alluding here to what we now call the Financial Revolution of the middle 1690s, which saw the foundation of the Bank of England and the successful and lasting creation of a system of public credit whereby individuals and companies could invest money in the stability of government and expect a return varying in proportion to the success of the government's operations.[7] Over the quarter-century that followed, contemporaries came to hold that this had led to the creation of what they called a "monied interest," and that this new class of creditors and speculators was tending to dominate politics. This conviction led critics like Swift[8] and Bolingbroke to say what had certainly not been said before, that a new form of property had arisen, one unknown in previous history. Consequently the relation of property to power, studied by Harrington, and the relation of property to the need for government, studied by Locke, seemed to have been transformed and to need reconsideration. This was a momentous intellectual event: there had been a sudden and traumatic discovery of capital in the form of government stock and a sudden and traumatic discovery of historical transformation as something brought about by the advent of public credit.

The century that followed the Financial Revolution witnessed the rise in Western thought (something not dissimilar may have been occurring in contemporary Japan)[9] of an ideology and a perception of history which depicted political society

[7] P. G. M. Dickson, *The Financial Revolution in England: A Study in the Development of Public Credit, 1688–1756* (London, 1970).

[8] Jonathan Swift, *The History of the Four Last Years of the Queen,* ed. Herbert Davis (Oxford, 1964), pp. 68–78.

[9] See Masao Maruyama, *Studies in the Intellectual History of Tokugawa Japan* (Tokyo and Princeton University Press, 1974).

and social personality as founded upon commerce: upon the exchange of forms of mobile property and upon modes of consciousness suited to a world of moving objects. This eighteenth-century perception of "commercial society" was not based in the first instance upon a perception of trade, or upon an increased hold which market values were gaining upon the thought of social theorists. If we pay attention to the actual records of debate, to the concerns which were expressed and the doctrines which were developed, we find that the origins of commercial ideology lay largely in the controversy between "virtue" and "corruption" and in the associated debate between "landed interests" and "monied interests" which was revitalised by the Financial Revolution.[10] There existed an ideal of the social and political personality epitomised by the term "virtue," entailing a conception of property which had more to do with Harrington than with Locke and more to do with classical than with feudal values. It extolled the image of the "patriot," the individual rendered independent by his property and permitted an autonomous engagement in public affairs. This image was regularly opposed to that of the man of commerce and the latter had to fight its way to political recognition in the teeth of the "patriot" ideal. Though the image of the patriot was of comparatively recent vintage, its roots were deep in classical antiquity, and on these grounds it asserted a rejection of feudal values as vigorous as anything in "commercial" ideology.

Thus we can no longer hold that the beginnings of a modern political theory of property are to be found in Locke's refutation of Filmer, or in any simple transition from feudal to bourgeois values. We must think instead of an enduring conflict between two explicitly post-feudal ideals, one agrarian and the other commercial, one ancient and the other modern. The roots of the conflict in the world of theory and ideology lie not in the perception of two conflicting ways of gaining wealth, so much as in that of two conflicting ways in which property might determine the relations of personality to government. The ideal of the patriot or citizen entailed the image of a personality free and virtuous because unspecialised. The function of his property was to give him independence and autonomy as well as the leisure and liberty to engage in public affairs; but his capacity to bear arms in the public cause was an end of his property and the test of his virtue. As far back as Harrington, we find it stated that while in principle the function of assuring arms and leisure can be discharged by property in goods as well as in land, in practise merchants and craftsmen will find it harder than will landowners and tenants to leave their productive activities to engage in self-defence. Therefore a commercial and manufacturing society like Holland is likely to be defended by mercenaries and governed by oligarchs. By the end of the century, this had been expanded into a general history of society. Medieval Europe was presented in a strangely non-feudal light as a society of warrior freehold-

---

[10] J. G. A. Pocock, *The Machiavellian Moment* (Princeton University Press, 1975), pp. 436–61.

ers. But with the revival of commerce and culture in the fifteenth century, these freeholders succumbed to the temptation to pay mercenaries to defend them while they pursued the profits and pleasures of civilization, and so they passed under the rule of absolute kings, the specialists in government by whom the specialists in warfare were paid.[11] The freeholders' loss of liberty was identical with a loss of virtue.

Here for the first time we hear that there is a process of specialisation in history and that specialisation may be incompatible with the unity of the moral personality which can only be found in the practice of civic virtue. It is also clearly implied that moral personality in this sense is possible only upon a foundation of real property, since the possession of land brings with it unspecialised leisure and the opportunity of virtue, while the production and exchange of goods entails activities too specialised to be compatible with citizenship. The merchant and the consumer are mistrusted as liable to pay the mercenary and the bureaucrat; yet it is seldom dogmatically stated that they constitute an inferior and banausic class. It was not the merchant trading upon his own stock who transformed and corrupted the relation of property to government; he might — though he would find it difficult — retain his civic virtue, his autonomy and his right to keep and bear arms. The danger lay with the owner of capital, great or small, who invested it in systems of public credit and so transformed the relations between government and citizens, and by implication those between all citizens and all subjects, into relations between debtors and creditors. It was not the market, but the stock market, which precipitated an English awareness, about 1700, that political relations were on the verge of becoming capitalist relations; and this awareness could never have developed as it did without the unspecialised agrarian ideal of the patriot to serve as antithesis. The merchant became involved in the indictment of capitalism, and the credit society became known as the "commercial" society, because it was observed that there was a fairly obvious relation between trade and credit. However, an obstinate conviction survived that the individual entrepreneur ought to be free from the machinations of those who determined the rate at which capital might be got. There was always urban as well as agrarian opposition to the alliance of government and bank.

If this alliance — developed with varying degrees of success by Dutch, English, Scottish and French projectors — was to be successfully defended against its critics, an ideological defence of specialisation, speculation and exchange would have to be provided. Though Locke took a hand in the Recoinage of 1696, one of the major proceedings of the Financial Revolution, he did not engage in the ideological manoeuvres which characterise the defence of credit politics. To understand this profound shift in sociological and historical perspective, we have to turn to

[11] *The Machiavellian Moment,* pp. 427–32.

other publicists, such as Daniel Defoe and Joseph Addison. Defoe argued vigorously that society could defend itself better against its own professional soldiers by controlling the money that paid them than by sending its citizens to serve in their place. Out of this thesis he developed a contrast between a commercial society which could pay to have services performed and one without money which could secure them only in return for grants in land.[12] The stereotype of a precommercial "feudal" society – or one more primitive still, like that of the Scottish Highlands – was in large measure the invention of defenders of the Whig system of government. It was harder to meet the neo-Harringtonian argument that a people who paid others to rule them would be exploited in both purse and liberty by their rulers. Here Defoe was on the brink of depicting a people engrossed in their commercial and personal concerns, who maintained a constitutional system of government with a view to keeping their rulers in leading-strings by retaining the power of the purse.

The conventional wisdom of today refers to this image as "liberalism" – though the word was unknown in this sense during the eighteenth century – and encourages us to think that it obtained paradigmatic dominance during the century which divided John Locke from Adam Smith. The challenge of virtue to commerce and specialisation remained constant and only half met; otherwise there would never have been a Rousseau. The reason of most importance to our purposes emerges quite clearly from the record of debate. The criticism based upon the concept of virtue presented a clear and coherent image of the unity of human personality, in its relation to both society and property. Arguments like Defoe's, which clearly implied that the ideal of patriot virtue was being abandoned and treated as historically unreal, could not be complete until an alternative image of personality had been provided. It is possible to show how this was done, and the story is in some respects familiar. Yet we cannot tell it properly if we ignore the complex struggle between the two images, or treat one as antique and the other as taking its place; both were formulations of the late seventeenth century. There is, however, extremely strong pressure from the existing paradigms to take the triumph of "liberalism" for granted. Both the classical and the socialist critics of modern society appear to need the "liberal" antithesis so badly, as a prelude to stating their own positions, that they exaggerate its paradigmatic control while simplifying and antedating the history of its emergence.

We have now to consider what problems necessitated the construction of a new image of social personality and why these problems were hard to overcome. It was common ground that the political individual needed a material anchor in the form of property no less than he needed a rational soul. If he found that anchor in the shape of land, it guaranteed him leisure, rationality and virtue. If he

---

[12] *The Machiavellian Moment*, pp. 432–5.

acquired land by appropriation or by inheritance, these things were guaranteed him as part of a natural order. Locke had argued that this was not enough to necessitate government and that a pattern of exchange relationships must figure among its preconditions. But Locke was ever indifferent to the ideal of patriot virtue, and it was this which the Financial Revolution seemed to challenge. Government stock is a promise to repay at a future date; from the inception and development of the National Debt, it is known that this date will in reality never be reached, but the tokens of repayment are exchangeable at a market price in the present. The price they command is determined by the present state of public confidence in the stability of government, and in its capacity to make repayment in the theoretical future. Government is therefore maintained by the investor's imagination concerning a moment which will never exist in reality. The ability of merchant and landowner to raise the loans and mortgages they need is similarly dependent upon the investor's imagination. Property – the material foundation of both personality and government – has ceased to be real and has become not merely mobile but imaginary. Specialised, acquisitive and post-civic man has ceased to be virtuous, not only in the formal sense that he has become the creature of his own hopes and fears; he does not even live in the present, except as constituted by his fantasies concerning a future. The National Debt has rendered society more Hobbesian than Hobbes himself could ever have envisaged, since it has placed the performance of covenants forever beyond the new Tantalus's reach and left him to live by dreaming of it.[13]

When the stability of government in the present became linked to the self-perpetuation of speculation concerning a future, something happened which forms an important part of the history of ideas concerning unlimited acquisition and accumulation. Government and politics seemed to have been placed at the mercy of passion, fantasy and appetite, and these forces were known to feed on themselves and to be without moral limit. This is not to suggest that this was the origin of the idea of unlimited acquisition or of the need to legitimate it; Joyce Appleby's studies of early market theory may well have shown that observation of mercantile behaviour itself generated a good deal of thought upon this question.[14] But it was observance of the revolution of public credit that generated the idea that political relations were becoming relations between debtors and creditors – a thought which the publicists of Queen Anne's reign discussed unendingly – and this was seen as leading not merely to corruption, but to the despotism of speculative fantasy. Booms and busts, bulls and bears, became the determinants of politics. The value of public stock – the Dow Jones ratings of the eighteenth century – became the index to the stability or instability of gov-

[13] See the preceding chapter.

[14] Joyce Oldham Appleby, *Economic Thought and Ideology in Seventeenth-Century England* (Princeton University Press, 1976).

ernments, and all this was seen as placing politics at the mercy of a self-generated hysteria (in the full sexist sense).

The intellect of the early eighteenth century can be seen applying itself to the stabilisation of this pathological condition. Defoe and others wrote about the conversion of "credit" into "opinion,"[15] Montesquieu about the conversion of *"crédit"* into *"confiance."*[16] Defoe, a moralist, meant that men should behave in such ways as to give one another good grounds for believing that promises would be performed and expectations fulfilled; Montesquieu, a Machiavellian, meant that by making themselves promises, men would discover that they had increased their credit, wealth and power. Both had in mind the conversion of the pure fantasies of speculation upon the future into the well-grounded opinions of continued experience in an on-going and dynamic political economy. It was the problem of how the bags of wind, which we meet in the imagery of Addison as well as Montesquieu, might be filled, and seen to be filled, with real gold.[17] (The problem of paper currency is acutely relevant here.) Such thinkers had recognised that, in the credit economy and polity, property had become not only mobile but speculative: what one owned was promises, and not merely the functioning but the intelligibility of society depended upon the success of a program of reification. If we were not to live solely in terms of what we imagined might happen – and so remain vulnerable to psychic crises like those of the Darien Scheme, the South Sea Bubble and the Mississippi Company – experience must teach us when our hopes were likely to be fulfilled, and *confiance* teach us that we might create conditions in which their fulfilment would be more likely.

The conversion of passion into opinion was only one of the programs which theorists devised for the remedy of the situation. Albert Hirschman's *The Passions and the Interests*[18] suggests another, and there is a clear relation between the problem of speculative politics and economics, and the existence in the eighteenth century of so many moral and philosophical writings on the conversion of passion into reason and of rational egoism into socially desirable behaviour. But there was far more at work here than a mere recognition that English society had been taken over by hard-faced *homines economici* obedient only to the laws of market behaviour. These laws were present and there was thought about them. There was an anxious desire to discover what these laws were; but it is equally true, and perhaps more prominent, that it was the hysteria, not the cold rationality, of economic man that dismayed the moralists. Systems of rational egoism were devised less to explain and legitimise what he was doing than to offer him means of controlling his own impulses. It might be possible to distinguish between "hard" and "soft" rationalisations of this order, of which the former accepted the uncontrollable acquisitiveness of entrepreneurs who knew what they were doing,

[15] *The Machiavellian Moment*, pp. 440–1, 454–6.   [16] *Esprit des Lois*, XIX, 27.
[17] *The Spectator*, no. 3; *Lettres Persanes*, CXLII.   [18] Princeton University Press (1976).

and the latter hoped to teach self-discipline and self-understanding to entrepreneurs who did not. Mandeville might be a "hard," Addison a "soft." But there
is reason to believe that the latter might preponderate; and certainly a main
theme of Hirschman's study is the emergence of a strategy whereby passion and
commerce could be presented as self-limiting forces in a new and remarkable way.

Economic man as masculine conquering hero is a fantasy of nineteenth-century
industrialisation (the *Communist Manifesto* is of course one classical example). His
eighteenth-century predecessor was seen as on the whole a feminised, even an
effeminate being, still wrestling with his own passions and hysterias and with
interior and exterior forces let loose by his fantasies and appetites, and symbolised
by such archetypically female goddesses of disorder as Fortune, Luxury, and most
recently Credit herself. Pandora came before Prometheus: first, because to pursue
passions and be victimised by them was traditionally seen as a female role, or as
one which subjected masculine *virtù* to feminine *fortuna;* and second, because the
new speculative image of economic man was opposed to the essentially paternal
and Roman figure of the citizen patriot. Therefore, in the eighteenth-century
debate over the new relations of polity to economy, production and exchange are
regularly equated with the ascendancy of the passions and the female principle.
They are given a new role in history, which is to refine the passions;
but there is a danger that they may render societies effeminate – a term whose
recurrence ought not to be neglected.

A contrast in these terms between "patriot" and "man of commerce," between
"virtue" and "politeness" or "refinement," emerges during the first half of the
eighteenth century, with Montesquieu as not the first but an authoritative exponent. The patriot's virtue – his autonomy and engagement – cannot well be
questioned, so long as there exists a *polis* or republic in which it may be exercised;
but it can be shown to have rested on an archaic and restrictive foundation. The
ancient city existed in a world where neither commerce nor agriculture were
properly developed, and for this reason, argues Montesquieu[19] (Josiah Tucker
half a century later greatly enjoyed turning this argument against the Virgini-
ans),[20] the virtuous citizen was usually a slaveowner. His devotion to the laws of
his city was characteristic of a world in which neither commerce nor culture –
frequently bracketed as "the arts" – furnished social ties capable of holding men
together and only the "stern *paideia*" (the phrase is Marvin Becker's) of civil
discipline could perform the task. It was a world in which there was no god but
Lycurgus and Plato was his prophet. With the rise of commerce and culture, new
forms of social relationship emerged and virtue in the antique sense became archaic. Yet Montesquieu, though he describes at length how *"le doux commerce"*[21]

---

[19] *Esprit des Lois*, IV, 8.   [20] *A Treatise Concerning Civil Government* (1781), pp. 167–8.
[21] This phrase is not Montesquieu's (for its history, see Hirschman, *op. cit.*), but "partout où il y a
des moeurs douces, il y a du commerce; et partout où il y a du commerce, il y a des moeurs douces"
(*Esprit des Lois*, XX, 1).

refines and moderates behaviour – how *polis* is replaced by politeness, even as *oikos* is absorbed by economics – does not give the name of "virtue" to that which takes the place of the old. Consequently, though we can glean from his text that something comes after the republic whose principle is virtue, he does not explicitly categorise what it is and does not escape from the possibility that modern refinement corrupts antique virtue without replacing it.

Notions of refinement and politeness, then, were crucial elements in the ideology of eighteenth-century commerce. We have examined some epistemological reasons why this should have been so. If speculative man was not to be the slave of his passions, he had to moderate these by converting them into opinion, experience and interest, and into a system of social ties which these things reinforced; and the reification followed by exchange of the objects on which his passions focussed was an excellent means of socialising them. When the polite man of commercial and cultivated society looked back into his past, what he necessarily saw there was the passions not yet socialised, to which he gave such names as "barbarism" and "savagery"; and his debate against the patriot ideal could be far more satisfactorily carried on if he could demonstrate that what had preceded the rise of commerce and culture was not a world of virtuous citizens, but one of barbarism. To demonstrate that the citizens of antiquity were barbarians themselves was plausible, but for most people too destructive. The apologists of commerce therefore preferred, to any scheme of history based on civic humanism, those schemes of natural law and *jus gentium* propounded by Grotius, Pufendorf, Locke and the German jurists, which stressed the emergence of civil jurisprudence out of a state of nature, since the latter could be readily equated with barbarism.[22] The tradition of natural jurisprudence thus makes its reappearance in the story – though there are scholars who would say that I ought to have been telling it in these terms all along – joining hands with many moral philosophies which focussed on the notion of passion, and using the state of nature to show how the passions were moderated in history by the progress of commerce and politeness.

We are contrasting a conception of property which stresses possession and civic virtue with one which stresses exchange and the civilisation of the passions, and thereby disclosing that the debate between the two is a major key to eighteenth-century social thought. What is perhaps of greatest concern in the present context is the spectacle of property moving from a situation in a structure of norms and rights to a situation in a process of history, of which changes in its character and function are seen as being largely the occasion; but we have not yet reached the point where the concept of property becomes absorbed into the larger scheme of productive relations. That point lies only a little way ahead, however, and we shall not have to distort the history of social theory in order to get there.

[22] See Hont and Ignatieff, eds., *Wealth and Virtue* (Cambridge University Press, 1983), for several essays on this theme.

It may have been the injection into the debate of a concept of barbarism, that social or pre-social condition in which there was neither ownership nor exchange – or so it was thought – which helped occasion the still imperfectly-understood appearance in Western theory of the famous four-stages theory of human history: that men were first hunters, then shepherds, farmers, and finally merchants.[23] To us, and soon to contemporaries, this meant a series of stages of production; but it is in the logic of the historical debate that it should have been primarily a scheme of the rise, diversification and control of the human passions, which the preoccupation with property served to anchor in history. It was by this time common ground that the passions were aroused and satisfied (if satisfied at all) by material goods and by perceptions and expectations of human behaviour importantly, if not exclusively, associated with the distribution of these goods, their reality or non-reality being an important part of the problem. The relation between commercial society and its possible predecessors had done much to make this a historical problem and to make it hinge upon the refinement of the passions. The four-stages theory marked an important step in the direction of a historicisation of the human personality, in which the character and control of the passions, together with the psychologies and epistemologies associated with the notion, were organised into a historical sequence of the modes of production.

The ninth chapter of Gibbon's *Decline and Fall,* in which he elaborates upon Tacitus's account of the primitive Germans, is an excellent specimen from which to illustrate what operations could be performed with the aid of this schema.[24] Gibbon tells us that the German tribes were pre-agricultural and illiterate; consequently they lacked both money and letters, the two principal means of communication by which goods and information are exchanged within more civilised societies. By placing exchange ahead of ownership, Gibbon indicated a historical perspective in which agriculture, which he calls "the useful parent of the arts," is seen rather as a necessary pre-condition of commerce than as a stage of society existing in its own right. He places himself in that tradition which we have traced from Defoe rather than from Locke and in which to exchange is seen as more important than to possess. But he does not neglect to emphasise that because the Germans lacked an effective agriculture, they lacked a sense of property which could reinforce and moderate the sense of self. The tribesman's passions were violent but unfocussed; he alternated between periods of lethargy and melancholy and moments of uncontrolled warrior action which roused him, says Gibbon, to "a more lively sense of his existence." For this *Angst* the only remedy was property. Had the German possessed land of his own to till, productive labour would have cured his physical and psychic lethargy. The sense of honour

---

[23] Ronald L. Meek, *Social Science and the Ignoble Savage* (Cambridge University Press, 1975).

[24] For the following references, see J. B. Bury's edition of the *History of the Decline and Fall of the Roman Empire* (London, 1902), vol. 1, pp. 218–26.

– of an exposed and vulnerable personal identity – which Gibbon tells us was all that the tribesman understood of liberty, would have been transformed into a sense of law and a capacity for military discipline by an awareness of responsibility for his material possessions and for the relations with others which possession involved.

There are obvious enough echoes of Locke here, though Gibbon does not make them explicit by citation. It may be added, on the one hand, that he is repeating Machiavellian doctrine about property as the sole source of social responsibility in the warrior as well as Machiavelli's views about mercenary and citizen militias. But on the other hand, a level of sophistication, not to be derived simply from Locke, is to be found in Gibbon's association between property and the passions. Property as such does what *"le doux commerce"* was seen to do by writers such as Montesquieu: it refines and moderates the passions by making us aware of what we share with others; without it there can only be a barbaric sense of honour based upon a profound psychic insecurity. Unless the passions are focussed upon objects outside the self, the self cannot be socialised or reconciled to its own existence. This is not the moment to embark upon a history of the concept of alienation, but certainly the above is an early statement of its association with the notion of property. If we are to be social beings, then we must become what we own in relation to others, what we share and exchange with others; and since the concept of labour has put in an appearance (though I do not ascribe to Gibbon a labour theory of value) the step from exchange to production is not far away.

In the same chapter, when writing of the history of sexuality, Gibbon makes further use of the concept of honour – the only value which can arise from the pre-social and pre-commercial self's awareness of its identity.[25] Echoing Tacitus on the role of women in primitive German society, he tells us that they were as warlike as the men and were respected as their equals. This occurred because warrior honour was literally the only value available at this stage of human development and was consequently adopted as one by either sex without differentiation. Since honour and equality are valuable, the tribal women were and are to be respected; and they added another value possessing a sexual basis: that of a ferocious chastity, since "the first honour of the sex has ever been that of chastity." But what was the role of women as property relations developed in society? We know that it was the perceived function of property and commerce to refine and polish human passions and behaviour. At this point Gibbon joins himself to a widespread and momentous tendency in eighteenth-century thought – that of ascribing precisely the same role to women and associating their performance of it with the rise of commercial society. It would be easy, and entirely justified, to point out how far this association was based on the still surviving view of women

[25] Bury ed., I, pp. 227–8.

as a species of property, or as a medium of exchange between proprietors. However, a case might be made for the view that women could expect more mobility, and even active agency, from a commercially conceived society than from the alternative model of the masculine and self-contained classical patriots.

The Enlightenment certainly saw women in the role of cultural entrepreneurs, encouraging the exchange of politeness and refinement in a variety of forms. The notions of commerce and culture were, as we have seen, intimately allied. But it is noteworthy that Gibbon, having remarked that the women of the German tribes might be admirable but not very feminine, goes on to express the fear that as property and commerce civilise society and as women play their role in the promotion of refinement, the latter may grow less chaste. Chastity's "most dangerous enemy," he says, "is the softness of the mind. The refinements of life corrupt while they polish the intercourse of the sexes." Gibbon is saying about sexuality precisely what Montesquieu had said about commerce itself, and there is more at work here than the standard imbalances of intersexual perception. We are being told that something is lost with the disappearance of barbaric honour and that the process of civilisation is at the same time a process of corruption. The unity of the undifferentiated personality − whether property or sexuality be seen as the source of differentiation − may have been relegated to a savage and irrecoverable antiquity, but it has not lost its uniqueness as a value.

The associations in Gibbon's ninth chapter between property and personality and between commerce and sexuality are not the only threads which may guide us in tracing the history of the ideology of commerce, and they are far from being confined to his writings alone. His contemporary William Robertson, for example, in his *History of America*, goes so far as to indicate (following Buffon) that the savage − in this case the Amerindian − is sexually cold, or at least devoid of affection in his sexual relationships, because he is not producing and distributing a sufficient diversity of goods to permit his passions to begin growing towards sociability and civilisation.[26] The point in the four-stage series (or was it really a cycle?) at which the sexual and economic Arcadia might be found, Robertson (as it were) left Rousseau to determine; but in his companion work on India he depicted an Asian society so far civilised by commerce that Europeans might trade with it and be neither impoverished nor corrupted.[27] Given the presumptions of the time, he would have to admit that Indians understood law but not liberty, private but not public virtue, thereby raising the question of whether European public values could have existed without the antithesis of the commercial principle − without barbaric and feudal honour, without classical citizenship and virtue.

[26] *The Works of William Robertson* (London, 1824), IV, pp. 297−8.
[27] "An Historical Disquisition concerning Ancient India," Section II; *Works,* IX, pp. 44−86; cf. Gibbon, Bury ed., I, pp. 54−56.

In his *View of the Progress of Society in Europe*, Robertson attempted what may in the proper sense be called a "bourgeois" interpretation of history by isolating the growth of trading towns as the agency which had introduced into feudal society the principles of modern liberty.[28] But the contrast with Asia was alone enough to show that the pre-commercial component must be allowed some positive role in the process. Gibbon touched on the same problem when he wrote, in language once again significantly sexual, that "the fierce giants of the north" – the savage Germans – "broke in" to a Roman world privatised to the point where personality had been stripped of its civic relationships. "They restored a manly spirit of freedom; and after the revolution of ten centuries, freedom became the happy parent of taste and science."[29] What happened during those ten centuries, whether savage freedom became civic virtue, and whether freedom fertilised politeness or politeness freedom, Gibbon does not tell us, since the later *Decline and Fall* does not focus on the history of the medieval West; but the essays of David Hume on the relations between liberty and the arts are enough to tell us that the problem was a difficult one.

We have seen how property moved from being the object of ownership and right to being the subject of production and exchange, and how the effect of this on the proposition that property was the basis of social personality was to make personality itself explicable in terms of a material and historical process of diversification, refinement and perhaps ultimate decay and renewal. We have now to consider more closely the politics of the commercial ideology, and in this regard it is crucially important to recall that the ideological necessity throughout had been to provide an alternative to a view of politics as founded upon the autonomy and unity of the patriot personality. The relegation of that unity to a barbaric or economically primitive past, in which it must itself disintegrate and seem never to have existed, was a powerful critical weapon in the hands of the modernists. Yet the ideal of unity obstinately refused to disappear. We find this interestingly illustrated in the writings of Josiah Tucker, a vigorous and original conservative – he calls himself a constitutional Whig – of the era of the American Revolution.[30] In *A Treatise Concerning Civil Government* which he completed in 1781, Tucker set out to deny that political capacity could be immediately anchored in human personality; but he did not locate the doctrine he attacked – as his language shows he knew he might have done – in concepts of classical citizenship or of man as by nature a political animal. He located it instead – as his choice of a title reveals – in the political theory of Locke, whose doctrine of property he did not explore because he believed himself confronted by English and American democrats who were using Locke to divorce property from personality and make

[28] *Works*, III, pp. 36–46; IV, pp. 52–54. [29] Bury ed., I, pp. 56–58.
[30] He was one of those insignificant Englishmen of whom the history of political thought so largely consists. This remark is dedicated with irritated affection to Judith N. Shklar.

the latter alone the sufficient and necessary condition of political right. If moral personality entailed a right of consent, and if without that consent government could have no authority over the individual, then government would be forever philosophically as well as practically impossible, for moral rights and obligations could not be deputed by one individual to another, whereas all government was founded upon the transfer of rights to representatives and rulers. Talk of "inalienable rights" was therefore political nonsense, and if — as Tucker believed — it was as a moral being that Locke supposed the individual to possess the right of consent, that premise made the latter incapable of choosing a representative to exercise his rights for him: a truth which only the "honest, undissembling" — but unfortunately mad — Rousseau had been able to perceive and declare. The capacity to transfer rights and become the subject and beneficiary of government must be sought for in man not as a moral, but as a social being; and the two, declared Tucker, who was an Anglican clergyman with an acute sense of sin, were not simply identical.[31]

Tucker was not a stupid man, and we should have to work hard to demonstrate that Locke was on his side and not, as he thought, against him. But when he puts forward his account of the social origins of government, he says things which the conventional wisdom of modern scholarship has encouraged us to deduce largely from the supposed principles of Locke. Government, he says, originates not in the inherent moral nature of men, but from the diversity of social activities in which they engage. These set up a variety of relationships among men, in which some individuals necessarily exert greater authority than others; in their origin these may be violent and unjust, but by experience men learn to recognise their necessity and conduct them properly. The various patterns of authority cohere into what may be called a "government" or "state," which experience similarly vests with codes of rules and systems of elaborate conventions. Though certainly constitutional in character, nothing prevents this government from exercising an ultimately uncontrolled sovereignty. At least it is not controlled by any rights or other moral characteristics inherent in men, which need be understood as preceding and going into the making of government.[32]

Tucker was a correspondent of Hume's, and we may recognise the latter's voice in some of the things he says. But it is of greater importance to see that he was situating himself in a by no means discontinuous tradition descending from Sir William Temple, who had written a hundred years before that nothing but opinion could prevail upon property to submit itself to authority; and what had happened during the interval was that it had become increasingly possible to see how property might itself be the source of opinion. Tucker uses the term "natural authority" when describing its civil and social genesis, but he repeatedly makes

[31] *Treatise,* pp. 27, 32–3, 167–8, 236–8.
[32] *Treatise,* section II, generally. Tucker relies heavily on Robertson's *America.*

it clear that the "natural society" which this term entails can only exist by becoming a commercial society. Not only is the paradigm of commerce necessary in order to describe the diversity of activities which generate "natural authority"; Tucker also emphasises that in the pre-commercial society – and here he mentions the classical *polis* to which republicans appeal – the exchange of goods and services is so underdeveloped that the normal human relationship is that between master and slave, lord and serf.[33] Only as commerce develops do social relations become capable of generating civil authority. Tucker uses no English equivalent for *bourgeoisie,* because there is none, but he does argue at length that it was the growth of the borough, under the patronage of the kings and barons of medieval England, which permitted the conversion of the latter from barbaric into civil rulers, exercising "natural authority."[34] Commerce, and the complexity of exchange which it generates, teaches both rulers and subjects the conventions according to which government must be conducted. Being rooted in experience, these lessons take the form of opinion, and we have heard enough by now of the process through which it had been decided, since Temple, that the conversion of passion into opinion was the function of commerce.

In this projection, the personality was related to government only through a series of social relationships of which commerce was the paradigm if not the efficient cause. Government was restrained and determined by convention but not by natural right; and far from there being any such things as "inalienable rights," the very foundation of government lay in the alienation of rights and, in a certain sense, of personality itself. For if government is merely the aggregate of the diverse forms of "natural authority," there is no one social or political relation to which the personality as a whole, or in its unity, is naturally committed.

Today we call this political theory "liberalism," and though the word itself was not so used in the eighteenth century, the criticisms which we use it to express were in many cases already in circulation. The indictment to be levelled against such a system would be not only that it denied the individual his natural right and his liberty of consent, but that it denied him his virtue. Commercial man might be a social but he could never be a wholly political being. There was no moment at which he addressed himself undividedly to the public good; consequently he risked the privatisation which Gibbon had seen overcoming the Romans of the middle empire and which Adam Smith thought a criticism to be most validly levelled at the conditions of life in commercial society.[35] He might under modern conditions have the social solidarity necessary to resist the barbarian invaders who had brought down ancient society, but it was a good deal less certain that he could resist the corruption of society from within. For if all his

[33] *Treatise,* pp. 130–2, 167–8, 170–201.   [34] *Treatise,* section III.
[35] "Of the Influence of Commerce on Manners," *Lectures on Justice, Police, Revenue and Arms,* Part II, Division 2, section 3.

political relationships were mediated, he must in the last analysis be governed by intermediaries, whether these took the form of mercenaries, courtiers, clergy or representatives; and every theory of corruption, without exception, is a theory of how intermediaries substitute their own good and profit for that of their supposed principals. The theory of surplus value itself may be considered an extension of corruption theory from the political to the economic realm. Virtue – a synonym for autonomy in action – was not merely a moral abstraction, but was declared to be a human necessity.

To all this the apologists of commerce replied that the unity of personality in political action was imaginable only under conditions so archaic and remote that it could not currently exist and, if we looked closely, would appear not to have existed even then. They added that the growth and diversification of human potentialities through the development in history of the capacity to produce and distribute was the true story of the human personality in society and that any loss of virtue which specialisation entailed was a price well paid for the increase in economic, cultural and psychic capacity. But the fact that the apologists so regularly admitted the possibility of a loss of virtue is a proof that the ideal of the undifferentiated personality, even when driven from history, refused to disappear as a norm. Montesquieu had called it "le plainte de Platon" that "le commerce corrompt les moeurs pures,"[36] and we may call it "le plainte de Rousseau" that "les moeurs pures" had never been fully realised in a history conceived as a process of commerce and specialisation. There were innumerable treatments of the tension between virtue and commerce, and innumerable attempts to resolve it, some of which satisfied their authors and may satisfy the modern critic; but there is no greater and no commoner mistake in the history of social thought than to suppose that the tension ever disappeared, that the ideals of virtue and unity of personality were driven from the field, or that a commercial, "liberal" or "bourgeois" ideology reigned undisturbed until challenged by the harbingers of Marx.

We have been tracing, from the era of Hobbes and Harrington to that of Hume and Rousseau, a complex dialectic based first, on the perception that there were now two ways – an ancient and a modern, a classical and a commercial – in which property might be seen as the foundation and determinant of social and political personality, and second, on an increasing awareness that the latter way furnished the human creature with a history, the former with a means of protesting against it. Real and mobile property formed the substratum of a quarrel which ended as that between the unity of personality and its increasing diversification in history, and it is hard not to link the problems perceived by Rousseau

---

[36] *Esprit des Lois,* XX, 1: "On peut dire que des lois du commerce perfectionnent les moeurs, par la même raison que ces mêmes lois perdent les moeurs. Le commerce corrompt les moeurs pures: c'était le sujet des plaintes de Platon: il polit et adoucit les moeurs barbares, comme nous le voyons tous les jours."

and Smith with Marx's indictment of specialisation and diversification, though I shall not attempt to consider how this link might be established. The problem of personality persisted as the core of the matter. But by the time of Marx there existed the powerful paradigm of the classical economics, of which Adam Smith was said to be the father and Locke the somewhat shadowy ancestor.

There is an enterprise, to which Joyce Appleby is the most recent contributor, of providing Smith with a pedigree of earlier analysts of market behaviour; but she does not seem to have shown how the analysis of the market could become a problem in political theory, and her dismissal in a footnote of anti-commercial ideologists as diverse as the Diggers studied by Christopher Hill and the country ideologists studied by myself as "reactionary" (and so presumably not worth thinking about) appears to hinder her from doing so.[37] I suggest that we cannot understand the vindication of commercial society unless we understand the grounds on which it was assailed and acknowledge the attack's continuous vitality. This obliges us to take a route which leads through Mandeville and Hume to Ferguson and Smith, and to encounter classical economics at the end of it, after long debate between virtue and commerce, virtue and corruption, virtue and passion. In a recent work by Donald Winch,[38] Smith is interpreted in this light, and we are reminded that he was a professor of moral philosophy and his first major work was a study of the theory of moral sentiments.

But if classical economics emerged in this way, if the last of the civic humanists was the first of the Scottish economists, if the quarrel of the ancients and moderns furnished the context in which the developing understanding of market relations took on problematic meaning, then the classical economics seem rapidly to have hardened into a paradigm which operated to deny the ambivalent historicism of late Whig culture. Bentham and the elder Mill, as well as McCulloch and Ricardo, would seem to have much to do with this, and we are left trying to see how their thought emerged in history. The space from Smith to Ricardo is replete with problems and possibilities.

---

[37] Appleby, *Economic Thought,* p. 268, n. 61.
[38] Donald Winch, *Adam Smith's Politics: An Essay in Historiographic Revision* (Cambridge University Press, 1978).

7

◁══▷

Hume and the American
Revolution:
The dying thoughts of a North Briton

This essay begins by exploring the second part of its title and then enlarges upon some wider implications of the first. That is to say, I want in the first instance to consider Hume's perception of the crises in English and American politics that marked the last decade and a half of his life and were at a crescendo when he died; and I want to consider what doing so may tell us about his perception of the historical world he was about to leave. I have emphasized the words "English" and "American" in order to hint, by exclusion, at something already implied by the title: that Hume's view of the British world in disruption was very much a view from Edinburgh; and my concern will be with Hume as publicist, historian, and political theorist, prior to Hume as philosopher. From Hume's perception of the American Revolution, I shall turn in conclusion to say something about his role in the ideological history of that great event, one as replete with paradox as even Duncan Forbes[1] could desire.

The thrust of this paper is historicist, in the sense that it emphasizes Hume's consciousness of history and of the moment in history that his individual life had occupied and was about to leave. Neither his historiography nor his philosophy is historicist in any of the principal senses that word was later created to express. But Hume was a historian as well as a philosopher and, in the former role as well as the latter, one of the greatest of his century. Edward Gibbon, who thought Tacitus the greatest historian of all time, once called Hume "le Tacite de l'E-cosse,"[2] and he did not mean the compliment to be an empty one. Discussions of Hume are predominantly discussions of his philosophy in the strict sense.

From *McGill Hume Studies*, edited by David Fate Norton, Nicholas Capaldi, and Wade L. Robison, pp. 325–43. © 1979 Austin Hills Press; reprinted by permission.

[1] *Hume's Philosophical Politics* (Cambridge: Cambridge University Press, 1975).
[2] *The Letters of Edward Gibbon*, ed. J. E. Norton, 3 vols. (London: Cassell, 1956), 2:107.

which may perhaps appear as much a contemporary as a historical phenomenon. But it seems desirable to draw attention to Hume as a historian, as a historical figure, and as a figure in history as he himself perceived it. The second related point that needs to be made is that, as well as a philosopher, Hume was a *philosophe*, a leader in the great eighteenth-century secularization of the intelligible universe, when secular man, ceasing to be the subject of a miraculous redemption, became instead an actor in civil history. The earthly city with its ideals of political virtue and cultivated taste replaced the heavenly; and the political city, or commonwealth, together with the opportunity for virtue it afforded, had since the Florentine Renaissance been seen as involved in increasingly complex historical contingencies. These – the processes that built up or broke down commonwealths – had come, from about a century before Hume's lifetime, to be discerned more and more in terms of political economy, or of the interactions between polity and economy. Like his bicentennial peers Gibbon, Smith, and Jefferson, Hume was deeply involved in patterns of thought that had descended from Machiavelli, Harrington, and Montesquieu. He both employed and criticized these as historian, essayist, moralist, and commentator on his own times; and in so employing them, he took part in their profound and important modification. We therefore have a Hume who was an analyst of his own moment in history and in the same act a maker and changer of intellectual history. It is this historical Hume I mean to discuss. The aim will be to consider his handling of the historical and political vocabularies of his age, without making very much attempt to connect this with his analyses of natural and moral philosophy.

A superficial reader of Mossner's still unsurpassed *Life* might gain the impression that, following the disastrous imbroglio with Rousseau and his final stint as an amateur diplomat, Hume retired to Edinburgh in the late 1760s and did little more than potter amiably about the New Town until the onset of his fatal illness. Hume's letters, however, leave a different impression; there is much about them in these concluding years that is not particularly cozy. Hume wrote many letters to his London publisher, William Strahan, that are outstandingly though not abnormally cantankerous in their kind,[3] though he was always distressed when he discovered he had distressed his correspondent. Poor Strahan indeed lived to be denounced by David Hume as an English Whig, and by Benjamin Franklin as a British Tory, a fate perhaps unduly severe even for a London Scot with ambitions in eighteenth-century politics. Hume, for instance, affected to hold Strahan blameable for the City of London's 1770 petition for a dissolution of Parliament and the removal of evil ministers.[4] This letter comes close to one

[3] For letters in this tone on business as opposed to political matters, see *The Letters of David Hume*, ed. J. Y. T. Greig, 2 vols. (Oxford: Clarendon Press, 1932), 2:212, 218f., 223f., 225, 227f., 236, 277f., 279f., 359–61 (hereafter cited as *Letters*).
[4] Ibid., pp. 217–18.

addressed to Gilbert Elliot, in which Hume declares from Edinburgh: "Our Government has become a Chimera; and is too perfect in point of Liberty, for so vile a Beast as an Englishman, who is a Man, a bad Animal too, corrupted by above a Century of Licentiousness. The Misfortune is, that this Liberty can scarcely be retrench'd without Danger of being entirely lost . . . I may wish that the Catastrophe shou'd rather fall on our Posterity; but it hastens on with such large Strides, as leaves little Room for this hope."[5] There is little reason to think that the philosopher's feelings were more moderate in the last months of his life.

Hume tells Elliot that he is revising the text of his *History*, with sentiments like the above in mind, and is bent upon purging it of the last taint of Whig prejudices. He is blowing off steam, no doubt, but there is too much of this kind of thing to be neglected. The vigor with which he denounced the excesses of liberty have led some readers to suppose that he swung to a reactionary and even a Tory political attitude in his last years, though Giuseppe Giarrizzo's attempt to relate this to changes in his philosophy has been vigorously opposed by Duncan Forbes.[6] I shall not try to consider whether Hume's philosophy, in the technical and academic sense, can be said to have changed in ways that can be politically explained, but it will further my theme if I offer some consideration of why both the word "reactionary" and the word "Tory" fail to do justice to the ambivalence of contemporary political thought in general, and of Hume's political thought in which it is many times redoubled. Giarrizzo's study was an admirable contribution to the study of this ambivalence, which Forbes has carried into further degrees of elaboration.

Ambivalence indeed is our keynote; we have to understand how it was that the fierce enemy of popular liberty also wrote, "I am an American in my Principles, and wish we would let them alone to govern or misgovern themselves as they think proper," adding in the same letter that "to punish those insolent Rascals in London and Middlesex" was a far worthier object of government in October 1775.[7] The entirely typical letter of 1770, from which I first quoted, can help us reach this goal if we analyze two of its components: first, its Anglophobia, which in Hume's case is never to be forgotten; second, the thinking it reveals on the relations of authority and liberty, which the English constitution had carried to greater heights of fruitful complexity than had been attained elsewhere. If Hume thought the English a bad lot, he considered their constitution a marvellous creation in its way – ambivalence again, which can be explained in terms of national identity.

Hume may be termed a North Briton, a term signifying a Scotsman who in

[5] Ibid., p. 216.
[6] Giuseppe Giarrizzo, *Hume politico e storico* (Turin: Einaudi, 1962); review by Forbes, *The Historical Journal* 6 (1963):280–95.
[7] *Letters,* 2:303.

the eighteenth century believed that the Union of 1707 had established either a
common nationality or an equality between two nationalities. But the insecurity
of referring to Scotland as North Britain is underlined when we consider the
unsuccessful experiment (which was also made) of referring to England as South
Britain. Eighteenth-century Scotsmen had no reason to believe that they had been
admitted to an equal partnership, nor did the English attempt to persuade them
that they had. Not the least revealing fact uncovered by Mossner is the circumstance that Hume all his life conversed in broad Scots and yet gave anxious care
to the complete Anglicization of his and his friends' written and spoken language. He advised William Robertson on the elimination of Scotticisms from
the latter's histories; and he was active in the importation of an Irish elocutionist
to Edinburgh to teach a perfectly English manner of speech,[8] the reason being that
any trace of a Scots accent was considered a bar to professional or political advancement in London, supposed to be the British capital. Hume's generation, in
short, confronted a problem in bilingualism, but once it was considered a matter
of the relation between the metropolitan and a provincial version of the same
culture, the Scots had no alternative to outplaying the English at their own
games. That is what lies behind Hume's pronouncement that this was the historical age and this the historical nation.[9] There was no political nationalism in
Scotland because no Scot had any belief in his country's ancient constitution or
any desire to hear the auld sang sung again. But from David Hume to John
Millar, the Scottish historical intellect developed enormously, in part as a consequence of the attempt to understand the English constitution better than the
English did themselves. It was the abrasive Hume who wrote a *History of England,*
the far smoother Robertson who wrote a *History of Scotland,* and there is no question to which of the two the English paid attention.

   A North Briton, then, was a Scotsman committed to a restatement of English
culture in such terms that it would become British and that Scotsmen would
make their own way in it. The vehement Anglophobia that Hume at times allowed himself to express may be attributed to insuperable doubts about whether
this enterprise was succeeding. The place of men of letters in eighteenth-century
society was always of profound concern to him: as a young adult he diagnosed his
own psychosomatic disorder as entirely occasioned by this problem,[10] and as a
classical humanist of his age he saw it as very largely a question of political order.
It is desirable to stress how many of the *Essays Moral, Political and Literary* are
essays about the politics of culture. This concern persisted to the end of his life,
as when in March 1776 he wrote to congratulate Gibbon on the first volume of
the *Decline and Fall* and expressed surprise that it was possible for an Englishman

[8] E. C. Mossner, *The Life of David Hume* (Austin, Texas: University of Texas Press, 1954), pp. 370–
75.
[9] *Letters,* 2:230.   [10] Mossner, pp. 66–88.

to write history in a society given over to faction for more than a generation.[11] Perhaps we should not make too much of Hume's disappointment, some thirty-five years before, over the failure of his *Treatise* to attract public attention; but when in 1741–42 he set about reestablishing his reputation with the *Essays,* he addressed himself to the great paper war among Walpole, Bolingbroke, and the wits of England, kept alive as an issue by Walpole's recent fall from power. He warned both parties against factionalism, in language showing that his sympathies were already leaning toward Walpole's side of the constitutional issue. But the 1742 volume contained a "Character of Sir Robert Walpole," in which we find the judgment that under this minister "trade has flourished, liberty declined, and learning gone to ruin."[12] Hume suppressed this verdict in later years, but in 1742 it clearly if mildly echoed the hatred that Pope, Gay, and Swift had felt for Walpole as for one whose corruption of politics was destroying the arts. Hume's judgment of Walpole is ambivalent, and the *Essays* are in large part a reconsideration of the relations of the three elements he had named: trade, liberty, and learning. Here is as good a point as any at which to begin our journey over that "terrible campaign country" that Forbes has described Hume as presenting to the reader,[13] in the hope of arriving at some understanding of that hatred of English faction so evident in the letters of Hume's last years.

The political ideology – Commonwealth and Country, Old Whig and Tory in restless but stable combination – which had united Bolingbroke and the English poets in the denunciation of Walpole,[14] supposed that the constitution was founded upon a principle of balance between independent parts. To abandon balance or to compromise independence was to corrupt both constitution and virtue, since the political balance offered the only conditions under which the individual could flourish as a moral and civic being. To think of the poet, scholar, or man of letters as engaged in the practice of public virtue was to affirm that he, too, was corrupted and frustrated by the rule of a corrupt minister; hence the great polemics of the so-called Tory satirists. Walpole was supposed to be wielding two great instruments of corruption, of which the first was parliamentary patronage and the second public credit. The latter, which produced rule by a class of investors interdependent with the executive, had much to do with the expansion of trade,

---

[11] *Letters,* 2:309–11.

[12] For the bibliographical history of this passage see Mossner, pp. 142–44. See also Bertrand A. Goldgar, *Walpole and the Wits: The Relation of Politics to Literature, 1722–1742* (Lincoln, Nebr.: University of Nebraska Press, 1976).

[13] *Hume's Philosophical Politics,* p. viii.

[14] Isaac F. Kramnick, *Bolingbroke and his Circle: The Politics of Nostalgia in the Age of Walpole* (Cambridge, Mass.: Harvard University Press, 1968); Maynard Mack, *The Garden and the City: Retirement and Politics in the Later Poetry of Pope, 1731–1743* (Toronto: University of Toronto Press, 1969); Caroline Robbins, *The Eighteenth-Century Commonwealthman* (Cambridge, Mass.: Harvard University Press, 1959); J. G. A. Pocock, *The Machiavellian Moment* (Princeton: Princeton University Press, 1975).

though the two were logically separable. The Commonwealth ideology, which appealed to urban and suburban Old Whigs, was also a Country ideology with appeal to Tory gentry, because the ideal of independence within balance suggested that ultimately the civic individual should be a proprietor of land – real property conferring independence, mobile property tending to corruption and dependence. But at this point there arose a contradiction within the politics of culture. The financial politics of Walpole might be said to corrupt the arts: but were not the arts themselves a source of corruption? It was widely held that at the end of the agrarian Middle Ages the revival of trade and the revival of learning had tempted the warrior freeholders to pay others to defend and govern them, sacrificing liberty and virtue the better to enjoy commerce and culture. The arts might therefore be the cause of their own decline, and trade, liberty, and learning might be at odds rather than in harmony.

Scots were less liable than Englishmen to the temptations of agrarian primitivism. It was all too easy to remind them that if they wanted to know what a society of warrior peasants was really like, they had only to look north of the Highland Line, and that the journey to Darien or Hudson Bay was well worth making in order to overcome such barbarism. The Scotland of 1707–45, in which Hume grew up and began to write, was one deeply committed to the pursuit of trade and taste, commerce and culture; and Hume's own commitment to the life of a man of letters must hold him back from any kind of primitivist romanticism. This was why he was never happy with his friend Adam Ferguson's *Essay on the History of Civil Society*,[15] and why his emotions discharged themselves on the evident fraud of Macpherson's *Ossian* with something like relief.[16] And yet, his deep fascination with the personality of Rousseau shows that he was anything but insensitive to the underlying dualities of his age; on the contrary, he was like every other philosopher of the time seeking to work them out in his own terms. He could not join with the Bolingbroke circle in the desperation of their assaults on Walpole and preferred to suggest that both parties were overstressing the importance of a single minister's impact on the health of the constitution.[17] To say this was to undermine the ideology of virtue and corruption at its source, and if it was Tory to assail Walpole and Whig to affect a pose of moderation, then Hume's argument at this point is Whig in a somewhat Addisonian sense. But he could not deny that Walpole had been the enemy of letters; for it was an evident fact that English letters at their most polite – and Hume held that the first author of polite English prose had been Swift[18] – considered Walpole their enemy. To

---

[15] *Letters*, 1:304, 308; 2:120, 125–26, 131–32, 133, 136.   [16] Ibid., 2:310–11.

[17] See the latter part of Hume's essay "That politics may be reduced to a Science," in *The Philosophical Works*, ed. T. H. Green and T. H. Grose, 4 vols. (London, 1886), 3:98–108 (hereafter cited as *Works*).

[18] "Of Civil Liberty," *Works*, 3:159 and note.

grasp the next stage in the analysis of paradox, it is necessary to understand that the ideology of the anti-Walpolean polemic was quite as much republican as it was Tory. Bolingbroke's nominally Tory circle had embraced the ideology of constitutional balance to the point of representing the principles of English government as those of a commonwealth based on a landed interest. To defend monarchy in the teeth of such an assault was to defend the commercial oligarchy of the Hanoverian Whigs, of which the Anglo-Scottish Union was one of the props.

We may consequently abridge[19] the Hume of the *Essays* as, first, adopting the position — from which he was never altogether to retreat — that a virtuous and frugal republic is in theory the ideal form of human government; and second, as arguing that it is under republican government that commerce and culture initially flourish. Because republics are ruled by public law, property and expression are guaranteed their safety, and prosperity and politeness can develop. The foundations of the republic are therefore not in agrarian austerity, and we find in the *Essays* the beginnings of the suggestion, to be carried further by Montesquieu, that where ancient republics were violent and harsh in their politics or their manners, it was precisely because commerce and politeness were lacking. It is therefore not certain that the growth of civilization necessitates the continuance of the ancient republican form; there are ways in which polite letters and manners can be seen to develop best under monarchy, and it is possible for monarchies to learn from republics the discipline of public law.[20] Hume can be seen at this point sharing with Montesquieu and Gibbon the widespread eighteenth-century conviction that Bourbon France is the most friendly, gracious, and polite to men of letters of all societies the world has seen.[21] In republican and partly republican societies, on the other hand — and England is one of these — liberty and equality beget a necessary ungraciousness,[22] a social style unfriendly to the man of letters (especially, we may surmise, if he is a provincial or a foreigner). It may be observed, first, that virtue is still political and has found no other supportive environment than the free republic; second, that the gap between liberty on the one hand and culture on the other has in no sense been bridged. It seems of importance to the interpretation of Hume to put forward the suggestion that it never was to be.

Hume was no ideologue and could not for obvious reasons carry out the schematic logic of suggesting that Walpole's commercial society was more friendly to politeness than were its adversaries. But he did not join with the poetic counterculture of Pope and Gay (one wonders if he knew how bitterly its members despise Scotsmen who were not as Anglicized as Arbuthnot). By the end of his

---

[19] "Of Civil Liberty," "Of Eloquence," and "Of the Rise and Progress of the Arts and Sciences" contain most of what is summarized here.
[20] "Of Civil Liberty," *Works,* 3:157–59; "Arts and Sciences," *Works,* 3:176–81, 184–87.
[21] "Of Civil Liberty," *Works,* 3:159.   [22] "Arts and Sciences," *Works* 3:187–88.

life he was to decide that both government and opposition in England were altogether incapable of politeness in any form, but one suspects that this was a discovery of the 1760s. Meanwhile, the *Essays* contain two important adjustments to the anti-Walpolean polemic: Hume accepts one and rejects the other of the great devices of corruption attributed to Walpole, but he does both in a manner that implies rejection of the pure country-commonwealth tradition. He accepts the premise that government in a society such as that of eighteenth-century England requires a plentiful supply of parliamentary patronage, in the form of offices the executive may distribute to aspiring politicians.[23] This was to reject the opposition thesis that government must be a pure balance, and to concede that the executive must have a dominant role; and it was to reject the republican ideal that government must rest on a foundation of virtue, and to concede that passion and interest must be recognized and even harnessed. But the ideal is rejected only as incapable of realization, not as an ideal in itself, for Hume is conceding that a measure of corruption is necessary and beneficial in a world of commerce – and we already know that commerce is a prerequisite to the development of culture. Virtue and politeness therefore remain nonidentical, and the latter has taken an important step away from the republican matrix in which it developed.

The second great device of Walpolean government was supposed to be public credit, which brought the executive and its creditors into dependence one upon another. Here Hume is unqualified in his condemnation, though he characteristically remarks that it is republics rather than monarchies that tend to contract increasing public debts: a despot can declare himself bankrupt with impunity, but in commonwealths, where the public authority rests upon the public faith, the machinery of public credit becomes irreversible.[24] Hume never receded from this position. Duncan Forbes, who sometimes yields to the temptation to torpedo a conclusion before we know exactly what it might have been, emphasizes the circumstance that Hume invested in the public funds and wrote a letter about selling part of his holdings at a profit.[25] But the philosopher's awareness of the gulf between ideal and practice is surely enough to make it clear that he knew what he meant when he wrote such sentences as "Either the nation must destroy public credit, or public credit will destroy the nation."[26] Hume was on friendly terms with Isaac de Pinto, the only political economist of the age to argue that national debt was a thoroughly healthy phenomenon,[27] but he retained a vivid

---

[23] "Of the First Principles of Government," *Works*, 3:112–13; "Of the Independency of Parliament," *Works*, 3:120–21; "Whether the British Government inclines more to Absolute Monarchy, or to a Republic," *Works*, 3:123–26.

[24] "Of Civil Liberty," *Works*, 3:162–63.   [25] *Hume's Philosophical Politics*, pp. 126–27.

[26] This sentence was added in 1764 to "Of Public Credit" (Forbes, *Hume's Philosophical Politics*, pp. 174–75; *Works*, 3:370).

[27] See Richard H. Popkin, "Hume and de Pinto," *Texas Studies in Literature* 12 (1970) 417–30; idem, "Hume and Isaac de Pinto: Five Unpublished Letters," in William B. Todd, ed., *Hume and the*

image of a society destroying itself by heaping up the public indebtedness to the point where trade and agriculture were both brought to ruin. We shall see that this was an important feature of contemporary interpretations of the American Revolution.

But if virtue and culture are ultimately unreconciled, and if the commerce the republic begets leads to a condition of public debt that destroys both liberty and prosperity, we are left with an account of the forces at work in history that is based upon a fundamental and acknowledged contradiction. The civilized monarchy Hume has begun to show signs of preferring is no more than a temporary compromise with these warring forces. To summarize the contradiction in a single sentence is to express it in more dramatic and dialectical a form than was congenial to the mind of Hume, yet his essay "Whether the British Government inclines more to Absolute Monarchy, or to a Republic" clearly indicates that it must incline one way or another, and must end sooner or later in an easy death or a violent one.[28] Hume's temperament, his politics, and his philosophy were such that he chose to express the historicist contradiction of his age in terms not of the dramatic juxtaposition of opposites but of the inexhaustibly subtle ambivalence that provides Forbes with his "terrible campaign country." There is no statement that does not contain its own ambiguity or is not offset by another statement somewhere else. But there is Hume's fascination with the personality of Rousseau, inviting the explanation that he recognized him as one who sensed as many and as complex contradictions as he did and who dramatized every one of them in his own personality. Rousseau was the undramatic Hume's antiself; the tragic farce of the encounter arose from the circumstance that Rousseau was by this time so paranoid that he was antiself to everybody he met. If we follow Forbes through the debatable marches and borderlands of the Hume country, it is to study one who converted his awareness of the ambivalent forces at work in history and personality into polite letters, skeptical philosophy, and magisterial history. We may try to pursue some of these themes down to Hume's farewell to existence in 1776.

A historicist explanation of Hume's philosophy − that is, one that related it to his historical awareness − would be a bold attempt if pursued in detail and would certainly encounter far more phenomena than it could hope to explain. But if we see him as one aware, like so many others in his age, that virtue must give way, for good and ill, to the commerce and refinement it generates in the course of history, we can add that trade and letters were perceived by the age as resting upon imagination and the passions, and as necessitating forms of government unlike those that rested upon republican austerity. A Marxist explanation of Hume would certainly stress that the eighteenth century was caught between

Enlightenment: Essays Presented to Ernest Campbell Mossner (Edinburgh: University of Edinburgh Press; Austin, Texas: University of Texas Press, 1974).
[28] *Works*, 3:125−26. The same antithesis occurs in "Of Public Credit," *Works*, 3:372−74.

an intensely realistic conception of the rationality of real property and an equally intense awareness of the mobile character of the property that was coming to replace it (and eighteenth-century thinking is sufficiently proto-Marxist to convince non-Marxists such as myself that it often invented Marxist explanations of itself). In this sense there is a relationship between the shift from real to mobile property and Hume's thought on the connection between reason and the passions.[29]

In Hume's social history of ideas the independence and self-knowledge of the virtuous citizen helped bring into being a commerce and culture bound to transform his nature because they rested upon passion and imagination rather than on reason. An empire of reason had raised up one of passion to succeed it. But it followed that reason was incomplete without the passion it partly generated, especially once it was decided that the virtuous citizen was less rational, because less polite, than the inhabitant of a commercial society. History would here reinforce any epistemology that might otherwise suggest that reason required the imagination to feed on, but a history that started from the ancient citizen would retain the precommercial republic as a paradigm of virtue. The world of imagination would continue to require the discipline of classical criticism; the civilized monarchy – the form of government best suited to a polished and commercial nation – would continue to require the discipline of republican freedom. But if this suggested that liberty was linked with freedom and government with the passions, it would be equally convincing to equate liberty with the empire of the passions, government with the insecure supremacy of reason. Hume held that authority and liberty could never be reconciled and that neither could replace the other.[30] Following Sir William Temple, he reworded Harrington to suggest that property and force were on the side of the governed and that it was opinion and interest that operated in favor of the government,[31] and he held a very similar view of the unstable relations of reason and passion. His historicism was therefore in a double relationship with his skepticism: he held that reason always gave way to passion and therefore had never really preceded it; but his image of the role that reason might enjoy was classical as well as modern.

Consequently, Hume saw history as the work of passional forces converted into rationality by a variety of agencies of which government was the chief. Commerce and culture were important but could not do its work for it and contained their own tendencies toward unreason. The Commonwealth and Country ideology, to which Hume was attracted, but which he could never accept, professed an eighteenth-century version of Ancient Constitution thinking, according to which the principles of balance were original to a constitutional system that must be pre-

---

[29] Cf. *The Machiavellian Moment,* chaps. 13–14.
[30] "Of the Origin of Government," *Works,* 3:116.
[31] "Of the First Principles of Government," *Works,* 3:109–12.

vented from moving away from them. But Hume had no belief in original rationality; he saw governmental forms as disciplining the original dynamism of passion, whose primacy was so complete that only experience and custom, rather
than rational prudence or legislative wisdom, could bring government into being
and maintain it. He therefore preferred to see government as modern and to look
back in time toward periods when it had been less coherent than it was now.
This modernism, however, did not originate with Hume or with his philosophy.
It had been the position of Walpole's apologists about 1730, and half a century
earlier of the High Tory historians around Robert Brady, who had defended the
monarchy of the 1680s by arguing that feudal history made it impossible that
there should ever have been an Ancient Constitution. Writers of the eighteenth
century, both English and American, did not fail to notice the curious way in
which Tory arguments in one age had become Court Whig arguments in another,
and Hume's cautious sympathy for the Walpolean position laid him open to the
charge of being a seventeenth-century Tory at a time when eighteenth-century
Tories were using Commonwealth arguments. He was not without sympathy for
the latter position, for it contained elements no eighteenth-century mind could
altogether reject. But it may be true – at least we have his word for it – that as
he grew older he eliminated from his *History* more and more elements he had
come to regard as Whig, at a time when he considered English Whiggism increasingly factious.[32] The ambiguity of the word "Tory" in England, however,
coupled with its relative inapplicability in Scotland, should warn us against considering that Hume became a Tory in any eighteenth-century sense as his interpretation of the past became more Tory in a seventeenth-century one.

The changes in the *History of England,* it has been thought, tend to shift the
emphasis from the view that the pre-Civil War constitution was ambiguous and
incoherent toward the view that, given its ambiguity and incoherence, the case
for the prerogatives of the crown was much stronger than Whig historiography
would admit. Hume saw political history as a tug-of-war between authority and
liberty, and it appears as if his sympathy for the element of authority increased
as his disgust with faction – which is the excess of liberty – grew. The opinion
that the English constitution allows too much to liberty, which we find in the
letters about 1770, is echoed nearly thirty years before, in such essays as "Whether the British Government inclines more to Absolute Monarchy, or to a Republic." We read here that the balance between authority and liberty is inherently unstable – as philosophically it must be. Property and the passion for
liberty are all on one side, and the government has only its command of patronage
and the power to corrupt leaders of opposition with which to counter the impulses of the governed. However, patronage is on the way to becoming so dom-

---

[32] "My Own Life," *Works,* 3:5.

inant a species of property that an absolute monarchy having the whole kingdom in its grip is perhaps the likeliest outcome, and very arguably we should prefer this "easiest death" or "euthanasia" to the violent death of faction and republicanism. This essay, however, could easily be read as a pessimistic version of a Country tract; and when we find it claimed in Tom Paine's *Common Sense* that the King of Great Britain exercises despotic authority because he has come to monopolize parliamentary patronage,[33] we must recognize that Paine is saying (consciously or otherwise) that Hume's prophecy has been already if violently fulfilled. By the year of his own decease, on the other hand, Hume saw British government as threatened by the violent death of faction if not by that of bankruptcy as well. To understand his attitude to the American crisis we must consider how this came about.

Hume saw liberty and authority as in unstable relation, and liberty as always liable to break down in faction, because he saw both philosophy and history as necessarily — he was no pessimist — the partial discipline of passion by reason. He thought in this way because he was a historian of enlightenment as well as of civil society; and the *philosophe* historian had to explain the persistence of religion, just as the historian of taste had to explain the persistence of the barbaric. To account for the persistence of irrational elements in culture and politics he had to resort to the combination of passion with habit. The undisciplined imagination generated absurd ideas in the mind; the personality then folded itself around them; and the undisciplined sociability of mankind led to the rise of combative sects, in taste and philosophy[34] as well as in religion and politics,[35] that pitted one irrationally retained habit of mind against another. Hume knew far too much about the role of imagination in creating liberty, commerce, culture, and knowledge itself to take a merely negative and repressive view of the need for rational and political discipline. The great originality of his history of the Puritan Revolution is his insistence that the fanaticism of the Puritan sects was both an excessive threat to rational freedom and a necessary step toward its establishment. But like other observers of the first three decades of George III's reign, Hume was troubled by the revival of quasi-revolutionary slogans in the confused politics of the time. Here we may link him directly with the tradition of Bolingbroke; for he concurred with that analyst[36] in thinking of parties and factions as irrational survivals of seventeenth-century principles in an age when they had lost their meaning, and also in thinking that the equilibrium of eighteenth-century society was threatened by corruption from above as by faction from below, so much so that it might have to choose the manner of its death. But where Country and Commonwealth thinkers united in considering corruption the enemy, it is part

---

[33] *Common Sense*, chap. 1.   [34] "Of the Dignity or Meanness of Human Nature," *Works*, 3:150–51.
[35] "Of Parties in General," *Works*, 3:129–33.   [36] See Bolingbroke's *Dissertation upon Parties, passim.*

of Hume's skeptical Whiggism (rather than his conservatism) that he saw faction as the principal danger.

It is safe to suppose that part of Hume's detestation of the London radicals, in whom he saw English liberty as mere licentiousness, originated from the savage anti-Scotticism of Wilkes and Churchill and of Number 45 of *The North Briton.* Hume had always been careful not to carry his *History* into the era between 1688 and his own time, or to give his analysis of recent and contemporary British politics. But his acquaintance Tobias Smollett, the London Scot, had not hesitated to publish an avowed continuation of Hume's *History*,[37] in which he analyzed post-Revolution Britain in terms more Tory and Country than Hume would have permitted himself. This had left him in the role of professional apologist for Lord Bute and the young George III; and faced with the anti-Scottish frenzies of *The North Briton,* Smollett had been destroyed. His health and his position in journalism were wrecked, and he retired to Italy to complete *Humphry Clinker* – a novel of the interactions of Scotland and Wales with a highly corrupt England – and to die soon after. Hume was not especially close to Smollett or to Bute, and his political outlook was very different from theirs, but the incident is very likely to have been connected with Hume's conviction that political faction was making the life of the man of letters impossible in England.

We may think of the leaders of the London radicals at this juncture as a breakaway movement originating among the followers of William Pitt, who throve on patriot and Old Whig rhetoric until he destroyed his position by accepting a peerage. But if Pitt was a lost leader to the Londoners and Americans, in Hume's eyes he was the evil genius – "that wicked Madman, Pitt"[38] – who had done most to precipitate the crisis of the sixties and seventies. If we anatomize the sins and lunacies of Pitt as Hume saw them, we shall find three elements. In the first place, he had encouraged the growth of populist, factious, and fanatical rhetoric and had quite obviously done so for his own ends, in the manner of the classical demagogue. In the second place, however, he had been responsible for a vast and unneeded expansion of empire; for it was clear to Hume that a mixed form of government, in which authority and liberty, reason and passion, stood in a precarious relationship, ought not to expand,[39] because – as Polybius had accurately prophesied in the case of Rome – to do so placed too great a strain on the relationship among its components. When empire was a popular cause it meant the expansion of liberty and faction at the expense of reason and authority. Hume wanted to see the Americans independent not because he thought the London radicals right but because he thought them foolish and wicked, like their evil angel Pitt, and wanted to see them deprived of their rallying cry. There are some

[37] Tobias Smollett, *A History of England* (1757).
[38] Hume to Wm. Strahan, 26 October 1775, *Letters*, 2:301.
[39] Ibid., pp. 300–301, and the following two letters, pp. 303–5.

remarkably splenetic passages in the letters, in which Hume hopes to see America in revolt, London depopulated, and authority restored to the nobility and gentry of both kingdoms.[40] Empire breeds faction, and faction fanaticism.

Like Adam Smith in Scotland and Josiah Tucker in England, Hume desired American independence for the strictly Tory reason – Tory, that is, as that word would be used in the generation following his own – that empire had come to be a radical burden on the structure of British politics. The Whig regime had been among other things a balance between the forces of landed oligarchy, making for stability, and London commerce, making for empire. Faced with a choice between the two, the conservative mind would sacrifice empire to stability without hesitation – especially if it meant jettisoning Pitt's and Wilkes's radical Londoners along the way. Hume's increasing Anglophobia – his conviction that English factions were the enemy of Scottish intellect – makes him prophesy the violent, not the easy, death of the constitution; but it would probably be a mistake to impute to him any nationalist desire to see the Union undone, even if he was disposed to think the Anglo-Scottish experiment a failure. We make him a man of theory rather than practice, however, when we stress his inability to visualize any *via media* between the violent and the easy death; he did not foresee the Britain of the younger Pitt, and he did not live to see it.

Hume had stiven all his life to adhere to the mainstream of Court Whig thinking, accepting the rise of commerce and politeness in full awareness of the moral and political price they exacted. But the repudiation of empire, even in the form of a repudiation of faction, was bound to aggravate the anti-Whig and anti-commercial strain in his opinions. The third of his reasons for calling the elder Pitt a wicked madman turns out to have been that the great war for empire that Pitt had waged had increased the national debt to near the point at which Hume thought it must prove ruinous to society.[41] Like Adam Smith on the one hand and the English radicals on the other, Hume may have thought the American crisis had originated in an attempt to make the colonies contribute revenue toward the debt's reduction. Smith thought this demand not in itself unreasonable. If the colonists would not contribute to the costs of imperial partnership, they should cease to form part of it. Not being an Englishman, Smith did not feel it so imperative to maintain Parliament's authority as a necessary shibboleth.[42] But no less vehemently than Smith, Hume contended that empire was not worth having at the price of expanded debt and ought to be repudiated as the main

---

[40] Hume to Gilbert Elliot, 22 July 1768, *Letters,* 2:184; Hume to Strahan, 25 October 1769, *Letters,* 2:210; Hume to Adam Smith, 8 February 1776, *Letters,* 2:308.
[41] Hume to Strahan, 11 March 1771, *Letters,* 2:237; Hume to Strahan, 22 July 1771, *Letters,* 2:248.
[42] *The Wealth of Nations,* concluding chapter, "Of Public Debts," and the closing sentence of the entire work.

cause of debt's expansion. Hume here seems to step right back into the tradition of Swift and Bolingbroke, denouncing Pitt, as they had once denounced Marlborough, as the author of war, debt, and corruption; but there are important dissimilarities, as well as similarities, between the positions.

Hume's conviction that national debt could reach the point of subverting the whole fabric of society may be thought of as a blockage in his economic thinking, one that not even Smith could quite overcome or de Pinto persuade him to abandon. But there is evidence that it had a wider meaning. As far back as Anne's reign, we find signs that the overinvested society was perceived as one in which the value of everything was reducible to the fluctuating loan rate or the daily price of government stock and was no more than an index to the state of confidence in society's ability to meet its obligations in an unforeseeable future. Such a society could be governed only by imaginary hopes and fears; it was the economic equivalent of religious superstition. Many analysts, and Hume among them, had argued that speculation, like other modes of the empire of passion, could be disciplined and rendered creative by subjection to the checks of political control by the owners of land; but if the empire of debt expanded to include the value of land, all might still be lost. We can now see why Hume might feel that the expansion of debt in the war for empire was, if not a cause, at least a linked phenomenon with faction in politics, barbarism in taste, and fanaticism in religion. The demagogues of London – like those of Boston, if he ever thought about them – were part of the state of things they affected to denounce, and it was a marvel that Gibbon should have produced a great work of letters in so insane a society.[43] The seventeenth- and eighteenth-century strands of Toryism in Hume are beginning to come together, in a pattern not altogether unlike that of Swift's rhetoric under Marlborough or Pope's under Walpole.

"Among many other marks of Decline," wrote Hume to Gibbon that March, "the Prevalence of Superstition in England, prognosticates the Fall of Philosophy and Decay of Taste."[44] The language suggests that of Pope at the close of the *Dunciad,* but what is more curious is that the fear of a revival of Puritan fanaticism had not yet reached the heights it was to attain. Had Hume lived to hear about the Gordon Riots in 1780, he would have had a new item to add to his jeremiad. It is therefore the more piquant to discover, as a warm admirer of Hume's diagnosis of the American crisis, none other than Dr. Richard Price – dissenting minister, radical Whig, torchbearer of the natural rights of Americans, Englishmen, and Frenchmen, Unitarian millennialist, and future object of the passionate denunciations of Josiah Tucker and Edmund Burke. And what

---

[43] Hume to Gibbon, 18 March 1776, *Letters,* 2:309–10; Hume to Adam Smith, 1 April 1776, *Letters,* 2:312.
[44] Hume to Gibbon, *Letters,* 2:310.

Price most applauded in Hume was the support he could give to the reduction of the whole crisis to the single issue of the National Debt.[45] Needless to say, Price believed that the growth of debt had corrupted the executive and set it conspiring to take away the liberties of Americans first and Englishmen after; whereas Hume's point was that debt had encouraged faction and fanaticism – the very characteristics that, though he liked Price personally, he might well have joined Tucker and later Burke in seeing him as embodying – while leaving the euthanasia of executive corruption as the only if preferable alternative. Hume and Price are the two sides of the Tory-radical medal; and the question with which we are left in conclusion is that of how far Hume's irony, ambivalence, and skepticism were contained within tensions that, in the year of his death, he saw as having passed out of control. He died peacefully, without patriotic lamentations for the fate of his country. But that may mean simply that he found it easier to surrender existence than to trouble about solving the riddles of history. Gibbon, whether as an Englishman or as an expatriate, probably knew in his heart that what was happening to Britain was not a Decline and Fall. Hume seems to have built himself the scenario of an almost insuperable contradiction. That his philosophy enabled him to quit the scene with equanimity we know; whether his history permitted him to prognosticate the next act is a question we may leave open.

Hume was a name to conjure with among the American founders, and I will revive the theme of ambivalence by adding a few words about that by way of coda. The late Douglass Adair showed[46] how he might be considered a contributor to Madison's tenth *Federalist Paper,* in which the conversion of passions and interests into a multiplicity of groups checking and balancing one another becomes a solution to the problem of the republic of great size, at payment of the usual cost of compromising the ideal of classical virtue. In Gerald Stourzh's masterly study of Alexander Hamilton, we see how the reading of Hume helped the greatest of Federalists accept the view that the United States must be a commercial empire, with a strong system of executive patronage and public credit finance.[47] But though Hume could live with a politics of patronage, the combination of empire and public credit sat ill with him. These were the very points at which Madison broke with Hamilton and moved into his alliance with Jefferson. To that purest of Commonwealth and Country thinkers, Hume was the posthumous ideologist of a conspiracy of British exporters, American merchants, and Federalist politicians to fasten the horrors of a Walpolean constitution upon the infant republic. Jefferson was at pains to exclude him from the reading of

[45] Price, *Two Tracts on Civil Liberty, the War with America, and the Debts and Finances of the Kingdom* (London, 1778); "Additional Observations," pp. xiii–xiv, 25, 38–39, 47, 51–52, 153n.
[46] *Fame and the Founding Fathers* (Williamsburg and New York: Institute for Early American History and Culture, 1974), pp. 93–123.
[47] *Alexander Hamilton and the Idea of Republican Government* (Stanford: Stanford University Press, 1970).

students at Charlottesville, and he encouraged the publication of a revised version of the *History of England* by an obscure London democrat, with all the facts left in and all the conclusions corrected.[48] After death, as in life, Hume was a master of the ambiguities of eighteenth-century historiography. It may be doubted that he expected to escape them.

[48] Craig Walton, "Hume and Jefferson on the Uses of History," in D. Livingstone and J. King, eds., *Hume: A Re-evaluation* (DeKalb, Ill.: Northern Illinois University Press, 1976). It would be appropriate, if iconoclastic, to apply to Jefferson Hume's observation that William Tytler "confesses to me & all the World that I am . . . right in my Facts, and am only wrong in my Inferences" (Hume to [Lord Elibank?], [late 1759 or early 1760], *Letters,* 1:321).

8

◁══════════════════════════════════════▷

Gibbon's *Decline and Fall* and the world view of the Late Enlightenment

In that otherwise memorable year, 1776, Edward Gibbon published the first volume of *The Decline and Fall,* carrying the narrative to the conversion of Constantine and concluding with the two famous chapters on the rise of Christianity. In 1781, he published the second and third volumes, carrying the narrative to the deposition of Romulus Augustulus and concluding with a chapter which anatomizes Merovingian Gaul, Visigothic Spain, and Anglo-Saxon Britain, and is itself closed by what is really a separate essay – the "General Observations on the Fall of the Roman Empire in the West." The three remaining volumes – which are concerned less with the Latin-Germanic West than with the "world's debate" between Byzantium and Islam in the East – did not appear until 1788. Gibbon died in 1794, at the outset of what would otherwise have been an exile from his beloved Lausanne occasioned by the wars between old Europe and revolutionary France. These dates reveal that *The Decline and Fall* is in chronology a product of the last years of the Enlightenment, the uneasy years between the American and French revolutions; this essay will examine the respects in which it is that also in spirit.[1]

Gibbon was a conservative in politics if a radical modernist in philosophy and religion, and his scholarship belonged in some ways to a generation earlier than his own: to Oxford – however he may have disliked it in his own time – of the Ancients against the Moderns and to Paris of the great years of the Académie des

From *Eighteenth-Century Studies,* vol. 10, no. 3, pp. 287–303. © 1977 American Society for Eighteenth-Century Studies; reprinted by permission.

[1] This essay develops and elaborates some points put forward in "Between Machiavelli and Hume: Gibbon as Civic Humanist and Philosophical Historian," in *Edward Gibbon and the Decline and Fall of the Roman Empire,* ed. G. W. Bowersock and John Clive (Cambridge, Mass., 1977). I hope to complete a full-length study, to be entitled *Barbarism and Religion: Civil History in Gibbon's Decline and Fall.*

Inscriptions et des Belles Lettres. But it is possible to disentangle from his volumes a historical sociology – or "philosophy of history" as the age would have it – based on the most advanced ideas of the French[2] and Scottish Enlightenments: on Buffon and Mably rather than Montesquieu – whom he greatly if critically admired – and on David Hume and Adam Smith rather than Voltaire – whom he came to despise. And this sociology is also an ideology; that is, it presents a clear image of the world view of the Late Enlightenment – its view of its own place in history and of the forces which threatened its future. Gibbon was sometimes evasive, but he was never complacent; he knew very well why he should think of civilizations as fragile, and the most he allowed himself to hope was that in the greatest of catastrophes, there were gains this side of savagery which could never be entirely lost. But it cannot be without a sense of irony and pathos that we read the words in which, on 1 May 1788, he presented his last volumes to the public and wondered aloud if he would write any more history: "I am fairly entitled to a year of jubilee; next summer and the following winter will rapidly pass away."[3] Within not much more than a year, Gibbon's Europe was to be destroyed by events which he certainly did not foresee; but in examining the fears for the future which he did entertain and temperately consider, we may inquire not only into the extent of his pessimism, but into the extent to which his fears foreshadowed what was to come.

Peter Gay has termed the Enlightenment "the rise of modern paganism," and it could not have persisted without that profound concern for the ancient world which moved Gibbon to write his history. The rejection of Gallican and Tridentine Catholicism, Calvinist and sectarian Protestantism, necessitated the erection of a secular ideal which found its location in the ancient city. In Voltaire and Hume, as well as in Gibbon, we find an avowed preference for Greco-Roman polytheism as permitting philosophy to develop independently of the gods, whereas the assertion – whether Platonic or Semitic – of a single godhead condemned it to the embrace of theology. Ancient philosophy, in the proper sense, is therefore a problem for Gibbon; since by "philosophy" he means nothing more or less than a methodical skepticism which frees the mind for its proper concerns, he is obliged to recognize it only in Lucretius or Cicero, and to dismiss the whole Athenian and Alexandrian endeavor as metaphysics and *esprit de système*.[4] The revival of Platonism ranks among the forces which destroyed ancient civilization, and seems

---

[2] For Gibbon's relation to French thought see the contributions of Robert Shackleton, Giuseppe Giarrizzo, Jean Starobinski, and Frank E. Manuel to Bowersock and Clive, eds.; and Giuseppe Giarrizzo, *Edward Gibbon e la cultura europea del Settecento* (Bari, 1954).

[3] *Decline and Fall*, Vol. IV (1788), v (introduction). Subsequent references to *The Decline and Fall* are given as *"DF,"* followed by the chapter number, and the volume and page number in the fifth edition of J. B. Bury (London, 1902–09). The quotation above may be found at Bury, I, xiii.

[4] *DF*, ii (Bury, I, 30). See also Gibbon's *Essai sur l'étude de la littérature*, chs. xlvii, lxxx, *The Miscellaneous Works of Edward Gibbon*, Vol. IV (London, 1814).

at times an agency even more subversive than the Christian combination of revelation with superstition. Gibbon comes nearest to a tragic awareness when he finds himself obliged to condemn the Emperor Julian — for whom he felt something like love — as a neo-Platonic metaphysician and magician who betrayed the philosophic paganism he struggled to revive, and the inferior of Athanasius in statemanship and public morality.[5]

It is possible to discover the sociology of religion — even the sociology of ideas — which enabled Hume and Gibbon to explain why the philosophy that flourished in an age of superstition must be flawed by systematization and metaphysics. Before we do so, however, we must consider the second reason why the secular ideal of the Enlightenment had to be located in the ancient city. Philosophic man in a secular universe must act and contemplate the reason for his actions, and it was in Athens and Rome that the philosophy of this combination had been worked out with the greatest finality. The hatred of metaphysics, however, combined with a Polybian veneration for the laws and arms of Rome, ensured that political philosophy would be admired in its Roman and Stoic rather than its Athenian and Academic form; the ideal city of the Enlightenment is populated not by illumined and contemplative philosopher kings, but by judiciously skeptical senators and magistrates. In consequence, the Anglo-French Enlightenment (including its American variant) was condemned to carry on the civic humanist and classical republican tradition of the Renaissance, and to see the failure of ancient philosophy as one with the failure of ancient politics.

This does not mean that all *philosophes* were doctrinaire republicans: Voltaire remained in spirit a man of the *grand siècle* and the *thèse royale* to the end of his days. But it does mean that every *philosophe* was in some degree involved in the contradictory vision of history which arose from accepting the Montesquieuan premise that virtue was the principle of republics; Gibbon, as we shall see, was no exception, and *The Decline and Fall* is written around this thesis. Ideally to be virtuous — as either the Renaissance or the Enlightenment understood this crucial term — a man should be the citizen of a republic. Property should give him independence and the ability to bear arms in the city's cause, and the community of arms-bearing proprietors should be the community of citizens obedient to the laws which they themselves made. The citizenry might be distributed into an aristocracy and a democracy, and a superstitious many might worship gods whom a philosophic few knew to be only modes of worshiping the city, but this did not detract from civic virtue so long as there was equality in arms and under the laws. The philosopher needed to be a senator, but was quite content to be a citizen. The element of contradiction in this vision — in which the Enlightenment was deeply entangled — arose from the republic's historical fragility. The republic was

[5] *DF*, xxi–xxiii; see particularly Bury, II, 361–81, 432–50, 473–78.

vulnerable to corruption, to political, moral, or economic changes which destroyed the equality on which it rested, and these changes might occur not accidentally, but in consequence of the republic's own virtue. Because it was virtuous it defeated its enemies; because it defeated its enemies it acquired empire; but empire brought to some citizens – chiefly military commanders and economic speculators – the opportunity to acquire power incompatible with equality and uncontrollable by law, and so the republic was destroyed by success and excess. This was why Gibbon's original Capitoline vision of writing the history of the decline and fall of the city[6] became a commitment to write the history of the decline and fall of the empire; quite simply, the empire had absorbed the city and destroyed its virtue, as Polybius had prophesied, Sallust and Tacitus had narrated, Machiavelli and Montesquieu had analyzed; and it is why his final verdict on the Western empire was that "the story of its ruin is simple and obvious . . . the natural and inevitable effect of immoderate greatness."[7]

But had this been all, Gibbon's history would have been an essentially simple narrative of the effects of corruption – a corruption arising from the separation of civil from military virtue, started by Marius and Sulla, completed by Caesar and Pompey, and institutionalized by Augustus, under whom the military institution began to govern the empire independently of the republic and so embarked on the long history of its own decay. This is Gibbon's narrative; it is his explanation, whenever he pauses to look back and analyze the Decline since the conquests of the republic. To the extent that this is so, he is still writing in the tradition of Tacitus whom he admired above any other historian; he can see only one locus of civic virtue, only one city destroyed by interaction with its empire, and Alexandria and Constantinople are part of the ruin because they are not cities in the political sense and have no virtue. But in fact this is not all. By the time we reach the "General Observations on the Fall of the Roman Empire in the West," from which the last quotation was taken, we know that the theme of corruption does not explain everything, and that there are strands in Gibbon's pattern with which the "General Observations" themselves – found slightly disappointing by nearly every reader – fail to deal. The corruption of the republic and the principate will not explain why Gibbon persisted in his design – after hesitation – through three more volumes of mainly Eastern history, or why, seven years later and near the end of his labors, he was moved to the famous remark that he had "described the triumph of barbarism and religion."[8] To find the strands in the pattern from which these concepts emerge, we must return first to the instability of virtue, and second to the relation between virtue and philosophy; and at each point we shall encounter Gibbon's response to the greatest mind of his genera-

[6] It does not seem to matter whether or not he had this vision on the day or at the place he claimed.
[7] *DF,* xxxviii (Bury, IV, 161).   [8] *DF,* lxxi (Bury, VII, 308–9).

tion, that of David Hume, to whom he paid the highest compliment in his power by calling him "le Tacite de l'Ecosse."[9]

It was not only the mutation of republic into empire as the main theme of ancient history which impressed the eighteenth-century mind with a sense of the mutability of virtue. It was widely held that virtue had subsequently been restored in a barbaric form by the Gothic and Germanic invaders, who had set up primitive but effective communities of armed freeholders, to which feudal relationships had been no more than marginal. There are traces of this perspective in Gibbon's first volume: he tells us that "the fierce giants of the north broke in and . . . restored a manly spirit of freedom; and after the revolution of ten centuries, freedom again became the happy parent of taste and science."[10] But the image of Gothic freedom, like that of primitive Roman virtue, rested on the assumption that the form of property which gave the individual arms and independence, liberty and virtue, must necessarily be land; and since the last years of the seventeenth century, it had been a commonplace to inquire what had been the consequence of the rise of commerce and of movable forms of property at the end of the supposedly agrarian Middle Ages. A quarrel of the ancients and moderns ensued: to some it seemed that the rise of commerce had spelled the end of virtue, as formerly free arms-bearing citizens had become content to pay mercenaries to defend them and absolute monarchs to govern them, the better to enjoy the wealth, leisure, and cultivation which commerce made possible. To these ancients – Thomas Jefferson among them – Europe under the enlightened monarchies was like Gibbon's age of the Antonines, enjoying an interlude of prosperity and politeness under the protection of a military establishment which law and liberty no longer controlled, and which must sooner or later become tyrannous and degenerate. But there were moderns – Defoe, Montesquieu, Hume, Smith, and Gibbon – who conceded that virtue had rested upon a foundation of arms and agriculture, but insisted that it had been so inhumanly harsh and restrictive as hardly to deserve the name; hence, they said – and Jefferson agreed – the nightmare utopias of Lycurgus' laws or Plato's republic.[11] The rise of commerce and culture had been worth the loss of virtue which it had entailed; it had vastly enhanced the human capacity for production and consumption, exchange, interdependence, and sympathy, and on this foundation there might be erected new ethical systems which displayed how man's love of himself might be converted into love of his fellow social beings. But the ancient image of virtue was never overthrown or abandoned, and in consequence it had to be recognized that the virtue of commercial and cultivated man was never complete, his freedom and independence never devoid of the elements of corruption. No theory of human

[9] J. E. Norton, ed., *The Letters of Edward Gibbon* (London, 1956), II, 107.   [10] *Df*, ii (Bury, I, 58).
[11] Montesquieu, *Esprit des Lois*, IV, 6, 8; V, 19; XX, 1; *Machiavellian Moment*, pp. 491–92.

progress could be constructed which did not carry the negative implication that progress was at the same time decay, that culture entailed some loss of freedom and virtue, that what multiplied human capacities also fractured the unity of human personality. The philosophers of the Enlightenment had not restored this unity, but had learned to live, resignedly or hopefully, with personalities sundered by history. They were already finding themselves cast in the role of Faust to the Mephistopheles of Jean-Jacques Rousseau.

Gibbon, in this analysis, emerges as a modern, and one relatively untroubled by the accusing finger of Rousseau; Lausanne was at a safe distance from Geneva. That is, he accepts the thesis that the Decline and Fall was ultimately due to the expansion of the empire, the professionalization of the armies, the institution of the principate, and the decay of virtue, but while he agrees that commerce, politeness, and luxury grew up behind the shield of the principate and the legions, he will not accept that luxury is to be considered a major cause of the Decline. There were more radical contemporaries who held that it was the affluent society which paid mercenaries to defend it, so that wealth was a cause of the loss of virtue; in their view of Roman history, the rise of the mercenary legions went together with the rise of the *equites* and the *publicani,* and they started from Sallust rather than from Tacitus. Gibbon – though he had written an essay about the dubious financial dealings of the tyrannicide hero Brutus[12] – resisted this interpretation. He was regularly at pains to point out that it was despotism, not luxury, which corroded the ability of ancient society to defend itself, and that the relation between despotism and luxury was not a simple one. When he paused, in the chapter which recounts Alaric's sack of Rome, to review the last stage in the history of the senatorial aristocracy, he made or strongly implied two striking points: the first, that the luxury of the senators was the effect of their living in an economy of conspicuous consumption, not of profitable exchange; the second, that if we look back into the primitive age of republican virtue, we find that the warrior yeoman was regularly plunged into debt because he preferred going off with the legions and seizing the lands of others to peaceably increasing by industry the yield of his own farm.[13] Virgil's *Georgics* – Gibbon had written in his youth – were written at Augustus' instance to persuade the soldier-farmer to civilize himself.[14] We can infer from this that Gibbon was awake to the modern argument – found in Defoe, Montesquieu, Hume, and others – that ancient virtue was warlike because it was economically primitive, and that a productive market economy had no need of virtue in this sense and would not be corrupted by its disappearance.

An implication would be that eighteenth-century commercial Europe was not threatened, like Rome, by corruption from within. Gibbon in 1781 had some

---

[12] "Digression on the Character of Brutus," *Miscellaneous Works,* IV, 95–111.
[13] *DF,* xxxi (Bury, III, 292–95, 302–3).   [14] *Essai,* pp. xix–xxii; *Miscellaneous Works,* IV, 32–37.

personal motivation for presenting this argument. The author, possibly Charles James Fox, of some satiric verses on Gibbon's dual role as historian of the Roman empire and parliamentary placeman under the North administration had written: "His book well describes / How corruption and bribes / O'erthrew the great empire of Rome; / And his writings declare / A degen'racy there / Which his conduct exhibits at home."[15] The revolt of the American provinces, as a matter of historical correctness, faced Britain with a Social War rather than a Decline and Fall, and came about precisely because the institutions of British liberty had not merged in those of imperial government; but it would not have been surprising if Gibbon had been at pains to destroy the very fashionable, almost radical-chic, parallel between contemporary Britain or Europe and Sallustian or Tacitean Rome. We have found that he had the means of doing so. But his historical intellect was a good deal stronger than its ideological promptings, and when we reach the "General Observations" at the end of Volume Three, we find this theme present indeed, but played down almost to vanishing point. Gibbon does indeed stress that the late empire was a military despotism which had destroyed its own capacity to replace and renew its virtue, whereas modern Europe is, he says, a great republic,[16] composed of diverse states which by emulation maintain each other's military virtue – though he also says that the advanced technology of war has rendered this virtue neither possible nor necessary[17] – correct each other's forms of government, and by trade and competition strengthen each other's economies.[18] In this peaceable and progressive society, military and political virtue are, in a way which recalls Montesquieu, kept at a level of moderate but not essential importance, and there is no need to worry too much about their necessary imperfection. But what renders the "General Observations" puzzling and disappointing to most readers is, one suspects, that this theme is dealt with in terms far less of internal decay than of the extreme improbability of barbarian assault from without. Gibbon elects to consider how Europe would stand up to a new nomad invasion, though he prefaces his observations with the admission that the Russians and the Chinese have reduced the nomads to a species verging on extinction.[19] American critics like to believe that he did this in order to avert his eyes from the painful spectacles of Saratoga and Yorktown;[20] but it is hard to find that the British cared enough about America to experience its loss as a trauma, and this emphasis on the nomads can be explained – the explanation will be

---

[15] There are various printings of these verses, of which the first ("King George, in a fright / Lest Gibbon should write / The story of Britain's disgrace . . .") is the best known. They are said to have been written in Fox's copy of *The Decline and Fall,* and found there when his books were auctioned.

[16] *DF*, xxxviii, "General Observations" (Bury, IV, 163).   [17] *DF*, xxxviii (Bury, IV, 166–67).

[18] *DF*, xxxviii (Bury, IV, 165–66).   [19] *DF*, xxxviii (Bury, IV, 164, note 6).

[20] See Bowersock and Clive, eds., pp. 30, 65, 182–83, 239–40. I am unpersuaded by the contention that Gibbon means "America" when he mentions "Armorica."

partly ideological – in terms of Gibbon's developing ideas on the sociology of barbarism.

Theorists in search of a modern equivalent for ancient virtue had already placed themselves on a road which, for Anglophones at any rate, led from John Locke to Adam Smith. The mind formulated its ideas in response to the sensations and objects encountered in experience; as men advanced in productive capacity through the successive stages of history, they enlarged their own minds by multiplying the objects to which they responded. In chapter nine of *The Decline and Fall,* Gibbon reviewed Tacitus' *De moribus Germanorum* in the light of this body of theory. The Germans were savages, he said, possessed of neither money nor letters, the media of exchange which multiplied and preserved the objects nourishing the mind,[21] and this was the case because their social condition was preagricultural.[22] They neither labored nor produced, and were consequently totally incapable of contemplation and almost incapable of action. Self-awareness was an existential burden of which they could discharge themselves only by violence;[23] war was their only activity, and honor – which was a fierce sense of personal though hardly of civil liberty – as near as they got to virtue.[24] If honor and liberty are precivil characteristics, Gibbon is devoid of serious nostalgia for the primitive virtues; he would have rather liked to believe in the authenticity of Ossian,[25] but he knew too well what Hume would have to say on the subject[26] and his own thesis commanded him to believe that virtue was civil and could exist only when the barbarian had been socialized into productive capacity and cooperative labor. He next considered the subject of barbarism in the very important chapter twenty-six, near the end of Volume Two, when the approach of the Goths obliged him to analyze the Huns and write a chapter on "the manners of the pastoral nations."

The notion of a pastoral, shepherd, or nomad stage, preceding agriculture in the order of historical development, was one recently discovered by eighteenth-century social theorists.[27] Adam Smith, as Gibbon could have known, argued that this was the stage at which private ownership and specialization of function, class division and consequently government, first made their appearance;[28] but Gibbon put forward a very different evaluation. All shepherd societies, he argued, were essentially alike,[29] because they presented humanity at its nearest to

---

[21] *DF,* ix (Bury, I, 218–20).   [22] *DF,* ix (Bury, I, 222–23).   [23] *DF,* ix (Bury, I, 221).

[24] *DF,* ix (Bury, I, 225–26). Note (a) the closeness of this argument to Montesquieu's concept of *honneur;* (b) its application to the condition of women in barbaric and civilized society (Bury, I, 227–28).

[25] *DF,* vi (Bury, I, 129–30).

[26] See Hume's letter as given in Gibbon's *Memoirs of my Life,* ed. Georges A. Bonnard (New York, 1966), p. 168.

[27] R. L. Meek, *Social Science and the Ignoble Savage* (Cambridge, 1975).

[28] Smith, *Lectures on Justice, Police, Revenue and Arms,* I, 1, 2; *Lectures on Jurisprudence,* ed. R. L. Meek, D. D. Raphael, and P. G. Stein (Oxford, 1978), 404–5.

[29] *DF,* xxvi (Bury, III, 71). See also Pocock, "Gibbon and the Shepherds: The Stages of Society in the *Decline and Fall,*" *History of European Ideas* II, (1981), 193–202.

the animal condition; since herdsmen did not labor but followed their grazing flocks, they developed no cultural individuality or diversity and their principal characteristic was a uniform mobility and ferocity in war. Gibbon was merely repeating in a cruder form the analysis he had already given of the Germans, and when he lays it down that this is the final analysis of barbarian society, to which by the nature of the case there can be nothing to add, we may feel that he is narrowing and indeed closing his equipment as a historian of culture. As a matter of fact, he is vastly enhancing his spatial capacity; chapter twenty-six is the prelude to the great panoramas of the later *Decline and Fall,* in which we see the interactions of the Desert with the Sown reaching all the way from Rome to China – Joseph de Guignes's *Histoire des Huns*[30] is one of the seminal books in Gibbon's reading – but as regards the history of Western Europe, the reduction of barbarism to a negatively characterized pastoralism does indeed enable him to carry out a gigantic and tendentious abridgment. As he describes, in chapters thirty-seven and thirty-eight, Germanic society taking shape in the conquered provinces of the West, the Gothic or Frankish settler is consistently presented as a hunter, shepherd, and warrior, exploiting an agrarian society he could never shape for himself. The first feudal lords who appear in Merovingian Gaul are essentially hunters, who conduct *razzias* to supply themselves with serfs and cattle, and let land revert to forest to supply themselves with game.[31]

Gibbon is systematically if not avowedly destroying the myth of Gothic agrarian virtue, by whose means feudal society had so often been equated with the primitive republic of warrior freeholders. His modernism appears at its extreme when he virtually confronts nomadism with urbanism and permits agriculture, "the foundation of manufactures,"[32] to appear only as the precondition of the latter. A determination to have none of the fashionable thesis that commercial society had degenerated from an agricultural condition helps explain why the "General Observations" do not consider Europe as threatened from within, but only by a purely conceptual nomad danger from without. Agriculture appears in the "General Observations" in two roles only: first, as the instrument by which civilization eradicates savagery – the Russians are plowing up the steppe, English navigators are introducing useful plants and animals to Polynesia;[33] second, as the indestructible germ by which civilization survives catastrophe – since it depends neither on individual genius nor on complex social diversification, the peasant household is unlikely to forget what it has learned about the arts of tillage in even the greatest of disasters.[34] The happy peasant, virtuous because unspecialized, yet specialized above the level of savagery, has made his reappearance

---

[30] *Histoire Générale des Huns, des Turcs, des Mogols et des autres Tartares Occidentaux. Par M. de Guignes* . . . , 5 vols. (Paris, 1756).
[31] *DF,* xxxviii (Bury, IV, 131–33).   [32] *DF,* ii (Bury, I, 53).
[33] *DF,* "General Observations" (Bury, IV, 164, 168–69 and note 15).
[34] *DF,* "General Observations" (Bury, IV, 168).

after being held back to the last page of Volume Three. Not even Gibbon could exorcise him from the eighteenth-century mind forever.

The relation of barbarism to religion can be explored when we realize that the Enlightenment's sociology of barbarism, which Gibbon knew very well, was also a sociology of superstition, and rather less certainly of fanaticism; superstition and fanaticism being the two categories into which the *philosophes* distributed most religious phenomena. In Gibbon's early *Essai sur l'étude de la littérature,* and in the two masters to which that work chiefly refers, Fréret and Hume[35] – we can read how the savage, idly and fancifully (because nonproductively) responding to the phenomena of experience, erects the multitude of gods and myths which make up the religions of superstition. Later in the progress of society appears the archaic philosopher, who endeavors to reduce religion from absurdity to rationality, but constructs the system of abstract ideas and occult qualities to which the *philosophe* gives the name of metaphysics. Should the metaphysician excogitate as part of his system the otherwise reasonable concept of a single god, there will arise a theology – one of those fatal unions of superstition with metaphysics for which the correct term is fanaticism or enthusiasm.[36] This was the baleful legacy of Plato, whose error was to think the godhead a subject for systematic philosophy;[37] it was an error natural enough in the historical context, but not one to which the ancient city was condemned. As empire and commerce made possible the comparative study of gods and metaphysics, the philosopher-magistrates of the ruling city could reduce philosophy to that rational and tolerant skepticism, and methodical curiosity, which is all Gibbon ever means by the word.[38] The skepticism of the ruling few forms a happy enough partnership with the superstition of the unreflective many, because neither attribute much truth-status to what they say; but the metaphysicians persist outside the pale, fanatically asserting the truth of what they take to be philosophy. The Platonic legacy is the potential enemy of the Roman order.[39]

Outside the natural history of religion altogether lie the great Semitic and Iranian[40] monotheisms, founded not on philosophy but on revelation. There is no sociological explanation of the prophet: he must be either a madman or an impostor – preferably, because more rationally, the latter;[41] but he erects a fanaticism more terrifying than that of the metaphysician, because it has no share in the progress of society from superstition to philosophy. The Jews, for whom

---

[35] For this relationship see Giarrizzo's volume and his essay in Bowersock and Clive, eds.

[36] Hume's *The Natural History of Religion* was one of Gibbon's principal sources; and see the quotation from Fréret in *Miscellaneous Works,* IV, 16n.

[37] *DF,* ii (Bury, I, 30); xv (Bury, II, 76); xxi (Bury, II, 335–36).

[38] *DF,* ii, is Gibbon's chief account of this ancient *esprit philosophique.*

[39] See the account of the neo-Platonic revival at the end of *DF,* xiii (Bury, I, 392–93).

[40] *DF,* viii, is largely an account of Zoroastrianism (Bury, I, 197–203).

[41] See the accounts of Zoroaster, Odin (*DF,* x; Bury, I, 240–41) and especially Muhammad (*DF,* 1; Bury, 333–96).

Gibbon has the *philosophe*'s total abhorrence, kept their god to themselves so jealously that the wars which destroyed them did nothing to the fabric of an empire in which they had no part;[42] but they left behind them the dangerous knowledge that the unity of the godhead might be more convincingly asserted on the foundation of prophecy than on that of philosophy. The way was prepared for that union of Mosaic revelation with Platonic metaphysics which was what Gibbon really dreaded in Christianity.

Gibbon saw the Decline and Fall as the failure of ancient skepticism, but not merely as the triumph of popular superstition. In the history of Christianity, superstition played a late and ambivalent role; it was preceded in the patristic era by fanaticism and enthusiasm. At a time when the populace of the empire, robbed of belief in their gods by the belated discovery that their masters thought them ridiculous,[43] were becoming exposed to a variety of restatements of the Jewish and Persian revelations, the masters themselves – perhaps because their role as magistrates was ceasing to satisfy in the decay of the principate – were turning to a variety of neo-Platonic and Gnostic metaphysics; and this apostasy of the philosophers played a major role in both the triumph of Christianity and the Decline and Fall. The great heresies which destroyed both civil and ecclesiastical discipline were all, Gibbon emphasizes, of neo-Platonic and Gnostic origin;[44] and the same disastrous ways of thinking were responsible for the failure of Julian to restore philosophic magistracy and virtue. Julian was the inferior of Athanasius in these qualities, and Athanasius is one of a chain of Church Fathers – Ambrose,[45] Gregory the Great,[46] and John Chrysostom[47] are others – of whom Gibbon writes with far more respect than mockery. The reason seems to be that these Fathers were leaders, effective and not without statesmanship, of their peoples in Alexandria, Milan, Rome, and Constantinople; the Christian republic – as Gibbon repeatedly calls it – was being led by Christian virtue.[48] It is true that this virtue was fanatical; both leaders and people were governed by a union of prophecy and metaphysics. It was anticivic and otherworldly, and could not be harnessed to the defense of the empire. But Gibbon was beginning to make use of Hume's distinction[49] between enthusiasm, which was fanatical and intolerant but drove men to assert their liberties against their rulers, and superstition, which

---

[42] Gibbon's main account of Judaism is in *DF*, xv (Bury, II, 2–6). All other references to the Jews display occasional pity and unvarying contempt. Observe that Hadrian's Jewish war is not considered an exception to the general peace of the empire (*DF*, i; Bury, I, 29 and note). I suspect this footnote to be deliberate and not an afterthought; cf. Bowersock and Clive, p. 64, n. 17.

[43] *DF*, xv (Bury, II, 55–56).

[44] *DF*, xxi (Bury, II, 336–54); xxxvii (Bury, IV, 95); xlvii (Bury, V, 96–106).

[45] *DF*, xxvii (Bury, III, 155–61, 174–76).

[46] *DF*, xlv (Bury, V, 33–38).   [47] *DF*, xxxii (Bury, III, 374–80).

[48] For this language see *DF*, xv, passim; and cf. *DF*, xix (Bury, II, 328).

[49] Hume, *Essays*, "Of Superstition and Enthusiasm." See also Pocock, "Superstition and Enthusiasm in Gibbon's History of Religion," *Eighteenth-Century Life* VIII, 1 (1982), 83–94.

was passive and law-abiding but disposed men to accept their rulers even when these were priests. Christian enthusiasm wins its greatest victory in *The Decline and Fall* when the temples of paganism are destroyed under the Theodosians; but almost immediately it is transformed into superstition, as the cults of saints and relics and shrines and miracles renew ancient polytheism in a Christian guise.[50]

About all this it is evident that Gibbon had ambivalent feelings, and saw history as an ambivalent process. Religion as superstition had originally been an aspect of barbarism, and it would be possible to see its revival as a return to barbarism. In chapter thirty-seven Christianity is shown reaching its nadir in the form of monasticism, and it is emphasized that the monk, deprived of property, the reward of his labor, and all membership in society, regresses to an apathy very like that of the savage; we are even told that one or two monks were of shepherd origin, and that a certain sect of solitaries grazed in the field like beasts.[51] But in the same chapter Christianity is shown helping to convert the barbarians, and Ulfilas is called the Moses of his branch of the Goths because he taught them letters and led them across the Danube to fertile pastures where their nomadism might become settled.[52] The image of agriculture has flashed across the page again, and it is used to distinguish between religion as a decivilizing and as a civilizing agency.

But religion as enthusiasm belonged to a more complex, because more civilized, phase in the historical process. Once Gibbon's knowledge of Hume reminded him that liberty and virtue might rest – as in the Reformation and the Puritan Revolution they had rested[53] – on a foundation of fanaticism, he was bound to remember his modernist skepticism on the subject of virtue. There was something to be said for superstition, if it was compatible with the rule of enlightened and tolerant magistrates; but in recounting "the corruption of Christianity" (his own phrase)[54] in the Theodosian age, he had reached the brink of that standard Protestant polemic against the rule of superstition by priests, to which as a *philosophe* he was in no way indisposed. In the later volumes of *The Decline and Fall,* however, this polemic, while of course present, is relatively undeveloped. These volumes carry out a plan, laid down as far back as Volume One in 1776,[55] of pursuing the history of the Eastern Empire beyond the fall of the Western; we are not to look to them for a history of how modern Europe, that great republic of states, emerged from the *respublica christiana* which had succeeded the Roman empire. But there is an extraordinary chapter in Volume Five – chapter fifty-four – in which Gibbon deduces the history of Protestantism

[50]*DF*, xxviii (Bury, III, 188–215).
[51]Bury, IV, 70–73. The shepherds turned monk may be found at pp. 64, note 30, and 73 (Simeon Stylites).
[52]Bury, IV, 76–77.   [53]*DF*, xvi (Bury, II, 138–39).   [54]*DF*, xxxvii (Bury, IV, 57).
[55]Bury, I, v–vii.

from origins not only Greek but neo-Platonic. The Gnostics begat the Paulicians, it seems, the Paulicians the Albigensians, the Albigensians the Western heretics in general, and these begat the Protestants.[56]

Gibbon is examining the interweavings of the rational and the enthusiastic components in Protestantism. At the end of this chapter he indicates what he applauds in contemporary religion – the restoration of the Antonine Enlightenment as the rule of an undogmatic clergy over congregations who no longer know or much care what they are meant to believe – and what he fears: those "Arminians, Arians and Socinians . . . who preserve the name without the substance of religion, who indulge the license without the temper of philosophy." A footnote draws the attention of the civil magistrate to the teachings of Joseph Priestley.[57] It is not known what Gibbon said if he ever heard that mobs, set on by magistrates, had destroyed Priestley's house in Birmingham, but this was just the sort of thing he feared. In Priestley's blend of unitarianism, materialism, and millennialism, he diagnosed the union of philosophy with fanaticism, and the structure of this chapter tells us that he saw Priestley as a second Arius, who would have been quite at home in the streets of fourth-century Alexandria. Gibbon as an undergraduate had been converted to Catholicism by reading Bossuet, and his return to Protestantism, even as a convenient home for an English *philosophe,* had never been free from uneasiness. He chose after 1781 to write the history of barbarism and religion in a new form: the history of how a prophet-legislator had civilized a pastoral people by teaching them enthusiasm for a religion of their own, and set the house of Islam at war with the city of Constantine.

Gibbon feared in Priestley exactly what Burke feared in Richard Price: the democratic fanaticism which they and many others thought was latent in English Dissent. After the Gordon Riots Gibbon wrote: "forty thousand Puritans, such as they might be in the time of Cromwell, have started out of their graves";[58] after the French Revolution, Burke wrote that nine-tenths of the Dissenters were devoted to its principles.[59] This analysis of *The Decline and Fall* – which disentangles some of its preoccupations without suggesting that these explain why it was written – indicates that Gibbon thought his world had laid the ghosts of virtue and corruption, but still went in fear of the spirit of fanaticism. The thesis of chapter fifty-four is not anti-Illuminist nonsense; there was enough neo-Platonism and Gnosticism abroad in the England of Blake, Shelley, and Coleridge to give us something to think about. But of the French Revolutionaries themselves, Gibbon said that they were fanatics, and also that they were barbarians; and he endorsed, like most gentlemen of his time, Burke's analysis and denun-

[56] Bury, VI, 110–29.
[57] Bury, VI, 129, note 49. See also *Letters,* II, 320–23, and *Memoirs,* pp. 171–72.
[58] *Letters,* II, 243.
[59] *The Correspondence of Edmund Burke,* ed. T. W. Copeland (Cambridge, 1958–69), VI, 418–22.

ciation of the fanaticism of natural right.[60] But there was room for another analysis, which Gibbon might perhaps have written: that of the fanaticism of civic virtue. We cannot regret that Gibbon died when he did; to think of him eking out an exile in a London he never much liked, aware that some nasty French commissary was living in the villa at Lausanne, and obliged to meet Wilberforce at dinner parties, should convince us that the age of Pitt was no age for him. But we must wish we had his account of Robespierre at the Feast of the Supreme Being.

[60] *Letters*, III, 321; for Burke, III, 216. Epithets such as "wolves," "savages," "cannibals" abound in Gibbon's correspondence in 1792.

9

Josiah Tucker on Burke, Locke, and Price
A study in the varieties of eighteenth-century conservatism

I

Early in 1946, an assistant lecturer and a lecturer in history found themselves sharing an office, as it would now be called, of Victorian granite and fiberboard partitions, forming part of what had been a gallery running above the archway of the Rolleston Avenue entrance to the old buildings of what was then Canterbury University College in the University of New Zealand. Both were newly appointed to their duties, the one just graduated and the other just returned from the wars. Between them, they increased the teaching members of their department from two to four. Both were men of independent personality who came to think it a matter of credit to each that they shared their quarters so cordially. In time, however, their ways parted. The assistant lecturer went in pursuit of a doctorate and entered upon a complex orbit that was to pass through Canterbury's gravitational field again. The lecturer, a more stable and powerful luminary unafraid of dog days, remained to become a professor of history and in due course vice-chancellor of the University of Canterbury in the times of its centennial and its migration to a new campus. Under whatever signs are now in the ascendant, the assistant lecturer offers the lecturer an essay upon a subject, and related to a personality, both of which have always meant much to him.

If the writings and addresses of Neville Phillips were to be collected, the language and mind of Edmund Burke would be found to have colored them deeply, and there would also be found a continuing concern with the conservative temper, coupled with the knowledge that this temper commands something more complex than surrender to it. In his writings on eighteenth-century history, there

This essay, in an earlier form, first appeared in *Essays Presented to Professor N. C. Phillips,* edited by Marie Peters, S. A. M. Adshead, and J. E. Cookson and printed for limited distribution at the University of Canterbury. Reprinted here by arrangement with the editors.

may be found the troubled and often troubling presence of Burke as a political actor, who not only responded unforgettably to the melee of his times but generated from the depths of a tormented personality a secondary melee of his own. "From chaos and cobwebs could spring even Burke."[1] He was capable of extravagance and even radicalism, and some modern exponents of the political order to which he belonged have detested him for these qualities;[2] yet it is a commonplace that conservatism, properly understood, can exist only in response to radical challenge, and to find a potential radicalism latent within the conservative himself is not therefore surprising. But the commonplace just mentioned raises a problem concerning conservatism in the age of Burke, which cannot be resolved through the study even of Burke alone. In the American and still more in the French Revolution, there appeared for the first time a predominantly secular revolutionary challenge, but the regimes against which it was directed were Whig as well as Anglican, Enlightened as well as Tridentine, and had just been celebrated by Gibbon as the most secular ruling order Europe had known since Roman antiquity.[3] We are not to forget the religiosity of Burke or Coleridge, Maistre or Chateaubriand, but we are faced with the problem of diagnosing both revolution and conservatism for the first time as secular principles, at work in a world where society and history counted for more than the church. There is an apparent paradox, however, in speaking of conservatism's existing "for the first time"; it cannot be a simple continuation of established ways and manners, but must mobilize them to meet a challenge never presented before. In the language of Joseph Levenson, a traditionalism is other than a tradition.[4]

We think of Burke as the philosopher of traditions: natural law and common law, Roman piety and prudence, Christian faith and medieval chivalry; no doubt this is how he intended his readers to think. But we must also see him as the active exponent and defender of Whig aristocratic politics, and not only was his attitude toward this order marked by the ambivalence of the *novus homo,* but the order itself was in fact far from traditional. Its pillars were the Revolution Settlement, the Toleration Act, the Bank of England, and the Septennial Act, and although the first of these might (but need not) be defended in the name of the ancient constitution, the others were in increasing degree defiantly modern and needed to be defended against "country," "Commonwealth," and "patriot" attacks whose appeal was to the symbols of Roman and Gothic antiquity. If conservatism is the defense of the existing order, the conservatism of the eighteenth century was the defense of a revolution. If this revolution had (like not a few

---

[1] From verses by Hester Thrale, quoted by Douglas N. Archibald, "Edmund Burke and the Conservative Imagination: Part II," *Colby Library Quarterly* XIII, 1 (1977), pp. 19–41, p. 19.

[2] Namier's dislike of Burke was vehement and transmitted to his pupils.

[3] See in particular, "General Considerations on the Fall of the Roman Empire in the West," *History of the Decline and Fall of the Roman Empire,* vol. III (1781), chap. 38.

[4] Joseph R. Levenson, *Confucian China and Its Modern Fate,* 3 vols. (London, 1958), vol. 1, p. xiii.

others) ended in oligarchy and the restriction of politics, this was not enough to make its defense a simple exercise in traditionalism. There was much to be defended that was not traditional at all, but must be defended on the grounds of its modernity. We already know how the apologists of Walpole developed a strategy in which modernism itself becomes a conservative argument,[5] and we are told that we must defend what is because it is all that we have achieved – all, indeed, that we have. To reconcile such an argument with piety toward the "little platoon" (by which Burke meant the French and English aristocracies) is difficult, but not impossible. Once we see it, however, as a central strand in Whig conservatism, a dilemma must necessarily arise within the accepted interpretation of Burke as traditionalist. If such elements are present in his thought, how do they coexist with those we have learned to recognize? If they are not present, why are they absent?

II

This essay is designed to explore these problems by confronting Burke with one of the most extraordinary and pungent personalities of his times: an intellect as conservative as his own, yet both like and unlike it in a challenging combination of ways. Josiah Tucker (1711–99), who became dean of Gloucester in 1758, is remembered as the author of economic tracts that rank him as a lesser pioneer of the free-trade school, but he was a good deal more than that.[6] The Seven Years' War gave him a passionate hatred of wars for the sake of trade,[7] and of the political alliance between Pitt and the London aldermen and liverymen that seemed to others (including Hume) to combine the worst elements of chauvinism and democracy. At least from 1766 Tucker believed that the problem of relations with America could be solved only by a total separation:[8] a declaration of Britain's independence from her colonies rather than the other way around. He came to believe that American resistance to parliamentary authority, English clamors for parliamentary reform, and Dissenting pressures for relief from the Test and Corporation Acts were aspects of a single conspiracy against the constitution by what he called "new-light men" – those ultraliberal descendants of the Puritans whom Burke had named "the very dissidence of dissent." Tucker also believed that the

---

[5] Isaac Kramnick, *Bolingbroke and His Circle: The Politics of Nostalgia in the Age of Walpole* (Cambridge, Mass., 1968), pp. 127–37. Kramnick considers Walpole to be the author of the ideas published in his defense – a doubtful ascription.

[6] See George Shelton, *Dean Tucker and Eighteenth-Century Economic and Political Thought* (New York, 1981), which reached me after all but the last part of this essay was completed.

[7] See the letter of February 11, 1758, in which Tucker tells Kames that his Bristol parish "is become a hell on earth," since the wealthier inhabitants are investing in privateers to plunder French trade and in brothels to provide them with seamen. Quoted in Shelton, *Dean Tucker*, pp. 166–7.

[8] *A Letter from a Merchant in London to His Nephew in America* (London, 1766), esp. pp. 44–9. Reprinted in *Four Tracts together with Two Sermons on Political and Commercial Subjects* (Gloucester, 1774), pp. 128–30. (The sermons are separately paginated.)

ideological foundation of their knavish politics was Locke's theory of the formation of civil society, against which he wrote a *Treatise Concerning Civil Government*,
published in 1781. This seems to be the first major refutation of Lockean politics
since that of Charles Leslie, the nonjuror, nearly eighty years before,[9] and it is
certainly the first to find in Locke the radical populist and democrat who has
begun to reemerge in recent research.[10] Tucker's primary bête noire came to be
the tradition of individualist natural right, which he insisted had been inherited
from Locke by Richard Price, Joseph Priestley, Benjamin Franklin, Jean Jacques
Rousseau, and other "republicans," "patriots," and "democrats" of the 1770s.
He respected Priestley and had an ironic admiration for Rousseau.[11] Price he
disliked personally as well as ideologically,[12] and the *Treatise Concerning Civil
Government* is a blast against Price in his pro-American vein, just as Burke's *Reflections on the Revolution in France*, a decade later, is a blast against Price's pro-
French utterances. Yet Tucker had an equal and associated antipathy to Burke;
he thought Dissenting propaganda had contributed to Burke's election for Bristol,[13] and in 1775–6 Burke's *Speech on Conciliation with America* and Price's *Observations on Civil Liberty* seemed to him to reveal the two men in hypocritical alliance. There is a strange triangle of repulsions here, which furnishes this essay
with its title; yet it takes us only to the brink of the differences between Tucker's
defense of civil authority and Burke's.

Tucker was an original, independent to the point of eccentricity. His works
were nearly all printed in Gloucester to be sold in London, an indication that he
wrote unsupported by any party connection, and when accused by Burke of being
a court flatterer intriguing for promotion, Tucker declared in print that he would
accept no preferment offered him, "SO HELP ME GOD."[14] He was, perhaps, in

[9] J. P. Kenyon, *Revolution Principles: The Politics of Party, 1689–1720* (Cambridge, 1977), pp. 63–
4; Gordon J. Schochet, *Patriarchalism in Political Thought* (Oxford, 1975), pp. 220–2. Hume's
essay "Of the Social Contract" may be considered another refutation.

[10] John Dunn, *The Political Thought of John Locke* (Cambridge, 1969); Julian H. Franklin, *John Locke
and the Problem of Sovereignty* (Cambridge, 1978); Richard Ashcraft, "The Two Treatises and the
Exclusion Crisis: The Problem of Lockean Political Theory as Bourgeois Ideology," in Pocock and
Ashcraft, *John Locke: Papers Read at a Clark Library Seminar* (Los Angeles, 1980), and "Revolutionary
Politics and Locke's *Two Treatises of Government*: Radicalism and Lockean Political Theory," *Political
Theory* VIII, 4 (1980), pp. 429–86.

[11] *A Treatise Concerning Civil Government* (London, 1781), p. 22: "Dr. PRIESTLY, the fairest, the
most open, and ingenuous of all Mr. LOCKE's Disciples, excepting honest, undissembling ROUS-
SEAU . . ." Cf. p. 236: ". . . except honest ROUSSEAU, who is generally consistent, whether in
Truth, or Error, and *perhaps* also Dr. PRIESTLY." For the full title of Tucker's *Treatise* see n. 52,
this chapter.

[12] *A Series of Answers to Certain Popular Objections against Separating from the Rebellious Colonies* (Gloucester,
1776), pp. xii–xiii, xiv, 87: "And you too, my ingenious Doctor, you, a Writer on moral Obligation, could condescend to lend your assisting Hand in this good Work"; pp. 88–93.

[13] *A Series of Answers*, p. 70.

[14] Burke's innuendo is in the speech on American taxation (*The Works of the Rt. Hon. Edmund Burke*,
Rivington edition, London, 1826, vol. II, p. 413); Tucker's oath in *A Series of Answers*, p. 97. See
Shelton, *Dean Tucker*, pp. 194–5, 197, 243–5.

no great danger of a bishopric. His belief that it was as foolish to make war for the subjugation of the colonies as it was wicked to support their claims to immunity was too much even for Samuel Johnson,[15] who had no aversion to independence of mind. But Tucker had no aversion to seeing himself as the one sane man in a wilderness of fools and scoundrels; he liked to recall how the great Bishop Butler, during an evening stroll in his garden at Bristol, had suggested to him that a whole nation might go mad just as an individual might.[16] Tucker was a florid, abusive, and egocentric writer, in addition to being an extremely funny one; we must remind ourselves that he is to be taken seriously. His reputation has further suffered from the inadequate growth of the history of ideology as a serious scholarly discipline. Robert Livingston Schuyler once edited a selection of Tucker's writings from which the whole third book of the *Treatise,* which deals with the history of medieval government, was omitted on the grounds that, being neither economics nor political theory, it could be of no possible interest to anybody.[17] Now that we know a little more about how to write the history of political thought, there is much to be found in Tucker that is worth studying both as history and as theory.

The key to Tucker's mind must be found in the unity he effected between the need for economic freedom and that for submission to civil authority. The first of these principles convinced him (with David Hume)[18] that those who made war for commercial empire were wicked madmen, and (with Adam Smith)[19] that to maintain empire in order to regulate colonial economies was costly futility. The second persuaded him (with both Hume and Smith)[20] that if the Americans would not submit to the authority of Parliament they should become separate and independent states – not indeed because they possessed any of the rights they were claiming, which would soon lead them to declare their independence, but because they were a set of dangerous anarchs with whom Britain, for both commercial and civil reasons, should have as little as possible to do. Neither Hume nor Smith was far from sharing the belief that independence was desirable, not as an American right but as a British convenience, and Hume agreed with Tucker that it would spike the guns of the potentially revolutionary agitators in London and Middlesex; but the dean of Gloucester proclaimed at the top of his voice what Smith knew was not politically practical to say before public opinion was

[15] Johnson, *Taxation no Tyranny* (1775) in *The Yale Edition of the Works of Samuel Johnson,* ed. Donald J. Greene (New Haven, Conn., 1977), vol. X, *Political Writings,* p. 451.

[16] *An Humble Address and Earnest Appeal* . . . (Gloucester, 1775), p. 20n.

[17] Robert L. Schuyler, ed., *Josiah Tucker: A Selection from his Economic and Political Writings* (New York, 1931).

[18] ". . . that wicked madman Pitt . . ." (Hume to Strahan, October 26, 1775); J. Y. T. Greig, ed., *The Letters of David Hume* 2 vols. (Oxford, 1932), vol. II, p. 301; see also pp. 303–5. *Four Tracts and Two Sermons,* pp. 75–88.

[19] *An Enquiry into the Nature and Causes of the Wealth of Nations.* especially the concluding paragraphs.

[20] Duncan Forbes, *Hume's Philosophical Politics* (Cambridge, 1975), pp. 133–4, 190n.; Donald Winch, *Adam Smith's Politics: An Essay in Historiographic Revision* (Cambridge, 1978), pp. 146–63.

ready for it. In this respect, Tucker's personality was more eccentric than his
intellect, but it must be added that he believed in the need to cast off the Americans for a formidable and fascinating collection of reasons. He took seriously, for
example – and why should he have been the only Englishman to do so? – Franklin's vision of a future in which the population of America would so far exceed
that of Britain that the seat of empire would be transferred across the Atlantic.
Tucker returned again and again to this theme;[21] it meant, he insisted, that the
contest with the colonies was a contest for empire,[22] not liberty, and that all
proposals for conciliation were part of an American strategy of remaining within
the empire, without acknowledging its authority or contributing to its defense,
until the time should come when they could take it over.[23] For his part, he added
for good measure, he would rather see Britain a French province than an American one.[24] Tucker never commented directly on the Declaration of Independence,
but it would have been perfectly consistent (given the military situation of July
1776) had he regarded it as a triumph for British arms; Yorktown he certainly
considered a fortunate defeat.[25] Before dismissing Tucker as an overintelligent
crank with one idea, it might be well to ask ourselves what effect Franklin expected his geopolitical prophecies to produce on the minds of Englishmen.

Tucker's reasons for wanting the Americans cast out of the British community
and obliged to assume the rank of independent states – enemies in war, in
peace friends[26] – begin at a level of envenomed antipathy but become deeper
and more interesting as we study them. In 1766, he gave a series of indignant
accounts of the American propensity for smuggling, for trading with the enemy
in time of war, for trying to force British investors to accept colonial paper currency in payment of debts;[27] and these, as we have seen, were already linked with
a vigorous response to Franklin's talk about a transfer of the seat of empire. All
these grievances recur to the end of Tucker's writing career, and in his later works
the specter of Franklin is merged with warnings against the colonies' encouragement of massive immigration from Britain and Ireland.[28] But the tones deepen

---

[21] A Letter from a Merchant, pp. 14, 42–3, Four Tracts and Two Sermons, pp. xii, 128–30; Humble
Address and Earnest Appeal . . . , p. 40; A Series of Answers, pp. xi–xii, 58–9.

[22] A Letter from a Merchant, p. 42 (Four Tracts and Two Sermons, pp. 128–9): ". . . you want to be
Independent: You wish to be an Empire by itself, and no longer the Province of another." Humble
Address and Earnest Appeal, p. 41: "His Majesty is graciously disposed to join with Great Britain
against America in this Contest for Empire, (for in Fact, that is the real Dispute, whatever may be
the Pretence)."

[23] A Series of Answers, pp. xi–xii, 58–9; Humble Address and Earnest Appeal; The Respective Pleas and
Arguments of the Mother Country and the Colonies . . . (Gloucester, 1775), p. vi.

[24] Four Tracts and Two Sermons, p. 194.

[25] Cui Bono? . . . Being a Series of Letters Addressed to Monsieur Necker (Gloucester, 1782), p. 140.

[26] Humble Address and Earnest Appeal, p. 5: "Offering at the same Time, to enter into Alliances of
Friendship, and Treaties of Commerce with them, as with any other sovereign, independent States."

[27] A Letter from a Merchant (see also Four Tracts and Two Sermons); A Series of Answers, pp. 88–93.

[28] E.g., Cui Bono? p. 26.

with *A Letter to Edmund Burke, Esq.* of 1775. Here Tucker carries out a devastating autopsy upon the great *Speech on Conciliation,* in which every one of Burke's explanations of the Americans' "fierce spirit of liberty" becomes a reason for having nothing more to do with them. He lingers with peculiar affection on that admittedly very odd passage in which Burke envisages the trans-Allegheny settlers' becoming a race of "English Tartars," a wild nomad cavalry raiding the outposts of settled government.[29] Even had British explorers yet encountered the Comanche and Kiowa, the landscape of Ohio and Kentucky[30] would hardly have justified this application of the "shepherd-stage" theory then becoming established in French and Scottish historical sociology,[31] and Tucker has some merciless fun with Burke's premature invocation of the cowboy West.[32] More serious disagreements, however, are soon to come. Burke's use of the argument from population growth plays right into Tucker's hands, and his suggestion that the spirit of liberty in the southern colonies may be directly connected with the institution of slavery enables Tucker to open up an argument that will soon become a favorite: that if slaveholders are generally republicans, history shows that republicans are generally slaveholders.[33] We should note the following:

As to the Institution of Slavery in any of our Colonies; let them be Advocates for it, who approve of it. For my part, I am thoroughly convinced, that the Laws of Commerce, when rightly understood, do perfectly coincide with the Laws of Morality; both originating from the same good Being, whose Mercies are over all his Works. Nay, I think it is demonstrable, that *domestic* or *predial* Slavery would be found, on a fair Calculation, to be the most onerous and expensive Mode of cultivating Land, and of raising Produce, that could be devised. And I defy you, with all your Learning and Acuteness, to produce a single Instance from History either antient or modern, of a Country being well cultivated, and at the same Time abounding in Manufactures, where this Species of Slavery (I mean the

[29] "They would wander without a possibility of restraint; they would change their manners with the habits of their life; would soon forget a government by which they were disowned; would become Hordes of English Tartars; and pouring down upon your unfortified frontiers a fierce and irresistible cavalry, become masters of your Governors and your Counsellors, your collectors, and comptrollers, and of all the Slaves that adhered to them." *Works* (Rivington edition), vol. III, pp. 63–4.

[30] Ibid.: "You cannot station garrisons in every part of these deserts. If you drive the people from one place, they will carry on their annual Tillage, and remove with their flocks and herds to another . . . they behold before them an immense plain, one vast, rich, level meadow; a square of five hundred miles." Burke may mean that this regression to the shepherd stage is less the consequence of the terrain than of the abdication of a civil government that might otherwise promote agriculture.

[31] See R. L. Meek, *Social Science and the Ignoble Savage* (Cambridge, 1975); J. G. A. Pocock, "Gibbon and the Shepherds; The Stages of Society in the *Decline and Fall,"* in *History of European Ideas* II, 3 (1981), pp. 193–202.

[32] *A Letter to Edmund Burke, Esq., Member of Parliament for the City of Bristol . . . in Answer to his Printed Speech . . .* (Gloucester, 1775), p. 43; *A Series of Answers,* pp. 24, 79–80; *Humble Address and Earnest Appeal,* p. 28.

[33] *Letter to Burke,* pp. 22–3; *A Series of Answers,* pp. 22, 103–6.

domestic or *predial*) is preferred to the Method of hiring free Persons, and paying them Wages.[34]

Tucker detested slavery, but this is no isolated explosion of his abhorrence. He would soon be developing a highly specific theory in which the rise of a wage economy goes with that of proper ideas concerning submission to civil authority, and the prevalence of slave or serf labor is linked with an erroneous theory of political liberty. Burke had enabled Tucker to accuse him of being on the latter side; the same strategy could be employed, in a remarkable fashion, when he dealt with Burke's suggestion that the northern colonists valued liberty because their Puritan forebears had emigrated in search of liberty both religious and civil.[35] Tucker's language shows how he was able to identify political radicalism with degenerate Puritanism and to accuse Burke (of all people) of complicity with both.

Our first Emigrants to *North-America* were mostly Enthusiasts of a particular Stamp. They were of that Set of Republicans, who believed, or pretended to believe, that *Dominion was founded in Grace.* Hence they conceived, that they had the best Right in the World, both to *tax,* and to *persecute* the *Ungodly.* And they did both, as soon as they got Power into their Hands, in the most open and atrocious Manner.

In process of Time, the Notion, that Dominion was founded in Grace, grew out of Fashion. But the Colonists continued to be Republicans still, only Republicans of another Complection. They are now Mr. LOCKE's Disciples; who has laid down such Maxims in his Treatise on government, that if they were to be executed according to the Letter, and in the Manner the *Americans* pretend to understand them, they would necessarily unhinge, and destroy every government upon Earth . . .

When the Emigrants fled from *England,* they were universally Calvinists of the most inflexible Sort. But they were very far from being of that Species of Protestants, whom you describe; and of which spreading Sect, there are but too many Proselites both in *Great Britain, Ireland,* and *America;* I mean the modern *new-light* Men, who protest against every thing, and who would dissent even from themselves, and from their own Opinions, if no other Means of Dissention could be found out. Such Protestants as these are very literally PROTESTERS; but it is hard to say, what they are besides . . .

The present Dissenters in *North America* retain very little of the peculiar Tenets of their Forefathers, excepting their Antipathy to our established Religion, and their Zeal to pull down all Orders in Church and State, if found to be superior to their own. And if it be this you mean, by saying, that the dissenting Interests [in America] have sprung up in direct *Opposition* to all the ordinary Powers of the World; — and that the Religion most prevalent in the Northern Colonies is a *Refinement* on the Principles of *Resistance;* the *Dissidence* of *Dissent,* and the *Protestantism* of the *Protestant* Religion:[36] — In short, if you ascribe the fierce Spirit now raging in the Northern Colonies to these Causes, I make no Objection

---

[34] *Letter to Burke.* [35] *Works,* vol. III, p. 53.
[36] Tucker is of course quoting a famous passage in Burke's speech.

to your Account of the Matter; provided you will allow, that the Religion of the Gospel is a very different Thing from theirs.[37]

This is not the last we shall hear of Tucker's belief that Locke's errors, or heresies, as a political theorist sprang from a confusion between the principles of civil and religious liberty. For the moment we are concerned with his onslaught upon Burke, and here the first point to notice is that he would have had no difficulty in accepting the contention of John Dunn and Quentin Skinner that Locke's *Treatises* form "the classical text of radical Calvinist politics,"[38] provided the word "radical" was interpreted so as to fall in line with Alan Heimert's contention that the American Revolution sprang from the soil of the Great Awakening.[39] By "the modern *new-light* Men," Tucker meant those Dissenters, English as well as American, for whom religion was now a kind of enthusiastic free inquiry; who held, as he had put it in an *Apology for the Present Church* written three years before, "that every Person, who was to teach, or preside in that Assembly, should engage, to *teach nothing but what appeared to him to be true,* and *agreeable to right Reason,* (which Words you know are a parody on a favorite Expression of yours relative to the Scriptures),"[40] and that religion was a perpetual search after truth no more to be finally concluded than Sir Hudibras's reformation. By inserting the words "in America" in square brackets in the last paragraph just quoted, Tucker probably meant to convey that English Dissent had gone over less completely to new-light rationalism than had the American congregations.[41] We may still hold that he exaggerated the case; but in the *Letter to Burke* he carefully excerpted the whole passage from the *Speech on Conciliation* in which Burke had described "the Dissidence of Dissent" as justifiable "only on a strong claim to natural liberty" and (with Tucker's emphasis added) as *"agreeing in nothing but in the Communication of the Spirit of Liberty."*[42] Here Tucker would see the religious origins of Locke's political theory; he would also see, in Burke's account

[37] *Letter to Burke,* pp. 18–20. Tucker's printer generally used square brackets, and these are repeated in this essay.

[38] Dunn, *Political Thought of John Locke;* Skinner, *The Foundations of Modern Political Thought,* 2 vols. (Cambridge, 1978), vol. II, *The Age of Reformation,* p. 239.

[39] Alan E. Heimert, *Religion and the American Mind: From the Great Awakening to the American Revolution* (Cambridge, Mass., 1966).

[40] *An Apology for the Present Church of England as by Law Established, occasioned by a Petition . . . for Abolishing Subscriptions, in a Letter to one of the Petitioners* (Gloucester, 1772), pp. 15–16. The "you" addressed is not Burke this time.

[41] *A Series of Answers,* p. 69n.: "It is remarkable, that the younger Dissenters of all Denominations, both Clergy and Laity, are [I do not say *Universally* but] *too generally* tainted with levelling republican principles respecting the *State,* and with various wild Heterodoxies in Point of *Religion.* The Elder, the more experienced, and those, who are in every respect the wiser, and better Part of them greatly lament this general Defection in their Brethren." Tucker goes on to say that this does not apply to the Scots, against whom the patriots display violent prejudice. This passage might be compared with Burke's estimates of the extent of pro-French feeling among Dissenters after 1789.

[42] *Letter to Burke,* p. 17.

of the state of American Puritanism in 1775, a diagnosis identical with his own. As he tells Burke, not only at the end of the passage quoted, but throughout the dissection of the *Speech on Conciliation,* they do not differ on the facts, only on the conclusions to be drawn from them. All that Burke finds to make the Americans formidable, Tucker finds to make them abominable; every one of Burke's arguments for conciliation Tucker finds to be an argument for separation.

But if Burke, recognizing the true character of American society, still wants to retain it in organic association with the established order in church and state, what is the explanation? Here Tucker's eye falls on the leading English apologists for American civil and religious liberty, and for colonial claims against the authority of parliament: Joseph Priestley and Richard Price. These "Republican Doctors"[43] have reduced religion to a species of enthusiastic speculation; they profess what Tucker considers a "Lockian" political philosophy that denies the legitimacy of all civil government by making consent its necessary precondition; they are the allies of those London radicals who, after joining with Pitt to promote the great war for empire, are now using the crisis in imperial government to demand far-reaching political change and even new forms of political association. It is clear that Tucker in the 1770s found Dissenting claims for reform on grounds of natural right and liberty deeply disturbing, exactly as Burke was to do a decade later; the words and actions of Richard Price helped spark Tucker's *Treatise Concerning Civil Government* in 1781, just as they did Burke's *Reflections on the Revolution in France* in 1790. But in 1775–6 Tucker found Burke expounding Price's brand of religion as a constituent of the American character, and Price praising Burke as a friend to liberty. Not even Tucker at his most explosive could call Burke a "Lockian"; but if the member for Bristol was not a republican, it seemed pretty clear to the dean of Gloucester that he was a "patriot," a self-serving politician who had joined with the republicans for reasons of his own. These reasons might be profoundly ambivalent and hypocritical. If in the *Letter to Burke* Tucker told him that "both the *American* and the *English* Republicans expect great things from you,"[44] in a tract of the following year he held Burke responsible for all plans involving a number of independent parliaments under the same crown, which he said would inevitably lead to the despotism of either

---

[43] ". . . your celebrated *American* Fellow Labourer . . ."; *Letter to Burke,* p. 12. The phrase "Republican Doctors" is in *Four Letters on Important National Subjects Addressed to the Right Honourable the Earl of Shelburne* (Gloucester, 1783), p. 23.

[44] *Letter to Burke,* pp. 14–15: "On the other hand, it is equally certain, that you are endeavouring to make Use of these factious Republicans, as the Tools and Instruments of your own Advancement." In *A Series of Answers,* pp. xii–xiii, Tucker says that Burke was personally responsible for the Declaratory Act and that Price lacks "the Ingenuity to acknowledge it." In *A Treatise Concerning Civil Government,* p. 254, appears the figure of a false patriot who, rather than advocate a separation from the colonies, "would warmly recommend a Reform in the K—g's Kitchen, in his Cellar, in his Household Servants, and his Household Furniture; – nay, I had almost said, in his Dog-Kennel." The allusion to Burke is obvious.

ministerial influence or royal prerogative, and probably to the triumph of Franklin's plan for the subjugation of Britain by America.[45] These charges were not as contradictory as may appear. When an eighteenth-century writer expresses fear of republicanism or democracy, he is usually expressing fear of a conspiracy by degenerate aristocratic politicians, "desperate *Catilinarian* Men."[46] By 1783 Tucker saw the role of patrician demagogue being played by Lord Shelburne, that patron of subversive intellectuals (like Shaftesbury before him),[47] who was supposed to have said that monarchy might prove unnecessary. This fear was to be shared by Burke; we know that the *Reflections* were in part intended to expose the evil designs of Shelburne and his creatures, Price and Priestley.[48]

Tucker's charges against Burke might not be acceptable, but they would not be unintelligible to a contemporary mind; yet we can see the doctrinaire element in them well enough. It seemed so clear that Britain should separate from the colonies, and the case for doing so had been so cogently stated in Burke's own oratory, that only sinister motives could account for his persistence in trying to keep them within the empire; *Common Sense,* which Tucker attributed to Franklin and Adams (he does not say which Adams), was a refreshingly honest work by comparison.[49] What is striking and important for our purposes, however, is that, ten to fifteen years before the *Reflections on the Revolution in France,* Tucker could make so "Burkean" a case against ideologies with which he held Burke to be in complicity. We return to the comparison between the two men's extended statements of the "conservative" position.

III

The name of John Locke does not occur in Burke's *Reflections* and, even where he is considering the proper interpretation of the events of 1688, it taxes the ingenuity of modern scholars to contend that a rebuttal of the *Treatises on Government* was what Burke had principally in mind. Tucker's *Treatise Concerning Civil Government* is another matter. Since at least 1775, the dean of Gloucester had been announcing his intention of publishing a systematic refutation of Locke's theory of politics at the earliest possible opportunity,[50] and had given several foretastes

---

[45] *Humble Address and Earnest Appeal,* pp. 10–11, 33–40.
[46] *Treatise Concerning Civil Government,* p. 238.   [47] *Four Letters on Important National Subjects.*
[48] Frederick Dreyer, "The Genesis of Burke's *Reflections,*" *Journal of Modern History* L, 3 (1978), pp. 464–6.
[49] *A Series of Answers,* p. 50: "In this single Assertion, tho' in very few others, I entirely agree with the Authors . . . IT IS TIME TO PART." See also p. 59.
[50] *Pleas and Arguments,* p. 13n. This is also described as "Tract V," in succession to *Four Tracts and Two Sermons,* and the treatise against Locke was evidently intended to be a sixth. See *Pleas and Arguments,* pp. 25ff., 38–9. In the "Advertisement" prefixed to the *Letter to Burke* (pp. 11–13), Tucker says: "The present critical Juncture obliges the Author to postpone his Animadversions on Mr. LOCKE's Theory of Government for some Time longer." See *A Series of Answers,* sig. A2.

of his arguments. Significantly, the anti-Lockean treatise was originally to have taken the form of an "address to the Protestant Dissenting ministers of North America," but any intention of addressing American audiences had disappeared with the increasing virulence of Tucker's feelings on the subject; and to judge from the four hundred pages it finally occupied, he had found composition a bigger task than he had anticipated. A draft was privately printed for circulation among the author's friends and predictably fell into hostile hands,[51] but the text that appeared in 1781 represented Tucker's final recension of his views.[52]

Tucker makes a somewhat simplistic statement of the position he desires to rebut. Locke is taken to have said that the individual cannot be deprived of his freedom without his own consent; that he inherits no obligation to obey civil authority from the fact of his father's obedience; that he cannot acquire membership in civil society from any period of living under its laws, without "actually entering into it by positive engagement"; and that he cannot be taxed or deprived of his property without his consent.[53] Tucker repeatedly cites the *Second Treatise* in support of this reading of Locke's intentions,[54] but he is less concerned with the structure of Locke's argument than with conclusions derived from and (in his opinion) compatible with it, which he claims to find in Priestley's *Essay on Civil Government*,[55] Price's *Observations on Civil Liberty*,[56] and other works.[57] These conclusions are (a) that there may be conceived an ideal form of government, founded on the individual's right to consent to the creation of authority and to acts of legislation and taxation, in which he is as far as possible his own legislator in matters concerning himself; (b) that governments obtaining in the actual world are legitimate only insofar as they conform to this model, which most of them

---

[51] Tucker included responses to criticisms already published by John Cartwright (*The People's Barrier against Undue Influence and Corruption* [London, 1780]) and James Dunbar (*Essays on the History of Mankind* [London, 1781]). See *Treatise*, pp. 385–6.

[52] The full title runs *A Treatise Concerning Civil Government in three parts. Part I. The Notions of Mr. Locke and his Followers concerning the Origin, Extent, and End of Civil Government, Examined and Confuted. Part II. The True Basis of Civil Government Set Forth and Ascertained; also Objections Answered; Different Forms Compared; and Improvements Suggested. Part III. England's Former Gothic Constitution Censured and Exposed; Cavils Refuted; and Authorities Produced; also the Scripture Doctrine Concerning the Obedience Due to Governors Vindicated and Illustrated.* By Josiah Tucker, D.D., Dean of Gloucester (London, 1781).

[53] *Letter to Burke*, pp. 11–12, 12–13; *A Series of Answers*, pp. [ix]–x; *Treatise*, pp. 1–2, 3–5.

[54] *Treatise*, pp. 5–10. The citations are from Locke's *Second Treatise*, chap. VIII, secs. 95, 98, 116, 119–22; chap. IX, secs. 123, 127; chap. X, secs. 138, 140; chap. XVII, sec. 198.

[55] *Treatise*, pp. 13–17, citing "2nd ed., 1771," pp. 6, 11, 40. For citations see *Pleas and Arguments*, pp. 38–9; *Letter to Burke*, pp. 12–13; *A Series of Answers*, pp. 60–4.

[56] *Treatise*, pp. 18–21, citing "the 5th edition," pp. 1, 3, 4, 7, 15. For earlier citations see *A Series of Answers*, pp. xii–xiv and (allusively) 60–74; also 88–93.

[57] Chiefly William Molyneux, *The Case of Ireland's Being Bound by Acts of Parliament in England* (1698). See *Pleas and Arguments*, pp. 25ff.; *Treatise*, pp. i–ii, 11–13, 96–101. Tucker attached much importance to proving Locke's complicity with Molyneux's writings, and argued incessantly for a parliamentary union with Ireland.

are far from doing; and (c) that when a government is such that it defrauds or deprives a people of its rights, they, or any individual acting in their name, are free to take action designed to recover these rights and establish a government that will actualize them. Tucker firmly asserts that Locke was the author and originator of these doctrines, but he is more concerned with the continuity and development of "Lockian" thought than with the exegesis and analysis of the *Treatises of Government* themselves. The problem he raises for us is less that of Locke's own intentions than that of the role he played in the history of thought in the eighteenth century: Had it or had it not been radical in the way that Tucker supposes?

Tucker's central criticism of the "Lockian" position is one we have long been accustomed to consider essentially Burkean: namely, that a systematic application of a theory of natural right centering in the individual must end by delegitimating all existing governments and all existing systems of institutionalized social relationships.[58] Burke was to put it thus: "They have the rights of men. Against these there can be no prescription; against these no agreement is binding; these admit no temperament and no compromise; any thing withheld from their full demand is so much of fraud and injustice."[59] As far back as 1775, Tucker had found a passage in Priestley that suggested that lawyers were not to be consulted when the requirements of nature were antecedent to any mere precedent of fact;[60] and in 1781 he quoted Price as saying: "In general, to be *free* is to be guided by one's own Will, and to be guided by the Will of another is the Characteristic of Servitude. This is particularly applicable to Political Liberty."[61] The question was, he wrote, whether any government was to be accounted usurpation that could not meet such criteria of natural right and freedom. Burke would have concurred (at least in 1790); the pages of the *Reflections* are thick with denunciations of the "metaphysician," whose wickedness knows no bounds because he will subject any human relation or affection to abstract criteria such as natural right, and as often as not this "metaphysician" is a figure constructed from that of Richard Price himself. A decade and more earlier, Tucker had found Price guilty of the same errors, but his imagination was coarser and less apocalyptic than Burke's, and the "metaphysician," instead of being an embodiment of Luciferian

---

[58] *Letter to Burke*, p. 12: Priestley teaches that "as all Governments whatever have been in some Measure compulsory, tyrannical and oppressive in their Origin, THEREFORE they ought to be changed"; Rousseau suggests doing this annually. *A Series of Answers*, p. 64. *Treatise*, p. 4: "The Question, therefore, the *sole* Question now to be decided, is simply this, 'Whether THAT Government is to be justly deemed an USURPATION, which is not founded on the *express* mutual Compact of all the Parties interested in, or belonging thereunto?' "; p. 17 (summarizing Priestley): "And in Circumstances, where *regular Commissions* from this abused Public cannot be had, EVERY MAN, who has Power, and who is actuated with the Sentiments of the Public, may *assume a public Character*, and bravely redress public Wrong."

[59] Burke, *Reflections on the Revolution in France: Works*, vol. II, p. 60.

[60] *Pleas and Arguments*, pp. 38–39 and note.   [61] *Treatise*, p. 20.

pride and hypocrisy, is simply a figure of the contemporary scene – the heir of Locke, the expositor of a socially dangerous error which Tucker proceeds to explain.

The error is that of making the individual, his rights, and his personality, anterior to the formation of civil society. Tucker presents this error as arising in two ways. In the first place, it is predicated on a fundamentally antisocial view of human nature. The naturally free individual is by nature free, and very little more; he desires to be free and to rule himself, he asserts a series of rights to the satisfaction of these desires, but he and those like him are by nature no more than so many "independent and unconnected" beings (the words are Priestley's), who

do not spontaneously, and, as it were, *imperceptibly* slide into a Distinction of Orders, and a Difference of Ranks by living and conversing together, as Neighbours and social Beings: – But on the contrary . . . naturally shew an Aversion, and a Repugnance to every kind of Subordination, 'till dire Necessity compels them to enter into a solemn Compact, and to join their Forces together for the Sake of Self-Preservation.[62]

It may be worth remarking at this point that Tucker shows no particular interest in Hobbes and does not find it necessary to invoke his specter as part of an indictment of natural-rights social theory. He is asserting that men are naturally sociable, that they naturally learn to accept differences of rank and authority as part of the experience of social life, and that government and submission to authority arise naturally out of the network of relationships and subordinations thus formed. By comparison, such an author as Priestley

supposes Government, to be so entirely the work of Art, that Nature had no Share at all in forming it; or rather in *predisposing* and *inclining* Man to form it. The Instincts of Nature, it seems, had nothing to do in such a complicated Business of Chicane and Artifice, where every Man was for driving the best Bargain he could; and where all in general, both the future governors and governed, were to be on the catch as much as possible . . . In short, they did not feel any Instincts within themselves kindly leading them towards associating, or incorporating with each other.[63]

Here are Burke's "sophisters, oeconomists and calculators";[64] but they do not occur where Burke seems to place them, at the moment of transition from a feudal and chivalric to a commercial and philosophical society, but rather at the moment of Lockean compact, where we are to imagine society as being formed by a multitude of "independent and unconnected" beings. Tucker hammers away at the unhistorical character of such a compact, because he wants to emphasize that we cannot imagine it without imagining the individual out of history, and consequently out of nature. The state of nature is profoundly unnatural. It is clear to him how this error has arisen.

[62] *Treatise*, p. 22.   [63] *Treatise*, pp. 23–4.   [64] *Reflections; Works*, vol. II, p. 89.

But if Mr. LOCKE and his Followers have not granted much to human Nature in one Respect, they have resolved to make abundant Amends for their Deficiency in another. For tho' they have not allowed human Nature to have any innate Propensities towards the first Formation of civil Society; – yet they do most strenuously insist, that *every Man,* every individual of the human Species hath an unalienable Right to chuse, or refuse, whether he will be a member of this, or that particular Government, or of none at all.[65]

As unequivocally as could be desired by any modern follower of Leo Strauss or Russell Kirk, Tucker identifies the "Lockian" error as the divorce of the individual from society brought about by the substitution of natural right for natural law. It is not by accident that the penultimate chapter of his *Treatise* is designed to rescue "the judicious Hooker" from the republican and individualist company he has too long been obliged to keep,[66] and restore him to his proper place in the succession from Aristotle and Cicero to Grotius, as "a Constitutional (though not a Republican) *Whigg.*"[67] Here we may be tempted to assign Tucker, as he assigns Hooker, to the grand "classical tradition of natural law," to which Burke too is held to have addressed himself when he protested against the "sophisters, oeconomists and calculators." But Tucker's role as a pioneer of free-trade economics may perplex us here, since we have been for so long encouraged to see the decomposition of classical politics in the eighteenth century as brought about by the rise of classical economics – as an affair of the revolt of economy against polity,[68] of the rise of possessive individualism[69] and market ideology.[70] Tucker is so far from fitting into this scenario that he presents a problem worth exploring. We should begin by noting the second explanation he offers of the rise of natural-right theory, one that entails a rather different account of its history. In a relatively benign account of Locke's historical role, he writes:

Mr. LOCKE in his early Days was a Witness to grievous Persecutions inflicted on the Score of Religion. He saw the Right to private judgment exposed to continual Vexations; and he saw likewise, that the Interests of the State were not at all concerned in maintaining that rigid universal Conformity in Religion, for which the Bigots of those Times so fiercely contended; – nay, that the Principles of Humanity, justice, and Truth, as well as the Suggestions of sound Policy, plainly required a more extended Plan of religious Liberty: All this he clearly saw: And hence he inferred, and very justly, that every Man had a Right not only to think, but even to act for himself, in all such religious Matters as did not oppose, or clash with the Interests of civil Society. And had he stopt there, and gone no further, all would have been right; nay, he would truly have deserved the Thanks of Mankind for pleading their Cause so well.

[65] *Treatise*, p. 25.   [66] *Treatise*, Part II, p. iii.   [67] *Treatise*, p. 409.
[68] Joseph E. Cropsey, *Polity and Economy: An Interpretation of the Principles of Adam Smith* (The Hague, 1957).
[69] C. B. Macpherson, *The Political Theory of Possessive Individualism: Hobbes to Locke* (Oxford, 1962).
[70] Joyce O. Appleby, *Economic Thought and Ideology in Seventeenth-Century England* (Princeton, N.J., 1978).

But alas! he extended those ideas, which were true only in what concerns Religion, to Matters of a mere civil Nature, and even to the Origin of civil Government itself, – as if there had been the same Plea for Liberty of Conscience in disobeying the civil Laws of one's Country, as for not conforming to a Church Establishment, or an Ecclesiastical Institution; – and that the Rights of private judgment [I mean the open and public Exercise of those Rights] are equally unalienable and indefeasible in both Respects.[71]

Tucker was what he had called Hooker, a constitutional Whig: a resolute defender of toleration, a resolute opponent of the Dissenting claim that civil rights should be accessible to all on grounds unconnected with church membership. What seemed to be a separation of church and state, he held, was in fact a confusion between the two, namely, the error of holding that civil liberty could be claimed on the same grounds as religious liberty; and this was an error to which Dissent, for theological reasons as well as in consequence of its civil position, was especially prone. We have noted Tucker's suggestion that New Englanders had passed from believing that dominion was founded in grace to believing that religious liberty was a civil and natural right. There is something to the same effect in a highly entertaining passage of the *Treatise* where he imagines his opponents objecting that though natural society may grow imperceptibly through the processes of human interaction, civil or political society is different in kind and cannot come into being without specific acts of consent and engagement by individuals. Tucker imagines his reply:

When Mr LOCKE was a very young Man, it was the Custom of the Pastors of his Time to make the junior Part of their Congregations to undergo the following strange Examination, "At what Day or Hour did you feel the Influxes of Saving Grace, and receive the Seal of your Election and Justification?" Something like the same Question is couched under this Objection, founded under Mr LOCKE's System.[72]

The acts of divine grace – however much the Puritans distorted their operations – may well occur and take effect outside the normal processes of social experience and education; but to suppose that the political acts of free individuals can only be thought of as acts of consent rooted immediately in nature is an error that may very well arise from a confusion between grace and dominion. The result is not only that we separate the political institution from

that *progressive* Course of Civil Society, which like the infant State of Man (*moral* and *intellectual* as well as natural) grows up gradually from small beginnings to Maturity . . . As well may you pretend to define, where the Night ends, and the Day begins, as to assign the exact Period when that Society which is *natural* puts on the Dress and assumes the Form of the Political.[73]

It is also that we confound the actions of the moral being with those of the political. By this Tucker does not of course mean that political actions are inde-

[71] *Treatise*, pp. 30–1.   [72] *Treatise*, p. 153.   [73] *Treatise*, p. 158.

pendent of moral constraints; he means that moral personality is not by itself a sufficient foundation for political capacity and membership. It is the fundamental "Lockian" error to suppose that it is; for not only does this mean that an equal political role must be accorded to every moral agent – every sentient human creature, rich and poor, male and female, young and old[74] – but in the last analysis it makes political action and capacity impossible. The reason is that moral action is not alienable, whereas political action is:

> In the Affairs of Conscience no Man can act, or be supposed to act as Proxy for another; no Man can be a Deputy, Substitute or Representative in such a Case; but every Man must think, and act personally for himself. This is the Fact; and in this Sense it is very true, that the Rights of private Judgement are absolutely unalienable . . . because they are *untransferable*.[75]

But all systems of political action, all distributions of civil authority among human beings, depend upon my capacity to recognize that another has the right to act for me and the authority to commit me by his actions. To say that all my actions must be performed by me as a moral agent not only denies another the authority to command me; it also denies me the authority to commission another to act in my name; for if my rights are unalienable I am not free to alienate them. To identify political capacity with moral agency therefore destroys both authority and representation at a single blow.

> Honest, undissembling ROUSSEAU clearly saw, where the Lockian Hypothesis must necessarily end. And as he was a Man who never boggled at Consequences, however extravagant or absurd, he declared with his usual Frankness, that the People could not transfer their indefeasible Rights of voting for themselves to any others: and that the very Notion of their choosing Persons to represent them in these Respects, was a species of Contradiction. According to him, a Transmutation of Persons could not be a greater impossibility than a Translation of those Rights, which are absolutely incommunicable.[76]

Rousseau is the Priestley of Geneva, the dissidence of dissent in its alpine form. Both theorists leave the individual "independent and unconnected," claiming to choose a government for himself but in fact incapable of doing so without "chicane" and "contradiction." Tucker does not examine Rousseau's solution of

---

[74] *Treatise*, pp. 26–7: "Now, according to the Principles of Mr. LOCKE and his Followers . . . the Right of voting is not annexed to Land, or Franchises, to Condition, Age, or Sex; but to human Nature itself, and to moral Agency: Therefore, wherever human Nature, and moral Agency do exist together, be the Subject rich or poor, old or young, male or female, it must follow from these Principles, that the Right of voting must exist with it: For whosoever is a moral Agent is a *Person;* and *Personality* is the only Foundation of the Right of voting." Tucker frequently hints that women would have the right to vote on these principles. He does not seem to think that they should, though he notes (*Treatise*, p. 249n.) that women shareholders vote in elections of East India Company directors; his point is not that women are not moral persons, but that moral personality confers no right to vote. See his debate with Cartwright on the subject; *Treatise*, pp. 358–65.
[75] *Treatise*, pp. 32–33; cf. p. 21n.   [76] *Treatise*, p. 39.

the problem, but if he had we may imagine him commenting acidly on the radical separation between the general will and any scheme of social relations on which human beings could be supposed to enter as the result of their own activities. He now returns to these relations as he claims they really are, and considers them as naturally engendering authority and political capacity, subordination and right.

IV

There is no distinction between natural and political authority, because the latter arises as humans, in the ordinary course of social interaction, recognize that inequalities of capacity exist among them and acknowledge the authority for specific purposes of those possessing superiority in the capacity for which each purpose calls.[77] Natural society is therefore deferential, and the state is the consolidation of those groups of authoritative persons to whom deference is paid. This does not mean that it is a simple aristocracy; Tucker is a good enough Aristotelian to be aware that authority comes in many forms and is lodged in many groups of persons, who need not cohere in a single governing class or institution. Consistently throughout his writings he affirms the superiority of a mixed constitution or state;[78] but this does not exist chiefly to ensure the internal restraints which its component parts exert upon each other, and Tucker has no objection to saying that "we must stop somewhere"[79] and attribute to some governing organ a final authority from which there is no appeal – the *ne plus ultra* that every parliamentarian found he must sooner or later assert and defend against American claims. The value of a mixed-constitution doctrine is that it appropriately expresses the idea that political authority is the coalescence of various forms of natural authority and is thus natural itself. There is nothing particularly architectonic about the political art; deference and authority are products of the natural sociability of human creatures pursuing their diverse activities and associations. Tucker would not satisfy any believer in the primacy of political philosophy as a ruling art, but then he was a Christian priest and not a pagan Platonist.

This natural society, in which people conduct their own activities and find their own heads of association, might remind Socrates of the "city of pigs," and it may if we are not careful remind us of Locke's state of nature. It is of course the antithesis of the latter, because it contains everything necessary to the constitution of civil government, without recourse to compact, contract, or consent. Tucker lays great emphasis on the civil-law notion of a "quasi-contract,"[80] in

[77] *Treatise*, pp. 130–5; p. 134: ". . . there is found to exist in human Nature a certain ascendancy in some, and a kind of submissive Acquiescence in others."
[78] *Treatise*, pp. 207, 242; *Four Letters to Shelburne*, pp. 100–1. [79] *Pleas and Arguments*, p. 12.
[80] *Treatise*, pp. 139–43.

which contractual relations and rights may be presumed to exist though no formal agreement to enter upon them has ever been signed; they exist because social relationships are found to have progressed to that degree of complexity and sophistication, and there is no need to posit the individual and his natural freedom as anterior to their formation. But we might still suppose that the "natural society" entails no more than a "natural economy": that relatively simple state of appropriation of the earth and cultivation of its fruits, which in Locke's system precedes the growth of monetarized exchange and the consequent need of more complex forms of government. Noting that Tucker has nothing whatever to say about this aspect of Locke's theory, an exponent of the view that Locke is the theorist of commercial society might wish to argue that Tucker misunderstood the nature of his doctrine, exaggerated the distinction between contract and quasi-contract, and allowed the apparently unhistorical character of Locke's individualism to mislead him – as perhaps it misled Priestley, Price, and Paine – as to the width of the gap separating Locke's thought from his own. Such an exponent might question whether Locke was the radical egalitarian and natural-rights individualist Tucker took him to have been.

Nothing, however, could be more inaccurate than to take Tucker to have been content with a simple "natural economy," and we cannot understand the character of his polemic against Locke until we understand the character of the debate over political economy in England and Scotland since Locke's time. During the last years of the latter's career, and with some assistance from him,[81] there had come into being a new system of public finance, based on the Bank of England and the national debt, which involved the growth of a new class of public creditors and the ability of the state to maintain its political and military enterprises by anticipating its revenues. This system had proved so stimulating to economic as well as political growth that the phrase "a commercial society" had come to denote not merely one engaged in trade and commerce, but one maintained by the system of public credit and capital flow that was now seen as essential to commerce in the ordinary sense. But the Whig political regime that credit supported had been created fairly rapidly and to the exclusion of many previously entrenched political groups, and the publicists of the eighteenth century engaged in a perpetual and bitter debate over the merits of its existence.[82] Its opponents,

---

[81] Locke was active in the Great Recoinage and one of the first shareholders in the Bank of England.

[82] There is now a sizable literature on this debate. See Caroline Robbins, *The Eighteenth-Century Commonwealthman* (Cambridge, Mass., 1959); Kramnick, *Bolingbroke and His Circle;* J. G. A. Pocock, *Politics, Language and Time* (New York, 1971); and *The Machiavellian Moment* (Princeton, N.J., 1975); John Sekora, *Luxury: The Concept in Western Thought from Eden to Smollett* (Baltimore, 1977); H. T. Dickinson, *Liberty and Property: Political Ideology in 18th-Century Britain* (London, 1977); Lance Banning, *The Jeffersonian Persuasion: Evolution of a Party Ideology* (Ithaca, N.Y., 1978); Drew McCoy, *The Elusive Republic: Political Economy in Jeffersonian America* (Chapel Hill, N.C., 1980); Istvan Hont and Michael Ignatieff, eds., *Wealth and Virtue* (Cambridge, 1983).

variously known by such epithets as "country," "Commonwealth," and "patriot" ideologues, included dissatisfied elements of both rural gentry with Tory antecedents and urban merchants and artisans with Dissenting connections and radical leanings; and this accounts for the widespread belief (which Tucker vigorously shared) that Tory and patriot, Jacobite and republican, were closely allied and at times virtually interchangeable.[83]

The ideology of opposition was moral and neoclassicist in its arguments and assumptions, and had little if anything to do with the debate between Locke and Filmer. To the image of the individual as client, dependent and corrupt, it opposed that of the individual as citizen, independent and virtuous. It located this image first, in classical antiquity, when the *oikos* had served to support the *polis* and the *ager* the *quiris,* and second, in a simplified and idealized version of medieval society, when the "Gothic" freeholder had been at one and the same time his own warrior, judge, and legislator. This was less an idealization of feudalism than a defeudalization of medieval reality,[84] and it is important to bear in mind that the economy invoked to assail the growth of public credit represented, in Marxist terms, the ancient rather than the feudal stage of production. But the defenders of the new order[85] saw from an early time that what they were required to vindicate was a rentier society in which the individual found it worth his while to pay others, and to invest his money in the system by which they were paid, to conduct a professionalized system of government that left him free to pursue his profit, leisure, and cultivation. If the Goths, Spartans, and early Romans had been free and virtuous, they had been neither enlightened nor polite; and it came to be argued that neither material freedom nor intellectual development had been possible in ancient economies, where the warrior-citizen had been obliged to discharge all functions in his own person, instead of paying others to discharge some of them for him.[86] In such an economy, moreover, the dearth of monetarized exchange relationships meant that the performance of personal services inevitably became a principal means of receiving a benefit or paying a debt.[87] The ancient city rested on a foundation of slavery, the Gothic polity on one of serf

---

[83] *A Series of Answers,* p. 93: "But the patriotic Dean SWIFT had almost raised a Rebellion in Ireland under the like shameful Pretence, with that which is now maintained by the patriotic Dr. PRICE, viz. That Copper Money and Paper Money will drain us of our Gold and Silver . . . And thus it appears but too plainly, that *Mock-Patriots* in every Country, in every Age, and of every Denomination, are much the same"; pp. 94n.–95: "And I have had the Mortification to find, that not a few of those, who formerly wore all the *Insignia,* and drank all the *Healths* of Jacobitism, now give as evident Proofs of their being Republicans." See also Thomas R. Cleary, "Henry Fielding and the Great Jacobite Paper War of 1747–49," *Eighteenth-Century Life* 5, 1 (1978), pp. 1–11.

[84] D. W. L. Earl, "Procrustean Feudalism: An Interpretative Dialogue in English Historical Narration, 1700–1725," *Historical Journal* XIX, 1 (1976), pp. 33–52.

[85] Of whom the leader was Daniel Defoe; Pocock, *The Machiavellian Moment,* pp. 432–6, 452–8.

[86] Melvin Richter, *The Political Theory of Montesquieu* (Cambridge, 1977), presents Montesquieu's treatment of this question.

[87] *Treatise,* p. 51.

labor. It was, then, as a means of defending rentier and "commercial" society against criticism in the name of the classical citizen ideal that the idea came to be generally put forward that personal liberty and intellectual progress depended on the increase and development of exchange relationships, and these in turn on the progressive increase of specialization of function and division of labor.[88]

In the growth of this debate, and the very important role it played in the history of political economy, Locke took no direct part. He appears to have been totally indifferent to the clash of ideas about ancient virtue and modern commerce, and though it is possible to imagine how his accounts of the origins of government might have been fitted into the defense of modernity, there is remarkably little sign of its being used in its construction. Lockean ideas about the role of labor in the appropriation of property, and more important, his ideas about the role of epistemology in the formation of personality, may have been extensively drawn upon by the Scottish philosophers as they formulated a theory of human progress in which labor became increasingly specialized and the human capacities for passion, production, and the organization of ideas increasingly complex and sophisticated.[89] But in the present state of research it is not at all clear whether or how this happened; we have for so long taken it for granted that the intellectual history of the eighteenth century is to be organized around the figure of Locke that we do not in fact know how to do so. Josiah Tucker, who was a keen student of the growth of the Scottish school,[90] a vigorous exponent of political and economic modernism, and a man of strong opinions about the history of political thought over the preceding hundred years,[91] was able to assume that Locke had played a wholly reactionary role and could be denounced as an exponent of archaic politics.

Tucker's refutation of "Lockian" politics contains many arguments directed at an ideal of classical citizenship that Locke himself had never affirmed. He contends that republican Rome was not a virtuous but an economically primitive polity, in which the constant demands of military service forced the citizen to neglect his smallholding and go into debt, thus preparing the way for his subsequent corruption.[92] It would have been better had he employed his industry in

---

[88] The classics here are John Millar, *The Origin of Ranks* (1771, 1787), and Adam Smith, *The Wealth of Nations* (1776). For Tucker, see *Four Tracts and Two Sermons*, p. 25; *Treatise*, pp. 130–1.

[89] For recent studies of the growth of this interpretation, see David Kettler, *The Social and Political Thought of Adam Ferguson* (Columbus, Ohio, 1965); Duncan Forbes, ed., *Adam Ferguson's Essay on the History of Civil Society* (Edinburgh, 1966); Forbes, *Hume's Philosophical Politics;* Meek, *Social Science and the Ignoble Savage;* Winch, *Adam Smith's Politics;* Albert Hirschman, *The Passions and the Interests;* Hont and Ignatieff, *Wealth and Virtue;* and chap. 6, this volume.

[90] Tucker corresponded with Kames, debated with Hume, and read Robertson. Cf. *Treatise*, p. 376.

[91] Tucker held that Filmer and Locke had fallen into the same error of making a right to rule anterior to the being of government, and differed only as to its location. *Treatise*, pp. 81–8, 427–8; *Four Letters to Shelburne*, pp. 97–8.

[92] *Four Tracts and Two Sermons*, pp. 60–5; *Treatise*, pp. 226ff.

increasing the yield of his farm; but Tucker quotes Cicero on the ignobility of all mechanical and useful arts.[93] The ancient republics all possessed governments profoundly unsuited to the encouragement of commercial society,[94] and the Gothic polities after them can only be compared to the slave-worked Jamaican and Virginian estates owned by such patriots as Beckford and Washington.[95] Tucker gleefully declares that Locke was the author of the *Fundamental Constitutions of Carolina* and as such – like Andrew Fletcher of Saltoun and other modern republicans – an apologist for slavery; he knows the answer to Dr. Johnson's question, "How is it that we hear the loudest yelps for liberty among the drivers of negroes?"[96] From his point of view it does not matter that the rhetoric of Roman virtue and independence is singularly absent from Locke's writings. In the rhetoric of Americans, Dissenters, and Londoners Tucker finds the two converging; there is a union between the classical ideal of the citizen (merged with the Gothic ideal of the freeholder) who commands his own lands and arms, so that he can be involved in government only in his own person, and the "Lockian" ideal of the individual whose rights to personality and property are anterior to the being of civil society, so that he can be brought under government only by his own consent. Tucker does not bother to distinguish between the two, rooted though the distinction may be in that between virtue and right, because he sees both as equally archaic. Such a precivil command of property is possible only in a precommercial world of slaveholding latifundists or serf-commanding barons. In the last of his published works, a group of open letters to Shelburne, Tucker links Locke with Algernon Sidney as nostalgic for "Polish liberty"; both were ideologues for a group of desperate aristocratic radicals, the Catilines of their age.[97] The dreadful truth that Russell and Sidney had taken French money was long since out,[98] and Tucker did not scruple to hint that the patriots of the American war had done the same.[99]

He would clearly have had difficulty in recognizing Locke as a "bourgeois ideologist," whatever that terminological inexactitude may imply. Tucker employs a basically Scottish theory of the progress of commercial society as a means of destroying the positions he attributed to Locke, Price, and Priestley, by affirming the priority of natural law over natural right. He was able to do this because he believed that natural society was commercial society, and that commerce was a natural human activity. It seems to have been said of him by Bishop Warburton

---

[93] *Treatise,* pp. 226–30.   [94] *Treatise,* p. 202 (chapter heading).

[95] *Series of Answers,* p. 106; *Treatise,* pp. 168, 218–224. Comparisons between Gothic barons and modern planters are found in *Treatise,* pp. 167, 210, 302.

[96] *A Series of Answers,* pp. 103–6; *Treatise,* pp. 167–8; *Four Letters to Shelburne,* pp. 92–4. For Johnson, see *Taxation No Tyranny,* in *Works,* ed. Greene, p. 454.

[97] *Four Letters to Shelburne,* letter IV.

[98] Sir John Dalrymple's *Memorials of Great Britain and Ireland* had been published in 1771.

[99] *Cui Bono?* p. 12.

that "he made religion a trade, and trade a religion;"[100] and though he displayed indignation at this piece of rather brutal perspicuity,[101] he did not conceal his belief that exchange relations between men were part of the providential plan for government of the universe. They came into being as humans discovered the diversity of their situations and capacities,

a great Difference of Talents; and, if I may be allowed the Expression, a wonderful Variety of Strata in the human Mind,[102]

and set up relations among themselves by exchanging the goods and services each was best fitted to provide. Though commercial progress tended to the dissolution of hereditary authority, it was in the practice of exchange that men learned to identify and respect their betters, and Tucker saw nothing in commerce incompatible with deference;[103] on the contrary, it was only through the cementing of these natural relations between men that government could come into being, without the "chicanery" and "contradiction" inherent in the idea of a compact between "independent and unconnected" individuals. Exchange among humans was a natural, providential, and divine necessity.

And how are the Ends both of Religion and Government to be answered, but by the System of universal Commerce? – Commerce, I mean, in the large and extensive Signification of that Word; Commerce, as it implies a general System for the *useful* Employment of our Time; as it exercises the particular Genius and Abilities of Mankind in some Way or other, either of Body or Mind, in mental or corporeal Labour, and so as to make Self-Interest and Social coincide. And in pursuing this Plan, it answers all the great Ends both of Religion and Government; it creates Social Relations, it enables Men to discharge their Duty in those Relations, and it serves as a Cement to connect together the Religious and Civil Interests of Mankind.[104]

V

But what is natural is also historical; Tucker's economy moves through a series of stages of development and attains greater fulfillment as it becomes more modern. There is consequently no such thing as a state of nature, conceived as a norm of departure; Tucker devotes no less than thirty pages of the *Treatise Concerning Civil Government*[105] to repudiating the thesis that the American Indians display society in its natural condition. Here he bases himself wholly on William Robertson's *History of America*, a classic of Scottish four-stages theory in which it is

---

[100] Shelton, *Dean Tucker*, pp. 164–5.   [101] *Four Tracts and Two Sermons*, p. xiv.
[102] *Four Tracts and Two Sermons*, p. 67.   [103] *Treatise*, pp. 41, 124, 126, 130–1, 159–60.
[104] *Four Tracts and Two Sermons*, p. 11.
[105] Pp. 170–201. Robertson's *America* had been published in 1777. See *The Works of William Robertson, D.D.* (London, 1824), vols. VI and VII.

said of the Indians (as Gibbon had written of the primitive Germans)[106] that because they do not labor, they neither appropriate nor produce and consequently have never developed their passions past a level of gloomy frigidity, to the point where the exchange of commodities makes possible the beginnings of sympathy and sociability. When Tucker wrote that commerce "creates social relations," he meant to be taken literally. He was no less clear that the beginnings of appropriation marked the beginnings of dispute over property and of the need for civil government; he quoted, ironically but by no means dismissively, the famous passage from the *Discours sur l'origine de l'inégalité* in which Rousseau prophesies the fatal consequences flowing from the first man's erection of a fence around land he calls his own.[107] That Rousseau thought this the true fall of man does not trouble Tucker unduly; it is an event occurring naturally in the process of primitive economics, and is not preceded by the construction of a fictitious scheme of rights.

If there is no state of nature, there is no "Machiavellian moment." We have already considered Tucker's refutation of the theory that early Rome or Sparta could be considered an era of civic virtue, with citizen-warriors commanding their own land and participating in their own government. Exchange relations had not yet developed to the point where the yeoman could be kept from sinking into debt, or the wealthy from commanding the labors of countless slaves; the ancient patrician, like the feudal baron, belonged to an era when the performance of personal service to a patron had not yet been replaced by the receipt of wages for one's industry or a price for one's produce, out of which a tax could be paid for the support of civil government. If no Machiavellian moment, then no "ancient constitution." Most of the third book of the *Treatise Concerning Civil Government* is spent in demolishing the myth of Gothic liberty, on which the patriots of 1781 still heavily relied. Locke had written nothing on this subject, and we do not even know if he meant to communicate his indifference to others; but it was prominent in that convergence of "patriot" with "Lockian" rhetoric with which Tucker supposed himself to be dealing.

What Tucker has to say here is in part a replay of a debate fifty years old, and of another fifty years older still. He was a keen admirer of Sir Robert Walpole, whom he saw as the first minister in history to have understood the principles of taxation and the proper government of a commercial society;[108] and in the paper war against Bolingbroke and the *Craftsman* about 1730, Walpole's journalists had helped defeat the country appeal to the "original principles" of the constitution by arguing that liberty in England was modern, not ancient, and that

---

[106] *Decline and Fall*, chap. 9; see J. G. A. Pocock, "Between Machiavelli and Hume; Gibbon as Civic Humanist and Philosophic Historian," in *Edward Gibbon and the Decline and Fall of the Roman Empire*, ed. G. W. Bowersock and John Clive (Cambridge, Mass., 1977).

[107] *Treatise*, pp. 46–7.   [108] *Four Tracts and Two Sermons*, p. 71n.; *Treatise*, pp. 78, 222n., 242–3.

constitutional government had emerged out of feudal disorder.[109] To make this case they had drawn upon the arguments of Robert Brady and the Tory historians of 1680 and after, who had been involved in the defense of one part of Filmer's writings when Locke was attacking the other.[110] This adoption of Restoration Tory arguments by Hanoverian Whigs to defend themselves against Common-wealth Whigs and their country Tory allies is, of course, a crucial and confusing move in the development of eighteenth-century polemics.[111] A hundred years after Brady, fifty years after Walpole, and twenty years after Hume (whose *History* he does not seem to cite), Tucker carries on the strategy; but he does so in a context transformed by the growth of Scottish historical sociology and a growing debate over the role of boroughs in the historical structure of English parliamentary government.

Before the growth of commerce, society could at most be feudal, and in an England of lords and serfs – vassals, copyholders, and villeins – Parliament in its modern sense could have no place. To understand the history of that institution, it was necessary to understand the history of the House of Commons, and since this assembly brought together the representatives of shires and boroughs, it was necessary to decide whether its history was to be written in terms of the increasing role of country gentry or of urban burgesses. The Scottish historians, Robertson among them, were advancing the generalization that "the progress of society in Europe" was due to the increasing commercial activity of the trading inhabitants of corporate towns[112] – the *bourgeoisie* in the institutional sense of the term, for which, significantly, no equivalent exists in English.[113] Tucker has no objection to this proposition in general, but as part of the patriot radicalism he had devoted himself to confuting, he was confronted by a demand for parliamentary reform which reiterated the allegation that the representation of boroughs was ancient and immemorial and could be traced to a time when they were independent and free before falling under royal and aristocratic influence. Tucker saw this argument not as expressing the claims of a rising class of burgesses, but as serving the interests of a miscellaneous political class of patriots, dissenters, and demagogues populating the great wen of London, Westminster, and South-wark,[114] whose influence had increased, was increasing, and ought to be dimin-

---

[109] See n. 6, this chapter; also Forbes, *Hume's Philosophical Politics*, pp. 233–49, 482–3. A good text is Lord Hervey's *Ancient and Modern Liberty Stated and Compared* (London, 1734).

[110] J. G. A. Pocock, *The Ancient Constitution and the Feudal Law* (Cambridge, 1957).

[111] Kenyon, *Revolution Principles*, pp. 200–8.

[112] Robertson, *Works*, vol. III, pp. 9–316, "The History of the Reign of the Emperor Charles V, with a View of the Progress of Society in Europe from the Subversion of the Roman Empire to the Beginning of the Sixteenth Century."

[113] *Bourg; bourgeois; bourgeois* (adj.); *bourgeoisie*. *Burg, Bürger; bürgerlich; Bürgertum*. Borough; burgess; no adjective; no collective or abstract noun. This exercise in historical semantics suggests further reflections.

[114] *Treatise*, pp. 258–60, 274, 291–2.

ished. Their rhetoric could at every point be confuted by advancing the thesis that commerce was the natural human state and that society progressed naturally from relations of personal service, dependence, and servitude to relations of independent association, voluntary deference, and monetarized exchange; but it was a central feature of this argument that trading towns had come late on the scene of history and could claim neither ancient nor natural right. As generally happened in the eighteenth century, the commercial interpretation of history was an argument in defense of the established Whig order, and to argue whether Tucker or his opponent (who in this case might be Cartwright) is the "bourgeois ideologist" is merely to play games with a double-headed penny.

Tucker accordingly depicts a process (based largely on the works of Brady and Madox in earlier generations)[115] in which the medieval boroughs, grudgingly founded by feudal lords in minimal recognition of the need for some division of labor, grew in importance during the period of "epidemical Madness" that seized on the unemployed warriors of Europe during the Crusades and were summoned to send representatives to the king's councils.[116] But far from eagerly pressing the demand for annual parliaments beloved of eighteenth-century radicals, they attended with the utmost reluctance and departed as soon as they could. For this Tucker assigns an interesting reason, in which the political behavior of barons and burgesses appears the reverse of what is sometimes portrayed.

The Fact was, to speak the Truth at once, the *landed* Interest, as it was *then erroneously* understood, was supposed to be directly opposite to the *trading* Interest of the Kingdom. For the personal and immediate Interest of the Barons, great and small, was to preserve their own Importance in the State, and their Authority and Jurisdiction over their Vassals and Dependents, in Contradistinction to the regal Power. Whereas Shopkeepers, Traders, and Mechanics, could have no such Views. Therefore the former were always desirous of having frequent Meetings of Parliaments, in order to consult and associate together against the Crown, whom they regarded as their common Enemy: [Magna Charta itself was owing to this very Principle.] Whereas the latter, the Corporate-Towns and Boroughs, which had Reason to esteem the Crown more their Protector than their Oppressor, had no such Motives, either offensive or defensive, for associating together. In one Word, the Crown, and the Law-Courts of the Crown, were then the only Security and Defence which trading Corporations could have had against the Power and Insults of the feudal Baronage.[117]

In this English version of the *thèse royale,* the trading classes are seen as tending to unpolitical passivity; Tucker had elsewhere observed that the proper conduct for a commercial nation was "to study to be quiet, and to mind our own busi-

[115] Robert Brady, *An Historical Treatise of Cities and Burghs or Borroughs* (London, 1690); Thomas Madox, *Firma Burgi, or An Historical Essay Concerning the Cities, Towns and Boroughs of England* (London, 1726). Tucker also cites Samuel Squire, *Enquiry into the Foundations of the English Constitution* (London, 1753); see Reed Browning, "Samuel Squire: Pamphleteering Churchman," *Eighteenth-Century Life* 5, 1 (1978), pp. 12–20; and Daines Barrington, *Observations on the More Ancient Statutes* (London, 1769).

[116] *Treatise,* pp. 262–5, 292–6, 309–16.   [117] *Treatise,* pp. 318–19.

ness."[118] An excess of political activity was the characteristic of the lazy, the ambitious and unemployed – of patrons and their clients, barons and their retainers. Tucker certainly did not consider the patriots of his own time a feudal class – there was none known to him nearer than Poland – but he did consider them a set of unproductive nuisances whose ideology was a great deal more feudal than they recognized; and the London mobs who followed them in politics seemed not unlike the *faeces Romuli* or the gangs of medieval retainers.

Unfortunately, he did not carry his account of English history past the unedifying picture of medieval politics necessary for the destruction of the Gothic myth, so that we do not know by what stages he thought England had achieved a form of government possible for a commercial society. We may imagine a somewhat Humean account of the process, with Tudor legislation against retainers at one end[119] and Tucker's insistence that the principles of taxation were not understood until the reign of George I[120] at the other. It is highly unlikely that the independent activities of the borough corporations would have played much part in it, since we know from the previously quoted passage that civil government itself – "the Crown, and the Law-Courts of the Crown" – was to be a crucial agency and that an important objective was the dispelling of the illusion that landed interest and trading interest were in opposition. Tucker had written one of his appeals for separation from America on commercial grounds in the form of the *Address to the Landed Interest*,[121] and it was one of his adversaries – Samuel Estwick, an agent for Barbados – who had argued that American taxation was a job of the landed interest, designed to reduce the land tax and the national debt.[122] In the long-term historical picture, the function of the rise of commerce was to civilize the landowning class and lead them in the paths of industry and exchange, and this need not entail any increase in the political role of the corporations; indeed, Tucker could have argued that it was perfectly compatible with the dominance of the borough representation by members of the landed gentry. There is certainly no sign that he found this phenomenon objectionable, and we should recall that he found the merit of commercial society to be that it promoted deference no less than industry.[123]

---

[118] *Treatise*, p. 52.   [119] *Treatise*, p. 314n.   [120] *Treatise*, pp. 67, 78.

[121] This is the page heading used in printing the work cited here as *An Humble Address and Earnest Appeal*. The full title was: *An Humble Address and Earnest Appeal to those Respectable Personages in Great-Britain and Ireland, who, by their Great and Permanent Interest in Landed Property, their Liberal Education, Elevated Rank, and Enlarged Views, are the Ablest to Judge, and the Fittest to Decide, whether a Connection with, or a Separation from the Continental Colonies of America, be most for the National Advantage, and the Lasting Benefit of These Kingdoms.* The tone seems to be defiant rather than sycophantic; the implication is that the landed aristocracy and gentry are the fittest to judge of the nation's commercial interests. Cf. *Treatise*, p. 212.

[122] Samuel Estwick, *A Letter to the Reverend Josiah Tucker . . .* (London, 1776).

[123] There is no shortage of evidence that Tucker's admiration for commerce did not make him (any more than Adam Smith) an admirer of tradesmen. *Treatise*, pp. 78, 212 and note, 232, 323–5, 327; *Cui Bono?* pp. 50–1, 53–4.

When Tucker meditated a reform of parliamentary representation, which was much under discussion in 1781,[124] he proposed a qualification of resident land-ownership for both county and borough members,[125] aimed at discouraging both the familiar demons of country ideology – "neither the Plunderers of the *East*, nor the Slave-Drivers of the *West*, nor the Privateering, trading Buccaneers of the *American* Continent, nor our *English Newmarket* Jockeys, nor *Change-Alley* Bulls and Bears"[126] – and the domination of Parliament by residents of London, West-minster, and Southwark, that fertile nursery of patriots.[127] For voters he proposed a qualification of forty shillings freehold in the counties, or payment of scot and lot in the boroughs.[128] "Any common Day-Labourer, or common Mechanic" might attain the franchise by industry before his old age. On the other hand,

It is indeed a melancholy Reflection, that in most Cities, and Borough-Towns, and per-haps in Counties, the far greater Number of Voters are such, whose Circumstances lead them to wish for a new Division of Property, because they have little, or nothing to lose, but may have much to get in Times of Confusion, and by a general Scramble. Therefore, every Rule of sound Policy, not to say Religion and Morality, suggests the Necessity of raising the Qualification of voting to such a Mediocrity of Condition, as would make it the Interest of the Majority of Electors, to assist in the Support and Preservation of Order and good Government, and not to wish their Overthrow.[129]

Tucker is not haunted by the specter of communism so much as by those of Gaius Gracchus, Catiline, and Julius Caesar. Nevertheless, it is hard not to hear the hoofbeats of the Manchester yeomanry when reading his proposals. Either the hopes of economic self-betterment must be such as to make the injunction *enrichissez-vous, et vous deviendrez des électeurs* convincing in the ears of every common day laborer or mechanic, or the scot-and-lot franchise must be a means of uniting greater and lesser proprietors in a class domination of those with little or nothing to lose. However, we should read the following in conjunction with the passage just quoted:

Though it would be highly absurd, to admit indiscriminately every individual Moral-Agent to be a Voter, yet true Policy requires that the Voters should be so numerous, and their Qualifications respecting Property be so Circumstanced, that the actual Voters could not combine against the Non-Voters, without combining against themselves, against their nearest Friends, Acquaintances and Relatives.[130]

The socializing and civilizing effects of commerce provide the razor's edge that civil government is to walk. Tucker is a progressive conservative, the defender of

---

[124] John Cannon, *Parliamentary Reform, 1640–1832* (Cambridge, 1972).   [125] *Treatise*, pp. 278–83.
[126] *Treatise*, p. 286.   [127] *Treatise*, pp. 291–2.
[128] *Treatise*, pp. 276–8, 284–5. Shelton (*Dean Tucker*, pp. 53ff.) shows that Tucker had argued for the use of a restricted franchise to encourage self-advancement in the poor as early as his *Essay on Trade* of 1749.
[129] *Treatise*, pp. 290–1.   [130] *Treatise*, p. 275.

a commercial order perhaps not much older than himself, which has certainly not finished evolving.[131] But because he sees no contradiction between nature and history – and thinks that Locke and Rousseau were wrong to impose it – he holds that the principles of economic progress are those of natural law. He sees no contradiction – nor, given the structure of English society, is there much reason why he should see it – between upholding the Whig commercial order and maintaining the primacy of the landed interest, or between proposing to reduce the electoral importance of London in favor of the agricultural shires[132] and writing:

Our exclusive Corporations, and Companies of Trades in Towns and Cities, have at present very little Power of doing Mischief, compared with what they formerly had. For Men's Eyes begin to be opened every where: And the flourishing State of those great Manufacturing Places in *England* (the greatest perhaps in the known World, certainly the greatest in *Europe*) where every Man enjoys PERFECT FREEDOM to follow that Course of Trade to which his Genius or Circumstances are best suited; I say, this flourishing State has made the *dullest* of us feel, that Industry and Ingenuity are best excited by constant Emulation, and that no Man ought to be armed with the Power of a Law, or with an exclusive Privilege, to crush his Rival.[133]

The age of the boroughs was drawing to a close, and one of the irritating things about the word "bourgeoisie" is that we are expected to use it precisely of the time when its semantic justification was beginning to collapse (if, in English, it ever had any). Its employment will not help us to understand why this shrewd and historically sophisticated mind saw no reason why the spread of manufacturing and wage relationships outside the older structures should present any threat to the principle of natural authority that it was his purpose to inculcate. He closed the *Treatise Concerning Civil Government* with the injunction the Revolution regime had maintained since 1688: that it was the duty of a people to obey constituted authority until, as a matter of utmost necessity, it became no longer possible to do so.[134] But the false principle, that there existed a body of rights that defined the legitimacy of any authority whatever, stemmed to his mind from premodern sources. The Americans and Dissenters were the heirs of the Puritans; Locke and the patriots were the heirs of the barons; and the Londoners inhabited no manufacturing city, but a great wen like ancient Rome. Commerce and manufacture upheld constituted authority, and it was natural that they should do so.

---

[131] In debate with Hume, Tucker had argued for a future of indefinite progress, which he thought Hume had denied. *Four Tracts and Two Sermons,* pp. 23, 41.
[132] *Treatise,* pp. 297–8. [133] *Cui Bono?* pp. 53–4.
[134] *Treatise,* pp. 3–4, 410–28. Kenyon, *Revolution Principles,* pp. 21–34. Reference may be made to what Burke has to say about 1688 in both the *Reflections* and *An Appeal from the New to the Old Whigs.*

VI

Old Dean Tucker was a fine old man; we study him both for the sake of his invigoratingly cantankerous intellect and for the light it is capable of throwing on the defense of the established order in late eighteenth-century Britain. Since when we think of conservatism we have to think of Burke, it is his intellectual as well as personal attitude toward the latter that renders Tucker an intriguing figure. Ten to fifteen years before Price addressed the Revolution Society, the dean of Gloucester had perceived that the Dissenting emphasis on natural rights was capable of challenging the legitimacy of all existing governments and the theoretical possibility of government itself. Perhaps he did not know that by 1781 or soon after, Burke was coming to see such arguments as "a preposterous way of reasoning and a perfect confusion of ideas"[135] in a prescriptive (or in Tucker's terms a quasi-contractual) system of government, or that he was beginning to regard Shelburne and his stable of intellectuals at Bowood with a mistrust as vehement as Tucker's own. It might have made very little difference if Tucker had known this; there was that about Burke he would never have liked, and in any case he ceased writing after 1785. Though Tucker lived until 1799, his energies seem to have failed him,[136] and we know nothing of his octogenarian responses to the French Revolution or to Burke's writings on that event; this limits our capacity to set the two conservatives in a common frame of comparison.

Born in the same year as Hume, Tucker is like him a conservative of the 1760s and 1770s, when patriots, republicans, Dissenters, and Americans seemed the enemies against whom the Whig order had to be defended. Richard Price, his doctrine of natural right, and his interpretation of the Revolution of 1688, had to be counterattacked in the course of this campaign, and there is a sense in which the sermon to the Revolution Society represents the response (almost the survival) of an older "Commonwealth" radicalism in the new world the French were creating. What Tucker had to say about Price in 1781 differed little from what Burke said of him in 1790, but the accidents of political alignment in 1776 and after enabled Tucker to stigmatize Burke as almost Price's ally. No doubt this was unfair, and one wonders whether Burke, whose allusions to Tucker are few, remembered it in 1790. Of far greater interest, however, is Tucker's decision to mount a full-scale assault on Locke. If he was right in perceiving that Locke had been a radical actor in 1683–8 and could be used in authorizing a radical interpretation of the meaning of 1688, we must ask why Burke, elaborating in both the *Reflections on the Revolution in France* and the *Appeal from the New to*

---

[135] *Works*, vol. X, p. 99.

[136] For the last phase of his life, see Shelton, *Dean Tucker*, pp. 255–7. He seems to have left no disciples, though a case might be made with regard to William Mitford, the historian of Greece; see Frank M. Turner, *The Greek Heritage in Victorian Britain* (New Haven, Conn., 1981), pp. 194–204.

the Old Whigs (an almost Tory account of the English Revolution), made no allusion to Locke one way or the other. Had Tucker's *Treatise* rendered Locke con-
troversial? Was he a figure too sacred or too little conspicuous in the Whig canon
to be brought back into debate? Our understanding of his reputation as a political
writer in eighteenth-century England is still too confused to let us say for certain.
Macaulay in the next century has likewise nothing to say about Locke's *Treatises
of Government* in the course of his generally Burkean interpretation of 1688, but
is insistent on clearing him of complicity in Monmouth's rebellion[137] (Tucker
insists on his guilt).[138] We may regard Macaulay as carrying on the Holland
House enterprise of reconciling the shades of Fox and Burke and reharmonizing
the shattered chords of Whig ideology; perhaps this necessitated a myth of Locke's
political respectability.[139] But to observe silence regarding the *Treatises* is not to
present them as a classic of moderate constitutionalism, and the stages by which
they acquired this reputation are still not well understood. Tucker saw them as
they have begun to reappear in the light of recent research, that is, as an essentially radical manifesto that appeared when their author and his cause were ceasing to be as radical as they had been.[140] There was not yet much contemporary
debate about their meaning, and Burke took no part in it.

  Tucker's Whiggism is of a different stripe from Burke's, and this must be
taken into account when we compare them as conservatives. When Tucker characterized himself as "a constitutional but not a republican Whig," he declared
himself as belonging to the generation of Hume, for whom the Whig order
required defense against patriots and Commonwealthmen, Tories and Jacobites,
all employing much the same ideology. He therefore situated himself in the
tradition of Brady, among those for whom the principles of constitutional liberty
were modern rather than ancient and for whom there could be no return either
to the customs and prescriptions of an ancient constitution or to the principles
into which these could (Burke said "preposterously") be resolved. Hume in his
History of England did the same,[141] but he also took a leading part in formulating
the Scottish perception of history as the progressive elaboration, through the
multiplication of commercial relations between human beings, of that growing
envelope of civilized and deferential manners that rendered ancient virtue no
longer necessary. Tucker, who believed himself to have surpassed Hume in showing that commercial progress knew no theoretical limits on its future,[142] joined

---

[137] Macaulay, *History of England from the Accession of James II*, ed. C. H. Firth (London, 1913), vol. II,
chap. V, pp. 538–9n.
[138] *Four Letters to Shelburne*, pp. 94–6.
[139] For this see Ashcraft's articles cited in n. 10, this chapter.
[140] See John Dunn, "The Politics of Locke in England and America in the Eighteenth Century," in
John Locke: Problems and Perspectives, ed. John W. Yolton (Cambridge, 1969).
[141] Victor L. Wexler, *David Hume and the History of England* (Philadelphia, 1979).
[142] See Istvan Hont, "The Rich-Country–Poor-Country Debate in Scottish Classical Political Economy," in *Wealth and Virtue*, ed. Hont and Ignatieff.

with the Scots in making this the means of rejecting the politics of nostalgia for republican antiquity; it is his peculiar originality to have seen that though Locke had been indifferent to the republican vision of history, his state of nature and theory of the origin of right to property could be made liable to criticisms identical with those brought against it. To this he added an even shrewder insight into the religious origins of Lockean thought and the leanings toward both republican and natural-rights theory displayed by the radical Dissenters and Americans of his time. Burke came in the path of Tucker's broadsides. Though we can say with confidence that he shared none of the views Tucker was concerned to attack, we cannot point to much that he had done by 1781 to associate himself with the polemic against them conducted by the "scientific Whigs," of whom Tucker was one.

It is arguable that he never did. The lucidity of Tucker's commercialism, and perhaps even his proposals for restricting the franchise so as to give the poor a motive for accepting a tighter work discipline, attracted the ironic approval of Karl Marx, who described him as "a Tory and a parson, but for the rest an honourable man," whereas he could see nothing in Burke except venality and hypocrisy.[143] Marx was wrong about Burke, who meant what he said, and the word "Tory" can be used of neither Burke nor Tucker until we understand how the Whig tradition fell apart and was reconstituted in the years of counterrevolution. But we cannot understand this either until we understand the far-reaching change in the Scottish perceptions of history that Burke helped to bring about at a time when Tucker had ceased to write. To Hume, Smith, Millar, or Tucker, commerce was the motor force behind the growth of manners and the progress of society. As it created increasingly complex social relations, the passions were refined, the sympathies developed, and human beings became increasingly capable of supporting the edifice of culture and the necessity of government. Commerce was the precondition of "the progress of the arts" and the elaboration of manners, in which the natural relations and subordinations of society were progressively discovered and actualized. But when Burke beheld the proceedings of the French revolutionaries, he very early saw in them a program for the systematic destruction of manners and the substitution of an altogether new and antinatural code of social behavior.[144] This had begun with an assault on the church, the nobility, and the royal family, but Burke was so far steeped in the belief that a modern commercial society was the ultimate efflorescence of manners that he accepted the corollary that the destruction of manners could not be accomplished without the destruction of commerce itself. He therefore took up certain hints dropped by Robertson and other historians, who had depicted the growth of chivalry and canon law as early movements toward refined manners and a better

[143] See Shelton, *Dean Tucker*, pp. 264–5.   [144] For a fuller treatment, see chap. 10, this volume.

circulation of goods, and used them in order to argue that church and nobility were necessary to the growth of manners and that manners formed a precondition of the growth of commerce itself. Burke was explicit in his revision of the Scottish sequence of history.

Nothing is more certain than that our manners, our civilisation, and all the good things which are connected with manners and with civilisation, have in this European world of ours depended for ages upon two principles, and were indeed the result of both combined; I mean the spirit of a gentleman, and the spirit of religion. The nobility and the clergy, the one by profession, the other by patronage, kept learning in existence, even in the midst of arms and confusions, and whilst governments were rather in their causes than formed . . .

If, as I suspect, modern letters owe more than they are always willing to own to antient manners, so do other interests which we value full as much as they are worth. Even commerce, and trade, and manufacture, the gods of our oeconomical politicians, are themselves perhaps but creatures; are themselves but effects, which, as first causes, we choose to worship. They certainly grew under the same shade in which learning flourished. They too may decay with their natural protecting principles.[145]

It is tempting to imagine an aged clergyman in Gloucester reading this passage, as he may well have done. "The gods of our oeconomical politicians," though intended probably to refer to the Scottish theorists as a group, might well strike him as meant for those who "made religion a trade and trade a religion." But what would Tucker make of the proposition that manners, learning, and above all commerce could survive only under the protection of the clergy and aristocracy? A Whig clergyman in the marrow of his bones — not least so in his refusal to pursue patronage too far — he had begun his career in controversy with the fathers of Methodism[146] and knew high fliers and High Churchmen when he saw them. What would he make of the proposition that the church was independent of commerce, and therefore of government, and was indeed their historical precondition along with an equally independent aristocracy? Here, he might have said with a flash of his old disgust, was the patriot up to his usual games, playing a baronial and papist card when the republican would not turn the trick. The University of Oxford declined to offer an honorary degree to Burke at the height of his counterrevolutionary fame because they were not sure of his churchmanship,[147] and his desire to relieve Irish Catholics was not unconnected with his desire for an ultimately civil religion.[148] Yet Burke could assign a historical role to the church; had Tucker done so?

---

[145] Burke, *Works*, vol. V, pp. 154–5.   [146] Shelton, *Dean Tucker*, pp. 17–36.

[147] Thomas W. Copeland, ed., *The Correspondence of Edmund Burke*, 10 vols. (Cambridge and Chicago, 1967); Alfred Cobban and Robert A. Smith, eds., vol. VI, pp. 193–5.

[148] So at least I read the relevant passages in the *Reflections* (*Works*, vol. V, pp. 173–8, 187–98), and see his avowal that his attachment to Christianity arose "much from conviction, more from affection" (*Correspondence*, vol. VI, p. 215). Cf. Frederick Dreyer, "Burke's Religion," *Studies in Burke and His Time* XVII, 3 (1976), pp. 199–212.

Tucker's misgivings may be imagined to increase as he read on and found in the *Reflections* an outburst – not the only one in Burke – against the brutality of Henry VIII's proceedings in the dissolution of the monasteries.[149] Very deep in the Anglican tradition lay the roots of the belief that the monastic lands should have been preserved and used to endow learning under clerical control; yet we can say with certainty that Tucker would have preferred even Warburton to Laud, although, to borrow a phrase of his own, "that is saying a great deal."[150] No Whig could support the idea of a church as independent as that, and Tucker saw the prosperity of learning as bound up with the progress of commerce and the arts; yet here was Burke saying that these forces could not maintain learning, or even themselves, unless protected by a wealth of land held in entail and mortmain. We might cite text after text showing Burke as aware as Tucker that the mainsprings of society were now in commerce,[151] and yet, by reversing the historical order in which Tucker's generation had ranked commerce and manners, Burke (whatever he thought he was doing) had opened the way to Coleridge's *Idea of a Constitution in Church and State,* to Arnold's *Culture and Anarchy,* and in our own time to Raymond Williams's *Culture and Society.* To the Enlightenment theorists commerce had appeared to be the force that refined the manners and extended the sympathies; now it could be argued that it was philistine and utilitarian, made use of a cold mechanical philosophy derived from Bacon and Locke, and did not protect culture and manners at all. Not even a leisured aristocracy was equal to the task, unless reinforced by Coleridge's "national church" and "clerisy," founded upon a "nationalty" of land reserved to maintain learning, which in an ideal history every nation would have established from its beginnings. *Ergo tua rura manebunt.*[152]

Could Tucker have lived to hear of notions of this kind – they were hardly formulated when he died in 1799 – he would have smitten the "nationalty" for the historical poppycock it was; and he might have noticed that Coleridge's "clerisy" is by no means the same thing as a Christian ministry. Even Burke (to continue the fantasy) may be imagined joining him here. He saw the French Revolution as a conspiracy of *gens de lettres* and monied speculators to get their hands on the lands of the church; to find the former setting themselves up as a new sort of landed clergy might not have seemed incompatible with this interpretation, or with Coleridge's Jacobin youth. But in this diagnosis, and later

[149] *Works,* vol. V, pp. 215–18; and *A Letter to a Noble Lord, Works,* vol. VIII, pp. 38–45.

[150] The Spartans treated the Helots "much worse, and with more *wanton* Cruelty, than the Planters do the Negroes in the *West-Indies;* – And that is saying a great deal"; *Treatise,* p. 219.

[151] See C. B. Macpherson, *Burke* (Oxford, 1981).

[152] These words from Virgil's *Georgics* form the motto of both the University and the Province of Canterbury, at whose foundation in 1850 a grant of lands was set aside for the maintenance of higher education.

when he defined Jacobinism as the rebellion of "talent" against "property,"[153] Burke raised a question unknown to Tucker and the generation of the Scottish Enlightenment. They had seen the cultivated intellect emerging as society was refined by the increasing complexity of property relations; but if, as Burke now desperately proclaimed, the intellect was turning to the destruction of property and social relations themselves, where was the property structure by which intellect might be disciplined? Burke was not the leader of a "revolt against the eighteenth century,"[154] but he announced that one had broken out and asked whether enlightened philosophy of history was capable of explaining or remedying it. From now on, there might be stern unbending Tories proclaiming the alliance of church and state as the only answer, and there might be Tory radicals castigating the existing church and state as quite incapable of providing it. Both brands of "Tory" were in fact Whigs, heirs of the latitudinarians and the neo-Harringtonians, respectively, but the Whiggism of Josiah Tucker had relatively little to say to the problem of culture and anarchy. Burke had discerned the advent of the politics of romanticism and alienated sensibility, which has preoccupied conservatives ever since; it is in Marxism, paradoxically enough, that we find continued the conservative assurance that intellect can again be disciplined by the processes of production. But Burke would have known what to say about the Great Cultural Revolution and the evacuation of Phnom Penh.

[153] *Works,* vol. VIII, p. 70.
[154] Alfred Cobban, *Edmund Burke and the Revolt Against the Eighteenth Century* (Oxford, 1929; revised, 1960).

10

The political economy of Burke's analysis of the French Revolution

There are, perhaps, in the end only two ways in which a historian may undertake the study of a document in the history of political thought. One may consider it as a text, supposed to have been intended by its author and understood by its reader with the maximum coherence and unity possible; the historian's aim now becomes the reconstitution of the fullest possible interpretation available to intelligent readers at the relevant time. Alternatively, one may consider it as a tissue of statements, organized by its writer into a single document, but accessible and intelligible whether or not they have been harmonized into a single structure of meaning. The historian's aim is now the recovery of these statements, the establishment of the patterns of speech and thought forming the various contexts in which they become intelligible, and the pursuit of any changes in the normal employment of these patterns which may have occurred in consequence of the statements being made.

Both approaches have their advantages and disadvantages. It is the second which will be attempted, in this essay,[1] to Burke's *Reflections on the Revolution in France* and subsequently to his *Letters on a Regicide Peace*. In 1960 the present writer published in *The Historical Journal* an essay entitled 'Burke and the Ancient Constitution: a problem in the history of ideas',[2] in which it was argued that important passages in the *Reflections*, together with passages from other speeches and writings by Burke, should be understood in the context of a tradition of common-law thought established in the age of Sir Edward Coke, and that they

---

From *The Historical Journal*, vol. 25, no. 2, pp. 331–49. © 1982 Cambridge University Press; reprinted by permission of the editors.

[1] Earlier versions have been presented to seminars at Johns Hopkins, Cornell and Cambridge, and to the Midwest American Society for Eighteenth-Century Studies. I am indebted to all these audiences for their comments and suggestions.
[2] *The Historical Journal*, III, 2, 125–43; reprinted in *Politics, language and time* (New York, 1971).

contained explicit and conscious allusions to this tradition and to their own place in it. The present essay will argue that comparably important passages in the *Reflections* and the *Letters* can similarly be situated in a quite distinct tradition of thought, which will be termed 'political economy'; but it will not be much concerned to inquire into the relations between the two traditions, or the possible consistencies and inconsistencies in Burke's text or thought occasioned by the fact that they are both present there. It seems more important to establish that Burke can be read in both of these contexts than to inquire whether he can be read in both of them simultaneously; the premises from which he argued and the messages which he may have transmitted can be given a thick description if we apply the first only of the procedures distinguished in this sentence. There is more to the method of interpretation followed both now and in 1960, however, than the singling out of one thread and then another in the texture of Burke's writings. A better analogy is the selection of one and then another facet from, and through, which a multi-surfaced and translucent artefact may be viewed. Burke's response to revolution looks different when considered as that of a common-law constitutionalist, and as that of an exponent of political economy; the prime need is to establish that it can be looked at in both ways.

The term 'political economy', as is well known,[3] can be used with reference to the late eighteenth century in varying degrees of specificity. We may use it, as it was then used, to denote either the emerging science of 'the wealth of nations' or the policy of administering the public revenue. Burke admired the work of Adam Smith, and the *Reflections* and the *Letters* contain lengthy passages devoted to analysing the state of the revenue both in revolutionary France (1790) and in belligerent Britain (1796). But it is and was also possible to use the term to denote a more complex, and more ideological, enterprise aimed at establishing the moral, political, cultural, and economic conditions of life in advancing commercial societies: a commercial humanism, it might not unjustly be called, which met the challenge posed by civic humanism or classical republicanism to the quality of life in such societies.[4] It will be argued that Burke was a defender of Whig aristocratic government; that Whig government was identified with the growth of commercial society; that Burke saw the Revolution as a challenge to the Whig order, arising within the conditions that order made possible; and that he employed the language and categories of political economy in order to analyse

[3] Here I am particularly indebted to members of the King's College Research Centre's project on the history of political economy, and to the conference which they held in May 1979. See Istvan Hont and Michael Ignatieff (eds.), *Wealth and virtue* (Cambridge, 1983).
[4] Cf. Albert Hirschman, *The passions and the interests, arguments for capitalism before its triumph* (Princeton, 1975); Duncan Forbes, *Hume's philosophical politics* (Cambridge, 1975); Donald Winch, *Adam Smith's politics, an essay in historiographic revision* (Cambridge, 1978); Drew R. McCoy, *The elusive republic: political economy in Jeffersonian America* (Chapel Hill and Williamsburg, 1980) and other works.

the revolutionary threat and respond to it. He did not do so, however, without using language which revealed tensions within Whig society and its ideology and furthered changes in the ways in which that language was normally used.

Political economy in eighteenth-century Britain was at one and the same time a nascent social science of a remarkably new order, part of an enduring though increasingly historicized science of natural morality, and an ideological defence of the Whig ruling order which took shape during the first quarter of the century. Burke's political and emotional loyalties were very strongly focused upon that order, and it was in its capacity as an ideological defence and moral vindication that he most keenly appreciated the new science of political economy and natural sociability. Far from being one in which the aristocratic and bourgeois principles were deeply at variance,[5] the Whig regime was founded on an assumed identity of interests between a managerial landed aristocracy and a system of public credit, in which rentier investment in government stock stimulated commercial prosperity, political stability, and national and imperial power. The defence of a commercial order in politics, society and morality, wherever it occurs down to Burke's time and after, is invariably a defence of the Whig regime and generally of natural aristocracy; and attacks upon the Whig regime are nearly as often conducted in the name of real or landed property against mobile or personal. The focus of these attacks, however, is not upon trade or the investment of capital in commerce, but upon its investment in government, patronage, and warlike expansion; from this, it was argued, arose the corruption which destroyed the commercial empires of Athens and Rome.

Because these attacks were based on an ideal of the ancient citizen, whose independence in arms and land assured his political virtue, it was necessary for the defenders of the Whig commercial order to find an alternative ideal.[6] They did so by characterizing the ancient citizen as an economically underdeveloped being. Because he lacked the ready credit and cash to pay wage-labourers, he was obliged to exploit the unremunerative labour of slaves and serfs. Because he was not involved in the multifarious social relationships which only an advancing system of commerce could bring, he could employ his leisure only in active statecraft and war, or in contemplative metaphysics or superstition. His personality lacked the multifaceted refinements and polishings which arose from encounters with other human beings in a multiplicity of exchange relationships and consumer activities; commerce, it was argued, was the sole agency capable

---

[5] See Isaac F. Kramnick, *The rage of Edmund Burke: the conscience of an ambivalent conservative* (New York, 1979).

[6] For other presentations of this argument see my *The Machiavellian moment* (Princeton, 1975) chs. 13 and 14; 'Between Machiavelli and Hume; Gibbon as civic humanist and philosophical historian', in G. W. Bowersock and John Clive (eds.), *Edward Gibbon and the Decline and Fall of the Roman Empire* (Cambridge, Mass., 1977); 'The Machiavellian moment revisited: a study in history and ideology', *Journal of Modern History*, LIII, 1 (1981), 49–72.

of refining the passions and polishing the manners. The central place — it is not too much to say — in Whig ideology between the English and French Revolutions was occupied by the concept variously expressed as manners, politeness or taste; this offered not only defence against criticism in the name of patriot virtue, but defence against that partially buried Titan haunting the imagination of the age, the explosive power of enthusiasm. The leading British and European exponents of the ideology of manners were the moral philosophers, conjectural historians and political economists of Scotland.[7] When Burke visited Glasgow as Lord Rector of its University in 1785 and dined with John Millar, and with Adam Smith in Edinburgh,[8] he was among celebrants of a historical view of the progress of society, in which the diversification of labour conducted the human race through four stages of production towards the refinement and enrichment of its manners.

The feature of the Whig regime which its ideologists found hardest to defend was the multiplication of the national debt. Queen Anne Tories, of the school of Swift and Bolingbroke, had thundered against Whig rule as that of a monied interest, made up of men who owned no property or rather had substituted property of an altogether new kind: the paper tokens of a fluctuating public confidence, in which the determinants of the rate at which money could be had, and the value of all property created, had themselves become a species of commodity. Richard Price, whose sermon to the Revolution Society spurred Burke to write the *Reflections,* had argued that the attempt to tax America was a product of the indebtedness and accompanying corruption which the elder Pitt's wars had brought upon England; and far-left Unitarian as he was, Price had been able to quote copiously from Hume, that most sceptical and therefore most resourceful of Whigs, as holding an almost indistinguishable position.[9] Neither David Hume, Adam Smith, nor as we shall see Edmund Burke,[10] was free of the nightmare that multiplying paper credit might end by destroying the value and even the meaning of property, the foundation alike of virtue, manners and the natural relations of society.

---

[7] N. T. Phillipson, 'Towards a definition of the Scottish Enlightenment', in P. Fritz and D. Williams (eds.), *City and society in the eighteenth century* (Toronto, 1973); 'Culture and society in the eighteenth-century province; the case of Edinburgh and the Scottish Enlightenment,' in Lawrence Stone (ed.), *The university in society* (Princeton, 1974); 'Hume as moralist; a social historian's perspective', in S. C. Brown (ed.), *Philosophers of the Enlightenment* (Hassocks, 1979); 'Manners, morals, civic virtue and the science of man', presented to the Fifth International Congress on the Enlightenment (Pisa, 1979); 'Adam Smith as civic moralist', in Hont and Ignatieff, *Wealth and virtue.* Also George Davie, *The Scottish Enlightenment* (Historical Association Pamphlets, General Series 99, 1981).

[8] The best account of this incident is in *The diary of the Rt. Hon William Windham* (London, 1866), pp. 60–1, 63–4. I am indebted to Mr. E. E. Steiner (Yale Law School) for this reference.

[9] Richard Price, *Two tracts on civil liberty, the war with America, and the debts and finances of the kingdom* (London, 1778), 'Additional Observations', pp. xiii–xiv, 25, 38–39, 47, 51–2, 153n.

[10] An exception must be entered to Macaulay's observation (*History of England,* ch. xix) that only Burke was 'free of the general delusion' that the debt would destroy society. He did not fear it in England, but did in France.

The revolution of 1688 had been secured by the foundation of the Bank of England and a system of public finance which encouraged investment in the future of the new regime and stimulated the growth of its prosperity and power. A century later, the French Revolution was perceived as having seized upon the lands of the French Church and made them its security for the issue of a national loan whose paper *assignats* were to be made legal tender everywhere. Now it is not possible to read Burke's *Reflections* with both eyes open and doubt that it presents this action – and not assaulting the bedchamber of Marie Antoinette – as the central, the absolute and the unforgivable crime of the Revolutionaries. The charge which appears as soon as Burke has completed his denunciation of the Revolution Society and Price's sermon is that in France we see

everything human and divine sacrificed to the idol of public credit, and national bankruptcy the consequence; and to crown all, the paper securities of new, precarious, tottering power, the discredited paper securities of impoverished fraud and beggared rapine, held out as a currency for the support of an empire, in lieu of the two great recognized species that represent the lasting conventional credit of mankind, which disappeared and hid themselves in the earth from whence they came, when the principle of property, whose creatures and representatives they are, was systematically subverted.[11]

Even the nocturnal attack upon Marie Antoinette – long notorious as the central firework display of Burke's rhetoric – if read carefully, will be seen as fitting into this context. His account of this partly imaginary atrocity leads on, as all readers know, to the even purpler prose of the lament for the decline of the age of chivalry and the triumph of the 'sophisters, oeconomists and calculators', which has driven so many commentators to Freudian and Marxist extremes in the attempt to discover what Burke was going on about. But an acquaintance with the Scottish historians would have solved the problem for them. Read on to the end of the paragraph, and we shall find 'the unbought grace of life', the 'chastity of honour which felt a stain like a wound', and all the rest of it, summarized in what follows by these perfectly sober remarks:

This mixed system of opinion and sentiment had its origin in the antient chivalry; and the principle, though varied in its appearance by the varying state of human affairs, subsisted and influenced through a long succession of generations, even to the time we live in. If it should ever be totally extinguished, the loss I fear will be great. It is this which has given its character to modern Europe. It is this which distinguished it under all its forms of government, and distinguished it to its advantage, from the states of Asia, and possibly from those states which flourished in the most brilliant periods of the antique world . . . Without force or opposition, it subdued the fierceness of pride and power; it obliged sovereigns to submit to the soft collar of social esteem, compelled stern authority

[11] *The works of the Rt. Hon Edmund Burke* (London, 1826; the Rivington edition), v. 88.

to submit to elegance, and gave a domination, vanquisher of laws, to be subdued by manners.[12]

This passage is one which might have come from any of the great historians of contemporary Scotland. In Robertson's *View of the progress of society in Europe* (1769),[13] or in Millar's *Origin of ranks* (1771),[14] Burke might have read − and he probably had − that the peculiar nature of feudalism differentiated the history of Europe from that of other societies, and that the rise of chivalry, with all its extravagances, was a revolution in manners occurring within the feudal world, by which barbarian warriors had begun to civilize themselves, to acquire more polished and humane modes of conduct towards the weak, the female and one another, and to promote the increased circulation of material goods and the skills entailed in producing them. It had been a major step in the direction of a commercial and polite society and the cultural characteristics that went with them. In the same way, wrote Robertson, the canon law, while doubtless promoted by the clergy to defend the riches brought to them by superstition, had promoted justice and respect for property and, by converting the struggle for ownership into the interpretation of a code by lettered men, had rendered manners more gentle and society more rational.

And Burke continues:

Nothing is more certain than that our manners, our civilisation, and all the good things which are connected with manners and with civilisation, have in this European world of ours depended for ages upon two principles, and were indeed the result of both combined; I mean the spirit of a gentleman, and the spirit of religion. The nobility and the clergy, the one by profession, the other by patronage, kept learning in existence, even in the midst of arms and confusions, and whilst governments were rather in their causes than formed. Learning paid back what it received to nobility and to priesthood; and paid it with usury, by enlarging their ideas and by furnishing their minds. Happy if they had all continued to know their indissoluble union, and their proper place! Happy if learning, not debauched by ambition, had been satisfied to continue the instructor, and not aspired to be the master! Along with its natural protectors and guardians, learning will be cast into the mire, and trodden down under the hoofs of a swinish multitude.[15]

The last phrase of course was to do Burke no good with his artisan readers; but observe that it is the revolutionary intelligentsia who are to play the role of Circe to the swine, and let loose a herd which only a fully organic society has the manners to educate. He goes on:

---

[12] *Works*, v, 151.
[13] *The works of William Robertson* (London, 1824), III, 28–33, 55–7 (chivalry and feudal law), 65–71 (canon law), 72–4 (chivalry). Note the association of both phenomena with commerce and towns.
[14] Text in W. C. Lehmann, *John Millar of Glasgow* (Cambridge, 1960), pp. 210, 212–18 (chivalry); Millar, *Historical view of the English constitution* (London, 4th edn, 1818), I, 109–26; II, 135–7.
[15] *Works*, v, 154.

If, as I suspect, modern letters owe more than they are always willing to own to antient manners, so do other interests which we value full as much as they are worth. Even commerce, and trade, and manufacture, the gods of our oeconomical politicians, are themselves perhaps but creatures; are themselves but effects, which, as first causes, we choose to worship. They certainly grew under the same shade in which learning flourished. They too may decay with their natural protecting principles. With you, for the present at least, they all threaten to disappear together. Where trade and manufactures are wanting to a people, and the spirit of nobility and religion remains, sentiment supplies, and not always ill supplies their place; but if commerce and the arts should be lost in an experiment to try how well a state may stand without these old fundamental principles, what sort of a thing must be a nation of gross, stupid, ferocious, and at the same time poor and sordid barbarians, destitute of religion, honour, or manly pride, possessing nothing at present, and hoping for nothing hereafter?[16]

Burke is asserting that commerce is dependent upon manners, and not the other way round; a civilized society is the prerequisite of exchange relations, and the latter alone cannot create the former. The political economists (or 'oeconomical politicians'), the historians of the Scottish school,[17] had as we have seen recognized clerical learning and feudal chivalry as preconditions of the growth of commerce; but Hume, Robertson, Smith, Millar – we may add Gibbon – had all isolated the growth of exchange, production and diversified labour as the motor force which created the growth of manners, culture and enlightenment. Burke characteristically regards this as preposterous, as mistaking the effect for the cause. He insists that commerce can flourish only under the protection of manners, and that manners require the pre-eminence of religion and nobility, the natural protectors of society. To overthrow religion and nobility, therefore, is to destroy the possibility of commerce itself. The assault upon Marie Antoinette betokens the destruction of chivalric manners, which is part of the destruction of the second estate; and this in turn leads, as Burke explains in more detail, to the destruction of the first, to the seizure of the lands of the church and their use to establish a despotism of paper currency, itself fatal to property, commerce, trade and manufacture. The *ancien régime* is a microcosm of the history of Europe: feudal conquest, clerical and political organization, commercial and cultural growth; all is organized around a historical edifice of manners, and it is the structure of European civility which the Revolution is in process of destroying.

We have next to inquire by what agencies this destruction is being carried out, and the possibility may arise that it is by something in the nature of a Marxist bourgeoisie. But if men of commerce are doing all this, Burke is insistent that

---

[16] *Works*, v, 155.

[17] So it seems proper to read the phrase; but 'the gods of our oeconomical politicians' may be a gibe at Josiah Tucker, who had attacked Burke bitterly in 1776 and was said to 'make religion a trade and trade a religion.' See George Shelton, *Dean Tucker and eighteenth-century economic and political thought* (New York, 1981), pp. 164–5.

they are destroying the possibility of commerce itself; and since we know that
the vocabulary of eighteenth-century England distinguished sharply between
commerce and speculation in the public debt – stockjobbing was to trade, Bolingbroke once wrote, as faction was to liberty[18] – it seems arguable that Burke
is presenting religion, chivalry and commerce as trodden down together by the
hoofs of a paper-money despotism. Following the next section of the *Reflections,*
concerned largely with the English determination to maintain an established and
landed church, Burke proceeds:

> By the vast debt of France, a great monied interest had insensibly grown up, and with it
> a great power. By the ancient usages which prevailed in that kingdom, the general circu-
> lation of property, and in particular the mutual convertibility of land into money, and of
> money into land, had always been a matter of difficulty. Family settlements, rather more
> general and more strict than they are in England, the *jus retractus,* the great mass of landed
> property held by the crown, and by a maxim of the French law held unalienably, the vast
> estates of the ecclesiastick corporations – all these had kept the landed and monied inter-
> ests more separated in France, less miscible, and the owners of the two distinct species of
> property not so well disposed to each other as they are in this country . . .
>
> In the mean time, the pride of the wealthy men, not noble or newly noble, increased
> with its cause . . . There was no measure to which they were not willing to lend them-
> selves, in order to be revenged of the outrages of this rival pride, and to exalt their wealth
> to what they considered as its natural rank and estimation. They struck at the nobility
> through the crown and the church. They attacked them particularly on the side on which
> they thought them most vulnerable, that is, the possessions of the church, which, through
> the patronage of the crown, generally devolved upon the nobility.[19]

There is no indication here that the revolutionary men of wealth are a class
seeking to maximize the profits of capital invested in commerce and manufacture.
They are described, in language drawn straight from the vocabulary of Queen
Anne Toryism, as a 'monied interest . . . grown up . . . by the vast debt' which
the government had contracted in order to wage its wars. Burke is employing,
here as throughout his diagnosis of the French Revolution as a conspiracy to
create a paper-money despotism, a language first created to attack the foundations
of the Whig order he is concerned to defend. He has told us, of course, that this
order is more stable than the *ancien régime* because it encourages the investment
of money in land and the conversion of land into money; it is this fluidity of
capital, compared with the rigid barriers between estates, which makes the political edifice of English manners more harmonious than the French, and on this
point Burke is as 'oeconomical' a 'politician' as any professor in Scotland. But his
'monied interest' is still situated between a landowning class on the one hand and
a debt-contracting government on the other, and it is this which differentiates it

[18] *Remarks on the history of England,* letter xiv (2nd edn, London, 1747), p. 169.
[19] *Works,* v, 204–6.

from a commercial or industrial bourgeoisie in the conventional sense of the word. In France, Burke's revolutionary monied interest grasps at power in order to carry out a vast expansion of public credit.

It does so by seizing on the lands of the church; and Burke must be aware that this can hardly be the main strategy for revolutionaries in England. The expropriation of the church there had been an episode of the sixteenth century, and the Puritan attempt to complete the process had fallen short of complete success. Deeply as Burke came to fear the revolutionary potential of English Dissent, he must have known that there were limits to what it could achieve by further disestablishment in the economic field. The vindication of a landed clergy, however, was an act to be performed, and it is of great interest to find Burke denouncing the 'tyranny' of Henry VIII's proceedings against the monasteries and quoting at length on this subject from Sir John Denham's *Cooper's Hill*.[20] The deepest discord in the Anglican tradition was the nostalgia for lands which might have been retained to endow a clergy and make them patrons of learning and the poor; and if Burke used the language of Swiftian Toryism to denounce the monied interest, here he used the language of the Laudians and stands on the brink of a high-churchmanship he could never have adopted[21] — one, moreover, capable of being put to radical use. No doubt Burke could have assured the Whig aristocrats whom he delighted to serve that their ancestors' seizure of church lands was justified by the merger of landed and monied interests which it had made possible, though this is rather far from what he told Bedford in *A letter to a noble lord* when that magnate permitted himself a sneer at Burke's pension.[22] It was in the logic of Burke's argument that from now on, landed aristocracy must either be praised for guaranteeing commerce and culture or condemned for failing to do so, and the voice of Denham was enough to make it clear that this would be no easy matter. Forty years later, William Cobbett was to denounce the English Reformation and all its fruits, precisely because it had facilitated the growth of capitalist landownership and the monied interest.[23] The Whig Burke had placed himself at a point from which Tory and Radical argument could take off.

Let us revert to Burke's account of France. His anatomy of the revolutionary movement does not stop with the affronted men of wealth; he writes:

Along with the monied interest, a new description of men had grown up, with whom that interest soon formed a close and marked union; I mean the political Men of Letters.

---

[20] *Works*, v, 215–18. For Denham and his poem, see Brendan O Hehir, *Harmony from discords: a life of Sir John Denham* (Berkeley, 1968) and *Expans'd hieroglyphics: a study of Sir John Denham's "Cooper's Hill"* (Berkeley, 1969).

[21] Frederick Dreyer, 'Burke's religion,' *Studies in Burke and his time*, XVII, 3 (1976), 199–212.

[22] *Works*, VIII, esp. pp. 38–45, where Henry VIII's tyranny recurs.

[23] William Cobbett, *A history of the Protestant Reformation in England and Ireland* (two vols., London, 1824).

Men of letters, fond of distinguishing themselves, are rarely averse to innovation. Since the decline of the life and greatness of Lewis the XIVth, they were not so much cultivated either by him, or by the regent, or the successors to the crown; nor were they engaged to the court by favours and emoluments so systematically as during the splendid period of that ostentatious and not impolitic reign. What they lost in the old court protection, they endeavoured to make up by joining in a sort of incorporation of their own; to which the two academies of France, and afterwards the vast undertaking of the Encyclopaedia, carried on by a society of these gentlemen, did not a little contribute.[24]

The circumstance that the *gens de lettres* were organized without being adequately patronized had been commented on by d'Alembert and has interested modern scholars.[25] Burke, who earlier observes that the English deists 'never acted in corps, or were known as a faction in the state',[26] explains that the *philosophes* constitute an anti-religious faction, and indeed an interest, distinct from the monied interest but intrinsically allied with it. Being organized for the destruction of the Christian religion, they supply an ideological justification for the speculators in the public credit, who seize on the church lands in order to increase the sphere of their operations. And there is reason to suppose that Burke sees this alliance between the two interests as more than an accidental convergence. Elsewhere in the *Reflections* occurs the following:

Nations are wading deeper and deeper into an ocean of boundless debt. Public debts, which at first were a security to governments, by interesting many in the public tranquillity, are likely in their excess to become the means of their subversion. If governments provide for these debts by heavy impositions, they perish by becoming odious to the people. If they do not provide for them, they will be undone by the efforts of the most dangerous of all parties; I mean an extensive discontented monied interest, injured and not destroyed. The men who compose this interest look for their security, in the first instance, to the fidelity of government; in the second, to its power. If they find the old governments effete, worn out, and with their springs relaxed, so as not to be of sufficient vigour for their purposes, they may seek new ones that shall be possessed of more energy; and this energy will be derived, not from an acquisition of resources, but from a contempt of justice. Revolutions are favourable to confiscation; and it is impossible to know under what obnoxious names the next confiscations will be authorised . . . Many parts of Europe are in open disorder. In many others there is a hollow murmuring under ground; a confused movement is felt, that threatens a general earthquake in the political world. Already confederacies and correspondences of the most extraordinary nature are forming, in several countries.[27]

[24] *Works,* v, 207.
[25] D'Alembert, *Essai sur la Société des Gens de Lettres* (1754, 1771); Orest Ranum, *Artisans of glory: Writers and historical thought in seventeenth-century France* (Chapel Hill, 1980). Burke's analysis begins here to anticipate the views of Augustin Cochin, *Les sociétés de pensée et la démocratie* (Paris, 1921), interest in which has recently been revived (n. 50, below).
[26] *Works,* v, 172.   [27] *Works,* v, 282.

And here there is a footnote:

See two books entitled, *Einige Originalschriften des Illuminatenordens — System und Folgen des Illuminatenordens,* München, 1787.

Burke is not known to have read German, and it is not clear from what source these references to the Illuminati reached him.[28] To know this is perhaps of less importance than to know whether continental European publicists perceived them as he did — namely, as typifying the alliance of organized but unpatronized intelligentsias with the machinations of discontented public creditors; for such is Burke's general perception of revolutionary movements about 1790. It would be valuable to know this for two reasons: first, it would help us to reconstruct Burke's understanding of *ancien régime* France in crisis, and the information on which he drew. Secondly, we need to know whether an extraordinary dread of the power of public credit to subvert the natural relations of society is peculiar to the English-speaking lands of the period or is dispersed through European society. In the passage just quoted, this fear is the occasion for the emergence of a key term in Burke's analysis of revolution: the term 'energy'.

There were two social forces which David Hume, pioneer philosophical defender of the aristocratic monied order, had identified as destructive of natural society. One was enthusiasm, which — he had written in the *History of England* — suspended all the normal relations between effects and their causes which accounted for social behaviour.[29] Though this usually appeared in the form of religious fanaticism, it was to be understood as occurring when the mind was left alone with its own creations and mistook these for real causes operating on it from without.[30] Burke's 'metaphysics' and 'preposterous way of reasoning' may be considered as descriptions of enthusiasm occurring in a non-religious form. The second destructive force recognized by Hume was public credit, which — he had written in an essay bearing that title[31] — was capable of substituting itself for all forms of property and for all the natural relations between men in society, of which he had named 'nobility, gentry and family . . . a kind of independent magistracy in a state, instituted by the hand of nature'[32] as constituting the three most vulnerable to the subversions of paper. Hume had seen this destructive force as issuing from the sovereign executive, and as reducing proprietors to 'a stupid and pampered luxury' and 'lethargy';[33] he had not discerned a connection between

---

[28] A possible candidate is August Ludwig Meyer, formerly a librarian at Göttingen, who visited England and was in touch with Burke during 1788–90. See *The correspondence of Edmund Burke,* VI (ed. Alfred Cobban and Robert A. Smith, Cambridge and Chicago, 1967), 256–7.

[29] David Hume, *History of England* (new edn, London, 1762), V, 55–6.

[30] Ibid., pp. 56–7.

[31] T. H. Green and T. H. Grose (eds.), *The philosophical works of David Hume* (London, 1875), III, 360–74 ('Of public credit').

[32] Ibid., p. 368.   [33] Ibid., p. 367.

public credit and enthusiasm. Yet it was precisely when property and natural subordination, the sources from which manners arose in society, had been subverted by paper that the mind was left alone with its own fantasies; what had the madness of the South Sea Bubble been but the enthusiasm of public credit? In the account Burke gives of the *gens de lettres, philosophes* and *illuminati,* the expansive power of the monied interest is being most expressly brought together with the uncontrollable energy of enthusiasm, the intellect divorced from all natural relations – from manners and subordinations, from the laws of nature and nature's God – feeding on its own fantasies and substituting itself for every other form of power.

At a later point in the *Reflections* Burke declares:

The whole of the power obtained by this revolution will settle in the towns among the burghers, and the monied directors who lead them. The landed gentleman, the yeoman, and the peasant have none of them habits, or inclinations, or experience, which can lead them to any share in this the sole source of power and influence now left in France. The very nature of a country life, the very nature of landed property, in all the occupations and all the pleasures they afford, render combination and arrangement (the sole way of procuring and exerting influence) in a manner impossible amongst country-people. Combine them by all the art you can, and all the industry, they are always dissolving into individuality. Anything in the nature of incorporation is almost impracticable amongst them.[34]

Now here it is hard to believe that Burke is describing English society. As a seasoned if unsuccessful Whig politician, he knew perfectly well that country gentlemen were entirely capable of combination, arrangement and influence, and in insisting on the 'miscibility' of landed and monied interests which differentiated England from France, he had given one very good reason for this. (He might indeed have asked himself whether French landowners would not be glad of the opportunity to invest in a public debt.) As for the striking word 'burghers', it had been adopted from the Dutch about 1600[35] to describe townsfolk, surely because the English 'burgesses' had been too far absorbed into its parliamentary context to do so, and because English contained no such category noun as the French *bourgeoisie* and felt little need for one. If we argue that Burke had complex and ambivalent feelings about the bourgeoisie, we must face the fact that he had no word for them, and as far as we know no concept. Is he struggling here to formulate one? He continues:

It is obvious that, in the towns, all the things which conspire against the country gentleman combine in favour of the money manager and director. In towns combination is natural. The habits of burghers, their occupations, their diversion, their business, their idleness, continually bring them into mutual contact. Their virtues and their vices are sociable; they are always in garrison; and they come embodied and half disciplined into the hands of those who mean to form them for civil or for military action.

[34] *Works,* v, 347–8.   [35] O.E.D., *sub voce.*

We do not usually think of the bourgeoisie as a standing army, or London and Bristol as garrison towns; no more did Burke. The burghers he describes here might exist in France or the Netherlands,[36] but never in England as he knew it; and as for their social composition –

All these considerations leave no doubt on my mind that, if this monster of a constitution can continue, France will be wholly governed by the agitators in corporations, by societies in the towns formed of directors of assignats and trustees for the sale of church lands, attornies, agents, money-jobbers, speculators and adventurers, composing an ignoble oligarchy founded on the destruction of the crown, the church, the nobility and the people. Here end all deceitful dreams and visions of the equality and rights of men.[37]

The 'burghers' here revert to being a Swiftian monied interest, rendered formidable by their alliance with an independently organized intelligentsia; it is not their desire to invest capital in commerce or industry that makes them a revolutionary class. But the word 'combination' must catch our eye. We may recall that it is when 'bad men combine' that 'good men must associate'.[38] If country people are incapable of 'combination', is there something in the conditions of town life favourable to a 'combination' of energies which is antisocial because not led by Hume's 'nobility, gentry and family . . . a kind of independent magistracy . . . instituted by the hand of nature'? If so, Burke would be lamenting the lack of an effective natural aristocracy in France, and intimating that one could only exist under conditions of Whig 'miscibility.'

The problem of energy and combination recurs, but is stated in rather different terms, in the *Letters on a regicide peace* of 1796–7 – that wild jeremiad of a mind at the end of its tether, in which Burke declares that what is going forward in Europe is not a war between nations but a civil war waged by a 'sect', 'conspiracy' or 'armed doctrine' of revolutionary fanatics, who aim at nothing less than the destruction of natural society itself. Before this – he had already written in *A letter to a noble lord* – men of property

were found in such a situation as the Mexicans were, when they were attacked by the dogs, the cavalry, the iron and the gunpowder, of a handful of bearded men, whom they did not know to exist in nature.[39]

And in the second of the *Regicide letters* is found a similar comparison with

the power by which Mahomet and his tribes laid hold at once on the two most powerful empires of the world . . . and, in not much longer space of time than I have lived, overturned governments, laws, manners, religion, and extended an empire from the Indus to the Pyrenees.[40]

---

[36] For armed 'burghers' in the Austrian Netherlands, see *Correspondence*, VI, 267.
[37] *Works*, V, 349–50.   [38] *Thoughts on the present discontents; Works*, II, 330.
[39] *Works*, VIII, 53.   [40] *Works*, VIII, 254.

Burke uses these historical instances of the utterly unexpected because he desires to say that something has happened unknown to previous history: something
unknown to history because it did not previously exist in nature, unknown in
nature because it is aimed at the destruction of nature itself; something which
seeks to carry out an entire revolution in manners, he informs us, and so to 'strike
at the root of our social nature'.[41] But this entirely demonic conspiracy has itself
a social origin, and the difference between the *Reflections* and the *Letters* may be
found in the way in which Burke's ideas on this subject have developed. The *gens
de lettres* are still there, to represent the power of the decivilized intellect; but the
role of the monied interest has diminished in visibility, and the 'burghers' have
vanished altogether from the page. In the *Reflections* Burke had spoken of the
confiscatory monied interest's search for governments possessed of greater 'energy', and his predominant concern in the *Letters* is to develop the idea of an
'energy' unchained from all the restraints of society. In place of the alliance
between monied interest and *gens de lettres,* we are now told that the Revolution
was made by 'two sorts of men . . . the philosophers and the politicians'. If we
ask who these 'politicians' were, we learn that they comprised

the active and energetick part of the French nation, itself the most active and energetick
of all nations . . . I am convinced that the foreign speculators in France, under the old
government, were twenty to one of the same description then or now in England; and few
of that description there were, who did not emulously set forward the Revolution. The
whole official system, particularly in the diplomatick part, the regulars, the irregulars,
down to the clerks in office (a corps, without all comparison, more numerous than the
same among us) co-operated in it. All the intriguers in foreign politicks, all the spies, all
the intelligencers, actually or late in function, all the candidates for that sort of employment, acted solely upon that principle.[42]

The monied interest has not disappeared, but it is now the bureaucrats and
technicians of national power who pursue confiscation as the means of national
aggrandizement. They have become revolutionaries by a route the ideological
opposite of that the monied interest might be expected to follow.

From quarrelling with the court, they began to complain of monarchy itself, as a system
of government too variable for any regular plan of national aggrandizement . . . They had
continually in their hands the observations of *Machiavel* upon *Livy*. They had *Montesquieu's
Grandeur et Decadence des Romains* as a manual; and they compared, with mortification, the
systematick proceedings of a Roman senate with the fluctuations of a monarchy.[43]

. . . What cure for the radical weakness of the French monarchy, to which all the means
which wit could devise, or nature and fortune could bestow, towards universal empire,
was not of force to give life, or vigour, or consistency – but in a Republick? Out the word
came; and it never went back.[44]

[41] *Works*, VIII, 172–3.   [42] *Works*, VIII, 240–1.   [43] *Works*, VIII, 244.   [44] *Works*, VIII, 246–7.

Republics, as Machiavelli well knew, were for expansion; but in eighteenth-century England the admirers of Livy's citizen warriors usually saw themselves at the opposite pole of social being from the speculators and stockjobbers of the monied interest. Burke, defender of the Whig order with its commerce and civility, can imagine the two coming into alliance. The republic expands through conquest, the monied interest through confiscation. Such a republic destroys man as social being, to reconstitute him as armed citizen; its nature is what we should call totalitarian.

> In that country entirely to cut off a branch of commerce, to extinguish a manufacture, to destroy the circulation of money, to violate credit, to suspend the course of agriculture, even to burn a city, or to lay waste a province of their own, does not cost them a moment's anxiety. To them the will, the wish, the want, the liberty, the toil, the blood of individuals, is as nothing. Individuality is left out of their scheme of government. The state is all in all . . .[45]

The *assignats* are now only one among the instruments of a despotism wielded by an alliance of literati, who aim not at the maximization of their investment in the public debts, but at naked power for its own sake. The Revolution is a *trahison des clercs:*

> Never can they, who, from the miserable servitude of the desk, have been raised to empire, again submit to the bondage of a starving bureau, or the profit of copying musick, or writing plaidoyers by the sheet.[46]

But the power of such persons may still have an origin in wider social change:

> A silent revolution in the moral world preceded the political, and prepared it . . . It was no longer the great and the populace. Other interests were formed, other dependencies, other connexions, other communications. The middle classes had swelled far beyond their former proportion. Like whatever is the most effectively rich and great in society, these classes became the seat of all the active politicks; and the preponderating weight to decide on them. There were all the energies by which fortune is acquired; there the consequence of their success. There were all the talents which assert their pretensions, and are impatient of the place which settled society prescribed to them . . . The correspondence of the monied and the mercantile world, the literary intercourse of academies, but, above all, the press, of which they had in a manner entire possession, made a kind of electrick communication every where.[47]

The 'electrick communication' is probably Mesmer's rather than Franklin's;[48] but is it in the term 'middle classes', purely English though it is, that Burke comes closest to formulating a 'bourgeois' theory of revolution? Thirty-five years later, at the time of the Reform Bill debates, the case for the measure was that there

[45] *Works*, VIII, 253.   [46] *Works*, VIII, 256.   [47] *Works*, VIII, 259–60.

[48] Robert Darnton, *Mesmerism and the end of the Enlightenment in France* (Cambridge, Mass., 1968) for an 'electric communication' as sympathy passing immediately from person to person.

had come to exist a 'public opinion', the political attribute of the 'middle class' or 'classes', which required only to be represented in parliament and neither should nor could be subjected to the restraints of 'interest', 'dependency' or 'connexion'. To this the Anti-Reformers replied that to permit such a 'public opinion' free and unconnected operation would be as revolutionary a measure as any undertaken in France. In the 1830s an ideologue or two can be found[49] who equates the rise of 'public opinion' with the 'history of civilization', with 'the middle class', with personal as opposed to real property and with command over the labour of others: the formula for a bourgeoisie in the Marxist sense of the term. Burke does not make any such equations, but he is visibly helping to lay the foundations for both sides of the 1832 debate. What interests him about 'public opinion' — a term which does not appear in the passage from which I have been quoting — is the occurrence of a revolution in communications: the growth of a society where, he says, 'there was no longer any means of arresting a principle in its course',[50] and enthusiasm, fanaticism and metaphysical politics could have free play. For the reformers of 1832, 'public opinion' was committed to a new system of property relations and therefore need not be feared; but in Burke's eyes it had nothing to do with manufacture and commerce at all, its agents were literati, bureaucrats and technocrats, and the form it took was 'energy', 'talent', 'a new, a pernicious, a desolating activity'.[51]

Jacobinism is the revolt of the enterprising talents of a country against its property.[52]

We have not considered as we ought the dreadful energy of a state, in which the property has nothing to do with the government. Reflect, my dear sir, reflect again and again, on a government, in which the property is in complete subjection, and where nothing rules but the mind of desperate men. The conditions of a commonwealth not governed by its property was a combination of things, which the learned and ingenious speculator Harrington, who has tossed about society into all forms, never could imagine to be possible. We have seen it; the world has felt it; and if the world still shut their eyes to this state of things, they will feel it more.[53]

'Dreadful energy' is the phrase whose meaning we have to penetrate. If, in some dialogue of the dead, Karl Marx be imagined explaining to Edmund Burke[54] that

---

[49] E.g. W. M. Mackinnon, *On the rise, progress and present state of public opinion in Great Britain and other parts of the world* (London, 1828); *History of civilisation* (two vols., London, 1846). For the aspect of the Reform Bill debate mentioned above, I am indebted to Professor Barton L. Boyer (College of Idaho), a member of my 1980 NEH Summer Seminar.

[50] Here again we are reminded of Cochin; n. 25, above. See Keith Michael Baker, 'Enlightenment and Revolution in France: old problems, renewed approaches', *Journal of Modern History*, LIII, 2 (1981), 281–303, for a study of François Furet's revival of Cochin's views.

[51] *Works*, VIII, 214.   [52] *Works*, VIII, 170.   [53] *Works*, VIII, 255–6.

[54] It is not easy to imagine, since most of Marx's surviving references to Burke are merely philistine; he impugned his motives without considering his argument. *Capital* (Moscow 1959), I, 170, quoted in Shelton, *Dean Tucker*, p. 264.

he had simply failed to recognize that one system of property relationships was replacing another, and that the 'dreadful energy' was that of the revolutionary and triumphant bourgeoisie, Burke must be imagined retorting that Marx was another 'learned and ingenious speculator' who had simply failed to recognize the spectacle of human energy disengaged from any system of property relationships whatever. Should Marx reply that this was impossible, since all human energy was by its nature involved in productive activity and the generation of new property relationships, Burke would declare that this comparatively liberal and relatively optimistic dogma failed to bring him any comfort, since he had seen a vision of human energy turned wholly and systematically destructive. It is a vision which many have had since his time, and sometimes with good reason.

And Burke saw the antithesis against which this energy was aimed as a liberal commercial society, the Whig order as ruled by Sir Robert Walpole and expounded by Adam Smith. The states of the civilized world, he declared, flourished by multiplying and by satisfying the needs of men, and the more effectively they did this, the greater the resistance they must overcome in mobilizing their resources to meet the challenge of revolutionary systems to which 'the state was all in all'. Britain could effectively meet such a challenge only because of the enormous taxable surplus which her affluence produced, and Burke silently pointed to the underlying problem of Pitt's strategy: was the expansion of British commerce an adequate substitute for the application of military power?[55] The *Letters* end with a review of the national resources, and we recall a passage towards the end of the *Reflections* in which 'virtue' is defined as most highly displayed in the management of the public revenue. Burke to the last was a man of his modern age, with little nostalgia in his make-up.[56]

This inquiry points to certain provisional conclusions, and to certain agenda for further research. Burke was a Whig, the defender of an aristocratic and commercial order which could be represented as at once natural and progressive and defended by reference to a system of civilized manners. 'Manners', he wrote, 'are of more importance than laws. . . . According to their quality, they aid morals, they supply them, or they totally destroy them. Of this the new French legislators were aware',[57] and had set out to inculcate a new system of manners altogether contrary to nature. The Revolution was the crime against society rather than against God; Burke's Christian feelings were real but not spiritual – they arose, he once declared, 'much from conviction, more from affection'[58] – and he tended to see religion mainly as the sacralization of man's social nature. Manners,

---

[55] *Works*, VIII, 251–3.

[56] This interpretation is reinforced by that of C. B. Macpherson, *Burke* (Oxford, 1981; in the Past Masters Series). Since the present writer has often differed from Professor Macpherson, it is a pleasure to record the closeness of their views on this subject.

[57] *Works*, VIII, 172.   [58] *Correspondence*, VI, 215.

then, offer us a key to his argument; but a strictly progressive theory of manners, such as Burke might have derived from his Scottish acquaintances, presented them as arising, and fulfilling the natural sociability of man, only in the course of the commercialization, refinement and diversification of society. In outlining his differences with 'our oeconomical politicians', Burke declared that manners must precede commerce, rather than the other way round, and that modern European society needed and must not sever its roots in a chivalric and ecclesiastical past. This move – to borrow a term now much employed – was historicist and traditionalist, but it was not reactionary. It anchored commerce in history, rather than presenting it as the triumph over history, and here we may cautiously link Burke's argument as studied in this essay with the appeal to prescription and immemorial usage studied in 'Burke and the Ancient Constitution'. If 'manners' were *mœurs*, refined and enriched by the progress of society, they were also *consuetudines*, disciplined and reinforced by the memory of society; and presumption, prescription and prejudice were signs and means of society's determination to keep its memory alive. Burke proposed to keep the past actual, but he did not propose to return to it; there is no neo-medievalist programme for reactivating an age of chivalry or an age of faith, only a declaration that to destroy the historical structure built up by older social forms must lead to the destruction of society in its modern character. It is 'manners', that key term in the defence of commercial humanism, which the demonic revolutionaries have set out to subvert, and it is the strength of a commercial Britain by which they must be defeated.

Nevertheless, Burke's 'view of the progress of society in Europe' constitutes a significant revision of the Scottish perception of history, and it would be interesting to know what the heirs of Robertson thought of his insistence that commerce had been and remained dependent upon aristocracy and established religion. To most eighteenth-century defenders of Whig civilization, the rise of commerce and the rise of polite culture went together, under the name of 'the progress of the arts', and required to be defended together, against those who hankered after the austere republicanism of Spartan or Roman antiquity. When Burke proposed to reverse the Scottish thesis that commerce had been the motor force behind the growth of manners, he went some way towards encouraging the view – soon to become widely held – that commerce might generate a 'mechanical philosophy' and a 'dismal science', hostile to the point of philistinism to 'the progress of the arts'. We have not therefore lost sight of the perspective in which Burke may appear to some degree involved in a 'revolt against the eighteenth century'.[59] If he held that aristocratic patronage and established religion were necessary links in the connexion between civilized manners and expanding commerce, he had, by calling attention – as he overtly did – to the problematic

---

[59] Alfred Cobban, *Edmund Burke and the revolt against the eighteenth century* (London, 1929, 1960).

relation in English history between Whig aristocracy and Anglican church, raised the question whether this alliance in fact held together. Both Tory and Radical neo-medievalists were now in a position to argue that it did not, though we ought probably to add that both were in their way mutants – 'romantic' mutants if the term is safe to use – of an essentially Whig stock.

The presence in Burke's argument of this problem – not to call it a contradiction – reopens one of the most difficult questions in Burkean studies: how far his writings on the Revolution form a commentary on English and how far on French affairs. On the one hand, the Whig 'miscibility' of landed and monetary property is said not to have been duplicated in France, so that weaknesses arising from their separation ought not to be feared in England. On the other, there are implicit weaknesses in the Whig order – the Church is not wholly out of danger – and Burke did end by falling into an acute dread of revolutionary activity in England. These fears, however, are not explained by his analysis of French affairs. His conviction that nine-tenths of Dissenters were Jacobins at heart[60] cannot be accounted for by supposing that he saw them as public creditors, incorporated *philosophes* or armed burghers. It may be, of course, that he feared the English radicals and anti-war Whigs less as revolutionaries in their own right than as fellow-travellers with someone else's revolution, anti-patriots judging by a double standard, which is exactly what some of them were. But the problem of relating Burke's analysis of French to his analysis of English affairs remains, and is heightened in proportion as we uncover the intense and idiosyncratic character of both. How far – again – is his account of that 'middle class' society, in which aristocratic patronage and segmentation have failed and 'electrick communication' ensures the instant explosion of opinion into enthusiasm, a diagnosis of the *ancien régime* in disintegration, how far a warning of what England may become?

To answer such questions, it would be valuable to know more about two things. The first is the reception of Burke's anti-revolutionary writings by his English readers, rather especially those sympathetic to them. Because we believe their impact to have been great, we have tended to take it for granted, and have not studied in detail exactly what messages they transmitted. An author is not necessarily read as he intended; but if we knew how responsive Burke's readers were to his doctrines about 'monied interest', 'armed doctrine' and 'dreadful energy', we might know how far he was writing in language shared with his contemporaries, and what the sources of that language were. The second area calling for investigation is Burke's understanding of the last phase of *ancien régime* society. There is clearly more here than sentimentalizing about the French royal family, or the complacent assumption that France could easily have been remodelled along Whig lines; more than he could have picked up from *émigré* nobles like

---

[60] *Correspondence*, VI, 419–20. Cf. *Works*, VIII, 141–2.

Lally Tollendal. What he has to say about the 'monied interest', the 'men of letters', the 'burghers' and the 'politicians' (or technicians of national power) may or may not be nonsense; but it is the product of information carefully arranged along systematic lines, and by no means all of it results from the application of English bugaboos to French affairs. He seems to have thought of the disintegrating *ancien régime* as one in which powerful combinations could be formed in the absence of royal and aristocratic techniques of control through patronage, and it would be desirable to know where he got his information regarding 'monied interest', 'philosophers' and 'politicians' as forming such combinations. He seems to have thought – at any rate while writing the *Reflections* – of the public debt as a powerful agent in bringing about this state of things, and it would be desirable to know how far this belief was an extension of the Anglo-Scottish obsession with debt as subversive of natural social relations and how far it was shared by French and European observers. Here Burke's dealings with the exiled finance minister Calonne might be explored; they corresponded (though not very intimately), and Burke made use of Calonne's *État de la France*.[61] His understanding of both French and English affairs, like his philosophy of society in general, is seen to have arisen from sources even deeper and more complex than has been suspected: more deeply and widely rooted in the language and thought of his time.

[61] For references to Calonne in the *Reflections*, see *Works*, v, 243, 245, 246, 334–5, 374, 413, 421 and n. For Necker's report on the finances, v, 219–21, 236–40, 244, 402, 410, 425.

PART III

11

◁ ════════════════════════════ ▷

The varieties of Whiggism from
Exclusion to Reform:
A history of ideology and discourse

I. From the First Whigs to the True Whigs

(i)

"But she is a Whig," an academic woman of high distinction once said to me of Caroline Robbins, whom this essay was first written to honor.[1] The description may have been culturally rather than historiographically apt; a case can be made for regarding Professor Robbins not indeed as a gravedigger, but certainly as a deconstructor of the Whig monolith – if, that is, it should not be thought "Whiggish" to maintain that there ever was one. Her major work, *The Eighteenth-Century Commonwealthman*,[2] appeared in 1959, and its function was to reveal to us the existence of a persistent tradition of Whig dissent, in which a succession of Old Whigs, True Whigs, and Honest Whigs – collectively known to us as "Commonwealthmen" – kept up a criticism of the principles and practices of the regime known to us as "the Whig supremacy," originating before its foundations in the Revolution of 1688 and audible well after the revolutions of 1776 and 1789. There was in fact a profound schism in Whig political culture, and we have been working out its implications ever since. Let us review the historiographical chronology.

Almost thirty years earlier, Herbert Butterfield had taught us to view with suspicion what he called "the Whig interpretation of history," and by 1959 we had begun studying its origin as itself a historical phenomenon. In the process its character had undergone a change, from the selective progressivism criticized in *The Whig Interpretation of History* to the antiquarian fundamentalism identified in *The Englishman and His History*[3] and further explored in *The Ancient Constitution*

---

[1] An earlier version was presented to a panel on Professor Robbins's work at the 1981 annual meeting of the North American Conference on British Studies.

[2] Caroline A. Robbins, *The Eighteenth-Century Commonwealthman* (Cambridge, Mass.: 1959).

[3] Herbert Butterfield, *The Whig Interpretation of History* (London, 1931); *The Englishman and His History* (Cambridge, 1944).

and the Feudal Law.[4] The problem of Whig historiography has since 1959 become increasingly an aspect of the problematic history of Whiggism, and two major caesuras may be detected in the development of the latter. In 1967 J. H. Plumb[5] established the paradigm of the "Whig oligarchy": after a period of broadly based and turbulent politics lasting through 1714, the Whig party hardened into a regime, and the Septennial Act and other measures of the early Hanoverian years formed a *governo stretto* of aristocratic patronage wielders not seriously shaken until after 1760. The fairly continuous and consistent ideology[6] of Caroline Robbins's Commonwealthman now appeared as the language of protest against this regime, employed alike by its Tory opponents in church and country and by its Old Whig critics in the boroughs now excluded from power, although the simplicities of this classification are now undergoing serious challenge. Between 1965 and 1970, Bernard Bailyn[7] established the paradigm of the "republican synthesis," in which the American Revolution was revealed as the repudiation not only of parliamentary sovereignty over the colonies, but of parliamentary sovereignty as an acceptable form of government – a repudiation that had made powerful and effective use of the language of Commonwealth and country denunciation of the corruptions of Whig parliamentary oligarchy.

To Caroline Robbins, the Commonwealthmen had appeared a succession of interesting but on the whole ineffective ideologues, and this interpretation has been independently but automatically followed by those historians for whom all politics are oligarchic and all ideologies ineffective. As early as 1949, however, Butterfield had drawn attention to the role of a radical brand of ancient constitutionalism among the Middlesex and Yorkshire petitioners of 1780, when the last of the old country movements had signaled a crisis with some drastic implications;[8] and after Bailyn's contribution, the republican synthesis vastly enlarged the possible significance of the Commonwealth ideology. Its criticism of executive patronage, public credit, and standing armies was seen as stemming from

[4] J. G. A. Pocock, *The Ancient Constitution and the Feudal Law* (Cambridge, 1957; New York, 1967).
[5] J. H. Plumb, *The Growth of Political Stability in England, 1660–1730* (London, 1967).
[6] The word "ideology" is here used loosely and perhaps casually, since it seems at least very difficult to employ consistently or rigorously. I use it in three senses that often overlap: (1) thought considered as rhetoric or speech in action; (2) thought determined and constrained by, and at times in tension with, the forms of speech available for its expression; and (3) a view of the world determined by the various factors that may be held to have determined it (there being no single preconceived theory as to what these may have been).
[7] Bernard Bailyn, *Political Pamphlets of the American Revolution*, vol. 1; no more published (Cambridge, Mass., 1965); *The Ideological Origins of the American Revolution* (Cambridge, Mass., 1967); *The Origins of American Politics* (New York, 1970). There is now an extensive literature on this time; for convenient bibliographies see two essays by Robert S. Shalhope in *The William and Mary Quarterly:* "Towards a Republican Synthesis: The Emergence of an Understanding of Republicanism in American Historiography," 3d ser., XXIX (1972), pp. 49–80; "Republicanism and Early American Historiography," 3d ser., XXXIX (1982), pp. 334–56.
[8] Herbert Butterfield, *George III, Lord North and the People, 1779–80* (London, 1949).

the republicans of the interregnum and even the Renaissance, and as capable of growing into a fully fledged republicanism. If this growth was stunted in Britain, it provided Americans with the language of genuine republican revolution; if Gordon Wood[9] and others demonstrated that it had to be drastically remodeled to become the language of Federalism, Lance Banning[10] and others demonstrated the profoundly country and Commonwealth character of Jeffersonian opposition to the programs of Alexander Hamilton, denounced as the heir of Walpole. At this point it became necessary to turn back to Britain and inquire how far the old radicalism (and, by implication, an opposed conservatism) was continued, or alternatively transformed, in the decades following 1784 and 1793. Among both American and British historians, then, debates continue that can be intimately related to the publication in 1959 of *The Eighteenth-Century Commonwealthman* and to historiographical events occurring since.

In that specialized domain inhabited by historians of political discourse, two developments may be noted as relevant. In 1960 Peter Laslett established that Locke's *Treatises of Government* must have been composed in the early 1680s.[11] From this it followed, first, that when written the *Treatises* must have expressed intentions far more revolutionary than could have been read into them when published at the end of 1689; second, that the Revolution was, as had long before been pointed out, justified in language more conservative, and involving far more reliance on historical continuity, than anything to be found in the *Treatises;* third, as we shall see further, that the Old Whig or Commonwealth criticism of the Revolution Settlement expressed itself in a distinct set of terms, whose radicalism was not necessarily derived from Locke. Caught in cross fire from three directions, the old view that Locke had provided the orthodox justification of the English Revolution, and by the same series of arguments had inspired the American Revolution,[12] necessarily dissolved, and it became apparent that his role, which was obviously great, in the thought of the eighteenth century would have to be reconstituted by means of a new description. How this is to be done remains a matter of much debate.

Lastly, the present writer, who ventures here to name himself among his betters, had by 1977 completed an elaborate synthesis, begun as early as 1964,[13] that offered to trace the history of the republican synthesis from its classical and

---

[9] Gordon S. Wood, *The Creation of the American Republic, 1776–87* (Chapel Hill, N.C., 1969).

[10] Lance Banning, *The Jeffersonian Persuasion: Evolution of a Party Ideology* (Ithaca, N.Y., 1978).

[11] Peter Laslett, ed., *John Locke: Two Treatises on Government* (Cambridge, 1960, 1963).

[12] It is always difficult to document one's straw men succinctly. A good example is Carl L. Becker, *The Declaration of Independence: A Study in the History of Political Ideas* (New York, 1922; several subsequent editions).

[13] J. G. A. Pocock, *Politics, Language and Time: Essays in Political Thought and History* (New York, 1971); *The Machiavellian Moment* (Princeton, N.J., 1975); *The Political Works of James Harrington* (Cambridge, 1977). See further "*The Machiavellian Moment* Revisited: A Study in History and Ideology," *Journal of Modern History* LIII, 1(1980), pp. 49–72.

humanist beginnings. It was a cardinal thesis with him that a persistent emphasis on the armed citizen, enshrined in perpetuity in the Second Amendment to the Constitution of the United States, had entailed as an ideological consequence the ideal superiority of real over personal property, and that this had imparted an agrarian and classical character to eighteenth-century republicanism, infecting it with ineradicable doubts and ambivalences regarding the growth of a world commerce that it otherwise ardently welcomed. Since the Whig oligarchy, now established as the dominant reality of Anglo-American history in the eighteenth century, was based on the management of a system of public finance by a class of great landed proprietors, this duality of mind among its critics and opponents had interesting implications and could be related to those other dualities of Tory and Old Whig, country and Commonwealth, Jeffersonian and Hamiltonian elements that the opposition to Whig oligarchy so manifestly contained. This interpretation, however, has proved too dialectical for those liberal and Marxist historians — in this respect curiously difficult to tell apart — who are wedded past separation to an ultimately "Whig" interpretation in which nothing counts except the rise of liberal individualism and the triumph of the bourgeoisie. These have incessantly accused the republican synthesis of doing less than justice to possessive individualism and of not assigning it the central role in the history of ideology in the eighteenth century. In a variety of essays the present writer has sought to explain how a system of commercial values, historicist rather than individualist in character, was formulated during the Enlightenment in the course of a complex dialogue with the classical republican criticism. This controversy is a further consequence of the fragmentation of our concept of "Whiggism" that occurred when the "oligarchy" and the "Commonwealth" were seen in opposition to one another. The essay to which this is the preface is devoted to accepting this fragmentation as a fact and to pursuing the history of "Whiggism" as a word denoting a diversity of realities. It will necessarily follow that a reevaluation of the changing meanings of "Toryism" must be undertaken as part of the enterprise.

(ii)

The history pursued will be presented in terms of ideology and discourse rather than behavior, on the presumption that what people claim to be doing and how they justify it is just as revealing as what they finally do. This approach of course in no way precludes asking who and what they were. Such a history of Whiggism would necessarily begin with J. R. Jones's "First Whigs,"[14] the men of Shaftesbury — unless there should be uncovered any significant links with the epony-

---

[14] J. R. Jones, *The First Whigs: The Politics of the Exclusion Crisis, 1678–83* (Oxford, 1961).

mous "Whiggamores" of the Scottish hills, a possibility to which the Anglo-centrism usual with historians tends to close our eyes. Who the First Whigs were and what they were attempting is a question notoriously hard to resolve; interpretation is currently turning back toward the view that the central facts of Restoration politics were the reestablishment of the church and the institutionalization of dissent, and that the First Whigs were a faction of former Presbyterians seeking to put together an alliance of Anglicans and Dissenters aimed at preempting the policy of indulgence, whereby the crown sought to make itself the patron of dissent and lessen its dependence on the church and church party.[15] If the religious rather than the constitutional establishment is to be made the central issue, we must downgrade (though we cannot ignore) the tradition of seeing the Whigs as primarily concerned with safeguarding whatever gains Parliament could be supposed to have inherited from the years of civil war and interregnum; religion was the issue on which Parliament was dragged back into self-assertion, and the Test Act was to stand beside the Toleration Act as pillars of the central pier of the Whig edifice – a perception quite generally held in the first half of the nineteenth century. However this may be, the experiment of making religion the central issue enables us to coordinate recent research in ways interesting to the historian of ideology.

We must now place at the center of the picture a phenomenon that in the years following the Restoration certainly could not have been called Whig, though it was later to form part of what we call an "Augustan" ethos and think of as an ideological buttress of the "Whig supremacy." This is the emergence of a latitudinarian churchmanship, a rational religion aimed at repressing, moderating, or replacing the "enthusiasm" now thought of as the essential characteristic of Puritanism: the claim to personal inspiration by an indwelling spirit, with all its chiliastic and antinomian capacity to turn the social as well as the metaphysical world upside down. Doctoral candidates – those straws who know which way the wind is blowing – are working with increasing concentration on what they term a Restoration "politics of culture," the redefinition of religious man as a polite rather than a prophetic being, whose communion with God is exercised from the midst of human society and culture, reinforced by and reinforcing their authority.[16] Important developments in philosophy occur as we pursue the growth of this world view through the Cambridge Platonists to Locke, with a detour by way of Bishop Cumberland and the revival of natural law; at the end of the path may be glimpsed the figures of Addison and the third earl of Shaftesbury, the Whig Erasmus and the Whig Montaigne. We are indeed dealing here with a

---

[15] I am indebted on this point to correspondence with Dr. Mark Goldie.

[16] See, e.g., W. Craig Diamond, "Public Identity in Restoration England: From Prophetic to Economic," Ph.D. diss., Johns Hopkins University, 1982; Lawrence E. Klein, "The Rise of Politeness in England, 1660–1770," Ph.D. diss., Johns Hopkins University, 1983.

strand of that Erasmian tradition of which the present master of Peterhouse has written so eloquently.[17] Research of this kind travels in convoy with the work of Margaret Jacob[18] and James Jacob,[19] both of whom have emphasized the emergence of a rational world order that ultimately reinforced the Whig political order, while it underwent persistent challenge from a more radical and illuminist rationalism of hermetic and spiritual origins. Though this radical illuminism is chiefly to be met with among excluded groups of republicans, it may also be found keeping Hobbesian and absolutist company; the revolutionary temper does not choose its allies in attacking the liberal. But if we are to acknowledge the existence of a Radical Enlightenment, and allow for a revival of enthusiasm in the age of the democratic revolutions, we must also admit that, in both British kingdoms, the Magisterial Enlightenment was a surprisingly clerical affair, owing quite as much to prelates as to *philosophes*: to English latitudinarians and Scottish Moderates in their unending warfare against antinomianism and enthusiasm.

In identifying (though hardly exploring) this surely most important of all ideological developments of the Restoration, we have traveled far enough from the company of the First Whigs, who had yet to cement an alliance with latitudinarian churchmanship. Their temper was neither irenic nor oligarchic and their radicalism owed a good deal to their alliances with London malcontents, though there are radical interpretations of Locke that may make a shade too much of the green-ribbon survivals of whom John Wildman was so questionable a representative. All attempts to synthesize the political arguments of the First Whigs have had to wrestle with the unstable blend of conservative and radical elements they seem to present, but yet another attempt may be offered here. The relevant chapters of *The Ancient Constitution and the Feudal Law*, published in 1957, emphasized the Whig appeal to the antiquity of the House of Commons but did not do much toward establishing the theoretical context in which it occurred; this has now, after nearly a quarter century, received its first restatement in *Subjects and Sovereigns*, the work of Corinne C. Weston and Janelle R. Greenberg.[20] Professor

[17] H. R. Trevor-Roper, "Religion, the Reformation and Social Change," and "The Religious Origins of the Enlightenment," both in his *The European Witch-Craze of the Sixteenth and Seventeenth Centuries and Other Essays* (New York, 1969).

[18] Margaret C. Jacob, *The Newtonians and the English Revolution, 1689–1720* (Ithaca, N.Y., 1976); *The Radical Enlightenment: Pantheists, Freemasons and Republicans* (London, 1981).

[19] James R. Jacob, *Robert Boyle and the English Revolution* (New York, 1977), and *Henry Stubbe: Radical Protestantism and the Early Enlightenment* (Cambridge, 1983); James R. Jacob and Margaret C. Jacob, "The Anglican Origins of Modern Science: The Metaphysical Foundations of the Whig Constitution," *Isis* LXXXI 257 (1980), pp. 251–67; and Jacob and Jacob, eds., *The Origins of Anglo-American Radicalism* (London, 1983).

[20] Corinne Comstock Weston and Janelle Renfrow Greenberg, *Subjects and Sovereigns: The Grand Controversy over Legal Sovereignty in Stuart England* (Cambridge, 1981).

Weston's earlier book, *English Constitutional Theory and the House of Lords* (1965),[21] remains the reigning study of Charles I's *Answer to the Nineteen Propositions of Parliament*, which Weston has elevated to the rank of a major document in the history of English political thought. In this memorable if ill-fated manifesto, the king was made to describe the constitution as a coordinated but not self-perpetuating balance of three powers, his own being but one. Research and interpretation since 1965 have shown that there were several directions in which argument could move from this point. The doctrine latent in the *Answer* could be used in dealing with the question of what was to happen when there was war between the three powers, which ultimately brought it into the context of the controversy over *de facto* authority. It could be used by radical republicans, of whom James Harrington was the most striking theorist, in contending that the historic constitution had failed to provide the equilibrium which it offered and that a new and perhaps socially based separation and balance of powers – a genuine republic – must be sought instead.[22] Lastly, and this is Professor Weston's contribution, it could be used to argue, necessarily in a parliamentarian interest, that King, Lords, and Commons found and affirmed their balance in a coordinate exercise of legislative sovereignty.

The authors of *Subjects and Sovereigns* contend that the last is the correct context in which to understand the so-called Brady controversy, the debate over the antiquity of the Commons in 1680–2.[23] In arguing that the Commons were immemorial, the Whigs Petyt and Atwood were not arguing for some McIlwainian doctrine of fundamental law or anticipating Burke's appeal to prescription – no doubt *The Ancient Constitution and the Feudal Law* can be read in one or both of these senses – but were trying to include them as coordinate in the exercise of legislative sovereignty; in denying their antiquity, Robert Brady was trying to exclude them from it. The debate concerned the location of sovereignty, a concept to which exclusionist First Whigs were as responsive as their opponents. The interpretation is an attractive one, especially if a Whig concern with parliamentary sovereignty can be made to coexist with a Whig adoption, occurring about the same time (1675), of arguments concerning the excessive influence of the executive ministry in parliamentary proceedings, their use of patronage and corruption, their designs to bring in standing armies, and the need for frequent, triennial, if not annual, parliaments as the only means of forestalling the ministers and their designs.[24] For it is in this coexistence that the conceptual origins of the later Whig schism may be found. Whigs who desired to rule employed

---

[21] Corinne Comstock Weston, *English Constitutional Theory and the House of Lords* (New York, 1965).
[22] Pocock, *Political Works of James Harrington*, pp. 15–42.
[23] Pocock, *Ancient Constitution and the Feudal Law*, chap. VIII; *Subjects and Sovereigns*, chap. VII.
[24] Pocock, *Politics, Language and Time*, chap. IV; *The Machiavellian Moment*, pp. 406–16.

arguments leading to the sovereignty of Parliament; Whigs who desired to oppose employed arguments about the independence of representative from executive and of property from patronage, which led ultimately to the separation of
powers and looked beyond it to republicanism. These arguments were not a Whig
monopoly; they were country in character and it still seems worth calling them
neo-Harringtonian;[25] but when Old Whigs, True Whigs, and Commonwealthmen desired to criticize Whig rule, the arguments were available to them. The
debate among Whigs of the next century may be summarized in the form: Was
parliamentary sovereignty possible without parliamentary corruption? Was parliamentary virtue possible this side of the republic? It was summarized in this
form by David Hume.

Petyt and Atwood affirmed the antiquity of the House of Commons; Henry
Neville carried out the move from Harringtonian to neo-Harringtonian positions
by professing that Petyt and Atwood had partially converted him to this doctrine,
which Harrington himself had only cautiously adopted. By locating the commonwealth of armed freeholders in a modified feudal past, however, Neville left
room for a doctrine of historical change, which in more simplistic hands could
become one of corruption or degeneration from original principles. This duality
is only one of several in the complex pattern of argument in the early 1680s.
Petyt's *Antient Right of the Commons of England Asserted* (1680), Atwood's *Jus An-
glorum ab Antiquo* (1681), and Neville's *Plato Redivivus* (1682) are, like James
Tyrell's *Patriarcha Non Monarcha* (1681) and more remotely, Locke's *Treatises of
Government* (not published until 1689) and Algernon Sidney's *Discourses of Government* (not published until 1698 and needing reaffirmation of its authenticity),
outgrowths of the debate that followed the republication of Filmer in 1679–80.
We may never have a complete study of this controversy in all its none-too-
coherent ramifications, for though it has been shown that Filmer was a serious
and intelligible thinker,[26] and that his arguments retained significance for the
first generation that debated the Revolution of 1688, he has not been made to
appear a key figure in any party's tradition or to have articulated positions central
or enduring in English thought. The transformations of Toryism have been too
many for that. In this survey of the variations of Whiggism, a crucial point is
that if Locke's *Treatises* were composed as early as we now believe, they envisaged
an "appeal to heaven" and a "dissolution of government" that had not yet taken

---

[25] For criticisms of this term, see J. R. Goodale, "J. G. A. Pocock's Neo-Harringtonians: A Reconsideration," *History of Political Thought* I, 2 (1980), pp. 237–60; J. C. Davis, "Pocock's Harrington:
Grace, Nature and Art in the Classical Republicanism of James Harrington," *Historical Journal*
XXIV, 3 (1981), pp. 683–98; Enrico Nuzzo, "La riflessione sulla storia antica nella cultura repub-
licana inglese del' 600," *Atti dell' Accademia di Scienze Morali e Politiche* XCI (1980), pp. 91–183.
[26] Gordon Schochet, *Patriarchalism in Political Thought* (Oxford, 1975); J. W. Daly, *Sir Robert Filmer
and English Political Thought* (Toronto, 1979). Both are based on Peter Laslett's edition of *Patriarcha
and Other Political Works by Sir Robert Filmer* (Oxford, 1949).

place, and therefore compassed and imagined rebellion to a degree not approached by any of the tracts published during the Filmerian controversy. It is this that has upheld attempts to read them as an appeal to London radicalism of an almost green-ribbon flavor,[27] and no doubt it explains why they long remained unpublished and why Locke was careful not to have them on his person when he went abroad in 1683; he could have shared the fate of Sidney if caught with such material in his cabinet. They were published, however, and it is now a difficulty about the *Treatises* that we have to read them as they were read — that is, as published after the miraculously bloodless appeal to heaven of 1688 — knowing that we are not reading them as they were written. This is not merely a problem in the interpretation of Locke's writings and career; it is a point of significance in understanding the transition from the First Whigs to the Revolution Whigs.

(*iii*)

Locke returned to an England (with the doings of Scottish Whigs we are not yet concerned) in which an appeal to heaven had been made but had not resulted in a dissolution of government, or in the civil war with which such an appeal was assumed to be coterminous. The appeal to heaven, however — the drawing but not the stroke of the sword — had rendered sharply problematic the legitimation not simply of the events preceding and following the flight of James II, but of the governing institutions, whether ancient or still to be established, that he had left behind him. From this perspective, which was not only a Tory one, the Revolution might seem to present first and foremost a problem in the legitimation of *de facto* authority, such as had engrossed debate after 1649, and this must explain the republication after forty years of so many works relating to the Engagement Controversy.[28] In *John Locke and the Theory of Sovereignty,* Julian H. Franklin has proposed to connect the *Treatises of Government* with George Lawson's *Politica Sacra et Civilis,*[29] a work of the late interregnum, and has traced the way in which a doctrine of original sovereignty, coined to show how a people might restore government after it had been dissolved, grew into a means of justifying their action in precipitating its dissolution. Resistance theory was not far re-

---

[27] Richard L. Ashcraft, "The *Two Treatises* and the Exclusion Crisis: The Problem of Lockean Political Theory as Bourgeois Ideology," in J. G. A. Pocock and Richard L. Ashcraft, *John Locke: Papers Read at a Clark Library Seminar* (Los Angeles, 1980); "Revolutionary Politics and Locke's *Two Treatises of Government:* Radicalism and Lockean Political Theory," *Political Theory* VIII, 4 (1980), pp. 429–86.

[28] See Quentin Skinner, "History and Ideology in the English Revolution," *Historical Journal* VIII, 2 (1965), pp. 151–78.

[29] Julian H. Franklin, *John Locke and the Theory of Sovereignty: Mixed Monarchy and the Right of Resistance in the Political Thought of the English Revolution* (Cambridge, 1978). For comment see Conal Condren, "Resistance and Sovereignty in Lawson's *Politica:* An Examination of a Part of Professor Franklin His Chimera," *Historical Journal* XXIV, 3 (1981), pp. 673–81.

moved from a profound acceptance of authority.[30] To read the *Treatises* in this way, however convincing as reconstruction, is not the same as weighing their contribution to the debate in which they were published; most recent scholarship on the Revolution controversy has dwelt on their relative inconspicuousness in that context.[31] The central point, of course, is that apologists preferred to argue that the government was not dissolved, that traditional institutions retained their authority, and that the actions taken and being taken were to be justified by reference to known law. The extent to which this argument was offered to sweeten the bitter pill of necessity and obligation *de facto* on Tory palates prevents our echoing the praise Macaulay lavished on the Revolution fathers for their anticipation of Burkean prudence and prescription; even Burke's interpretation of the Revolution is not as Burkean as that; but William Atwood, who is classified as a "radical Whig,"[32] emphasized in one of the few contemporary notices of the *Treatises* that their doctrine was admirable but unnecessary, since the government had not been dissolved.[33] Whigs were beginning to opt for leaving the English people under the authority of their own history. This had not been Atwood's point in upholding the ancient constitution against Brady, but by the end of his career he was beginning to maintain the authority of ancient English institutions over the other kingdoms of Britain.[34] The uses of history were many, and the authority of nature dangerous.

There were, however, substantial groups of Whigs who wished that the government had been dissolved and that the Convention had proclaimed itself something more than a parliament: a constituent assembly looking toward a radical remodeling of the constitution. Locke himself seems to have been in sympathy with this position and may well have printed the *Second Treatise* in an attempt to further it.[35] It is difficult, however, to discover much unity of ideology or program among these discontented Whigs, whose existence is of such importance to the story we have to trace. A few pamphlets issued from the vicinity of John

[30] Skinner, "History and Ideology in the English Revolution"; Martyn P. Thompson, "The Idea of Conquest in Controversies over the 1688 Revolution," *Journal of the History of Ideas* XXVIII, 1 (1977), pp. 33–46; Mark Goldie, "Edmund Bohun and *Jus Gentium* in the Revolution Debate, 1689–93," *Historical Journal* XX, 3 (1977), pp. 569–86.

[31] J. P. Kenyon, *Revolution Principles: The Politics of Party, 1688–1720* (Cambridge, 1977); Martyn P. Thompson, "The Reception of John Locke's *Two Treatises of Government, 1690–1705*," *Political Studies* XXIV, 2 (1976), pp. 184–91; Mark Goldie, "The Revolution of 1689 and the Structure of Political Argument," *Bulletin of Research in the Humanities* LXXXIII 4 (1980), pp. 473–564.

[32] Goldie, "The Revolution of 1689," so classifies him.

[33] William Atwood, *The Fundamental Constitution of the English Government* (London, 1690), p. 101; Franklin, *John Locke*, pp. 105–98.

[34] Atwood, *The History and Reasons of the Dependency of Ireland upon the Imperial Crown of the Kingdom of England* (London, 1698; a reply to Molyneux); *The Superiority and Direct Dominion of the Imperial Crown of England over the Crown and Kingdom of Scotland* (London, 1704, 1705).

[35] Ashcraft argues this case at length and convincingly; see n.27, this chapter.

Wildman and Richard Hampden;[36] Lois G. Schwoerer has identified a group of hard-core First Whigs who wanted to use the Declaration of Rights to effect a sharp reduction in the powers of the crown.[37] These were neither London radicals nor republican doctrinaires, but seasoned Exclusionists whose reliability had once been carefully noted by Shaftesbury himself with such marks as "worthy" or "honest." This is not enough to identify them with a further group of sometime Exclusionist pamphleteers – Robert Ferguson, Samuel Johnson, and others (identified by Mark Goldie in a crucially important article entitled "The Roots of True Whiggism")[38] – whose means of limiting the powers of the crown was to insist on the necessity of frequent parliaments, triennial if not annual, and who came within a few years to lament that the revolution of 1688–9 had failed to effect this restoration of what they claimed was an ancient constitutional liberty. Some of them, including Ferguson, even reverted to Jacobite plotting in the hope of achieving the radical program by means of a Stuart restoration – much as their Leveller predecessors had plotted with Royalist exiles in the 1650s. Goldie's group, as his choice of a title indicates, were the immediate predecessors of Robbins's Commonwealthmen and belonged to that world of London radicalism with which Shaftesbury and Locke had maintained close contacts; some of them had been in Holland with Locke in the years of exile and conspiracy after 1683,[39] and had promoted Monmouth's expedition with its radical and popular manifestos. Yet in laying the foundations of the Commonwealth tradition, they were at the same time laying those of the tradition we denominate "country." The independent gentry of the shires were to show themselves not unresponsive to the argument that frequent parliaments were necessary if the patronage of the crown was not to bring members into dependence on the executive, and the passage from republicanism to Jacobitism was to be a recurrent phenomenon in opposition conduct from 1689 to 1745. With the coexistence and interchangeability between urban and agrarian opposition of which it is an indicator we shall be much concerned.

Goldie's True Whigs did not borrow significantly from Locke's *Treatises of Government*. The one outstandingly radical doctrine these contain is that of the dissolution of government, and there may well have been those in the radical groups who wanted to bring it about as a means to the institution of frequent parliaments. Yet not only is the case for these best stated in language not to be found in the *Treatises*, but Locke himself explicitly rejects both the case and its language. There is a crucial difference here that needs underlining at this point.

---

[36] Franklin, *John Locke*, p. 103, n. 38 and p. 108, refers to these as "Lawsonian"; others see them as more authentically radical.

[37] Lois G. Schwoerer, *The Declaration of Rights, 1689* (Baltimore, 1981).

[38] Mark Goldie, "The Roots of True Whiggism," *History of Political Thought* I, 2 (1980), pp. 195–236.

[39] Ashcraft, articles cited in n. 27, this chapter.

As early as 1675, Shaftesbury and perhaps Locke – if we believe that he had any hand in writing the *Letter from a Person of Quality to his Friend in the Country*, a tract central to Shaftesbury's campaign to bring about a dissolution of Parliament when Danby seemed to be bringing its militant Anglicanism into alliance with the king – had been denouncing prolonged parliaments as tending to corruption; after their defeats in 1679 and 1680, they had equally denounced the arbitrary dissolution of parliaments by the prerogative. The logical remedy lay in the election and reelection of parliaments at frequent but regulated intervals, which Harrington had endeavored to provide by the devices of rotation and which the manifestos of the Good Old Cause, put out by discontented officers before and after the publication of *Oceana*, had presented as the principal objective of the politically militant soldiers of 1647–9.[40] Here we have the reason for the appearance of Harringtonian language in the Shaftesburean rhetoric of 1675–6, which – restated in the "neo-Harringtonian" form made necessary by the persistence of the historic constitution – was to make so great an appeal to urban and country oppositions in the eighteenth century. But we also have a link with something older and more urban than Harrington: a London-based radicalism looking back through the lens of the Good Old Cause to the Agitators and Levellers of 1647, of whom John Wildman was a living if battered reminder. With the small masters and old soldiers of London Shaftesbury and Locke kept up their association; if Locke was involved in plotting insurrection in 1683 or 1685, it was with representatives of this radical underground.

This had its own political language, as old as the Levellers, in which natural rights and historic birthrights merged in coexistence if not in consistency; there can be no greater error than to suppose that the argument from natural rights by its nature tended toward radicalism, the appeal to history toward conservatism. There arose a claim to the effect that frequent or annual parliaments were rooted in medieval or Anglo-Saxon antiquity, so that to deny them by prorogation or dissolution was to deny Englishmen their inheritance or birthright in the constitution. Here was an ancient constitutionalism more radical than Petyt's or Atwood's, closer to the concerns of the more violent Shaftesbureans and serving to link them with their Commonwealth antecedents. It was among men of these antecedents, and professing such language, that Locke moved when, in London or Amsterdam, he moved in conspiratorial circles. The *Second Treatise*, we must suppose, was written at some time during the years when Locke was keeping such company and associating himself with conspiracy and insurrection, as he perhaps did with the Rye House plot, and very probably with Monmouth's rebellion.[41]

---

[40] See "James Harrington and the Good Old Cause: A Study of the Ideological Context of his Writings," *Journal of British Studies* X, 1 (1970), pp. 30–48.
[41] Ashcraft, "Revolutionary Politics," reopens the question of Locke's involvement. See n. 27, this chapter.

Yet the thirteenth chapter of the *Second Treatise* explicitly rejects the position that the intervals between parliaments can be provided for as part of the original constitution of government. Though it leads toward Locke's concluding argument that failure to call a parliament at the proper time is one of the missteps by which a prince may put himself in a state of war with his people, it explicitly declares that the calling and dissolving of parliaments is a power that may be and has been reserved to the prerogative.[42] The chapter proceeds to declare that it is for the prerogative and executive power to reform the representation of the people in Parliament by erecting new corporations where old ones have become depopulated,[43] and is followed by the chapter headed "Of Prerogative," in which the existence of a power capable of setting laws aside is justified on the grounds that *salus populi suprema lex esto.* All that makes Locke's argument a revolutionary one at this important point is the further series of claims that the prerogative must be exercised for the public good; that it is entrusted to the prince in order that it be so exercised; that if it is exercised to the public harm, for example in the calling and dissolving of parliaments, the trust is dissolved and with it the government; and that the judges of whether this has happened are necessarily the people, who may by appealing to heaven – that is, by drawing the sword – proclaim that the prince has put himself in a state of war with them.

---

[42] ". . . for it not being possible that the first framers of the government should, by any foresight, be so much masters of future events, as to be able to prefix so just periods of return and duration to the assemblies of the legislative in all times to come, that might exactly answer all the exigencies of the commonwealth; the best remedy that could be found for this defect was to trust this to the prudence of one who was always to be present, and whose business it was to watch over the public good. . . . Thus supposing the regulation of times for the assembling and sitting of the legislative not settled by the original constitution, it naturally fell into the hands of the executive, not as an arbitrary power depending on his good pleasure, but with this trust always to have it exercised only for the public weal, as the occurrences of times and change of affairs might require. Whether settled periods of their convening, or a liberty left to the prince for convoking the legislative, or perhaps a mixture of both, hath the least inconvenience attending it, it is not my business here to inquire, but only to show that though the executive power may have the prerogative of convoking and dissolving such convention of the legislative, yet it is not thereby superior to it." *Two Treatises of Government,* chap. 13, sec. 156.

[43] "*Salus populi suprema lex* is certainly so just and fundamental a rule, that he who sincerely follows it, cannot dangerously err. If therefore the executive, who has the power of convoking the legislative, observing rather the true proportion than fashion of representation, regulates, not by old custom, but true reason, the number of members in all places that have a right to be distinctly represented . . . it cannot be judged to have set up a new legislative, but to have restored the old and true one, and to have rectified the disorders which succession of time had insensibly, as well as inevitably introduced . . . prerogative being nothing but a power in the hands of the prince to provide for the public good, in such cases which, depending upon unforeseen and uncertain occurrences, certain and unalterable laws could not safely direct; whatsoever shall be done manifestly for the good of the people, and the establishing the government upon its true foundations, is and always will be just prerogative. The power of erecting new corporations, and therewith new representatives, carries with it a supposition that in time the measures of representation might vary . . . and whenever the people shall chuse their representatives upon just and undeniably equal measures,

This is certainly a revolutionary doctrine, as well as a theory of revolution, but there is room for debate in which of several senses it is a radical one. Certainly it expresses neither a conservative nor a radical constitutionalism; at this point it is not a constitutionalist doctrine at all, but is advocating a prerogative exercised *pro salute populi* and tempered only by the threat of dissolution of the government and consequent civil war. It reads very like the language of desperate men in the early 1680s, turning to thoughts of civil war or the threat to use it – a threat easily countered by a government that called out its troops and appealed to the political nation with the perfectly justified cry "Forty-one is come again." But the conjunction of prerogative and revolution is a long way from the radical constitutionalism of the Levellers and the Good Old Cause; what kind of popular absolutist, one is entitled to ask, might King Monmouth have turned out to be? The problem is to explain why Locke rejected the language of his own radical associates, who continued to argue for frequent parliaments as a constitutional right on radical-historical grounds.

The Revolution of 1688–9 was accepted by Tories on the grounds that the ancient constitution had been set aside as an act of necessity rather than of right, and (or so they struggled to add) a *de facto* government erected until time should remedy the situation. It was justified by those whom we shall be calling the ruling Whigs as an act carried out within the structure of the ancient constitution, designed to preserve it and legitimated by it. Though these were the arguments of those whom the Revolution enabled to continue as rulers in England, neither was very complete or satisfactory;[44] and as we shall see, Burke and even Macaulay were still struggling to reconcile them with each other. John Locke, satisfied by neither argument and none too happy with the revolution taking shape in 1689, published (but did not admit having written) his *Treatises of Government* as a service to those who argued that there had been a dissolution of the government, a reversion of power to the people, and an opportunity for radical reconstitution. This act gave him a certain place in the continuum of English radical thinking. There were always those who held – sometimes on Lockean grounds – that what occurred in 1688–9 had been a dissolution of the regime if not the government, an election of a monarch by the people, and an affirmation of a right to do the same again should need arise.[45] The *Treatises of Government*

---

suitable to the original frame of the government, it cannot be doubted to be the will and act of the society, whoever permitted or caused them so to do." Ibid., sec. 158.

[44] This is the argument of Kenyon, *Revolution Principles*. Schwoerer, *The Declaration of Rights*, argues that perceptible changes in the prerogative were made in consequence of pressure from the more radical faction she has identified.

[45] See Richard Ashcraft and M. M. Goldsmith, "Locke, Revolution Principles and the Formation of Whig Ideology," *Historical Journal* XXVI, 4 (1983), pp. 773–800. This traces a continuation from Locke through Defoe of the view that James II had been deposed and replaced by his people. Occasionally expressed throughout the eighteenth century, it may be identified with that proclaimed by Price and attacked by Burke, but needs to be distinguished from the argument about frequent parliaments and executive corruption emphasized here.

exercised a special appeal in dissenting and nonconformist circles, and a hundred years later we will find this interpretation of the Revolution passionately debated between Richard Price on one hand, and on the other Josiah Tucker (who considers Locke the apostle of the radical cause) and Edmund Burke (who does not mention him at all). What the *Second Treatise* cannot do is to find Locke a place in the mainstream of English radicalism: the claim to "frequent parliaments regularly chosen by the people," which had been made on grounds of both natural and historical right in the manifestos of the army, the Levellers, and the Good Old Cause. It was this that had begun to reassert itself about 1675 and was now being restated by those Goldie has identified in "The Roots of True Whiggism" – all of them Shaftesbureans, Londoners, and former associates of Locke's – in language modified by the further claim that Parliament was threatened with corruption by the executive. At the roots of True Whiggism we find the link between the Good Old Cause and the eighteenth-century Commonwealthman; but just as Harrington himself can be connected with the Good Old Cause, so we shall find the Commonwealth critique of ruling Revolution Whiggism taken up and linked with the neo-Harringtonianism of the country Tories. Radical opposition could be Tory as well as Whig, rural as well as urban; it would be hard to say as much for the thinking of the *Treatises of Government*.

Locke, therefore, must be counted a First Whig who never became a True Whig or a significant contributor to their vocabulary; nor was he an original member of that "Whig canon" of seventeenth-century writers whom Caroline Robbins identified as the pantheon of the Commonwealthmen. This will become evident as we study the next phase of the formation of True or Old Whiggism; before we do so, however, an attempt must be made to fix his ideological role. Locke's career as a theorist and literary activist in the 1680s, it is evident, was very different from what it was in the 1690s, and the anonymous publication of the *Treatises* looks like an end rather than a beginning. Within a very short time he published the *Letter Concerning Toleration* and the *Essay on Human Understanding* (he even admitted authorship of the latter), and it is here, as well as in his writings on religion and his *Reasonableness of Christianity*, that his contribution to Whig culture – to say nothing of his true greatness as a mind – may best be found. If we adopt the perspective, mentioned earlier, that presents the Revolution as a move to stop James II from preempting Whig positions, and toleration as the Whig riposte to indulgence, the two most solid achievements of the Revolution Whigs must seem, first, that they retained Dissenter support and never lost it to the Jacobites, and second, that following the departure of the nonjurors they were able to create a latitudinarian episcopate that induced a sufficient number of the recalcitrant clergy to underwrite them. As the philosopher of toleration, Locke really was a pillar of the Whig order, which came to pair his name with that of Hoadly, while the epistemology of the *Essay* was clearly of incalculable if ambivalent importance in establishing that religiosity of the sociable man that we have seen to be the central theme of the latitudinarian counterrevolution.[46] Here, it may some day be agreed, were Locke's true accomplishments as an ideologue as well as a philosopher; the *Treatises of Government*, when recognized as his, were swept along in the wake of this mighty work in a manner that has made their radicalism (which was not the radicalism of the next seventy years) hard to recognize. It was Locke's pupil the third earl of Shaftesbury who thought his work as a moralist subversive unless carried further in the direction of sociability.

II. From the Financial Revolution to the Scottish Enlightenment

(i)

The next phase in the formation of an opposition ideology may be examined in the light of several events occurring about 1698: a moment, like 1675 or 1680–2, when a number of distinguishable threads came together to create a new pattern. As prelude it must be stated that William III, little as he may have reflected on what he was doing, is a revolutionary actor in the history of British monarchy. He obliged his new kingdoms to reorganize their military, financial, and political structures in order to achieve effective participation in continental and imperial warfare, and this is an important precondition of the formation of Whig oligarchy at the end of the reign succeeding his own. To Goldie's True Whigs in the aftermath of the Revolution we need impute no more than disappointment that features of the Exclusionist program were not being adopted; but the radicals of 1698 confronted the regime of the Junto Whigs and the powerful institutions that had been built up to conduct the Nine Years' War. The establishment of the Bank of England in 1694 had laid the foundations of that edifice of public credit which was to be incessantly debated until well after the French Revolution, but the most prominent theme of the 1698 polemic was the reduction of William's army. A Scot, Andrew Fletcher of Saltoun, and two Anglo-Irishmen, John Toland and John Trenchard, held forth on the vices of a standing army and the virtues of a militia, and this was to be of significance in the ideological history of all three kingdoms. Trenchard is a key figure in the history of neo-Harringtonian thinking; it is becoming usual to present the Scottish Enlightenment as a series of replies to positions taken by Fletcher; and though Toland did not here write in an Anglo-Irish context, Viscount Molesworth in Dublin had published his *Account of Denmark* and William Molyneux was about to publish his *Case of Ireland's Being Bound by Acts of Parliament in England*[47] – a work filled with Lockean

---

[46] A Marxist analysis of the *Essay* may be found in Neal Wood, *The Politics of Locke's Philosophy: A Social Study of "An Essay Concerning Human Understanding"* (Berkeley, 1983).

[47] For both these see Robbins, *Eighteenth-Century Commonwealthman*, pp. 88–108, 134–43. The character of Irish Whiggism might repay study at even greater length.

doctrine that Locke was obliged to disown and Atwood to castigate. The paper war of 1698 enlarges our subject into a British context and establishes themes that were to preoccupy the American mind.

The neo-Harringtonian reading of history was given its definitive form in Fletcher's *Discourse of Government in Relation to Militias;* the reading with which the Whig regime was to counter it obtained its first formulation in the reply Daniel Defoe directed against both Fletcher and Trenchard.[48] Fletcher located the Harringtonian ideal of armed civic virtue in a Gothic and medieval past whose feudal character he played down; he presented the rise of commerce and enlightenment at the end of the Middle Ages as phenomena admirable in themselves but entailing specialization and the loss of liberty as the freeholders permitted themselves to be defended and governed by professionals, who necessarily exploited and corrupted them. Defoe asserted that a society built on military service and tenure was not only feudal but baronial, uncultivated, violent, and repressive; true freedom was modern and could only be found in commercial society, where the individual might profit by wealth and enlightenment and did not risk his liberty in paying others to defend and govern him, so long as he retained parliamentary control of the purse strings. The defense of the Whig regime was beginning to find the once Tory feudal interpretation of medieval history usable for its purposes. In this debate neither side made any allusion to Locke – it is difficult to see why they should have – nor does it appear that Locke (who was still living) expressed any interest in it. The confrontation of Fletcher with Defoe supplies an antithesis between virtue and commerce, republicanism and liberalism, classicism and progressivism. The Old Whigs identified freedom with virtue and located it in a past; the Modern Whigs identified it with wealth, enlightenment, and progress toward a future. Around this antithesis, it is not too much to say, nearly all eighteenth-century philosophy of history can be organized, though it is obvious that in cultures other than the British, something other than Whig parliamentarism must be located as the precipitating cause; in France, perhaps, one could point to the growth of an enlightened court culture, with philosophic academies and *gens de lettres* in dialogue with absolute monarchy.[49] Nor must it ever be forgotten that, as the debate progressed during the next century, virtually every participant showed himself deeply aware of the values propounded by the opposing party. There can be no greater mistake than to turn this debate into a straw man by presenting it as a simple eristic, and nothing more like a "Whig interpretation" than to render the eighteenth century the progressive triumph of the Modern Whigs over their opponents.

The terms "Old Whig" and "Modern Whig" appear about this time in the satirical dialogues of Charles Davenant,[50] who was among the first to link the

---

[48] *The Machiavellian Moment*, pp. 427–36.
[49] Nannerl O. Keohane, *Philosophy and the State in France* (Princeton, N.J., 1980).
[50] *The Machiavellian Moment*, pp. 437–46.

growth of standing armies with that of a "monied interest" of investors in the public funds. Yet Davenant's own claims to be called any kind of Whig are uncertain, and we are at the point where the debate can no longer be adequately described as one between ruling Whig politicians and their doctrinaire Old Whig critics. The drive to disband the army came, after all, from a "country party" led by that complex and ambivalent figure Robert Harley, and both it and he were on their way from being something that could be called Whig to being something that could be called Tory. As the discontent of the "country" (a term that could bear urban as well as rural meanings) acquired in its growth a plethora of Jacobite and High Church resentments against everything that had happened since 1688, we enter that territory in which the opposition of court and country has to be interwoven with that of Whig and Tory, and to which the historiographical catchphrase "the rage of party" is peculiarly applicable. It is also that in which the categories Old Whig and Tory begin to penetrate one another. John Toland claimed in after years that the edition of Harrington he prepared between 1698 and 1700 had been undertaken as a service to Harley. He also dedicated this idealization of a gentry republic to the mayor, aldermen, and common council of the city, praising London as a Venice where Harrington had imagined England as a Rome.[51] Harrington, though he never said so, may have seen trade as bringing about the emancipation of the freeholders from their lords, but London was by now the center of the "monied interest," of which he had never heard. The field of debate was not simple, and we should not hasten to resolve it.

Toland's role in the militia debate is of less significance than other activities in which we find him engaged.[52] During the years to which his edition of Harrington belongs, he wrote a *Life of Milton,* he partly rewrote and then published the memoirs of Edmund Ludlow, and he was instrumental in producing the definitive edition of Sidney's *Discourses,* to which – as has been pointed out by Blair Worden, who has reestablished part of Ludlow's authentic text – we had better pay close critical attention.[53] Toland was in short the main actor in creating what Caroline Robbins has called "the Whig canon" of seventeenth-century writers venerated by the eighteenth-century Commonwealthmen; to the names just listed those of Vane, Marvell, Neville, and Nedham were soon to be added.[54] But this Whig canon was in fact a republican canon; every name upon it was that of a Commonwealthman in the sense of a defender of the regicide government, if not of the regicide itself. To understand its significance we must place its creation

[51] *The Political Works of James Harrington,* pp. 141–142.
[52] Robbins, pp. 125–8; Margaret C. Jacob, "John Toland and the Newtonian Ideology," *Journal of the Warburg and Courtauld Institute,* XXXII (1969), pp. 307–31, and works cited in nn. 18 and 19, this chapter. Robert E. Sullivan, *John Toland and the Deist Controversy: A Study in Adaptations* (Cambridge, Mass., 1982).
[53] Blair Worden, ed., *Edmund Ludlow: A Voyce from the Watchtower* (London, 1978).
[54] Robbins, *Eighteenth-Century Commonwealthman,* chap. II.

alongside that of the "Whig interpretation of history," which may be seen taking shape in the years around 1700. J. P. Kenyon has emphasized how incessantly Whigs of every stripe from the Exclusionists on were saddled with responsibility for the judicial murder of Charles I. The only way to escape it was to separate the parliamentary leaders from the army regicides and construct a vindication of the men of 1628 and 1641 on the grounds they themselves had alleged: that there was an ancient constitution and that the actions of Charles I had tended to break it. James Tyrrell, the friend of Locke, who had joined him in attacking Filmer's *Patriarcha* and had encouraged William Petyt to defend the ancient constitution against *The Freeholder's Grand Inquest* published with it, seems to have been one of the first to see the necessity of this strategy.[55] Even the publication in 1702 of Clarendon's *History of the Rebellion* did not inhibit its growth; Clarendon himself, after all, had behaved conformably to the Whig interpretation until the Grand Remonstrance. From Tyrrell to Rapin de Thoyras, Whig historiography was built up from the twin foundations of the ancient constitution and a judicious defense of Eliot, Hampden, and Pym; we all know that the myth proved very potent indeed.[56] But the "republican canon," built up by Toland and other Commonwealthmen to the time of Thomas Hollis, by implication both adopted the Whig interpretation and challenged it. It endorsed the ancient constitution and said little about the "Norman yoke," but it moved beyond Parliament to Commonwealth, beyond the antiquity of Parliament to neo-Harringtonian ideas of Gothic liberty; it also implicitly endorsed the regicide of 1649, from which Whig historiography was a sustained attempt to deflect attention.[57] Toland was the archivist and to some extent the myth maker of English republican theory.

He appears also as a leading activist of radical deism, the promoter in England and abroad of various secret societies that look like gathered congregations of illuminist rationalism. One of the dedicatees of his Harrington, the city magnate Sir Robert Clayton, was a leader of the established structure of English freemasonry at a time when Toland was seeking to organize hermetic groups within it. The ideological implications of this have been worked out by Margaret Jacob.[58] Religious unorthodoxy of any kind had obvious anticlerical connotations, and these were the years in which the church was most alarmed by the spread of what it called deism. But there was a profound if elusive difference between a "rational religion," however undogmatic, that supported the Whig latitudinarian ideal of

[55] A full-length study of Tyrrell would be worth having; there is J. W. Gough, "James Tyrrell, Whig Historian and Friend of John Locke," *Historical Journal* XIX, 3 (1976), pp. 581–610. His *General History of England* began appearing in 1696.

[56] There may well have been more "Tory" than "Whig" historians of seventeenth-century events during these years; we are dealing with three dominant interpretations.

[57] There is overlap here; many Whigs maintained "Calves' Head" attitudes and displayed copies of Charles I's death warrant, but such endorsements were more private than public.

[58] See works cited in nn. 18 and 52, this chapter.

a rational piety practiced within society and amenable to its authority, and a "religion of reason," or worse still "of nature," that offered to make the bold spirit master of its thinking in this world and denied the separateness of the next. The latter smacked of republicanism – though Toland and his friends were in retreat from the forum into the lodge – and of enthusiasm, albeit one of *prisca theologia* rather than biblical prophecy. There is a skepticism that tolerantly accepts the clergy and another that angrily proposes to disestablish them. What this distinction means is made very clear in the histories written by such thoroughgoing *philosophes* as Hume and Gibbon, not that even they are unequivocal about it.

(*ii*)

Between the Treaties of Rijswijk (1697) and Utrecht (1713), opposition polemic in England was directed against the regime that conducted the War of the Spanish Succession: a regime presented as a system of public credit and national debt, maintaining an ever-expanding professional army and parliamentary patronage, which waged and won great wars abroad but was held to pay for itself by imposing a land tax on the freeholders and gentry. However exact or inexact this description, the regime bears witness to the profound transformation in British politics brought about by involvement in the wars against France; the expansion of imperial power was made possible by devices that tended to the stabilization of parliamentary rule, and before the political crisis of 1710–15 we see the alliance of Godolphin and Marlborough with the Junto Whigs as anticipating the Whig oligarchy and the imperial parliamentarism of the Hanoverian reigns. The polemic against the wartime regime therefore presents itself as continuous with the polemic against parliamentary oligarchy, and we have looked back to the beginnings of the Commonwealth tradition to substantiate the Robbins thesis that this polemic was continuously conducted by Old, True, and Independent Whig critics of the Whig regime, revealing a sharp schism in Whig political culture. We shall see that this thesis can be, and indeed must be, maintained; yet we must now confront the problem that during the reign of Anne the polemic against the Whig monied interest – the alliance of urban dissent with great financial and military interests – was conducted by Tories, that is, by adherents of a country party that claimed to speak for the rural gentry and was moved by their discontents into High Churchmanship and the borderlands of Jacobitism. This was territory into which radical deists and republicans of the Toland stripe could not follow, and old Commonwealthmen and supporters of frequent parliaments are to be found in due course reluctantly endorsing the Septennial Act of 1716 as the only means of rendering the Jacobites harmless.[59] We might con-

---

[59] Robbins, *Eighteenth-Century Commonwealthman*, pp. 109–10; Sullivan, *John Toland*, pp. 37, 142, 153–57, doubts Toland's reluctance.

clude from this that the heirs of Shaftesbury and Neville had lost control of their neo-Harringtonian ideology to its natural proprietors, the self-appointed mouth-pieces of the country gentry; yet so long as the lineage established in *The Eighteenth-Century Commonwealthman* stands, this cannot be uncritically accepted. The relationships between urban and rural, and also (but not interchangeably) Commonwealth and Tory, elements in opposition polemic and ideology require a good deal more investigation.

The polemic of Anne's reign was directed against the monied interest: against a speculative society typified less by merchants – always figures of relative benig-nity – than by the stockjobbers, political adventurers, and investors in the public funds whose tense, grubby, avid faces begin to appear in caricature. The gener-alization has been ventured[60] that since by now property was acknowledged as the social basis of personality, the emergence of classes whose property consisted not of land or goods or even bullion, but of paper promises to repay in an unde-fined future, was seen as entailing the emergence of new types of personality, unprecedentedly dangerous and unstable. Hence the imagery of Credit as a female and hysterical figure, and (shared by Addison and Montesquieu) of the bags of gold that prove to be only bags of wind.[61] To all this the Roman mythology favored by a number of traditions, including the Harringtonian, offered a gallery of countertypes: self-mastered, stoic, public, and agrarian, whether called from the plow like Cincinnatus or retiring like Cicero to Tusculan philosophic leisure; Cato in all his manifestations the arch figure. The Whigs of the regime, at whom so much of this was aimed, strove to annex the Roman ideal to their own cause, and there was plenty in the Ciceronian ethos of *negotium* and *officium* that favored their doing so; Reed Browning has written a remarkable study of "Court Whig" thought as fundamentally Ciceronian.[62] But what was above all needed was a defense of urban life and politics as neither an ancient polis nor a *faeces Romuli* – a financial and military regime based, as both Fletcher and Defoe had realized, on a decisive abandonment of the classical (and at the same time Gothic) ideal of the citizen as armed proprietor, and his replacement by a leisured, cultivated, and acquisitive man who paid for others to defend and govern him. This could not be defended in Greco-Roman terms. Rather, it called for an understanding of commercial modernity, and the vindication of the regime entailed an opposi-tion between ancient and modern, resembling if not identical with that currently going on in the "battle of the books." Whig ideology now took a decisive turn toward social, cultural, and commercial values, one we associate especially with the name of Addison, among a group of great contending literary figures who were at the same time party journalists and cultivated essayists, catering in both capacities to a new urban public of the readers of periodicals. In reply to the Old

---

[60] See chap. VI of the present volume.   [61] Pocock, *The Machiavellian Moment*, pp. 452–7, 475.
[62] Reed Browning, *Political and Constitutional Ideas of the Court Whigs* (Baton Rouge, La., 1982).

Whigs and their Tory inheritors there appears a new category, which we may term that of the "polite Whigs."

The ideal of politeness had first appeared in the Restoration, where it formed part of the latitudinarian campaign to replace prophetic by sociable religiosity. This campaign is carried on by Addison, a sound churchman by the new Whig standards, whose supreme achievement we see as the advancement of a polite style, and so of a politics of style accompanied by a morality of politeness.[63] The polemic against enthusiasm was to continue for another hundred years – so deep were the scars of the Puritan interregnum on the governing-class mind – and the concepts of politeness, manners, and taste were to remain integral parts of its strategy. It is important to notice, however, that they could be directed at other targets. Satire against curmudgeonly old dons out of Anthony Wood could easily become polemic against Oxford clerical Toryism, while across the Channel the deist *philosophes* were seeking to substitute manners for religion as the key to the history of mankind. In Whig England, moreover, Addisonian politeness had a further set of adversaries. It could be used against the uncouth virtue of the Spartans and Romans – of Cato the Elder, with his distrust of all philosophers – being exalted by the neo-Harringtonian critics of the regime, and against the radical deists with whom some of them still associated. Politeness and enlightenment were irenic, established, and oligarchic ideals, capable of being employed against Puritan, Tory, and republican alike and of making them look curiously similar.

Placed in a counter-Harringtonian context, the ethos of politeness is seen to make an appeal to that historical movement discussed by both Fletcher and Defoe, in which the rise of commerce and culture had led to the replacement of the armed citizen by the leisured taxpayer under parliamentary government. But the exaltation of politeness is not just a way of saying that the acquisition of culture is worth the price; in the *Spectator* essays, politeness becomes an active civilizing agent. By observation, conversation, and cultivation, men and women are brought to an awareness of the needs and responses of others and of how they appear in the eyes of others; this is not only the point at which politeness becomes a highly serious practical morality, reinforced by an obviously Lockean epistemology, although just at this point Shaftesbury thought Lockean doctrine needed to be enlarged by a doctrine of sympathy. It is also the point at which Addison begins to comment on the structure of English society and the reconciliation of its diverse "interests." In the Spectator circle, Sir Roger the country gentleman and Sir Andrew the urban merchant meet and polish one another, and Mr. Spectator comments on the merits and shortcomings of each. His observation is his prac-

---

[63] Edward A. Bloom and Lillian D. Bloom, *Joseph Addison's Sociable Animal: In the Market Place, on the Hustings, in the Pulpit* (Providence, R.I., 1971) remains a convenient summary of Addisonian ideology. See also James Leheny's introduction to his edition of *The Freeholder* (Oxford, 1979).

tice; by observing his friends he heightens their awareness of self and other, and this sociable role is more important, both morally and socially, than any he could play as a politically engaged activist.

The Spectator circle also stands for what was coming to be called "the Town," the leisured urban environment spreading west from the old centers of Westminster and London as the result of the growth of the parliamentary aristocracy and the rentier classes; it was not the ferociously expanding London (also sometimes called "the Town") of Defoe, Hogarth, and Fielding. It is the setting in which gentleman and merchant meet to learn politeness, and at the end of the later *Freeholder* essays the loutish Tory squire, the Foxhunter, is brought to Town and taught the blessings of trade and the Protestant succession – which had intervened in emblematic form in the Vision of Credit at the outset of the *Spectator* series, and had caused the bags of wind to be filled with gold again. The Town was replacing the court as the meeting point of country and city; Macaulay's famous chapter on the bumpkin backwardness of the rural gentry and clergy is simply an extension of the Addisonian doctrine that an urbane and suburban Whiggism was necessary to teach church and country the culture without which they would be unable to exercise their liberty. Whiggism of the polite kind had no need of the Puritan, Tory, or republican virtues; the ideological importance of secular culture was a Whig, and paradoxically also an Anglican, creation.

There was as we shall see a Scottish component in Macaulay's thinking. Polite Whiggism gains meaning when read in the context of Defoe's reply to Fletcher of Saltoun, and Nicholas Phillipson, George Davie, and others have developed an interpretation of the Scottish Enlightenment that locates its beginnings in the need to find alternatives to the values expressed in Fletcher's speeches opposing the form taken by the Anglo-Scottish Union of 1707.[64] There are two respects in which the union is crucial to the formation of the Whig regime of the eighteenth century. It originated in an urgent Scottish desire to take part in the economic growth fostered by the new financial and military power of the southern kingdom, and because it took the form of an incorporation of the two parliaments, it ensured that the managers of patronage both controlled the politics of Scotland and enlarged the ministerial interest at Westminster. This accounts for the bitter dislike of Scotsmen in British affairs expressed by such critics of the coming oligarchy as Jonathan Swift, Charles Churchill, and Thomas Jefferson. Andrew Fletcher, however, based his opposition to the incorporating union on values more simply civic-humanist and neo-Harringtonian. He ardently desired mod-

[64] Nicholas Phillipson, "Towards a Definition of the Scottish Enlightenment," in *City and Society in the Eighteenth Century*, ed. P. Fritz and D. Williams (Toronto, 1973); "Culture and Society in the Eighteenth-Century Province: The Case of Edinburgh and the Scottish Enlightenment," in *The University in Society*, ed. Lawrence Stone (Princeton, N.J., 1974); "The Scottish Enlightenment," in *The Enlightenment in National Context*, ed. Roy Porter and Mikulas Teich (Cambridge, 1981). G. E. Davie, *The Scottish Enlightenment* (London, 1981).

ernization of the Scottish economy – he had after all been a promoter of the Darien Scheme, the equivalent of the English South Sea Bubble – but he no less ardently desired that the moral consequences of commerce and culture should be controlled by the disciplined virtue that only the maintenance of autonomous political and military institutions could preserve for Scotland. He therefore desired a federative union, with a regional parliament and militia. The program was politically foredoomed, but it is the contention of Phillipson and Davie that the values it expressed enjoyed such resonance that some alternative to them must be found. Scottish lay and clerical thinkers therefore set about defining a morality in which virtue might be shown arising from sources in society, culture, and commerce, and existing independently of the practice of autonomous politics.

The provincial elites of postunion Edinburgh, it is contended – juristic, landowning, mercantile, academic, clerical – can be seen founding a series of evidently Addisonian societies, dedicated to the furtherance of sociability, conversation, and moral and economic improvement. Though the combination is unmistakably Whig, it is the emphasis on the last that is distinctively Scottish; because in Scotland there was no Tory landed interest, but only Jacobites, Highlanders, Borderers, and a past remembered as more barbarous than it probably had been,[65] the Whig belief that conversation and commerce go together merged with a perception of economic improvement as immediately superimposed upon feudal, agnatic, and hunter-warrior states of society. This perception sensibly quickened after the Highland rebellion of 1745; but long before that, Addisonian, latitudinarian, Arminian, and Lockean theories of morality, religion, and sociability found themselves in a more direct confrontation than could possibly occur in England with the heavily armored Calvinism of the late Covenanting period. Here too the collision between modernity and tradition was more acute than anything known in the southern kingdom, though the rise of the Moderate faction among the Edinburgh clergy did much to cushion it; and finally, the rather rapid advent of an enlightened morality merged with a Scottish tradition of study in the Roman civil law, itself turning, under Arminian influences in the Dutch universities, which Scotsmen attended in numbers, toward the analysis of jurisprudence in terms of manners, morals, and sociability. So distinctively Scottish is this last that Duncan Forbes and Peter Stein have found it possible to describe the Scottish Enlightenment in terms of the modernization of jurisprudence and ethics, with minimal reference to the need to overcome a neo-Harringtonian critique of the Whig commercial order.[66] Indeed, the relative absence in Scotland of anything like the conjunction of Tory and Commonwealth-

---

[65] Jenny Wormald, *Court, Kirk and Community: Scotland, 1470–1625* (Toronto, 1981).
[66] Duncan Forbes, *Hume's Philosophical Politics* (Cambridge, 1976); Peter Stein, *Legal Evolution: The Story of an Idea* (Cambridge, 1980). See the present writer's "Cambridge Paradigms and Scotch Philosophers," in *Wealth and Virtue*, ed. Istvan Hont and Michael Ignatieff (Cambridge, 1983).

man in England may raise the question whether one Fletcher of Saltoun is enough to make a republican antitradition. It can be affirmed that the Moderate clergy and Whig lay elites of Edinburgh and elsewhere developed a powerful series of theses regarding the history of society, the psychological foundations of morals and aesthetics, and in due course political economy. These formed an ideological vindication of the Union of 1707, and when they moved south with David Hume, they took the form that Forbes has called "scientific Whiggism"[67] and that in England encountered a diversity of antagonists.

(iii)

From the Hanoverian succession of 1714 we are accustomed to date the rather rapid establishment of the "Whig oligarchy" or "supremacy," which may have been the outcome of long-term social processes but on the *evènementiel* level appears to us — as it did to the next generation — associated with such highly specific legislative measures as the Septennial Act of 1716 and the ultimately abandoned yet significant Peerage Bill of 1719. The lengthening of the duration of parliaments made possible a series of *pactes de famille* that were rapidly to make contested elections a good deal less common in counties and even in boroughs; we tend to see this as the effective disfranchisement of the borough electorates which for so much of the preceding century it had been the inclination of the gentry to strengthen, involve, and enlarge. The shrinkage of local influence could only weaken those families excluded from government patronage, and even a *pacte de famille* that might preserve a seat in Tory hands paid a price for it in the loss of ability to challenge a government by forcing a contest. Stamped with the suspicion of Jacobitism and demoralized by the loss of their leaders, the Tory gentry so conspicuous in 1709–14 rapidly dwindled into an authentically Jacobite rump of uncertain size, or were forced to make their peace with a series of Whig patronage masters if they desired to exhibit anything more than the passive virtue of independent country gentlemen. This perception of politics[68] has been challenged by twentieth-century research, which queries the extent to which patronage was centralized in a few identifiable hands, and by more recent works that maintain the active role of the Tories until 1745 or 1756; but it was quite widely shared by observers and critics of the Hanoverian regime in all three kingdoms. There was believed to exist a Whig "oligarchy" or "supremacy," the

---

[67] Forbes, *Hume's Philosophical Politics;* for the shaded differences between "sceptical" and "scientific Whiggism," see discussion later in this section.

[68] The representative works on this subject are Plumb, *Growth of Political Stability;* W. A. Speck, *Stability and Strife: England 1714–1760* (Cambridge, Mass., 1977); H. T. Dickinson, *Liberty and Property: Political Ideologies in Eighteenth-Century Britain* (London, 1977). The two latter authors advocate the view that a court–country replaced a Tory–Whig polarity about 1714.

effective dictatorship of a single if minimally organized party using as its instrument a parliament so far sovereign that it had prolonged its own duration without reference to the electorate.

The alliance of forces that established the Whig regime was that which had conducted the War of the Spanish Succession and had been attacked with all the resources of the polemic against a monied interest said to use war as a means of expanding its credit, its patronage, and its parliamentary and military power. Much of this polemic could be carried on even when the new oligarchy had adopted a policy of peace and French alliance; even though the South Seas Company was a Tory foundation with many Tory directors, the polemic against the monied interest could be directed against the Whig ministers who intervened to save the public credit. This polemic could be Old Whig as easily as it could be Tory, and there now appeared to give it an effective voice that founding father among Commonwealthmen John Trenchard, who until his death in 1724 conducted *Cato's Letters* and *The Independent Whig,* with Thomas Gordon as his coadjutor and his successor.[69] The former journal took parliamentary corruption as its chief target; the latter was directed against the alliance of Whig politicians with the established church and was anticlerical enough to be widely read and imitated in America, especially when one colony or another was active in opposing the threat of a crown-supported episcopacy.[70] It was also translated into French and published by Holbach; deists and Old Whigs continued to figure in the European Enlightenment.

The greatest of all polemics, however, against the regime consolidated and typified by Sir Robert Walpole was Tory to the extent that it was orchestrated by Bolingbroke, and High Church and even Catholic to the extent that it involved Swift, Atterbury, and Pope. There are many problems here crucial to the understanding of eighteenth-century ideological history. What so outspoken a deist as Bolingbroke had been doing at the head of an Anglican party in Anne's reign is a question that seems to transcend any answer (however justified) in terms of political duplicity. The grandfather of Edward Gibbon was a city Tory and South Seas Company director, and his family at Putney seems to have included two men of intellect: William Law, the nonjuring mystic, and David Mallet, the deist and Bolingbroke's literary executor.[71] This sharp dualism – oligarchy makes

---

[69] For them see Robbins, *Eighteenth-Century Commonwealthman,* pp. 115–24; Pocock, *The Machiavellian Moment,* pp. 467–77; Isaac F. Kramnick, *Bolingbroke and His Circle: The Politics of Nostalgia in the Age of Walpole* (Cambridge, Mass., 1968), pp. 243–51.

[70] See Milton M. Klein, ed., *The Independent Reflector . . . by William Livingston and others* (Cambridge, Mass., 1963). The Holbach translation is entitled *L'Esprit du Clergé* and is dated 1765; see Frank Manuel, *The Eighteenth Century Confronts the Gods* (Cambridge, Mass., 1959).

[71] Michel Baridon, *Gibbon et le Mythe de Rome: Histoire et Ideologie au Siècle des Lumières* (thèse présentée devant l'Université de Paris VII; Lille, Service de Reproduction des Thèses, 1975), vol. I, pp. 23–6, 39–42; Patricia Craddock, *Young Edward Gibbon: Gentleman of Letters* (Baltimore, 1982), pp. 8–9, 24, 36, 51, 87, 126.

strange bedfellows — may be associated with another, inherent in the character of the *Craftsman*, conducted by Bolingbroke and Pulteney, and in the *Dissertation upon Parties* and *Remarks on the History of England*, works by Bolingbroke that grew out of it. These were recognized by contemporaries as constituting a country campaign, a polemic designed to drive Walpole from power by mobilizing a "public opinion" that should include the independent country gentlemen still supposed to be an essential component of the political order. As such, they marshalled all the neo-Harringtonian arguments familiar to us since at least 1675: the danger of an executive ascendancy employing patronage and finance as means of corruption; the need for Parliament to be independent of the executive, and to this end composed of independent proprietors; the importance of landed even more than mercantile property in ensuring personal and parliamentary independence; and the need to return to the principles of an ancient constitution in which all these truisms had been institutionalized. Bolingbroke also, in *The Idea of a Patriot King*, engaged in the "Leicester House" maneuver becoming frequent with politicians out of power: He imagined a successor to the throne who should himself take the lead in rendering Parliament independent of ministerial and oligarchic control. However unimportant this "idea" may have been in shaping the conduct of George III before or after 1760, it played a real part in shaping others' perceptions of his conduct.

But the public opinion to which this printed polemic was addressed was necessarily made up of those in a position to read books and journals printed in London, and though an increasingly effective circulation industry might convey these views to a country public for whom they were intended, we must suppose that they had an urban public as well. This in turn might consist largely of recent arrivals, seasonal visitors, and suburban residents drawn to the Town by politics, business, and pleasure, while retaining much of the country outlook they had brought with them; but under the conditions presupposed by the thesis of Whig oligarchy, we must also take account of a longer-established city population, whose participation in politics and satisfaction by it were no longer what they had been in the days before the Septennial Act. To the real or fancied exclusion of country gentry by parliamentary oligarchs and the monied interest, we have to add that of borough electorates effectively disfranchised after 1714, and the crucial problem we now face is that of the relative significance of the ideologies generated by these two groups or offered to them.

Marxist and *marxisant* historians retain an apparently ineradicable allegiance to the idea of the rising bourgeoisie or middle class, without which, it seems — though one may want to ask why — not only their classical system but their entire way of thinking would disintegrate. They feel obliged to explain all social opposition or radical thought in preindustrial eighteenth-century Britain — unless it can be dismissed as "traditional" or outright "reactionary" — as the ideology of a bourgeoisie, to be contrasted with that of an aristocracy that must be shown to have been feudal, paternalist, or hierarchical; this bourgeois radicalism must further be integrated with a "liberal" possessive individualism associated as closely as possible with the name of Locke, who has become a necessary actor in their scheme of things. Historians of this persuasion have been offended by the suggestion that radicalism in the eighteenth century consisted largely of a polemic against a system of public credit dominated by a landed aristocracy, that it was conducted largely in the name of classical-republican and agrarian-military values, and that it was in the defense of the Whig aristocracy that an ethos of commercial individualism was first elaborated. Although none of these propositions would have disturbed Marx and Engels as much as they do their successors,[72] the latter have cast about for ways of depriving them of their force. Isaac F. Kramnick,[73] for whom every diminution of the role of Locke is an implicit attack on Marx and every criticism of the concept of bourgeois ideology an attack on that of ideology itself, has hit upon the strategy of representing all radicalism of the foregoing kind as reflecting the consciousness of an excluded country gentry, and all claims for republican virtue and independence as reflecting this gentry's "nostalgia" for an ordered, hierarchical, and paternalist society in which others were dependent on them. The republican critique thus shifted unthreateningly into the reactionary column, the way is clear for the emergence in the late eighteenth century of an essentially Lockean "bourgeois radicalism," a term Kramnick reiterates with all the fervor and unction of one testifying to the old-time religion. A more sophisticated version of the same thesis may be that put forward by E. P. Thompson, who accepts the view that the governing classes become deeply divided during a period with 1714 as one of its turning points; Thompson seems to contend, however, that the excluded fragment offered an ideology of paternal protection in opposition to the governing fragment's techniques of patronage and direct control.[74] Both these contentions operate by representing country and Commonwealth criticisms of the Whig order as the ideological tools of a Tory gentry, and by minimizing that duality of Tory and Old

[72] As is made clear at various points in R. S. Neale, *Class in English History* (Oxford, 1981).

[73] Kramnick, *Bolingbroke and His Circle;* "Religion and Radicalism: English Political Theory in the Age of Revolution," *Political Theory* V, 4 (1977), pp. 503–34, and "Republican Revisionism Revisited," *American Historical Review* LXXXVII, 3 (1982), pp. 629–64. Despite some kind words in the first footnote of the latter article, I consider the alliterative incantation that forms its title a clear indication that an orthodoxy is about to be reestablished; the word "revisionism" is synonymous with heresy. Joyce O. Appleby likewise tends to regard any diversion of emphasis from liberal capitalism as deconstructive of both English and American history; see her "What is still American in the Political Philosophy of Thomas Jefferson?" *William and Mary Quarterly*, 3d ser., XXXIX, 2 (1982), pp. 287–309. It was not and is not my intention to furnish or to demolish answers to that question.

[74] E. P. Thompson, "Eighteenth-Century English Society: Class Struggle without Class?" *Social History* III, 2 (1978), pp. 133–65.

Whig versions of the same argument around which this essay is being built.

Meanwhile a heavy blow at the nostalgia thesis, and to some extent at the oligarchy thesis on which it rests, has been struck in the recent work of Eveline Cruickshanks, Linda Colley, and J. C. D. Clark.[75] These authors contend that the Tory party did not decline and disappear by rapid stages after 1714, but remained a stubborn, active, and surprisingly radical political alternative until some time after 1745. Though they are not uniformly in agreement, they take seriously in varying degrees the contention that the Tories of these decades were actually, or in a high state of potentiality, Jacobite, or alternatively that the condition of politics was such that no statesman could afford to act as if Jacobitism were anything but a serious threat. Dr. Clark, the most methodologically polemical of these three scholars, further offers to carry on a version of the Namier thesis — he is critical of Namier, but for not being Namierite enough — that insists, first, that eighteenth-century politics were oligarchic, at least in the sense that the game of high politics is played according to rules intelligible only to those playing it; and second, that in the politics of oligarchy — indeed in all politics insofar as they are high politics — ideology and the rhetoric of issue, principle, and abuse have little or no place. A consequence for his argument is that though he indicates some scorn for the concept of Whig oligarchy, this scorn is reserved for those — as they might be G. O. Trevelyan or E. P. Thompson — who employ the term as one of condemnation and identify oligarchy with corruption.[76] He insists *à l'outrance* on the oligarchic character of politics and merely defers the advent of oligarchy without party from the years after 1714 to those after 1745, a move of greater narrative than interpretative importance (Clark usefully insists on the superiority of narrative over interpretation).[77] The return of Tories and Jacobites to center stage, supposedly the principal modification of the accounts of history given by Namier and Plumb, thus tends paradoxically to reinforce these historians' accounts of what eighteenth-century politics were like as a structure.

Clark lays great emphasis on the point that the players in the game of high politics are seldom much activated by their perceptions of the general issues implicit in the game's existence, least of all by the issues apparent to those who are critical of the existence of high politics or of high politics in their existing form. To the extent to which the players constitute an effective oligarchy, they can afford to ignore ideological issues, especially those used to question whether oligarchy should exist at all; if the issues, having been articulated, are admitted to a role in the game, they are admitted only by the action of one or more of the

---

[75] Eveline Cruickshanks, *Political Untouchables: The Tories and the '45* (London, 1979); Linda Colley, *In Defiance of Oligarchy: The Tory Party, 1714–60* (Cambridge, 1982); J. C. D. Clark, *The Dynamics of Change: The Crisis of the 1750s and English Party* (Cambridge, 1982).

[76] Clark, *Dynamics of Change*, p. 458, n.1.   [77] Ibid., pp. 18–19.

players, themselves motivated by their playing of the game. When issues and ideology appear in eighteenth-century politics, they tend to acquire a local, tactical, and oligarchic significance; some oligarch allows them to be heard, for purposes of his own. We should study this kind of perlocutionary force, rather than the ideological implications of the generalized utterances we hear.

To the extent to which this is true − and it must be true to a high degree if the term "oligarchy" is to be appropriate − two consequences follow. We must beware of supposing that the actors in high politics were motivated by the things they said, and we must beware of supposing that the categories of ideological rhetoric necessarily furnish either reliable description or reliable evaluation of the way the institution of high politics worked. The historian of ideology, however, is not necessarily making either of these suppositions, though there is a convention of taking it for granted that he is. Clark stresses that the game was extraordinarily hard for the players to describe, even to one another − in the words of John Nance Garner, "politics is funny" − and that therefore the language of the spectators was bound to be inadequate as a description of the game. He quotes Dodington[78] on the difference between bystanders, who can see only the backs of the cards, and players, who can see the markings. But those excluded from a game in which they are being governed are talking not merely about how the game is being played, but also about the fact that they are being excluded from it;[79] the fact that their awareness of the former is false does not mean that they have not something to say about the latter, or that what they have to say (even if false) is not an effective way of acting on their exclusion. Clark is not absolutist, any more than were the politicians he studies (though it seems only a matter of time before some genius informs us that absolute monarchy reached its height in England during the reign of George II). He does not think that the language world of high politics was altogether hermetic and unaccountable; it was a shibboleth with the men of letters they read that the ultimate foundation of government was in opinion. He very rightly emphasizes that outside the closed circle of high politics, there were social areas in which people were intensely aware of what might be going on within the circle and employed, in the attempt to characterize it, language and terminology in many ways drawn from the game itself; nor does Clark altogether preclude the possibility that this language might in turn counterpenetrate the circle and be employed within it. He quotes from

[78] Ibid., p. 11.
[79] "The minds of leading Whigs," says Clark (ibid., p. 4), "were dominated not by a canon of Whig doctrine drawn from the great seventeenth-century tradition − Harrington, Tyrrell, Moyle, Trenchard, Toland, Sidney and the rest − but by the practical details and daily techniques of their trades." The whole point of post-Robbins writing has been that this is true. The "canon of doctrine" was used by discontented Whigs to indict leading Whigs and the practice of their "trades" − and occasionally by leading Whigs to embarrass one another. Dr. Clark denies what has not been significantly affirmed.

governing-class sources well aware that there was such a thing as popular opinion and another such thing as press agitation, and although he shows that the rulers looked on both as irrelevant and offensive – imprudent and unnecessary corporate venalities – except insofar as they could be created and managed (as they often were) by high politicians, he displays his sources' awareness that they might not always be able to manage them.[80] This is why eighteenth-century fears of revolution regularly took a Catilinarian form; some member of the inner circle might betray his class. In the end, as we shall see, Catiline was a paper tiger; something else happened. But the criticism of oligarchy is not to be studied as a description of oligarchy but rather as one of its products, one furthermore that oligarchy does not always succeed in absorbing and that may in the long run have something to do with how oligarchy is modified. At this point narrative recedes and interpretation must step forward.

There is a rhetoric by whose means Outs – who are insiders – become Ins; there is a rhetoric that outsiders use to comment on insiders and on how the latter keep them out. In Hanoverian England these rhetorics not infrequently coincided, but even when it is necessary to distinguish between them – as Clark wishes to emphasize – the rhetoric of outsiders is worth studying as part of their political culture, whether or not it is the speech of men in power. In that society we note a rhetoric used by Tory oppositions, highly coincident as regards content with a rhetoric, often Old Whig in derivation and audience, that may have given voice to the discontent of urban populations diminished in importance by the Septennial Act. We encounter yet again the problem that Tory language, which ought to have been and often was High Church and Jacobite, ought not to have been but often was radical and republican, Commonwealth as well as country. There are Jacobite manifestos of 1745 that sound not unlike Monmouth's manifestos of 1685.[81] Indeed, Linda Colley, in a lecture published independently of her book, has contended that the story of "English radicalism before Wilkes" is to be found in the continuity of Toryism between 1714 and 1760.[82] But it is an essential part of the argument that this Toryism was if anything more urban than rural, that without ceasing to ascribe discontent to elements of the country gentry it gave a voice to those city and borough populations who found that the great financiers and the parliamentary oligarchs were depriving them of power.

---

[80] Clark, ibid., pp. 3–4, 12–15. See in particular p. 12, where a pamphleteer writes, "It is the controversy itself which is the SIN."

[81] F. J. McLynn, "Issues and Motives in the Jacobite Rising of 1745," *The Eighteenth Century: Theory and Interpretation* XXIII, 2 (1982), pp. 97–133. Mr. McLynn's facts may be studied to advantage by those who do not accept his conclusions.

[82] Linda Colley, "Eighteenth-Century English Radicalism before Wilkes," *Transactions of the Royal Historical Society*, 5th ser., 31 (1981), pp. 1–20. See also Robert M. Zaller, "The Continuity of British Radicalism in the Seventeenth and Eighteenth Centuries," *Eighteenth-Century Life* VI, 2–3 (1981), pp. 17–38.

Marie Peters has reminded us how much of the basis of William Pitt's London popularity was Tory and how many of these Tories joined in opposition with such West Indian plantation owners as the Beckford brothers and Sir John Phillips;[83] anything less nostalgic, hierarchic, or paternalist than a West India London alderman of the 1750s would be hard indeed to imagine. Marxists of the simpler kind will at this point toss their usual double-headed penny and proclaim that insofar as Tory rhetoric spoke for the country opposition it was nostalgic (so they were right after all), and insofar as it spoke for the urban opposition it was bourgeois (so they were right after all). The difficulty about this move is that it does not tell us why the same rhetoric served to articulate opposite systems of values, and this cannot be done by appealing to the common sophism that it does not matter what people say because the Marxist knows what they mean. Those of us who believe not only that people's language articulates their experience, but also that it has something to tell us about what that experience was, will have to resume our researches. Meanwhile it is clear that if a country-Commonwealth language could articulate urban discontents, there was less need to wait for a Lockean individualist language in which to do it; what role a Lockean language might play remains to be seen. It is also clear that if discontented groups in country and borough society chose to employ republican, classical, and nostalgic (meaning past-oriented) language in attacking an oligarchy of great landowners and great investors, a modernist, commercial, and polite language might be employed (as we have begun to see it was) in defense of the Whig aristocratic order. The perception goes with another, well known to Marx himself: that great landowners were often highly effective capitalist investors. We can see therefore that if there was "bourgeois" criticism of the Whig aristocracy, it might well include criticism of their capitalist behavior; but we cannot add that defense of the aristocracy was equally "bourgeois" without emptying the word of all useful meaning (if it has any). Our investigation must at this point turn once more to the relations of "ancient" to "modern" in mid-century polemic, and in particular to the character of Whig modernism.

(iv)

Bolingbroke and the Craftsman had argued in defense of an ancient constitution, which had ensured the independence of legislative from executive and to which a return must be made to protect the legislative and those whom it represented from reduction to a corrupting dependence. The argument could be made to support a demand for return to more frequent parliaments, and it looked back to a neo-Harringtonian past of proprietors armed and assembling to assert their

---

[83] Marie C. Peters, *Pitt and Popularity: The Patriot Minister and London Opinion during the Seven Years' War* (Oxford, 1980).

liberty. In reply, Walpole's defenders had argued that liberty was not ancient but modern, and that the past was feudal, not free. It followed that the constitution contained no principles to which return could be made and that its spirit was either pragmatic and empirical, or modern and progressive.[84] The latter argument had been anticipated by Defoe with his contention that liberty appeared only as proprietors emerged from feudal subordination and acquired through trade control over the movement of their own goods; at this point Defoe could have appealed to Locke, though there seems to be little evidence that he did. But as the oligarchy acquired control of the executive and the power to exercise a parliamentary sovereignty of which the Septennial Act was a signal expression, it appropriated the interpretation of history that the Charles II Tory Brady had once used to affirm royal sovereignty in the face of Parliament, and employed it to nullify the arguments with which the Queen Anne Tory Bolingbroke was challenging parliamentary politics in the name of the independent proprietorship – in city, one wants to add, as well as country. The defense of oligarchy and sovereignty went hand in hand with that of commercial society.

A problem that assumed prominence as part of the Walpolean polemic and counterpolemic was that of the relation between political regimes and the arts. Walpole was "Bob, the poets' foe"; nearly all the great writers of the age were his enemies,[85] and part of their extraordinarily obsessive presentation of him as a medley of clown and tyrant, Sejanus and Tiberius, was the contention that as virtue became corrupt under his control of politics, the arts lost integrity and language itself lost meaning. There is complexity and paradox here. On the one hand the qualities that the arts were thought in danger of losing were the "modern" virtues of clarity, order, and good taste; on the other, the danger stemmed from an alleged loss of the "ancient" and Roman virtues of political independence, liberty, and self-mastery. We find reason to suppose that the apocalyptic triumph of nonsense over language at the end of Pope's *Dunciad* has something to do with a society dominated by speculators in paper promises to repay which will never be made good before the end of time; if property is the foundation of personality, unreal property (in which nothing is owned except meaningless words) makes personalities unreal and their words meaningless. *Pape Satan, pape Satan aleppe!* Against this the image presented is that of Roman order, although the imagery stresses retirement from the corrupt city more than activity in a city whose virtue is to be restored.

---

[84] This point has been adequately dealt with by Kramnick, Dickinson, Zaller, and other writers cited.

[85] Bertrand A. Goldgar, *Walpole and the Wits: The Relation of Politics to Literature 1722–1742* (Lincoln, Nebr., 1976); Maynard P. Mack's, *The Garden and the City: Retirement and Politics in the Later Poetry of Pope* (Toronto, 1969) is the established interpretation of Pope's perception of literature as opposition. The possibility that Pope's political writing had a positively Jacobite character is advanced by Howard Erskine-Hill, "Alexander Pope: The Political Poet in his Time," *Eighteenth-Century Studies* XV, 2 (1981–2), pp. 123–48.

Yet the corruption of virtue was a concept carrying strong agrarian, anticommercial, and republican implications, and if we return, as recent Pope scholarship has been doing, to the hypothesis of a strong crypto-Jacobite component in the polemic against Walpole, the dualities of eighteenth-century opposition are once more made manifest. Furthermore, the proposition that the arts were being corrupted and destroyed in a speculative Whig society was hard to reconcile with the thesis, put forward by Fletcher and adopted by Defoe in 1698, that the growth of the arts was part of the growth of commercial society, and partook of both its benignant and its malignant characteristics. To say, as David Hume did in an early essay, that under Walpole "trade had flourished, liberty declined, and learning gone to ruin"[86] was to beg the question, posed by Hume and other Scots in later writings, whether trade and learning did not flourish together, thus rendering the nature of liberty problematic. We have so far considered politeness, and consequently the arts, as features of an Addisonian Whig ideology; it was a paradox characteristically Humean that "the first polite prose we have was written by a man who is still alive (N.: Dr. Swift)."[87] The paradox for which Swift stood, however, was that in attacking Walpole polite letters might be attacking the forces that had cultivated them.

There was a classical republican and humanist reply to the polite contention: that the arts, being of the nature of rhetoric, could flourish only under conditions of public liberty and must decline under tyranny or corruption. Tacitus had always been an authoritative source for this argument, and Thomas Gordon's translation of Tacitus, which won him some European reputation, seems to have been employed by d'Alembert in his examination of the condition of letters in the ancien régime.[88] It is here that we encounter the problem of Augustanism. Voltaire in the *Siècle de Louis XIV* had argued what would certainly be a "modern" thesis if read in Whig conditions, namely, that the great periods in the history of the arts had all occurred under strong manipulative rulers – Pericles, Augustus, the Medici, Louis himself – because they required peace, prosperity, and patronage and must be bought at the price of authority. In calling Hanoverian England "Augustan" we implicitly accept Voltaire's thesis, acquainted though he was with Bolingbroke and Pope; we imply that the arts flourished under Whig oligarchy and ignore the passionate asseverations of the wits that Walpole brought

---

[86] Hume, "The Character of Sir Robert Walpole," *Philosophical Works*, ed. T. H. Green and T. H. Grose (London, 1882), vol. IV, p. 396. This essay was subsequently withdrawn.

[87] Hume, "Of Civil Liberty," *Philosophical Works*, ed. Green and Grose (1875 edition), vol. III, p. 159.

[88] Orest A. Ranum, "D'Alembert, Tacitus and the Political Sociology of Despotism," *Transactions of the Fifth International Congress on the Enlightenment* (Oxford, 1980), sec. V, pp. 547–58. For an enlightened nobleman who ranked Gordon with Algernon Sidney, see Franco Venturi, "Le Adventure del Generale Henry Lloyd," *Rivista Storica Italiana* XCI, 2–3 (1979), pp. 369–433, esp. p. 429.

them to the point of death. Howard Weinbrot has found that in the England we call "Augustan" the image formed of Augustus himself is preponderantly negative and Tacitean; he is less the friend of Maecenas than the predecessor of Tiberius (and by implication of Walpole). Virgil himself does not escape blame, or the imputation of decadence.[89]

Nevertheless, Tacitus and Voltaire between them posed an awkward problem in the politics of culture under a commercial oligarchy. If the arts did not decline, did it follow that they could only flourish, in conditions restrictive of liberty and virtue? Rousseau's answer we know; it lies at the end of nearly every avenue opened by this question. More immediately, the first step in seeking a way out of the dilemma must be to find means of asserting that commerce and culture, prosperity, politeness, and the progress of the arts, themselves constituted modes of liberty and virtue that remained valid even under a *governo stretto*. Even republican theory might be enlisted in this enterprise; since the wars of the Maritime Powers with France, Englishmen had been acquainted with the idea, which Dutch writers had expressed before them, that the first republics had been trading cities asserting the freedom of the seas against Cretan thalassocracies and Persian empires.[90] Rhodes and Corinth might be set up instead of Sparta and Rome, and if the end result had been Athenian empire or Venetian oligarchy, Athens and Venice presented their own images of liberty. In mid-century Britain, however, the leading role in the identification of liberty with commercial culture was taken by Scots engaged, as we have seen, in the search for modes of freedom and virtue that could grow in the space left by a forsaken political autonomy. We encounter here forms of Whiggism not exclusively shaped by confrontation with the Tory-republican mixture that constituted opposition ideology in England.

Walpole was pulled down by forces combining country discontents and urban bellicosity, but the years succeeding his fall witnessed no revival of patriot virtue, merely the unencouraging rise of the Pelhams. The great age of literary satire seemed to have ended, and if there is a period of English history without significant ideological dispute it may have been the late 1740s and early 1750s.[91] In Scotland, however, the decade was punctuated by a mainly Highland Jacobite rebellion and a renewed effort to impose economic modernization on the moun-

---

[89] Howard K. Weinbrot, *Augustus Caesar in Augustan England: The Decline of a Classical Norm* (Princeton, N.J., 1978).

[90] Charles Davenant was an English expositor of this view; Pocock, *The Machiavellian Moment*, pp. 437–8. For the Dutch, see E. O. G. Haitsma Mulier, *The Myth of Venice and Dutch Republican Thought in the Seventeenth Century* (Assen, 1980). It is tenable – to say no more – that the British nations were idiosyncratic in owning a rhetoric both republican and agrarian. See Pocock, "The Problem of Political Thought in the Eighteenth Century: Patriotism and Politeness," with comment by E. O. G. Haitsma Mulier and E. H. Kossman, *Theoretische Geschiedenis* IX, 1 (1982), pp. 3–36.

[91] See, however, Maurice Goldsmith, "Faction Detected: Ideological Consequences of Robert Walpole's Decline and Fall," *History* LXIV, 1 (1979), pp. 1–19.

tains: an episode that served to intensify awareness of the historically contingent character of the Scottish union with England and of commercial society in general. Southward-facing Scots, like David Hume and Tobias Smollett, were well able to see the connection with the debates that had gone on in England since 1698, and the striking growth in Scottish literature occurring between the Jacobite rising in 1745 and the American Revolution in 1776 includes a reevaluation of English history and the formation of a distinctively Scottish way of viewing the history of society in general.

In the essays he began to write following the failure of his first philosophical treatise, Hume revised his earlier censures of Walpole and began to argue that a polite liberty – the freedom of a man to enjoy his property and his intellect – might flourish under commercial conditions, not merely in a Whig parliamentary oligarchy but even in a Bourbon absolute monarchy.[92] Liberty in this sense was intimately connected with the authority whose protection it required, but, for reasons that may be extended into the philosophical, Hume did not suppose the relation to be a simple one. In his essays on the English, which was now the British, constitution he stressed its ultimate instability. The balance of independent powers, of which it had been supposed to consist since the *Answer to the Nineteen Propositions*, might end in a republic or even an anarchy, and the parliamentary "influence of the crown," by which the edifice was supposedly held together, might end in an absolute monarchy or even in a despotism.[93] It is significant that Hume, in general so unmistakably a defender of the Whig commercial aristocracy, expressed unmistakably Tory fears of the power of public credit, which by rendering both real and mobile property valueless might destroy the natural aristocracy of land-inheriting families.[94] In his writings on the social character of religion, he showed superstition and enthusiasm, mythopoeic polytheism and philosophic monotheism, as both supporting and subverting the severed principles of authority and liberty.[95] The long polemic against enthusiasm was not at an end, and Hume represents the conservative character of enlightenment in Protestant countries; he reminds us at the same time that the inner dynamics of Protestantism were not yet worked out.

Hume held that commerce and enlightenment were producing a society preferable to anything in antiquity; he also held that the Whig regime in Britain was unstable for reasons partly historical and partly rooted in the constitution of society itself. His modernism therefore possessed a double face. He believed that the reigning order was progressive but at the same time that it was fragile. His

---

[92] Forbes, *Hume's Philosophical Politics;* and James Moore, "Hume's Political Science and the Classical Republican Tradition," *Canadian Journal of Political Science* X, 4 (1977), pp. 809–39.

[93] Hume, *Essays,* "Whether the British Government inclines more to Absolute Monarchy or to a Republic."

[94] Hume, "Of Public Credit."

[95] Hume, "Of Superstition and Enthusiasm," "The Natural History of Religion."

History of England, which began to appear in 1754, is the greatest of a series of writings that express impatience with any complacent synthesis that imputes to the Whig order a comprehensiveness it does not possess. He included Locke with Rapin, Hoadly and Sidney, among those authors whose compositions he described as "most despicable,"[96] though some strange simplifications here have suggested that it was a Scottish rather than an English Lockeanism he had in mind. But he held in equal contempt the writings of Whig historians such as Rapin de Thoyras,[97] and there is a sense in which the *History of England* carries on the contention of Walpole's defenders that liberty in England is little older than 1688.

Hume goes back to Harrington and even more to Brady in arguing that the government of England was feudal under the Normans, Angevins, and Plantagenets;[98] the doctrine of an ancient constitution is therefore untenable – or rather, he says in a footnote he must have enjoyed writing, at least three ancient constitutions can be made out in the English past.[99] Subsequently, what he calls "a revolution in manners," and describes, as do Fletcher and Defoe, in terms of the growth of enlightenment and trade,[100] brought about the Protestant Reformation, a period of almost Turkish despotism under the later Tudors, an interlude of confusion about the true distribution of authority and power, a decade of enthusiasm and hypocrisy in the 1650s, and finally the establishment of a relatively ordered liberty in 1688. Beyond that point Hume declined to go; the history of England since the Revolution was left to Tobias Smollett, whose Tory and radical ideas acquired in London led him to a greater neo-Harringtonian stress on corruption and the monied interest than Hume would have thought right to endorse.

Such is what we have learned from Duncan Forbes to call Hume's "sceptical Whiggism" (the phrase is ultimately Hume's own) and oppose to the "vulgar Whiggism" that confused Bourbon absolutism with despotism and upheld belief in an ancient constitution. But there are two kinds of "vulgar Whiggism." There is the ancient constitutionalism of the neo-Harringtonians – Old Whig with the Commonwealthmen and their republican canon, Queen Anne Tory with Bolingbroke and the *Craftsman* – who located in the past those principles from which ministers, standing armies, and the monied interest had brought the constitution to degeneration. The modernism of Walpole's defenders had been designed against this thesis, and Hume without doubt shared many of their intentions. On the

---

[96] Hume, *History of England from the Invasion of Julius Caesar to the Revolution in 1688* (new edition in 6 vols.; London, 1762), vol. VI, p. 443. A footnote identifying Locke and other authors aimed at was deleted from this edition.

[97] J. Y. T. Greig, ed., *The Letters of David Hume*, 2 vols. (Oxford, 1932), vol. I, p. 258.

[98] Victor C. Wexler, *David Hume and the History of England* (Philadelphia, 1980).

[99] Hume, *History of England*, vol. IV, p. 314n.

[100] *History of England*, vol. IV, p. 336; also III, pp. 63–7, 121–2; V, p. 68.

other hand, and far more central to the concerns of regime Whiggism, there is the ancient constitutionalism of the "Whig interpretation of history," which defended the parliamentary leaders of 1604–42 by endorsing their case for the antiquity of law and Parliament. Hume's bad reputation in English historiography for the next hundred years, until and including the time of Macaulay, arose from his attack on this way of interpreting the seventeenth century. Following a lead originally given by Harrington, he saw the reign of Charles I as a period in which historical change had rendered the dualisms of medieval government – Harrington's "wrestling ground between king and nobility," Hume's "absolute monarchy under which the people had many privileges"[101] – finally and decisively unworkable, so that its problems could no longer be solved by the traditional remedies. The more Hume reflected on this situation, the more he became persuaded that the king enjoyed just as good a case as the parliamentary leadership – given that neither had a very good case in that age of confusion – and his offense in Whig eyes was that he argued for king against Parliament and slighted the ancient constitution in so doing. Times had changed since the *Craftsman* controversy and the fall of Walpole. In the 1730s and even the 1740s oligarchy and ministerial rule could be defended by asserting the modernity of parliamentary freedom against the Tory and republican appeal to the ancient constitution. In the 1760s, when the reaction to Hume's *History* was at its height, something had happened to make defenders of a system no older than 1714 fall back on the appeal to antiquity and the "Whig interpretation of history." We shall have to consider what that was, as well as the curious transformation of terminology that was to lead to Hume's being branded a Tory. Meanwhile, we have to observe that the argument of modernity was far from being exhausted or given up.

From "sceptical" we turn with Forbes to "scientific Whiggism." During the two following decades Hume's friends and associates in Edinburgh and Glasgow, William Robertson, Adam Ferguson, Adam Smith, and John Millar – the present writer would add Edward Gibbon, as a star revolving in an intersecting orbit – produced the extraordinary series of works that together constitute their authors as "the Scottish historical school." These present a theory of history that ranges across the disciplines from moral philosophy to political economy, and arise from concerns transcending the ideological conflict between the regime Whigs and their critics; yet, as Forbes's nomenclature reminds us, they never cease to be illuminated by that conflict. Paying little regard to the ancient constitution, with which as Scotsmen they felt no great concern, they situated the transition from barbaric and feudal to commercial and polite society in the context of the four-stage scheme of history, in which a progressive division and specialization of labor had refined the passions, polished the manners, and multiplied the interactions

---

[101] Harrington, *Political Works*, p. 196; Hume, *History of England*, vol. V, pp. 110n.–112.

of human beings of both sexes, and in so doing had rendered them capable of the production and distribution of wealth. From the perspective adopted in this essay, their argument may be seen as an immense elaboration of the insight first reached in 1698: that the individual might (with Defoe) or might not (with Fletcher) be justified in abandoning the search for liberty in self-sufficiency in favor of one for liberty in increasing sociability and exchange; the weight of Scottish argument is, of course, almost wholly on the side taken by Defoe. Yet the claims of the individual self and its military and civic autonomy continued to be heard; there were controversies over the militia and the authenticity of Ossian; and perhaps the most alienated Scottish voice of the mid-century comes from London, where Smollett's radical Tory concern with corruption led him to equate civilization with corruption but freedom with savagery. Dumbarton he proposed as the point where Britons fleeing from Roman despotism had wisely but precariously stopped short of Gaelic barbarism.[102] In Edinburgh and Glasgow they proposed to keep moving along the lines of civilization, yet were never unaware of the dangers of doing so. Ferguson, Smith, and Millar all knew there could be such a thing as overspecialization. The mobilization of commerce and politeness in support of Whiggism and the union had nevertheless reached a state of imaginative completeness.

III.   From the Seven Years' War to the Constitution of the United States

(i)

We now return to the politics of Westminster, London, and England as they took shape in and from the late 1750s. The ensuing period, however one dates it, was one of dislocation and fragmentation, which has been subjected to a fragmenting historical analysis; to say anything suggestive of a pattern of development is dangerous. Nevertheless, it is possible to construct a scenario in which the polemic against the oligarchic regime remained in many ways the same, while displaying some major regroupings of opinion and beginning to undergo some deep-seated change. The elder Pitt's wartime ministry involved association between, on the one hand, the Pelham and Grenville-Temple connections among the great Whig families and, on the other, a faction of London aldermen, with support among the liverymen and in the streets among the "mobile," headed by William Beckford and others identifiable as urban Tories. In his role as opposition orator, Pitt had employed the usual patriot rhetoric aimed at independent

---

[102] The notion of Dumbarton as marking the frontier between Belgic or Cymric agriculture and Pictish or Gaelic pasturage may also be found in Thomas Carte, *A General History of England*, 3 vols. (London, 1747), vol. I, pp. 130, 175.

country gentlemen, supposed to waver in matters of foreign policy between blue-water strategies and outright avoidance of conflict, in either case inspired by distaste for continental wars that intensified the national debt and the Hanoverian connection. Since Pitt's London supporters had West and East Indian associations, they could be ardent supporters of war outside Europe, in America and India as well as at sea; the word "patriot" thus took on its mid-century (or post-Jacobite) meaning, combining the notion of a noisy blue-water bellicosity with the image of a quasi-republican supporter of his country against his king, or at least his king's ministers. It is not to assert that a republican revolution was ever likely in England to say that "patriots" often employed revolutionary and even republican language. The Beckfords began their public career as urban Tories, but it is in their journal the *Monitor* that hints have been found, as early as the fifties, of the notion of appealing to the nation, the people, and even a national convention against a corrupt and minister-dominated parliament.[103] By the time he died as Lord Mayor in 1771, William Beckford was using Commonwealth language and threatening the king with a radical evocation of 1688, if not 1641 or 1649, while the language of the Sawbridges was as startling in its way as the actions of the Wilkites. Tory and republican appear in this projection as remaining brothers under the skin; nevertheless, it is from the time of Pitt the Elder that the word "Tory" begins losing the meanings it had borne since the time of Bolingbroke and taking on new significances.

Perceptions, no doubt exaggerated or distorted, of the intervention in politics of the new king George III and his adviser Lord Bute had much to do with initiating these changes. It has many times been shown that the king was acting within the normal conventions of politics and had no thought of acting otherwise, but the fact remains that he was denounced, and that language was available to denounce him, for acting outside Whig rules.[104] That Bute was a Stuart made it possible to impute to him designs of restoring Stuart ideals of kingship, while the circumstance that George III was apparently using the authority and influence of the crown to break up constraints that Whigs imposed on him made it possible to see him, and believe that he saw himself, as a "patriot king" in the sense in which Bolingbroke had adumbrated that deeply paradoxical term. Here we have a first move toward the reunion of the seventeenth- and eighteenth-century connotations of "Tory." Once the "independence of the crown," a Bolingbrokean term, could be linked with the "prerogatives of the crown" fought for by the pre-1688 Stuarts, Charles II Tories and George II Tories could be seen as

---

[103] Marie C. Peters, "The *Monitor* on the English Constitution, 1755–65; New Light on the Ideological origins of English Radicalism," *English Historical Review* LXXXVI, 341 (1971), pp. 706–27. See also Nicholas Rogers, "Resistance to Oligarchy: The City Opposition to Walpole and his Successors, 1724–47," in *London in the Age of Reform*, ed. John Stevenson (Oxford: 1977).

[104] For the first half of this sentence see Richard Pares, *George III and the Politicians* (Oxford, 1953); for the second, Herbert Butterfield, *George III and the Historians* (London, 1957).

one and the same, and aristocratic politicians resentful of George III's policies could make believe they were fighting for the good old cause for which Hampden had died on the field and Sidney on the scaffold.[105] A new chapter, with new heroes and villains, could now be written in the Whig interpretation of history, but Walpolean modernism would have to be abandoned and Humean skepticism denounced. Scientific Whigs were liable to find themselves, without much repugnance, supporters of George III's ministries. It is testimony both to the intellectual power of Hume's *History*, and to the changing ideological climate in which it appeared, that almost a century later it still seemed to Macaulay his principal adversary and competitor.

There were deeper ambivalences still. The regime that had prevailed since the Septennial Act was above all a regime of influence and patronage. The extent to which patronage was concentrated in a few hands, and the efficacy of patronage whoever exercised it, may easily be exaggerated;[106] yet the regime was widely perceived as one in which "the influence of the crown" was exercised concurrently with the not dissimilar "influence" exercised by Whig magnates, with the result that those currently occupying the king's councils could be denounced as selfish "ministers," and those currently out of place denounced as a selfish "faction," each seeking to add the crown's influence to their own. This was the small change of political rhetoric, even when it was not far from the truth; but when George III displaced powerful groups of Whig politicians, they not only denounced him or his advisers for using his influence against them but contrived, sometimes by affecting to regard him as a patriot king in the making, to accuse him of designing a real change in the structure of politics. They said that the influence of the crown was being used to destroy the independent capacity of the aristocracy to form associations — by the use of patronage, party association, popularity, or any combination of them — that could then recommend themselves to the royal councils. For many years this complaint was regularly urged in Whig rhetoric and literature. Burke's *Thoughts on the Present Discontents* (1770) is a famous example, and leading Whigs now formed and long retained the belief that the use being made of royal influence was "Tory."[107] They had something Bolingbrokean in mind. The influence of the crown, which Bolingbroke had imagined capable of restoring the independence of Parliament, was in their vision being employed to

---

[105] This finds a late echo in Macaulay's description of the Rockingham Whigs as "worthy to have charged at the side of Hampden at Chalgrove, or to have exchanged the last embrace with Russell on the scaffold in Lincoln's Inn Fields." Macaulay, "The Earl of Chatham," *Critical and Historical Essays,* 3 vols. (Boston, 1901), vol. III, p. 654.

[106] J. B. Owen, "Political Patronage in Eighteenth-Century England," in *The Triumph of Culture,* ed. P. Fritz and D. Williams (Toronto, 1972); Clark, *Dynamics of Change,* p. 15.

[107] F. O'Gorman, *The Whig Party and the French Revolution* (London and New York, 1967) has some useful quotations from Portland, Fitzwilliam, and Lady Rockingham in the years 1793–4 (pp. 198–9, 211).

break up the independent associations of the aristocracy and their followings and subject Parliament to royal control. Burke shared this belief in an aristocracy natural because independent, and if there is anything new about the theory of party expressed in *Thoughts on the Present Discontents,* it is Burke's belief that aristocratic associations are more than combinations of patrons and clients.[108] Natural aristocracy may prefer *governo largo* to *governo stretto;* to this extent the Septennial oligarchy was showing signs of loosening up.

The Whig aristocracy, against whose oligarchy all patriot rhetoric had been directed, were now in a position to put themselves forward – or a faction among them identifying themselves with the whole could put them forward – as the true patriots or natural leaders of a free society, while stigmatizing the patronage of the state as a design to restore the excessive powers of the seventeenth-century crown. This enabled them to identify new (if fictitious) "Tories" with old, and to go (sometimes consciously) in search of the rhetoric of the First Whigs, with which Shaftesbury in 1675 had tried to turn the House of Lords against the ministerial corruption he attributed to Danby. The language of Whig opposition turned back toward the ancient constitution and republican virtue – those linked if disparate vocabularies – and there could appear noblemen expressing radical, republican, and even democratic ideals, the counterparts in fact of Milord Stanhope in Mably[109] and Milord Bomston in Rousseau. Some of these called for reforms in the system of representation, and even for manhood suffrage; as we shall see, there were followings to be gained by doing so. But no Whig aristocrat out of office would find it easy to break with the methods of rule by patronage and high politics exercised since the Septennial Act, or with the system of public credit that was twenty years older. They might deplore, and even propose to reform, the probably mythical enlargement of royal patronage under George III or the much more real enlargement of the national debt by the Seven Years' War, but they must go on administering these systems whenever they might come back into office. We may say, then, that the game of politics had not changed very much, but we must also say that the rhetoric employed in the game envisaged increasingly significant alterations in its rules.

(*ii*)

Like the language employed in parliamentary opposition, from which it cannot altogether be separated, the language of radical criticism of the regime began to

[108] See John Brewer, "Rockingham, Burke and Whig Political Argument," *The Historical Journal* XVIII, 1 (1975), pp. 188–201.
[109] "Stanhope" appears in Mably's *Des Droits et des Devoirs du Citoyen,* dated 1758 but published 1789. See Keith Michael Baker, "A Script for a French Revolution: The Political Consciousness of the Abbé Mably," *Eighteenth-Century Studies* XIV, 3 (1981), pp. 235–63.

change after 1760. The term "Tory," perhaps because it could now be applied to the policies of the crown, ceases being applied to the recurrent turbulence of London aldermen and their following, about the time when their perception of Pitt as a lost leader who had gone over to the oligarchy was producing a more vehement hostility to Whig aristocracy and even to aristocracy as such. Their rhetoric remained "patriot" in many ways, and it by no means shed all its Tory characteristics. The rabid anti-Scotticism of the *North Briton* had more to do with hatred of Hanoverians, especially when Scots and Hanoverians were both soldiers, than with hatred of Jacobites. But patriot radicalism was no less urban than Toryism had been before it, and as we pursue the explorations of popular politics conducted by John Brewer and others,[110] from the streets and clubs of London to those of provincial towns, we seem to be following the growth of a "public opinion," increasingly given to new forms of "association," which it is hard not to consider as the self-assertive voice of those borough populations whose political weight had been reduced since the not very distant time when the oligarchy had been established. Not only urban Toryism, but the "True," "Old," "Independent" Whiggisms of the Commonwealth tradition have by now been identified as semi-interchangeable modes of protest, dating from the late seventeenth century, against the increasing consolidation of an oligarchic Whig regime. It comes as no surprise, then, that the Exclusionist, country, and Commonwealth program of "more frequent," annual, or triennial parliaments began again (if it had ever ceased) to be the theme of polemic against the regime, and remained a staple of radical demand until the days of the Chartists; or that the interregnum heroes of the canon put together by John Toland began yet again to be cited by such radical sages as Thomas Hollis, James Burgh, Catherine Sawbridge Macaulay, and at a later period, the young William Wordsworth, some of whom even display an awareness that there had once been such people as Agitators and Levellers.[111] The independent and often Dissenting borough populations were, it might seem, once again finding their Old Whig and Commonwealth voices. We are tempted to conclude that the Tory interlude in their history was over, but to make such an assertion brings us once more face to face with the problem of telling Tory and Commonwealth apart.

---

[110] John Brewer, *Party Ideology and Popular Politics at the Accession of George III* (Cambridge, 1976); "English Radicalism in the Age of George III," in *Three British Revolutions: 1641, 1688, 1776,* ed. J. G. A. Pocock (Princeton, N.J., 1980). For further bibliography, see Albert Goodwin, *The Friends of Liberty: The English Democratic Movement in the Age of the French Revolution* (Cambridge, Mass., 1979), p. 533–4, and Zaller, "Continuity of British Radicalism," cited n. 82. For every discovery that a crowd was "manipulated," there is a corresponding need to know what was in its members' minds that made them willing to be "manipulated"; it may and may not have been what the manipulators sought to put there.

[111] A study of the extent in this century of historical knowledge concerning the interregnum radicals would be worth having; ours is largely dependent on the Thomason and other collections, which became available only with the opening of the British Museum.

The radical voice of the 1770s further complicates matters by uttering propositions not usually to be found in the rhetoric of early Georgian opposition. It is at times militantly hostile to aristocratic control of politics and does not differentiate very much between Whig aristocrats in opposition to George III and Whig aristocrats in office under him. That monarch's actions preclude any lasting attempt to appeal to him as a "patriot king" and he is seen less as a counterweight to the aristocracy than as their partner in operating a repressive and corrupt parliamentary regime. The attack is directed against the aristocracy, not so much a class of landholding seigneurs as one of borough owners, borough patrons, and boroughmongers; there are complaints, however, that men of landed wealth should use the borough system to dominate the parliamentary representation of the men of movable wealth — or, when the appeal is being made to artisans, the men whose wealth is in their labor — inhabiting the towns. In conjunction, perhaps, with this tendency to regard the borough as a repressive device, there is rejection of any "idea" of a patriot king or patriot minister and an insistence that the only true patriots are the "people" themselves. A radical Lockeanism makes its appearance, and the authority of the *Second Treatise* is often, though not necessarily, cited in support of the view that since the "people" are originators of their own government, they may resume the power to alter that government, not merely (as Locke had emphasized) when it becomes repressive, but when it becomes corrupt, when it fails to give effect to their natural freedom, or more simply still whenever they find good reasons for doing so. This ultra-Lockean radicalism, entailing a democratic doctrine of permanent reform if not revolution, is to be found, occasionally but not uncharacteristically, at the leading edge of the republicanism that now took shape; it helps shift republican doctrine (in what measure remains to be determined) away from the polity of independent powers and toward the sovereignty of popular will.

At this point the voice of liberal-Marxist historians is heard loud and jubilant. Their principal concern is to affirm the autonomy in history of a kind of practice (in this case its ideology) called "bourgeois," and to present history whiggishly (in the Butterfieldian sense) as the unidirectional movement toward, and later past and away from, the ascendancy of this practice. To do so has become so dominant an enterprise that Marxist historians may be recognized by their incessant use of the term "bourgeois," non-Marxist (or "bourgeois") historians by their care to avoid it. The function of the word in question is to denote the presence and action of those whose wealth is movable and employed in controlling the labor of others; we may agree that it is very important indeed to have means of denoting their presence and describing their action, without agreeing that the word "bourgeois" necessarily denotes and describes them satisfactorily. The word has, however, acquired a mystical value and become a test of orthodoxy. In the present case, the assumptions used by the liberal-Marxist historians are that an opposition to something called "aristocracy," an emphasis on the individual's possession of rights and property that government exists to protect, and the adoption of a Lockean brand of populism justify them — when these phenomena occur in conjunction — in using the magic word "bourgeois." The latent assumptions are (1) that all the foregoing phenomena entail an acceptance of movable rather than real property as the basis of social and political reality, and (2) that the historical complex so constituted is and should be described as bourgeois, on grounds that seem to be more than merely conventional. How the word entered the Marxist lexicon and came to be used as it now is offers a problem of which little seems to be known and which will not be discussed here, though the present writer's sense that it has become a mystical term is strong enough to make him wish to avoid it. How far the English radicalism that took shape in the 1770s ought to be described as bourgeois in the conventional sense, and how this interpretation ought to be operated if at all, are problems that do need to be examined if a history of the "Whig" cluster of ideologies is to be adequately constructed.

The latest to write on these matters in the liberal-Marxist perspective is, predictably, Isaac Kramnick. In "Republican Revisionism Revisited" he sets out to aver that the radicalism of the 1770s was "bourgeois" in the previously mentioned senses, and therefore sharply distinct from the country, Tory, and Old Whig criticism of the Whig regime that had preceded it.[112] He pursues this aim (as we have seen) by the adoption of two strategies. One is the dismissal of all brands of neo-Harringtonian criticism as Tory, agrarian, ancient constitutionalist, "nostalgic," and reactionary; the other is the repetition, more incantatory and liturgical than anything else, with which he introduces the terms "bourgeois" and "middle class" into every sentence in which he characterizes the radicals of George III's reign. Concerning the first strategy, enough has surely been said to establish that it simply will not do. Early Georgian opposition was both Tory and Old Whig; Toryism itself was both rural and urban; Kramnick's attempt to reduce republican rhetoric to fox-hunting nostalgia is doomed from the start. What remains not fully explained is how an ideology stressing Roman warrior — civic values and the independence that came best from real property possessed the appeal it visibly had for town dwellers; but if we have not fully explained the fact, Kramnick does not help by denying its existence. The present writer has preferred the argument that since the target of criticism was the manipulation of credit and the forms of dependence and corruption it could bring, the tradesman operating on his own stock could seem to share in the independence of the yeoman landholder; John Brewer in a significant article has shown the ways in which such a tradesman might feel his independence threatened by the private or public behavior of the aristocratic managers of debt.[113] It did not

[112] See sources cited in n. 73, this chapter.   [113] "English Radicalism in the Age of George III."

follow that the tradesman must necessarily characterize himself as creditor in the "public" sense, or abandon a view of the world in which debtors and creditors appeared almost equally dangerous. So long as professional men, tradesmen, and artisans believed themselves to be inhabitants of a domestic economy, a universe of masters and servants in which independence was to be pursued and dependence avoided, a plebeian version of the Roman republican ideal would make some sense to them and the argument that it was predicated on an obsolete agrarian economy would benefit only their rulers. This does not mean that a democratic radicalism furnishing the individual with the politics of life in a world of exchange relationships would not ultimately appear. Possibly it did appear in middle-Georgian London, and certainly we should be on the alert for its appearance; but we will not be well equipped to detect it if we fetishize the term "bourgeois" and construct a naive and crude antithesis between republican and Lockean forms of radicalism.

This mistake was not often made by critics and theorists in the later eighteenth century. James Burgh, a writer of the 1770s studied by Robbins, Kramnick, and others,[114] was indeed one of the early English authors known to have used the term "bourgeoisie,"[115] but he used it of the lesser citizenry of Holland, and why he used a French word in denoting Dutch social categories is as puzzling as why Burke used the Dutch word "burghers" to denote the inhabitants of French towns – or who first used the word with reference to England. It was Burgh who complained that borough patronage subjected townsmen to great landed proprietors, but in order to increase the representation of great cities, he envisaged, like many after him, a reduction of borough and an increase of county representation.[116] There began at this time a lively historical debate (which has still to be studied) regarding the role of boroughs in English history.[117] Were they originally independent communes or instruments of royal and aristocratic patronage? If we are to see in electoral reforms such as Burgh proposed the emergence of the "bourgeoisie" as a nationally acting "class," we must observe that they were destroying the boroughs to do so. Dialectical rhetoric will doubtless inform us that they

---

[114] Robbins, *Eighteenth-Century Commonwealthman*, pp. 364–8; Carla Hay, *James Burgh: Spokesman for Reform in Hanoverian England* (Washington, D.C., 1979); Martha K. Zebrowski," One Cato Is Not Enough; or, How James Burgh Found Nature's Duty and Real Authority, and Secured the Dignity of Human Nature against All Manner of Public Abuse, Iniquitous Practice, Vice and Irreligion," doctoral dissertation, Columbia University, 1984. Burgh quoted as freely from the Tories Brady, Carte, and Bolingbroke as from interregnum sources, Locke, and the Commonwealthmen.

[115] James Burgh, *Political Disquisitions*, 3 vols., (London, 1771), vol. I, p. 71.

[116] Burgh, *Political Disquisitions*, vol. I, pp. 51–4, 75–7. See generally John Cannon, *Parliamentary Reform, 1640–1832* (Cambridge, 1972).

[117] T. H. B. Oldfield's *History of the Boroughs* (published between 1792 and 1816 and then entitled *The Representative History of Great Britain and Ireland*), in time the encyclopedia of the reforming movement. It is noteworthy how Tucker relied upon Robert Brady's *Boroughs* (1690) and Thomas Madox's *Firma Burgi* (1726).

were emancipating themselves from the corporations in which their class had taken shape, but this rather easy move does not inform us how far mid-Georgian radicals claimed to be speaking for a historical class of "burgesses," a word that should have been developed in the formation of any English "bourgeois" consciousness. The operative historical myth remained ancient constitutionalist and neo-Harringtonian; it spoke of Anglo-Saxon tythingmen and hundredmen as rustic warriors governing themselves in village assemblies, among whom the freemen of ancient boroughs took their place almost as a detail. Burgh's generation indeed hesitated between this and a counterimage of the slow emergence of urban freedoms from feudal darkness; but the latter thesis did not explain why boroughs had rights or how they had lost them, and so entailed what did not occur, the abandonment of historic right and historic constitutionalism as radical arguments. It was not really possible (though it was sometimes tried) to attack the managers of public credit and the standing army as a feudal aristocracy, and rights were better ancient than modern if one aimed to overthrow the regime of the Modern Whigs (especially when they too claimed the authority of the ancient constitution).

Ancient rights, furthermore, could be as well enjoyed by a Roman republic as by a Gothic yeomanry, and Burgh took the next step this could imply. Alongside the Lockean image of the "people" retaining the right to form or reform governments, he set the unmistakably republican notion that their greatest need, as they recovered the rights that had been taken from them, was to form themselves into rhetorical and hortatory associations for the renewal of their moral and political virtue.[118] Where Burke feared that a camarilla of courtiers was plotting to deprive the aristocracy of their capacity to form associations – "where bad men combine, the good must associate"[119] – Burgh thought that borough and country populations bypassed by the Septennial Act must associate in the realm of moral virtue before advancing (as they would later do in the guise of public opinion) to a reform of the parliamentary representation. The logically separate notions of right and virtue could up to a point be unified by making each the precondition of the other; and if this could be done, Locke could be made into an Old Whig after all. As an acquisitive and commercial Modern Whig, however, he must continue to serve the Whig regime. The naiveté of Kramnick's feudal-bourgeois antithesis prevents his realizing that a democratic individualism which presupposed the individual's commitment to a society based on acquisition and exchange could come about only when democrats fully accepted that the commerce associated with Whig rule had transformed the social world, and they would not

[118] See the second and third volumes of *Political Disquisitions*, and Eugene C. Black, *The Association: British Extra-Parliamentary Political Organisation, 1763–93* (Cambridge, Mass., 1963).
[119] Burke, "Thoughts on the Present Discontents"; see Paul Langford, ed., *The Writings and Speeches of Edmund Burke*, 3 vols. (Oxford, 1981), vol. II, p. 315.

do that as long as they continued to employ neo-Harringtonian and Old Whig doctrine to indict the Whig aristocracy. Since the problems of mid-Georgian England remained so largely the problems of an agrarian society, it is not to be wondered at that rhetoric of this kind remained active until well after the Napoleonic wars. The emergence of a democratic ideology for mobile individuals, of whom some were proprietors of capital and others of labor, ought indeed to be looked for and can be found, but the imposition of the category "bourgeois," as if it were descriptive of the social tensions of English society, merely leads us to misunderstand the context in which this ideology emerged. To use "bourgeois" as a technical term for such proprietors is not to characterize any estate, order, or class in Georgian social or historical reality.

Josiah Tucker, whose arguments were studied in Chapter 9, assailed Locke's political theory in conjunction with the Commonwealth or classical republican position as if the two were interchangeable. He did so on the grounds that both were economically and historically archaic, and for the same reasons; no theory of political society that held individual rights and moral personality to be fully formed at the beginning, or even in the early stages, of the growth of productive and commercial relationships between human beings could lead to anything but a stunted and impoverished image of individual social personality. The classical citizen could not be other than a master of slaves, and this was why Roman republicanism appealed to Virginia and Jamaica planters; Locke had designed his individual for the slaveholding and feudal tenures of the *Fundamental Constitutions of Carolina,* and the only difference between his scheme and Filmer's was that the latter had made the rights of one individual, the former those of any individual, anterior to the relations natural to men in society, which were formed in the historical processes of commercial growth. Like his contemporary David Hume, whom he thought not quite modern and optimistic enough,[120] Tucker was an heir of the defenders of Walpole; he was a defiant modernist who held that sound political theory had been impossible before that great minister had discovered the true principles of government through taxation, and in nothing was he more truly a Whig than in his conviction that it was commercial society that taught men deference to a natural aristocracy and civilized the "landed interest" to the point where it could assume that role.

Kramnick characteristically supposes that Tucker attacked the "bourgeois" radicals because they taught disrespect to the "traditional" aristocracy,[121] but the whole point of Tucker's case for the Whig aristocracy and the landed interest, who in his mind are one, is that they are not traditional, feudal, or classical, but modern and progressive, and that deference increases with diversification. As for

---

[120] See his *Four Tracts together with Two Sermons on Political and Commercial Subjects* (Gloucester, 1774), pp. 41, 47–8, where he opposes his progressive to Hume's cyclical view of history.
[121] "Republican Revisionism Revisited," p. 653.

the contractarian and republican intellectuals, from Locke and Sidney to Price and Priestley, Tucker saw them as the reverse of what is meant by "bourgeois." They were the archaic and reactionary apologists of "desperate Catilinarian men," déclassé patricians who, from Shaftesbury to Shelburne, had employed an individualist rhetoric in leading mobs of underemployed Londoners not subject to the civilizing disciplines of the labor market. The malcontent "patriots" of 1776 – Whig oppositionists, London aldermen, American colonists – were inhabitants of an anachronistic equivalent of ancient Rome, with its *faeces Romuli* on the Thames and its *latifundia* in the Caribbean and the Chesapeake, where street crowds followed aristocratic demagogues and slaves were in bondage to their masters because free wage labor had not yet developed to the point where men knew their station and its duties, their interests, and the necessity of submission to recognized authority. Tucker saw such a political economy developing in the new manufacturing towns as the medieval selfishness of corporate boroughs disappeared, and he had no objection to seeing them enfranchised. To do so would not entail any false theory of pseudonatural (because precommercial) rights.

Tucker's function is to remind us that the aristocratic Whig order was defended as modern by men born before it was established, and as a commercial order against men who could be characterized as archaic and reactionary. The Scottish science of political economy, essentially a celebration of the progressive role played in history by the diversification of labor, was perfectly compatible with a theory of the natural aristocracy of a hereditary landed class,[122] and Hume's historicist skepticism regarding natural rights was easily turned against the individualist radicals who continued to find Whig rule repressive. Tucker saw the regime of the progressive aristocracy as threatened by a coalition of reactionary "patriots," among whom he included Whig patricians who were traitors to their class, London guild bosses untouched by the free market, American colonists whose wealth rested on smuggling and slavery, and a faction of religious radicals whose ideology turned out under his analysis as archaic as that of the rest. These were the English Unitarians like Price and Priestley, who employed Lockean theses to argue for a complete separation of civil rights from religious identity and the reduction of all worship to free speculation and inquiry, and with them the New England enlightened Puritans whom Burke had identified as "the dissidence of dissent, agreeing in nothing except the principles of liberty." Tucker despised Burke for furthering the coalition of transatlantic radicals, but found nothing wrong with his diagnosis. He himself held radical libertarianism to be a Puritan survival, a secularized form of the radical autonomy of the free spirit; there is a sense in which he was carrying on the Anglican polemic against enthusiasm, the insistence that private inspiration must be subject to the disciplines of

---

[122] See Hume's "Of Public Credit," in *Essays*.

polite, commercial, and deferential society. Scottish social thought contained nothing, except Hume's religious skepticism, which was unfriendly to the aims of the latitudinarian and Moderate clergies in either kingdom. In Price and Priestley Tucker (like others) detected the enthusiasts who of old had claimed that all authority must give way before the freedom of the spirit and were now insisting that all governments were illegitimate except insofar as they furthered the freedom of the mind and the rights of the individual. Ten years before Burke heard of the sermon to the Revolution Society, Tucker saw Price as prepared to challenge the legitimacy of any government that did not satisfy his ideals of liberty. The formation of a political culture based on moral dissent is arguably as significant in the long run as that of one based on the mobility of property; it may outlast it.

(iii)

Tucker wrote during the efflorescence of Scottish scientific Whiggism and during the rapid and revolutionary development of radical patriot Whiggism in America. The early phases of the latter's history are still curiously little known; we know a good deal about the doctrinal content and social function of American patriot culture as a fully fledged entity, but not much about the processes whereby it reached the colonies and subsequently took root there. What we can say about it is that it was Old Whig and does not raise for us the problems of seeing how a republican ethos could enter a High Church or Jacobite Tory mind; if there were no Tories in Scotland, there were none in America either, and it may have been there that the word "Tory" first took on its paradoxical later meaning of an authoritarian defender of the Whig order. Attempts have been made to derive American republicanism from Scottish origins, stressing the concepts of sympathy and sentiment to be found there,[123] but it is a difficulty that Scottish scientific Whiggism evolved in a commercial and unionist direction highly supportive of the Whig order, and we should be obliged to set the Enlightenment of Francis Hutcheson in opposition to that of Hume, Robertson, or even Adam Ferguson, and perhaps look behind Hutcheson to the radically Whig Irish environment, of Molyneux, Molesworth, and possibly Toland, in which his career began.

If we evaluate American political culture as an English transplant, it will seem to present the spectacle of a country Whiggism, desperately mistrustful of any kind of court but not immediately involved in confrontation or interaction with any such. Colonial gentries, clerisies, and artisanates adopted patriot rhetoric with alacrity, but were not at grips with the concrete reality of the regime it had been formed to oppose. The patriot gentry of Virginia praised civic virtue as the

[123] Garry Wills, *Inventing America: Jefferson's Declaration of Independence* (New York, 1978).

ethos of their class and spoke much of the horrors of corruption, but were not a landed interest fearing displacement by a monied, or still less a parliamentary, gentry of "independent country members" constantly faced by the ministerial authority their English equivalents rather half-heartedly denounced. In still Puritan Massachusetts, in religiously heterogeneous Pennsylvania, and even in Virginia where reigned that perfect gentry solution to the problem of ecclesiastical authority – an episcopal church without a bishop – patriot clergies and laities exploited the equation of religious with civic freedom, of congregation with republic,[124] and moved toward those deist and Unitarian solutions that equated faith with freedom to believe as one chose. None of them, however, was subject to the toleration of an established church that ranked among the governing institutions of a realm. Radical groups of merchants and artisans took shape in Boston and Philadelphia and corresponded with Londoners who spoke, as they themselves did, a language going back to the First Whigs and the Commonwealth; but those cities were not parliamentary boroughs subject to the Septennial Act and obliged to reexplore the history of parliamentary representation and parliamentary corruption as boroughs felt it in their intimate structure. An American political society was one that spoke the language of parliamentary opposition without being a parliamentary realm; its political culture was the criticism of a regime it experienced only at a distance.

Bernard Bailyn at the end of the 1960s found himself under considerable attack for having suggested that radical Whig ideology had operated to render the American Revolution inevitable because, given certain critical conjunctions, it made it impossible for Americans to regard British policy as anything but a design to destroy virtue and liberty and establish a despotism. To some scholars this carried the unwelcome suggestion that the Revolution was no more than an early instance of "the paranoid style in American politics";[125] to others it seemed to neglect other contributory causes and competing ideologies; to still others it appeared to disregard the functioning role of ideology within the structure of colonial society – and often they thought they already knew what that was. However, the proposition that an ideology may operate by itself and work both with and against realities instead of merely reflecting them is reinforced if we take up the suggestion made in the preceding paragraph: that Old Whig ideology in eighteenth-century America was in the nature of a Hartzian fragment,[126] divorced from a context it still presupposed and, if at all controlled by the context

---

[124] Alan G. Heimert, *Religion and the American Mind from the Great Awakening to the Revolution* (Cambridge, Mass., 1966); Nathan O. Hatch, *The Sacred Cause of Liberty: Republican Thought and the Millennium in Revolutionary New England* (New Haven, Conn., 1977).

[125] See, most recently, Gordon S. Wood, "Conspiracy and the Paranoid Style: Causality and Deceit in the Eighteenth Century," *William and Mary Quarterly,* 3d ser. XXXIX, 3 (1982), pp. 401–41.

[126] Louis B. Hartz, ed., *The Foundation of New Societies* (New York, 1964).

to which it had been transplanted, controlled by it in unpredicted and paradoxical ways. There are many serious problems with Hartz's model, and the debate
in which Bailyn became involved is not being continued here. But if we take up
the suggestion that Americans were conducting their political culture with the
aid of a rhetoric formed to criticize a Whig parliamentary order in which they
were involved only at a distance and in which they did not participate, it may
help us understand why the rhetoric of Old Whig parliamentary opposition became a means of republican revolution in America, at the same time as it was
becoming a language of franchise reform in England and of parliamentary autonomy in Ireland.

If we examine the roles of the various components of Whig doctrine in the
Revolution, we shall be obliged to separate contractarian and resistance theory
from republican theory, according to the purposes for which each was used. The
argument that parliament was not entitled to levy taxes in the colonies was originally constitutionalist, but expanded to the point where it was expressed in
terms of natural rights and the powers and obligations of the state to maintain
them. Locke took his place here with Grotius, Pufendorf, and Vattel, and the
end of the process was reached in the Declaration of Independence, when it had
to be maintained that what had been colonies were now states, fully empowered
to protect the peoples inhabiting them and their property; for this end they had
been established and it made them states. However, it had until very recently
been accepted that this function was rightfully discharged by another state, that
of Great Britain, and a decent respect for the opinions of mankind impelled
Congress to endorse a quasi-Lockean rhetoric that enumerated the wrongful acts
by which the government of that state had lost its lawful authority over the
American people (usually numbered in the singular, though organized into thirteen states). The result, however, was less the dissolution of all government over
that people[127] than the exaltation of their existing governments into states; rather,
it was contended – by arguments that made use of Locke's doctrine of a right to
emigrate – that these governments already existed in history and by right of their
historic origins enjoyed a contractual autonomy.[128] The chain of arguments to
this point was juristic; it deployed the concept of right rather than the republican
concept of virtue.

By the time of the Declaration of Independence the colonial governments were
being reorganized as those of states, a process in which many have discerned the
crucial step into revolution. These constitutions rejected the authority of the
crown, and in consequence it became a question whether they should acknowl-

---

[127] Only in some western districts, and for local reasons, was it much maintained that a dissolution
of government had occurred and a state of nature obtained. See Wood, *Creation of the American
Republic*, pp. 282–91.

[128] Jefferson's *Rights of British America* and Adams's *Letters of Novanglus* advance versions of these theses.

edge the monarchical principle, and if so in what form. Here we switch from the argument tending to independence into the argument tending to republicanism, but this is not the first point at which the effect of republican language and doctrine is to be felt. Prior to the Declaration – while, that is, he was still the commander of troops who had taken up arms in a civil war – George Washington was in the habit of referring to the forces opposing him as "the ministerial army." In Old Whig and Commonwealth rhetoric of eighteenth-century opposition generally, the sovereign's ministers were conventionally presented as menacing figures; it was they who disturbed the balance of the constitution, employed the influence of the crown to reduce Parliament to dependence, promoted standing armies, and sought to corrupt virtue and establish a general despotism. This is the rhetoric that, in Bailyn's presentation, could expand until it filled men's minds and could permit only a totally Manichaean interpretation of every event. In an age when it seemed that executive authority could maintain itself only by patronage, and that all patronage entailed the reduction of independence to dependence – when even David Hume held liberty and authority to exist in an irresolvable conflict – it was hard not to see virtue as perpetually threatened by a total subversion. In Britain, where the realms were anciently possessed of sovereignty, it could be said that the dualisms were necessary. Sovereignty might threaten liberty and virtue, yet sovereignty had to be maintained; the relations between the two were those of constant adjustment, not the warfare of light with darkness. In the American colonies, new states were grasping at sovereignty but, since they had not previously possessed it, were doing so with the aid of an ideology that stressed far more nakedly than in Britain the power of sovereignty to subvert. The logical outcome could only be republican. King and Parliament must be represented as totally corrupt and aiming at total corruption; the new states must establish sovereignty in the only form that aimed at the systematic institutionalization of virtue. For the reason that they must become states, they must become republics. The rhetoric of right as the precondition of independence merged with the rhetoric of liberty and virtue as the preconditions of one another.

From a time at least as distant as that of the *Answer to the Nineteen Propositions,* it had been possible to represent the King, Lords, and Commons of England as a balance of equal and independent powers; yet this concept is formally republican, and theoretical republicans such as Harrington had been moved to try to replace King, Lords, and Commons by agencies better suited to the roles it enjoined. A central problem, though by no means the only one, had been that of sovereignty. Three independent powers might seem better qualified to check than to reinforce one another's majesty, but, as Weston and Greenberg have shown us, the *Answer to the Nineteen Propositions* could be used to promote the doctrine of a conjoint exercise of sovereignty, in which it was debated whether the Lords and Commons took part in legislation as initiatory wills or merely through their functions of counseling the crown and giving or witholding consent to its actions. The problem was further complicated as language slid from describing King, Lords, and Commons as estates to vesting them with the executive, judicial, and legislative powers; for once the king was characterized as an executive, it became apparent that he also legislated and did so as King-in-Parliament, and any attempt to separate executive and legislative and place them in equilibrium as independent agencies must encounter the shock of reality. A rhetoric directed against ministers, placemen, and courtiers could for a long time obscure this contradiction; they could be represented as the minions and intermediaries of power, unknown to the constitution and liable by misusing the influence of the crown to destroy the balance of the constitution by bringing powers that should be independent into dependence on one another. From the circumstance that it was not known how the executive could subsist except by patronage, ministers (and public credit) acquired that supposed capacity for infinite malignity and subversion with which the age invested them. Once attention was paid, however, to the facts of legislation or fiscality, it became apparent that executive and legislative were not separate and could not be; the king was present in Parliament in the mediatory persons of his ministers, and acted there to pass laws and to execute policies. There was even a body of post-Harringtonian doctrine that contended that he needed influence and patronage, as his ancestors had needed the ties of tenure and vassalage, to attach members of the legislature to his interest and so get these things done.[129]

Once again we see why regime Whiggism took up pre-Whig constitutional doctrine, and why it was that Old Whig, Tory, and country oppositions were to a certain extent in bad faith; their rhetoric implied such criticism of parliamentary monarchy that it could be imagined that a republic might replace it, yet none of these oppositions had any program whatever for doing so. No bill for a general expulsion of placemen from Parliament ever got off the ground, and it becomes increasingly hard to believe that any was seriously intended; yet such bills went on being moved, and the rhetoric and doctrine that went with them continued being voiced. There was at least this to be said for Hume's belief that the balance of the constitution, though the best that could be hoped for, was inherently unstable: there was a persistent disjunction between language and reality, and practice contained disjunctions that theory could not explain away. The regime of oligarchy incessantly criticized itself, just as the commercial aristocracy criticized itself in the name of agrarian and republican values. Much of what we term ideology was in fact utopia (though we must not confuse utopia with nostalgia).

But Americans were not skeptical Whigs in the Humean sense; the very con-

---

[129] See Reed Browning's study of Samuel Squire, chap. V; n. 62, this chapter.

siderable skepticism of the Founding Fathers did not go beyond Franklin's famous apophthegm, "a republic, madam, if you can keep it." They took the left fork from the *Answer to the Nineteen Propositions* and having convinced themselves, for reasons that may have been partly Hartzian, of the thoroughgoing corruption of ministerial parliamentarism, they took the separation of powers seriously, excluded the executive secretaries from seats in Congress, and so rejected parliamentary monarchy forever and committed themselves to a republican experiment. Josiah Tucker, with his usual acumen, perceived both the American war and American independence as means to preserve the sovereignty of Parliament against enemies who were as much Tory as republican; if the colonies could not be subjected to a necessary sovereignty, then sovereignty itself must cast them out. The disruption of Whig empire was a disruption of the varying intimations of Whig political culture; if America could never again be a parliamentary monarchy, then Commonwealth radicalism in parliamentary Britain could never again be the same. It had been a pusillanimous idea, thought Jefferson, that America had friends in Britain worth keeping in with.[130]

The republican component in the Whig inheritance did not, however, control, though it did modify, the formation of governments in the United States. Gordon Wood[131] has examined the process by which several states set up bicameral legislatures in the apparent expectation of duplicating the ideal relationship of few to many that characterized the classical republican model, but discovered that even in Virginia a naturally leading elite and naturally deferential vulgar were no longer to be found.[132] Wood argues that republican theory presupposed a society of estates, but in some of its versions the aristocratic component need only be one of talent, whereas in others the few were defined by their political function rather than by their inherent virtue. What can be clearly seen is that post-Revolutionary thinking early showed itself acutely suspicious of the idea of natural aristocracy and unwilling to distinguish it from hereditary or otherwise entrenched aristocracy. John Adams, the most systematic thinker in the older republican style, who wished to warn that a natural aristocracy of some kind would always emerge, and that it must be anticipated and rendered harmless by being provided with a useful function, found himself accused of designs to restore a hereditary nobility.[133] Natural republics, as they may be termed, self-differentiated into patricians and plebeians, gentlemen and yeomen, signally failed to make their appearance in the constitution-making period; to many it seemed that a mobile and acquisitive bonanza was taking shape instead, and this was lamented

---

[130] Julian P. Boyd, Lyman H. Butterfield, and Mina R. Bryan, eds., *The Papers of Thomas Jefferson* (Princeton, N.J., 1950–), vol. I, p. 314.

[131] *Creation of the American Republic,* pp. 391–425.

[132] For the processes occurring there, see Rhys Isaac, *The Transformation of Virginia, 1740–1790* (Williamsburg, Va., and Chapel Hill, N.C., 1982).

[133] Wood, *Creation of the American Republic,* chap. XIV, pp. 565–92.

on all sides as a failure of virtue, the principle universally known to be cardinal to republics. Very cautiously, publicists began to examine what forms of government there might be that did not depend on virtue.[134]

What was taking shape would have to be a republic, in the sense that there was no other acceptable alternative to parliamentary monarchy. That constitution, from which the United States had just broken away, relied heavily on the concept that the nation, or the people, were represented both by the king as a public person and in his councils by persons elected to "represent" shires and boroughs. In Britain at this period, as the pendulum swung against the regime of the Septennial Act, it was being argued among the radicals both that the remedy for corruption lay in a better representation of the people – meaning one in which more members of the communities represented took part in electing their representatives – and that the ultimate authority to form and reform governments resided in this same people as an entity. If these two arguments were allowed to interact, there could emerge the idea of a people who constantly renew virtuous government, and their own virtue, by regularly choosing their representatives to constitute a government. Though Rousseau, far away in Europe, had already damned this concept for separating virtue from personality, it retained much of the republican's characteristic concern for virtue. The form of government that emerged from representation, however, was a sovereign to whom the people in the act of election transferred rights and powers they might otherwise have exercised for themselves, and there can be nothing further from the republican principle than the idea that a select body of persons can represent, impersonate, or stand for a body of autonomous citizens and claim that when it governs them, they are governing themselves. To the classical republican or the modern communitarian,[135] representation is little better than alienation, and there are still those who claim that in constructing a representative democracy, the American founders were saddling the people with a Hobbesian Leviathan.[136] The prepositions contained in the great phrase "government of the people, by the people, and for the people" can be made to form a trinity of consubstantial ambiguities.

As the Whig tradition separated into its dual constituents, the theory and practice of representative democracy were developed in the United States far faster than in Britain; but because they were developed in the context of a republican experimental structure, they encountered problems that did not confront the British a century later, when they set about the democratization of parliamentary monarchy. It was as a second best to the republican ideal that the people were

---

[134] J. R. Pole, *Political Representation in England and the Origins of the American Republic* (New York, 1966), pp. 531–2.
[135] Benjamin R. Barber, *The Death of Communal Liberty: A History of Freedom in a Swiss Mountain Canton* (Princeton, N.J., 1974).
[136] Frank M. Coleman, *Hobbes and America: Exploring the Constitutional Foundations* (Toronto, 1978).

proclaimed capable of representation in all branches of government; James Madison paid more than lip service to this truth when he calmly reversed accepted terminology and proclaimed that a polity in which the people governed themselves was a democracy, and one in which they were governed by their own representatives a republic.[137] There was a sense in which Madison was maintaining the republican paradigm by giving the representatives the role of a few and the electors that of a many; the former constituted a natural aristocracy (qualified by the fact of election) who made the decisions, the latter a natural democracy who evaluated the decisions after they had been made and the qualifications of those who had made them. Even the idea that representatives should be instructed by their constituents need not annul this relationship. But the few and the many are in a relationship of deliberation rather than of power, which does not define the capacity of representation to produce sovereignty. Madison had further to maintain that the people retained sovereignty in the act of choosing representatives to exercise it, and this had to be done in two ways: first, by elaborating devices to make the elected accountable to their electors – the idea of frequent elections was deeply embedded in the Commonwealth tradition; and second, by a separation of powers that ensured that the representatives could not corruptly consolidate themselves to monopolize the government. We have seen how separation of powers emerged together with conjoint sovereignty to give parliamentary monarchy its republican shadow; in this way too the oppositions of eighteenth-century Britain left their legacy to the American republic.

None of the states constituting that republic, however, presented by the end of the century the image of a classical or Harringtonian republic of interacting gentry and freemen, and if they had it was a recognized impossibility to draw several such republics together in any union more perfect than that of an Achaean league. The fact that government in each state was better constituted along representative than classical republican lines made it more possible to extend the principle of representative sovereignty to the point where it could define the relations of states to union; we reach the point where Whiggism is transformed into Federalism, and what was originally English becomes that which can only be American. The separation of powers, however – that oddly ambiguous legacy – left unsolved the relation of executive to legislature; to this day a parliamentary observer sees the United States government as consisting of an executive who persistently tries to legislate and a legislature that as persistently frustrates him, and the observer wonders how far this accounts for the growth of court and palace politics in the city where (as it happens) these words are being written.[138] An

---

[137] *The Federalist*, no. 10, *The Federalist Papers*, ed. Jacob E. Cooke (Middletown; Conn., 1961), pp. 60–1.

[138] As a fellow of the Woodrow Wilson International Center for Scholars, in the Smithsonian Institute in Washington.

attempt to solve the problem along regime Whig lines was made under the first presidency by Alexander Hamilton, who sought to establish in Congress something in the nature of a "presidential interest" made up of men who would find it in their interest to support measures proposed by the administration.[139] That Hamilton's project included use of executive patronage, a strong, federally controlled professional army, a funded national debt, and a Bank of the United States ensured a passionate polemic in which he was accused of a design to install all the techniques of government by corruption supposedly perfected by Walpole.[140] Americans once more showed how deeply they could fear a type of regime of which they had little direct experience.

It is interesting that the accusation of contriving to establish an office-holding and fund-holding aristocracy merged instantly with that of seeking to restore a hereditary titled nobility and king. Americans brought up to dread and detest the Whig oligarchy saw it as both ancient and modern, both feudal and fiscal, and feared both its despotism in the past and its corruption in the future. There could be no better illustration of how the republican mind located itself, and the modes of property on which it thought it rested, in a scheme of history still cyclical and degenerative; American optimism, of which there was plenty, consisted in the hope of escape from history into utopia, wilderness, or millennium. This is the moment at which to take up the problem of how far the political economy of republicanism persisted in America; how far, that is, the republic was held to presuppose an agrarian, unspecialized economy and to fear the corruptions of industry and commerce. We may pass over much of what has been urged to the effect that the Jeffersonian farmer was less a self-sufficient yeoman than a commercial producer for a market,[141] since it has never been alleged that republican virtue was incompatible with trade and industry. Jefferson could not be more anxious for economic modernization than Andrew Fletcher of Saltoun had been, and both considered slavery from the angle of its possible contribution to mercantile growth. The antipathy to what was called "commerce" in the eighteenth century arose, it must always be remembered, along two main lines of development. It was feared that men might become in various ways dependent through overspecialization, as they had been tempted to entrust their independent virtue to professional soldiers, governors, patrons, or – it was increasingly perceived – employers. The yeoman living off the produce of his farm was archetypally immune from this corruption, but that did not preclude the possibility of independence through exchange relations; the yeoman took his goods to market, the serf delivered them to his lord as payment in kind. The independence of

[139] Gerald Stourzh, *Alexander Hamilton and the Idea of Republican Government* (Stanford, Calif., 1970).
[140] Lance Banning, *The Jeffersonian Persuasion*.
[141] Appleby, cited in n. 73, this chapter. The best recent work on this question is Drew R. McCoy, *The Elusive Republic: Political Economy in Jeffersonian America* (Chapel Hill, N.C., 1980).

the small entrepreneur appeared in American values as an outgrowth of the independence of the small farmer,[142] and even the growth of water-powered mill industry in New England was idealized in terms of rustic independence and virtue. The pieceworker and his capitalist employer presented a graver problem in mutual corruption and interdependence – especially when they created a new type of urban environment – and Jefferson was concerned with the problem of how far his society should advance beyond domestic to factory manufactures. At all levels, independence and specialization remain the theme, and the workman sees himself as independent artisan rather than as proletarian struggling to transcend his overspecialization.

The second line of thought, which must never be lost to sight, is that "commerce" in the eighteenth century was held to entail the presence of an aristocracy: the Whig aristocracy Hamilton was accused of wishing to reintroduce to America. As late as 1813–14, John Taylor of Caroline unhesitatingly characterized as "capitalists" the privileged rulers of an aristocratic mode of government, perfected in Britain during the previous century and still threatening the virtuous agriculture (at once scientific and slaveholding, improving and Catonian) of which he was the advocate.[143] The ghost of the monied interest still walked, and it was a question of historical circumstance whether the improving landowner felt impelled to embrace the Whig aristocracy in Scotland or reject it in Virginia. The values of market society, which could reinforce yeoman independence in one set of circumstances, could be employed (as Tucker demonstrates) to reinforce the Whig order in another, and it does not seem to be a coincidence that Madison and Hamilton have been identified as students of Hume,[144] whereas it was Jefferson who wanted to exorcise him from the American mind. Hamilton, who wanted strong government and commercial empire, would be attracted by Hume's thoughts on the relation between liberty and authority and on how men were to live freely under government in a world where commerce counted for more than virtue. But though the American future might belong to Hamiltonian practice, it belonged to Jeffersonian ideology.[145] There is not to be found anything like the ideology of regime Whiggism, in which a modernizing aristocracy is rein-

---

[142] Rowland T. Berthoff, "Independence and Attachment, Virtue and Interest: From Republican Citizen to Free Enterpriser, 1787–1837," in *Uprooted Americans, Essays to Honor Oscar Handlin*, ed. Richard L. Bushman (Boston, 1979).

[143] John Taylor, *Arator: Being a Series of Agricultural Essays, Practical and Political* (Petersburg, Va., 1818; reprinted, Indianapolis, 1977), pp. 74, 79–81, 85, 98–110. In an *Inquiry into the Principles and Policy of the Government of the United States* (1814), Taylor distinguished between "capital created by industry" and "capital created by paper." "Capitalists" were those who robbed the former to create the latter and found a new species of aristocracy.

[144] Douglass Adair, *Fame and the Founding Fathers*, ed. Trevor Colbourn (New York; 1974).

[145] John M. Murrin, "The Great Inversion, or Court versus Country: A Comparison of the Revolution Settlements in England (1688–1721) and America (1776–1816)," in Pocock, ed., *Three British Revolutions*.

forced in possession of a strong executive government by the twin forces of commerce and politeness. This is one reason why Scottish social thought has been so
long misunderstood and Adam Smith set down as a rugged individualist. The
tremendous historical power of commerce was recognized and described in the
eighteenth century as a soft, civilizing, and feminizing force, and in the nineteenth as hard, heroic, and philistine: the gentle and the stern *paideia*.[146] The
advent of industry has much to do with this, but so has the role of a commercial
aristocracy, present in Britain but absent in America.

IV.   From the response to the American Revolution to the reaction to the French Revolution

(i)

Radical or patriot Whiggism in Britain and America confronted a Whig oligarchy that both cultures characterized in the same terms, but Americans had to do
with it at a distance and feared it as a specter, whereas Britons encountered it
head on as part of their own world of experience and were obliged to hear and
respond to what was regularly said on its behalf. Once the "ministerial" armies
had been discouraged from attempting to reduce the colonies to obedience, there
existed a space, if not a vacuum, that must be filled by extending – and, as it
turned out, transforming – the republican intimations latent in Whig discourse.
We have already begun to observe the reasons why this could never happen in
Britain. There existed no vacuum; political space was already filled with the
historic institutions of royal government and common law. The republican intimations of Whiggism called for a republic of separated powers, but where the
crown in Parliament already exercised a conjoint sovereignty, there could be no
real case for a classical republic, just as a few years later there was no point in
raising the Jacobin cry for a republic one and indivisible. England (if not Britain)
was one and indivisible already, aristocratic and corporate power notwithstanding, and the only serious Jacobins in the British Isles (to use that term) made
their appearance in Ireland, where a republic one and indivisible had much to
commend it before and even after the rise of Orangeism. The sovereignty of
Parliament being an effective fact, it might seem as if Commonwealth quasi-
republicanism stood revealed as a historical blind alley, and indeed it may never
have been the same after the American war. The Declaration of Independence
was a brutal slap in the face of those London radicals who had supposed that the
American cause was their own,[147] and Richard Price and those like him were
reduced to declaring that American independence was a punishment for British

[146] This phrase was coined by Marvin C. Becker, *Florence in Transition,* 2 vols. (Baltimore, 1967–8).
[147] Colin Bonwick, *English Radicals and the American Revolution* (Chapel Hill, N.C., 1977).

guilt. The relations between the component powers in Parliament could not be remodeled along republican lines once the spectacle existed of the experiment being carried out in American reality – not that the American constitutional experiments of the 1780s seem to have attracted much British attention – and the attempt to do so had always been largely a Tory affair. But, as we have already seen, royal influence and aristocratic corruption had always been exposed to Old Whig and patriot denunciations, and since the days of the First Whigs it had been held that the remedy for such things lay in more frequent parliaments and a reform of the representation. Before the American crisis became an American war, these habitual slogans were being developed into serious proposals for franchise reform, abolition of boroughs, and even manhood suffrage, and the electorate was being presented as not only a repository of republican virtue and Lockean power, but as a necessary and essential component in a political and social balance. If British radicalism could not significantly take a republican route, it could take a democratic one. The democratization of politics could occur on both sides of the Atlantic, but in the American republic the representation of the people became a mode of sovereign democracy, whereas in Britain the representation of the realm, with which the sovereign monarchy consulted to render its sovereignty effective, became a representation of the people. Even this took a long time.

Because British republican and democratic radicalism encountered an aristocratic oligarchy entrenched in control of a parliamentary system to which no alternative was possible, there could never be a republican revolution but must be a reform of Parliament. To say this, however, is not to say, as some have supposed, that British radicalism was a tame and reformist affair compared with the revolutionary daring of the Americans.[148] Nothing like the creative constitutional experimenting of the Founding Fathers is indeed to be found, but the experience of the next fifty years in exacting parliamentary reform from the oligarchy was tougher and more embittering than any undergone by the Americans, and it is possible to imagine that it might have led to more revolutionary conclusions. To smash and replace crown and Parliament, shire and borough, would have been as totally transforming a revolution as the smashing and replacement of the ancien régime, and there have always been British revolutionary dreamers who wonder what it would have been like.

> It may be we shall rise the last as Frenchmen rose the first,
> Our wrath come after Russia's wrath, and our wrath be the worst.[149]

But this seems to be dreaming against the facts. The strength of Whig and conservative interpretations of British history continues to lie in the general truth

---

[148] A view attributed to the present writer by Linda Colley, *In Defiance of Oligarchy*, p. 174, and "Eighteenth-Century English Radicalism before Wilkes," p. 2.

[149] G. K. Chesterton (scarcely a man of the left), in "The Secret People."

that no revolutionary alternative to the democratization of Parliament has ever been taken seriously, and it has remained plausible that the Whig regime, even at its most oligarchic, possessed a liberal flexibility that the ancien régime lacked. It can further be maintained that because the oligarchic regime disposed of powerful and articulate ideologies in which both its ancient and its modern character could be asserted and defended – rhetorics that ranged from the ancient constitution to the Wealth of Nations – the ideological debate in counterrevolutionary Britain was of a depth and texture unknown in revolutionary America. Thomas Paine, Jeremy Bentham, Adam Smith, Edmund Burke, William Godwin, William Blake, Thomas Malthus, William Cobbett, Samuel Taylor Coleridge, and James Mill form a gallery of radicals, conservatives, and revolutionaries hard to imagine in a simpler and more spacious world. America might produce prophets, but few dialecticians appeared until Tocqueville arrived to tell the republic what it was becoming. This is not being said to score points in a World Cup for political thinkers, but rather to establish the premise that a history of "the varieties of Whiggism" still has a long way to go.

Two authentic revolutionaries took part in the Anglo-American debate of the mid-1770s: Jean Paul Marat, a Frenchman resident in London, and Thomas Paine, an Englishman just arrived in Philadelphia. The former wrote a rather conventional radical Whig tract that he had to revise considerably to make into a French Revolution manifesto years later.[150] The latter remains difficult to fit into any kind of category. *Common Sense* breathes an extraordinary hatred of English governing institutions, but it does not consistently echo any established radical vocabulary; Paine had no real place in the club of Honest Whigs to which Franklin had introduced him in London, and his use of anti-Normanism to insist that Britain did not have a constitution but rather a tyranny does not permit us to think of him (as contemporaries might have) as a New Model soldier risen from the grave. Moreover, when the Revolutionary War was over Paine returned to live under "the royal brute of Great Britain" as if nothing much had happened, nor was he pursued by the authorities until the very different circumstances of 1791. One of the few practicing revolutionaries in English history, he performed no independent revolutionary action in England; his appearance on the scene, however, does indicate that things were beginning to happen for which neither branch of the Whig mainstream could properly account. In 1776, the year of *Common Sense,* there appeared Jeremy Bentham's *Fragment on Government,* the first shot in a long *guerre de course* against the ancient constitution, the balanced government, the common law, and all the icons of regime Whiggism as voiced by the latest of its expositors, Sir William Blackstone. In the same year, however,

---

[150] Luciano Guerci, "Marat prima della Rivoluzione: *Le Catene della Schiavitù,*" *Rivista Storica Italiana* XCI, 2–3 (1979), pp. 434–69. *The Chains of Slavery* was Marat's title in 1774, *Les Chaines de l'Esclavage* in 1793.

Bentham seems to have taken a hand in writing a government-sponsored rebuttal of the Declaration of Independence.[151] There was nothing venal about him and it is far too early to be speaking of Philosophic Radicalism or of Bentham as a radical of any kind; but no man and no tradition was his master. Some program for scientific legislation was already in the young man's mind, but his indifference to constitutional debate was all but absolute. We may do best to think of Bentham as a kind of conservative Jacobin, a bureaucratic reformer indifferent to history, but altogether without revolutionary aspirations or opportunities; yet we should not try to document, what this might otherwise suggest, an affinity with Walpolean or Scottish modernism – the rhetoric of modernism was Whig and his was not. The parameters within which occurred the mutation of discourse that produced him and his mind are hard to establish and seem not to belong to the history of English public debate. Like Paine, but like him only in this, Bentham concealed his origins if he had any.

The established patterns of radical speech and action outlasted the Declaration of Independence, and Herbert Butterfield in 1949 found it possible to characterize 1780 as the year of "the revolution that did not happen."[152] He came under considerable fire for doing so: Whig historians believe that revolution is precluded by the structure of English institutions, and Namierite historians find it difficult to believe that political beings ever think or act in a revolutionary manner. To say that no one intended revolution in 1780 is in a sense to beg the question, since revolutions are commonly conducted by those who had no intention of doing so; but without climbing into the cumulonimbus of the counterfactual, we can say that in 1780 there were those who knew that revolution might occur. The attempt made in that year to combine the petitioning activities of London and Middlesex radicals with those of Yorkshire gentlemen and freeholders suggests the classic formula for a country movement combining urban with rural discontent; in the highly traditional Old Whig and ancient-constitutionalist rhetoric which the movement employed may be discerned elements of the notion that the uncorrupt people may assemble, associate, and petition – petitioning was often a tumultuous activity – in order to bring about reform of a corrupt parliament. This was also the year of the Convention at Dungannon, when a virtuous militia assembled in arms to bring about – peaceably, it is true – a renewal of Irish parliamentary life (a revolution in the ancient sense of the term). It never became clear how far, supposing Parliament to be corrupt, a national convention could proceed through parliamentary channels or must substitute itself for them, and in the world as it looked after 1789, the charge of promoting a national convention was to become that of promoting revolution in

---

[151] Douglas Long, *Bentham on Liberty: Jeremy Bentham's Idea of Liberty in Relation to his Utilitarianism* (Toronto, 1977), pp. 51–4.
[152] Herbert Butterfield, *George III, Lord North and the People, 1779–80*.

the French or most modern sense of the word. Long before that, however, British and Irish patriot radicalism appeared to have shot its bolt. The Yorkshire movement failed; the Patriot Parliament ran itself into futility; the Gordon riots stirred up all the governing class's latent fears of religious enthusiasm. "Forty thousand Puritans as they might have been in the time of Cromwell," wrote Gibbon, "have started out of their graves."[153] The election of 1784, however it came about, in retrospect appeared to mean that the monarchy, the oligarchy, and the gentry had closed ranks and were prepared to distinguish ever more stringently between the reforms they were ready to concede and those they were not.

If we date the British counterrevolution from 1784, without waiting for the massive reaction against the news from France, we may take into account certain ideological indications of a hardening of attitude. Blackstone's successor in the Vinerian professorship had come out unequivocally for a high doctrine of sovereign authority, in framing which Samuel Johnson may have taken a hand.[154] In the domain of philosophy, the reality of divine will and the autonomy of moral values were being asserted in terms calculated to reinforce the authority of society; the advent of Scottish commonsense philosophy and the rapid adoption of William Paley's writings into the Cambridge curriculum are instances of this. There is an audible sternness and an unwillingness to accept opposition as legitimate, which suggests that the oligarchy was losing its tolerance for quasi-republican alternative programs; leaders of the aristocracy who found themselves in opposition might have to decide quickly whether to endorse or reject radical plans. This may have been a crucial moment in the reflective as well as the active career of Edmund Burke. Between 1781 and 1784 it became clear that he would have no part in proposals to enlarge the franchise. Thomas Reid and William Paley, nevertheless, were liberal as well as conservative philosophers, and Burke did not base his theoretical opposition to enlargement of the franchise on any intransigently modernist claim that the constitution had assumed its final form in 1688 or 1714 and could not thereafter be reformed. Rather, he affirmed that the constitution was prescriptive and immemorial, and that therefore it was conceptually impossible to speak either of natural rights it disregarded or of original rights from which it had fallen away.[155] The bedrock of ancient constitutionalism was being laid at the foundations of the prescriptive conservatism to which Burke would give classic expression a few years later and which, at a first and even a second reading, seems very remote from the Scottish scientific Whiggism hitherto an intellectual pillar of the post-Walpolean order. One would give much for

[153] J. E. Norton, ed., *The Letters of Edward Gibbon*, 3 vols. (London, 1956), vol. II, p. 243.
[154] I refer here to Sir Robert Chambers, whose subsequent career lay in India; for his association with Johnson see W. Jackson Bate, *Samuel Johnson* (New York, 1975), pp. 417–26. Johnson certainly helped with the writing and may have advised on the argument.
[155] Pocock, *Politics, Language and Time* (New York, 1971), pp. 226–8.

a report of the conversations that took place when Burke dined with Millar in Glasgow and with Smith in Edinburgh; the young William Windham, however, found his faculties not clear next morning.[156]

(ii)

The impact of the French Revolution between 1789 and 1793 brought about a disintegration and regrouping among the Whigs: one, to speak more precisely, in which a relatively organized entity known as the Whig party lost contact with several great Whig connections but contrived to retain its name. Whether the Grenville and Portland connections ceased being Whigs, and if so what they were said to have become, is a question we may consider. Whatever the high politics of these occurrences,[157] their history in the fields of ideology and discourse may conveniently be recounted from the obvious point: the publication of Burke's *Reflections on the Revolution in France* in 1790. Burke was spurred to write this by hearing of Richard Price's sermon to the Revolution Society, which presented the march to Versailles in October 1789 and the conducting of the French royal family to Paris as glorious events in keeping with the spirit of the English Revolution of 1688. If we ask what Price was doing when he delivered this address, part of the answer must be that his rhetoric may well have been "vulgar Whig" but was not Old Whig in the Commonwealthman sense. It was aimed at a king, not a king's ministers, and proclaimed that kings – in England, France, or nature – might be cashiered for misconduct: a doctrine of conditional rule and popular sovereignty, which paradoxically formed no part of the language that affirmed the separation and balance of the component parts of the constitution. Price may well have believed that he was preaching a Lockean sermon, and Josiah Tucker would caustically have agreed; there is a problem *ex silentio* in the circumstance that Burke at no time saw fit to mention Locke's name in this connection. He set himself, however, to repudiate what was certainly a radical Whig interpretation of the events of 1688–9, and there is evidence that, much like Tucker some years earlier, he saw Price as an agent of the earl of Shelburne.[158] There was a conspiracy afoot, both conservatives agreed, to damage the monarchy by using 1688 to assert natural rights of limitation and deposition, and Tucker had seen this as the work of aristocratic desperadoes conducting an ideological fronde. After Burke's conduct in the regency crisis, he was ill placed to defend himself had any such

---

[156] *The Diary of the Rt. Hon. William Windham* (London, 1866), pp. 60–1, 63–4: "Felt very strongly the impressions of a company entirely Scotch. Faculties not clear."

[157] For which see O'Gorman, *Whig Party and the French Revolution,* who never neglects the factor of belief.

[158] Thomas W. Copeland, ed., *The Correspondence of Edmund Burke,* 10 vols. (Cambridge, 1967); vol. VI, pp. 91–2.

charge been made; but his attitude toward aristocratic Whiggism was more complex than Tucker's.

Tucker and Burke both had recourse to an interpretation of 1688 so characteristic of regime Whiggism as to savor paradoxically of the arguments used by
Revolution Tories. That is, they argued that the Revolution had been an act of
necessity and had not established any general right to repeat the actions of which
it had consisted. To avoid the extremes of arguing either that it established a
right of deposition or that it set up a merely *de facto* regime, it must be argued
that the act of necessity was performed within a framework of historic constitu-
tionality that had not been dissolved. Here, however, the arguments pressed by
Tucker and Burke, in each case against Price, must be said to have diverged.
Tucker was a modernist of much the same school as Hume; he saw the principles
of constitutional liberty as recent in their formation, and the acts of 1688 and
1689 as important contributions to giving them shape. He saw the reliance on
abstract natural right, of which he suspected Price, as implying a violent repudiation of the processes of history, by which commerce was bringing a free and
ordered society into existence. Burke on the other hand had already subscribed
to the view that the constitution was immemorial and prescriptive; he could join
hands with Coke and Blackstone in presenting the men of 1688 as acting within
the framework of the ancient constitution and the *confirmatio cartarum*,[159] and the
history to which natural right did violence was a process of gradual adaptation
and piety toward precedents, far more natural and prudential and less dynamic
than those isolated by the theorists of scientific Whiggism, of whom Tucker was
one. Those who had acted out of necessity were seen to have acted out of reverence
toward precedent and custom.

Burke established a rhetoric of prescriptive conservatism with such intellectual
power and religious conviction, and found so large a public willing to endorse it
— even Gibbon, to his slight dismay, found himself a true believer[160] — that he
bade fair to displace Scottish social theory from its role as the chief ideological
support of the Whig order. This does not mean, however, that he was either
indifferent or hostile to it. As his understanding of the European civility threatened by the French Revolution developed and intensified, he saw that civility
increasingly as an edifice of manners and morality resting on a foundation in
commerce: precisely the theory advanced by Hume, Robertson, and Gibbon,
looking back to the age of Addison, Shaftesbury, and the philosophers of politeness. That the Whig order, as part of this civility, was based on a union of land
and commerce Burke had no doubt whatever, and he held that the virtue of the
state was displayed in the management of its revenue. But the management of

---

[159] Not much had in fact been said about Magna Carta in 1689. Schwoerer, *The Declaration of Rights*,
pp. 195–6.
[160] Norton, ed., *Letters of Edward Gibbon*, vol. III, p. 216.

Whig commerce must be in aristocratic hands, and Burke found increasing reason to fear the emergence of a "middle class" no longer responsive to their patronage and leadership. It was not, however, the entrepreneurial activity of this class that he feared or saw as directing their behavior, but rather their energy, their enthusiasm, and their unbridled capacity to form associations; the category "bourgeoisie" may be imposed on his thought but cannot be directly elicited from it. For these reasons, although he continued to accept and proclaim the civilizing power of commerce, he declared as early as the *Reflections* that commerce stood in need of its own history. It did not negate the feudal honor or the ecclesiastical piety and learning that had preceded it, and to destroy these – as a revolutionary monied interest and intelligentsia were doing in France – was to destroy commerce and civilization themselves. Burke's intellectual solution to the challenge presented by revolution was to enlarge scientific Whiggism in the direction of a deeper historicism; his common-law concern for custom and precedent and his Whig commitment to aristocratic manners and politeness have somehow to be fitted into this context.

As has been indicated in the preceding chapter, the point at which his thought comes closest to breaking with the Whig tradition to which he deeply belonged was that at which he articulated his concern for clerisy. Burke's religiosity – his awareness of the sacred, of the need for transcendent moral sanctions – was real although its roots do not seem to lie in direct religious experience; but to the need for a clergy to preach the discipline of transcendence he added the need of one to further that of manners through the maintenance of learning. Here he struck a chord which was Tory and Laudian rather than Whig and latitudinarian; Whigs knew that there must be polite manners and that the clergy had a role to play in furthering them, but they emphatically did not think – in the tradition of Anglican critics of Henry VIII – that there could be no manners without the learning of an established, beneficed, and landed church. Burke was to persuade many of them that there was such a necessity, but it may have been these among his disciples who found that they had become Tories in a real sense of the word. By denying that culture was dependent on commerce, and affirming the possibility of the converse relationship, he radically modified an important premise of scientific Whiggism, and in suggesting that a class brought into being by commerce might destroy itself by attacking the clerical foundations of culture he gave expression to a new problem in social theory. The barbarian was known; he existed before the growth of commerce had made culture possible. But what was to be said of the philistine, who existed after the relation between culture and commerce had become possible but who denied that it was a necessary one? Burke's demonic men of energy, destroying the framework of manners in the pursuit of power, are examples of what is meant; they appear within the process of history but almost as its negation. Later, however, it was increasingly felt that the growth of commerce might produce a class without manners or culture, and this was to form part of the conventional meaning of the term "bourgeoisie." The process of history itself must be reexamined in this light, and at the point where Burke's revision of perspectives forces scientific Whiggism to redefine itself as Tory stands Coleridge's *Constitution of the Church and State*,[161] a study of how a static landed and a dynamic commercial class must discipline themselves by endowing a clerisy charged with the perpetuation of culture. Coleridge's American disciples, however – such as there were of them – called themselves Whigs.[162]

Burke's immediate intention was to demolish the claim that the English Revolution of 1688 might be read in such a way as to provide justification for the French Revolution of 1789, and thus to assimilate the former event to the latter. Because he was an imaginative and neurotic genius, Burke saw, both rightly and wrongly, very much further than that; he recognized the Revolution in France as an event of vast ideological importance and endeavored to diagnose and resist it by far-reaching ideological statements. As regards actions his countrymen might or might not perform, however, he does not seem to have looked much further, initially at least, than the attempt to assimilate the two revolutions and justify the latter one; yet this issue was to prove sufficient to fragment the Whig political groupings along ideological lines that are by no means identical with those defining the fissure between regime and Commonwealth Whiggism that has concerned us so far. A number of problems meet us here. The myth of the French Revolution is of course no myth; it was instantly recognized as an event that transformed – in some minds it came to constitute – world history, and people in many political cultures found themselves living in terms of their responses to it. Yet the Revolution did not instantly assimilate all other political cultures into its categories, and English political culture was singularly idiosyncratic, tough, and resistant. English radicalism, no less than the defense of the ruling system, was as we have seen possessed of many idioms for expressing its values and demands, and these did not instantly disappear with the news from the Bastille and Versailles. We should therefore ask the question – and seek to answer it in terms of a serious theory of speech and discourse – exactly why radicals in England found it necessary to interpret French events as expressing their demands, and state their values in terms congruent with French discourse as they understood it. This program is probably too ambitious to be undertaken here. As regards Price, the Burkean diagnosis (i.e., that Price was abstracting concepts from one tradition of discourse and imposing them as criteria on all political societies whatever) is plausible as far as it goes, but carries more than

---

[161] *On the Constitution of the Church and State according to the Idea of Each* (London, 1830).

[162] The most recent studies are Daniel Walker Howe, *The Political Culture of the American Whigs* (Chicago, 1979), and Jean V. Matthews, *Rufus Choate: The Law and Civic Virtue* (Philadelphia, 1980).

one meaning. Burke condemned Price as a political rationalist, or as he called it a "metaphysician": one who would construct a theory and then use it to judge, sentence, and transform all practice. Burke had already brought this charge against English reformers, and Tucker earlier still had leveled it against Price himself. It would be useful to determine whether Price was guilty as charged, after which we would be free to determine that it was not necessarily a crime. Historically speaking, had a habit of arguing in the way described established itself in the discourse of English radical intellectuals, whether inclined to Platonism like Price or to associationism like Priestley?[163]

The notion of abstraction can be applied in another way. If we think of English radical sympathizers with the French Revolution as engaged in a species of comparative politics – as asserting that the speech and actions of the French had bases in common with their own speech and action – it is evident that this would entail an exercise in translation, and translating concepts from one mode of speech into another cannot be done without abstracting them, when it is easy to assert that they possess multicontextual if not universal significances. It was Mackintosh's complaint that Burke's language was so English as to leave no terms in which it was possible to understand scientifically what the French had been doing.[164] If we employ the concept of translation, however, we are once again affirming that the English had a discourse of their own, after which we must ask why they found it necessary to assimilate it to French discourse; exactly what was performed when English radicals addressed each other as "Citizen"? And if we affirm that English radical discourse possessed a continuing validity not identical with that possessed by the French,[165] we must sooner or later ask the question: Exactly how Jacobin were the English Jacobins? When it was suggested in the preceding essay that Burke feared the English radicals and dissenters less as revolutionaries than as fellow travelers,[166] the intention was to raise the problem of translation; for the fellow traveler is preeminently one who asserts that the parameters of a neighboring politics are relevant to, and more significant than, those of his own, yet does not leave his politics to inhabit those to which he refers himself. Translation entails the problem of the double standard; every one of those who replied to Burke's *Reflections* declared that the French must not be judged harshly for actions performed in the overthrow of despotism, but if this meant that they must be judged by standards intelligible to themselves, the mere fact that Englishmen did not fully comprehend them meant that they must judge the French

[163] For this dimension of the difference between the two men see Jack G. Fruchtman, *The Apocalyptic Politics of Richard Price and Joseph Priestley* (Philadelphia, 1982).

[164] See pp. 297–8.

[165] E. P. Thompson, *The Making of the English Working Class* (New York, 1964), and a plentiful literature of articles and monographs.

[166] See also Robert L. Dozier, *For King, Constitution and Country: The English Loyalists and the French Revolution* (Lexington, Ky., 1983), p. 69.

either less or more severely than they could ever judge themselves. This perplexity now entered political discourse as a constant and has never left it.

We are circling around the problem and have returned to the point of recognizing that Englishmen for all their idiosyncrasy of culture did evaluate their actions with reference to the pretensions of the French. This, which had moved Price to speak and Burke to write, is highly relevant to the fragmentation that now overtook the Whigs. Between 1789 and 1793 the followers of Charles James Fox moved away from Burke's condemnation of the French Revolution and into opposition to Pitt's policy of making war against it. Because they possessed a political organization[167] and a newspaper that were in the habit of using the phrase "the Whig party," they were able to arrogate the label "Whig" to themselves, and it was possible for the *Morning Chronicle* to announce that "the great body of the Whigs of England" had sat in judgment on the disputes between Burke and Fox and pronounced in the latter's favor; "the consequence is that Mr. Burke retires from parliament." Burke, who found this kind of party discipline as uncongenial as many still do, retorted with *An Appeal from the New to the Old Whigs*. The title is at variance with the terminology we have been using: Burke's "Old Whigs" are in fact the great families constituting the "Old Corps" of Whigs, and in particular their Revolution ancestors, whereas his "New" are still in many ways the heirs of the Old (True, Real, Independent, Honest) Whigs of the Commonwealth tradition.[168] The *Appeal* essays once more to demonstrate that the Revolution of 1688 was the antithesis of that of 1789, and the foundations it discovers for the dethroning of James II and the impeachment of Henry Sacheverell are, if anything, more consonant with the thinking of Revolution Tories than are those laid down in the *Reflections*. Regime Whiggism had long since absorbed Revolution Toryism and made it its own, but perhaps we have here one clue to the curious change that at some point overcame the term "Tory" and made it applicable to the great Whig families who took Pitt's path and also Burke's. The motives that led Fox to stand out in opposition to the war with France cannot be too simply stated;[169] among them may have been the feeling that the radical associations offered a power base still necessary to him, but we know also that he continued to see the policies of the crown and its ministers as "Tory," in the Bolingbrokean sense that they aimed to use royal influence to break up aristocratic associations. This would be the normal way of using the term; there is an evident sense of paradox in the remark made a few years later

[167] O'Gorman, *Whig Party and the French Revolution,* pp. 12–31.

[168] O'Gorman shows clearly that Burke's terminology was not idiosyncratic; the equation Old Whigs/Old Corps was perhaps more current than the use of "Old Whig" in a "Commonwealth" sense. He also shows that Burke's publication was by no means welcomed by the Old Whigs to whom he appealed; as usual, he seemed to them too strident.

[169] O'Gorman, *Whig Party and the French Revolution;* Herbert Butterfield, "Charles James Fox and the Whig Opposition, 1792," *Cambridge Historical Journal* IX, 3 (1949), pp. 293–330.

that the French Revolution "had made Gibbon a Christian and Windham a Tory."[170] But the word could also be used to denote more generally a supporter of the crown and its policies, as to Americans it had meant a supporter of royal authority exercised in Parliament. Nothing could be more Whiggish than the Grenvilles and Portlands who now rallied to support Pitt and the war with France; nothing could be more Whiggish than the existing parliamentary and ecclesiastical structures, reform of which came to be demanded by those who were opposed to the war. It is not yet fully understood by what stages the word "Tory" came, whether in contemporary or in historians' parlance, to be applied to stern unbending defenders of the Septennial Act, the Toleration Act, and the national debt.

The Foxite Whigs' decision to oppose the war with France reopened a problem closely akin to that of fellow traveling. What came to be termed "antipolemic" (meaning antiwar) argument could be, and was, expressed in language dating from the Queen Anne Tories: A war in Europe with subsidized allies corrupted the body politic; it multiplied patronage, pensions, honors, standing armies, and the national debt. Milton! thou shouldst be living at this hour; the Commonwealth voice was as audible as that of the country, and both remained so for the next twenty years. But at the same time the war was an ideological conflict, fought against what Burke was to term an armed doctrine; to oppose it, therefore, was to declare it as doctrinaire as its adversary and to place its opponents in the position of those who were above ideologies, or could choose between them without choosing either. This was more than ever the case when it appeared that the war must go on until monarchy was restored to France, and involved repressive measures against ideological dissentients at home, not all of whom succeeded in avoiding subversive actions. Quite unlike the opposition in the War of the Spanish Succession or even the American Revolution, the opposition to the Revolutionary and (with modifications) the Napoleonic Wars was in the predicament of a principled opposition to a principled war. It might very laudably oppose an ideological crusade that had become repressive of domestic liberties; yet once the opposition suggested that the ideological hostility of the adversary in the war was not so harmful as domestic repression, it was unclear what standards it was using to criticize the adversary, and it could be accused, without being certain of its reply, of thinking a few treason trials at home worse than a reign of terror or a military despotism abroad. Intelligent critics were aware of this problem, and when Napoleon seemed to have converted the war into one against tyranny, or the Spanish risings into a war for popular liberties, the critics could adjust their position without losing their principles; yet the problem of the double standard was almost structurally inescapable, as was that of the apparent defeatism that

[170] Paul Turnbull, "The Supposed Infidelity of Edward Gibbon," *Historical Journal* XXVI, 1 (1982), pp. 23–42. Quoted from Lord Glenbervie's diary.

arose when one doubted the military prospects of a war because one disapproved of its moral foundations. What Americans might term the Copperhead role dogged the antiwar Whigs to the end of the Hundred Days, and even William Cobbett, who was more like John Bull than most Englishmen, was habitually defeatist regarding the war in the Peninsula.[171]

Those who opposed the French wars were almost without exception patriots as the term was used in the nineteenth century (very differently, as we have seen, from its use in the prerevolutionary era to denote one whose ostensible concern for public virtue carried him to the point of republicanism). Their loyalty was to the national community and its values, and if they doubted the country's right to victory they did not desire its defeat. Yet there were those who, without doing anything to ensure defeat, spoke as if they expected it – as if the shortcomings of the regime ensured that it would and should fail; they began with a laudable desire to understand the enemy's point of view and ended by hero-worshipping Napoleon as their successors would Stalin. It is desirable, though it will not be welcome,[172] to dwell on this, because we are dealing with the origins of what has become an integral part of modern political culture.

From the age of the counterrevolutionary wars A. J. P. Taylor has traced the lineage of "trouble-makers" and "dissenters" (as he uses the terms), who object less to the misuse than to the use of national power, because they operate by moral standards that must always condemn it.[173] Richard Price was among the first of them, and it is tempting to explain them along Burkean lines: they erect the community's morals into a standard of theory by which its practice can only be condemned. But we must add to this by comprehending that these antipatriots were the heirs of the "patriots" so defined by eighteenth-century usage: the "Mock Patriots" as Tucker splenetically called them. Where the patriot followed public virtue to the point of rejecting his country's institutions, the antipatriot follows moral virtue to the point of rejecting his country's community. To the patriot in the modern or postrevolutionary sense, his country is his country right or wrong, and he is tempted to pronounce it always right. The antipatriot is tempted to pronounce it always wrong, because his notion of a country is a congregation engaged in moral censure and admonition, but ruled by politicians whose corruption is taken for granted. Tucker and Burke witnessed, and in their eyes Price personified, the formation of this mentality, which came about when the Old Whig and Nonconformist consciences were unified in the presence of the ideological problem imposed upon discourse by the revolution in France. Burke overstated but did not altogether misstate the case when he declared that the

[171] George Spater, *William Cobbett: The Poor Man's Friend,* 2 vols. (Cambridge, 1982).
[172] Contemporary writing about radicalism and repression in these years maintains a high temperature. The present writer finds popular discontent and popular patriotism equally understandable.
[173] A. J. P. Taylor, *The Trouble-Makers: Dissent Over Foreign Policy 1792–1939* (London, 1957).

opposition to the French war marked the end of patriotism as he had known it. The antiwar intelligentsia had been born, with their moral certainties, their double standards, and their love of vicarious capitulation. To that extent it was a new world.

A deservedly more benign — though in no way uncritical — account of these people has been given by J. E. Cookson.[174] He emphasizes their role in the development of nineteenth-century middle-class liberalism and the Nonconformist conscience, terms that go together in consequence of the predominant degree to which the antiwar movement was rooted in the radical Unitarian associations of the 1780s. He is thus enabled to bring out the essentially ecclesiastical character of the terms "Tory" and "liberal" at the beginning of their modern history. From the time of the first petitions for the relief of Dissenters from civil disabilities, a "Tory" came to mean one who insisted that a Toleration Act and a Test Act were interdependent, and that the Revolution Settlement implied a high degree of identity between the political nation and an established church. Most "Tories" in this sense were or had been Whigs, and it can even be doubted whether Burke, with his support for the relief of Irish Catholics, would have qualified for the term. A "liberal" thinker, on the other hand, was one who advocated a religion of free inquiry and speculation, and for this reason held religious freedom to entail an equality of civic rights. Though other meanings attached themselves with varying degrees of rapidity, it was long before the word "liberalism" took on the full range of political meanings, and longer still before it took on the full range of economic meanings, with which we now burden it.

Dr. Cookson's "liberals" were before anything else an antiwar movement, and he gives ample detail of the extent to which their opposition to war was an opposition to aristocratic control of a military and financial state, couched in the established language of attack on a monied interest. It follows that their criticisms were directed, much as were those of their Jeffersonian contemporaries in the United States, against a military and financial, even more than a landed, aristocracy; they did not need to echo, but would have fully endorsed, the American contention that the former sort of aristocracy would infallibly engender the latter. This is the context in which we should read their incessant praise of the "middle classes" as composed of self-reliant men of enterprise. They knew, as their peers in New England and the mid-Atlantic states were coming to know, that they were living in a society in which commercial relations were more and more preponderating over agrarian relations; but they acclaimed the investor of personal property in precisely the same language, and for precisely the same independence and virtue as opposed to corruption, as their neo-Harringtonian forebears had deployed in acclaiming the master of real property in land. In

---

[174] *The Friends of Peace: Anti-War Liberalism in England, 1793–1815* (Cambridge, 1982).

America if not in Britain, it is possible to discover antebellum Whigs who followed John Taylor in reserving the term "capitalism" for a system of public finance controlled by an aristocracy,[175] and in Britain we may allow ourselves to think of the later differences between northern and midland industry and London and Westminster banking.[176] There is a case for seeing praise of the individual entrepreneur as the country ideology of capitalism.

(iii)

Adopting language originally framed to excoriate the Whig order for which he stood, Burke had diagnosed the French Revolution as the conspiracy of a monied interest, aimed at establishing a new kind of despotism on the dissolution by power and paper of all the natural ties among men − including, of course, the natural ties of commerce. Paine retorted by directing this language back into its historic channels; he denounced the war against the Revolution as the conspiracy of a boroughmongering and patronage-wielding aristocracy, aimed at perpetuating the system of paper money and public credit on which its power rested. In the second part of *The Rights of Man* he outlined a scheme for democratic control of the fiscal structure and the institution of systems of worker insurance. The French Revolution had in a sense been a national and democratic takeover of the debts of the French crown, and schemes like Paine's, but even more ambitious, were being propounded by such as Linguet.[177] In English terms, we may read Part II of *The Rights of Man* as marking a decisive move away from any dream of a merely rustic, republican, or Anglo-Saxon democracy; revolutionaries must seize the credit of the state because they lived in a world that credit had transformed. Yet Paine's starting point (and in this respect Burke's) was in the country and Commonwealth denunciation of the credit structure, which continued to carry with it idealizations of the independence of the small proprietor, and quasi-Harringtonian democratic utopias continued to be constructed by Spence and others; to seize the credit structure might be to perpetuate, to transform, or to abolish it. Paine wrote several prophecies of the imminent collapse of British aristocratic war finance, and it was one of these that caught the eye of that quintessentially country democrat William Cobbett, during his second American so-

---

[175] Rush Welter, *The Mind of America, 1820–1860* (New York; 1975). For an interesting account of Joseph Priestley in his Pennsylvania years, seeking to reconcile the militia ideal with the idea of a commercial society, see Lawrence Delbert Cress, *Citizens in Arms: The Army and Militia in American Society to the War of 1812* (Chapel Hill; N.C., 1982).

[176] W. D. Rubinstein, "Wealth, Elites and the Class Structure of Modern Britain," *Past and Present* LXXVI (1977), pp. 99–126; and with reservations, Martin J. Wiener, *English Culture and the Decline of the Industrial Spirit* (Cambridge, 1981).

[177] Darlene Gay Levy, *The Ideas and Careers of Simon-Nicolas-Henri Linguet: A Study in Eighteenth-Century French Politics* (Urbana, Ill., 1980).

journ in 1817–19, and caused him to exhume Paine's bones and bring them back to England as relics.[178] To anyone but Cobbett it would have occurred – as to everyone but Cobbett it immediately did – that he was also bringing back the bones of the author of *The Age of Reason*.

The point of the incident is that British radicalism, throughout the age of counterrevolutionary war, agrarian misery and rebellion, and industrial change, continued to be expressed in terms of a sustained attack on the Whig oligarchy, variously known as "Old Corruption" and "The Thing." Aristocratic control of politics, patronage, and finance continued to be put forward as the root cause of moral evils such as corruption and material evils such as poverty; removal of aristocratic control was seen as the prerequisite if not the ultimate goal of all reform. We know that the language in which Old Corruption was defined was by this time a century old, and as much Tory as Whig in its origins and transmission; the time has now come to claim that it remained paradigmatic. Even had Cobbett been an isolated and eccentric exhibitionist, the depth of his indebtedness to Paine would demand our attention, but the phenomenon has a deeper meaning. Both men were asserting, in the eighteenth-century tradition, that the credit structure must soon collapse under the weight of its increasing debts, paper issues, and corruption; where Paine differed from Hume and Price was in his insistence that a national debt as such was benign and helped hold the nation together, and that only aristocratic mismanagement ensured disaster.[179] Cobbett was so certain of disaster that he offered to be broiled on a gridiron if it did not occur, and when Huskisson and others appeared to have held the system in equilibrium Cobbett hoisted a gridiron over his newspaper offices, partly as a gesture of defiance, partly as a declaration that if the financial apocalypse were not now, yet it would come.[180] The survival of the banking edifice through the 1820s made two things possible. One was the 1832 reform of the parliamentary structure by Whigs not acting on Commonwealth and country principles, a reform celebrated by Macaulay as an assurance of economic health and progress. The other was the sustained endeavor of Marx and many others to persuade the English working classes that the causes of immiseration lay not in the aristocratic structure of Old Corruption, but deeper within capitalism in the relations between capital and labor. There is a sense in which Whig recovery and reform were necessary conditions of Marx's intellectual system, and this is one reason why Marxists tend to be Whig historians.

A Marxist analysis encourages us to look for the supersession of a politics based on the confrontation between the oligarchy and its rural and urban opponents by

---

[178] Spater, *William Cobbett*, vol. II, pp. 289–90, 313–16, 346–7, 376–9, 387, 556n. 9.

[179] This may be traced as far back as *Common Sense;* see Philip S. Foner, ed., *The Life and Major Writings of Thomas Paine* (Secaucus, N.J., 1974), p. 32.

[180] Spater, *William Cobbett*, Vol. II, pp. 365, 413, 421, 424.

one based on that between two classes, one of employers and the other of workers, the one employing an ideology of the free market and the other an ideology of the exploitation of labor. We should indeed look for the emergence of both these ideologies, since it would seem that they did appear and the classes they presuppose may have appeared also. But to write of them Whiggishly – on the supposition that nothing matters except their appearance and that the transition from one politics to the other was rapid and complete in proportion to its assumed significance – is to divert the historian of ideology from his proper task, that of discovering and articulating the languages in which the inhabitants of an era did in fact present their society and cosmos to themselves and to each other. We have supposed that a version of the entrenched radicalism of Commonwealth and country presented the context in which – if not the matrix out of which – new radical languages must take shape; a sketch of the processes by which this occurred may be offered if we examine some of the replies to Burke's *Reflections,* and some of the ideologies that made their appearance soon after.

Paine's *The Rights of Man* is, of course, the most famous of these. It contained elements probably new and certainly unfamiliar in the context of Commonwealth and country radicalism, and these differentiate it from the reply to Burke written by that simon-pure representative of the old quasi-republican tradition, Catherine Macaulay;[181] but we have also seen how Paine inspired Cobbett to perpetuate the ideology that had Old Corruption at its center. Not all replies to Burke, however, were written by those Old Whigs whom he called New. Mary Wollstonecraft's *Vindication of the Rights of Man* permits us to look toward that revolutionary rationalism in which William Godwin a few years later was to blend a secularized millennialism with elements of Locke and Rousseau,[182] in a way that Tucker would have had no difficulty in recognizing. Wollstonecraft, however, had a quarrel of her own with Rousseau, which bore fruit in her far more striking *Vindication of the Rights of Women;* from the standpoint of the present volume, what is most noteworthy here is that the *rights* she claims for women are to the material means of independence and *virtue,* but that she further claims that the *manners* (and therefore the morals) of society need to be drastically revised before the virtues expected of women can be defined without profound falsity.

We are traveling away from the central and of course masculine structures of English and Scottish discourse, but a Rousseauist concern for the integrity of personality in the confrontation with society – itself not distant from the familiar concerns with virtue, corruption, and diversification – may serve to recall that there took shape at this time a kind of radicalism to which we attach the epithet "romantic." Godwin's early training as a Sandemanian makes us ask about the

[181] Catherine Macaulay (afterward Graham), *Observations on the Reflections of the Right Hon. Edmund Burke . . . in a letter to the Right Hon. the Earl of Stanhope* (London, 1790).
[182] Don Locke, *A Fantasy of Reason: The Life and Thought of William Godwin* (London, 1980).

religious origins of his rationalism and reminds us at the same time that Whig political culture unhesitatingly identified nearly all forms of radicalism as "enthusiasm." Nor was this diagnosis necessarily mistaken. The path that led from an inner and personal religion to a rationalist and secular libertarian individualism had been pointed out and marked with warning signs by Hume, Tucker, and Burke, and there are hints that the immanentism and hermeticism of Margaret Jacob's Radical Enlightenment were emerging from below ground to take shape in a rich variety of gnoses. It is not merely that the years of revolution and counterrevolution were fertile in millennialisms and illuminisms;[183] something even deeper was happening. The two greatest system builders among English romantics are assuredly Blake and Coleridge. In the one we hear voices coming from very old and deep layers in the archaeology of heretical and antinomian counterreligion, though some severance from these roots seems necessary in order to account for Blake's need to invent his own mythology and nomenclature; only great genius can make the difference between Golgonooza and Barsoom. In the other we encounter a scholarly endeavor, carried out at the levels of elite literacy, to uncover and recover what Coleridge claims to be the buried tradition of English Platonic and Neoplatonic thinking, to which a return must be made if a revolution (or counterrevolution) is to be achieved.[184] In both, we discover the invention of a countermyth, to which Coleridge's Platonism and Blake's Everlasting Gospel were alike opposed: the myth that English thought had been dominated since the early seventeenth century by the succession of Bacon, Hobbes, Locke, and Newton, the cold mechanical philosophers of rationalist individualism. How far from historic reality this myth was should by now be evident; Whig society had been philosophically defended on grounds of its richness, fecundity, and diversity, its capacity to develop sentiment and sympathy, transaction and conversation, taste and science, the polite together with the mechanical arts. It is not too much to say that commerce had been celebrated as poetry before it was denounced as pushpin. Yet Bentham and Mill were by now on the scene, and there was clearly a case for regarding them – though they were not Whigs – as cold mechanical philosophers. The myth of "the single vision and Newton's sleep" answered some deep needs of the imagination, which is not to say that we should allow it to write our history for us. Of all the inventions of radical thought at this period, it is the one most insistently and angrily maintained on right and left at the present day.

The attack on the four philosophers of the single vision was intended as an

---

[183] Clarke Garrett, *Respectable Folly: Millenarians and the French Revolution in France and England* (Baltimore, 1975); W. H. Oliver, *Prophets and Millennialists: The Uses of Biblical Prophecy in England from the 1790s to the 1840s* (Auckland and Oxford, 1978); J. F. C. Harrison, *The Second Coming: Popular Millenarism 1780–1850* (New Brunswick, N.J., 1980).

[184] To indicate the growth of Coleridge's thought in footnotes is a dangerous task, but see particularly *The Friend* and *On the Constitution of the Church and State,* cited in note following.

attack on reigning Whig culture and reminds us that romantic radicalism, like other radicalisms before it, flowed from both a republican and a Tory source; this may help us understand the movement of Coleridge, Southey, and Wordsworth from republican youth to Tory old age, but it further complicates the meaning of the word "Tory" at a time when it was increasingly used to denote a last-ditch defender of the Whig order. Burke, in his one major departure from the Whig mainstream, had declared that manners continued to rest on an ecclesiastical and chivalric foundation and had drawn upon Anglican tradition to present the clergy (or clerisy) as protectors of learning and culture; we saw how easily this could be turned into a criticism rather than a defense of the Whig aristocracy. A "Tory" in the post-Burkean sense might be one who sternly maintained that an established clergy was needed to preserve both moral and cultural discipline, but he would have to believe (as many did) in the conjunction of the clergy with the landed aristocracy and gentry in order to qualify as a conservative. If he did not, he might remain a Tory but would tend to become a radical: one who believed, in an enlargement of the Bolingbrokean tradition, that the gentry needed outside assistance in order to uphold the values for which they stood. Bolingbroke had seen a "patriot king" in this role, but it could be performed by a democracy, a clergy, or a clerisy. By 1828 Coleridge was devising a Tory utopia in which aristocracy, commerciality, and clerisy discharged separate but reinforcing functions; but his "national church" or clerisy is concerned to maintain culture rather than religion, and we move irrevocably out of the reigning and into the radical mode of thought once it appears that the three agencies operate independently of one another rather than in shared dependence on a central sovereignty. Coleridge's *On the Constitution in Church and State* is in many ways a counterpart to Harrington's *Oceana,* which he admired[185] and supposed to belong to his "Platonic" tradition (as possibly it does).[186]

A Tory radicalism – in the eighteenth century a means of maintaining Roman virtue in a fading partnership with Christian dynasticism – could in the early nineteenth century grow out of the fissures Burke had managed to open between aristocracy, commerce, and culture. It was post-Whig in the sense that it accepted and sought to exploit the primacy that Whig thought since Defoe and Addison had accorded to the notions of manners and culture, but it was also paternalist to the extent that it seemed to make culture dependent on gentry and clerical protection. Since a nostalgia for the Middle Ages was on the point of developing (for reasons to be examined in a moment) we seem to be finding merit at last in the theses of Thompson and Kramnick; but it is the defect of any

---

[185] *On the Constitution of the Church and State,* ed. and with an intro. by John Barrell (London, 1972), p. 51.
[186] See Pocock, "Contexts for the Study of James Harrington," *Il Pensiero Politico* XI, 1 (1978), pp. 20–35.

"paternalist" interpretation of Tory opposition that paternalism could be (and was) outbid by patronage any day of any week in the long years of Whig suprem- acy. Radical Toryism derived its republican content from the fact that it was an attempt to make clients act independently of their patrons, which was why read- ers of Cicero so easily saw it as Catilinarian. In ecclesiastical matters, silent though these may have been from Atterbury to Newman, its churchmanship could be so high as to make the church independent of the establishment, while in the rela- tions between classes the idea of a Tory democracy could at times go to surprising lengths. J. B. Bernard, an unusually deviant Fellow of King's, was in the 1830s close to calling for a workers' revolution in support of the landed interest.[187]

We are on the wilder shores here, but their sands stretch far away. The prob- lem of pauperism imposed itself on the English consciousness during the 1790s, and Malthus's *Essay on the Principles of Population* is a result. This may be charac- terized as a piece of pessimistic Whiggism, part of that "stern *paideia*" that max- imized the prices to be paid for civil order the better to emphasize that the prices would have to be paid. William Cobbett saw Malthus's *Essay* in that light, to- gether with the whole developing science of political economy, and like others he tried to imagine a rural society in which the cost in suffering and humiliation would be less high. Since it was a commonplace that the Whig aristocracy and the landowning class generally – whom he detested not as Norman conquerors but as paper-money upstarts – had risen to power on the dissolution of the mon- asteries, it was possible to imagine a time when the protectors of learning had also been the protectors of the needy. Cobbett did not join the neomedievalist gentry in nostalgia for a hearty and hospitable baronage whose doors had stood open to the poor (he knew too much about rural life for that), but he did persuade himself that charity to the unfortunate had been better managed by the monks than by the poor-law overseers. He enlarged this issue until it became his key to the understanding of history. His *History of the Protestant Reformation in England and Ireland* (1824) was a total indictment of English Protestantism (dissent no less than establishment), not merely for the destruction of medieval charity, but for the erection of capitalist agriculture, political oligarchy, corruption, borough- mongering, paper money, standing armies, and The Thing in all its aspects, with the Puritan, American, and French revolutions thrown in as "Reformations Two, Three, and Four." There is much more here than autodidact egocentricity; Cob- bett appears as the first Englishman to reject, by wholesale and with his eyes open, the three hundred years of history in which England had taken its modern shape. To do this, we may wish to assert, he needed a fully revolutionary con-

---

[187] James B. Bernard, *Theory of the Constitution Compared with its Practice in Ancient and Modern Times* (London, 1834). See Gregory Claes, "A Utopian Tory Revolutionary at Cambridge: The Political Ideas and Schemes of James Bernard, 1834–1839," *Historical Journal* XXV, 3 (1982), pp. 583– 604.

sciousness, and Marxism, with great plausibility, would have him find it in a proletarian class-consciousness that should recognize capitalism as the agency transforming the world and the proletariat as the victim, inheritor, and resolution of that transformation. But if there was a class present in Cobbett's thinking, it consisted not of proletarians but of cottagers, and the most revolutionary act they were likely to perform was to go to America and not come back (Cobbett himself returned to England twice). The cottager was not likely to see himself as inhabiting a world transformed by the cash nexus or as empowered by history to carry on the process of creating it; he would prefer to inveigh against the capitalization of agriculture and the corruption of the unspecialized labor he had once performed. The language of country opposition was suited to his purposes, and since he already possessed a politicized but not precisely a class consciousness, he found it far more natural to denounce his betters for corrupting the realm than for exploiting his labor; his ideology was wide-ranging and unspecialized, and it is entertaining to imagine Cobbett's observations on the phrase "the idiocy of rural life."

It was hard to condemn the destruction of rural society without engaging in some degree of nostalgia, and a wholesale condemnation of modernity necessarily entailed some degree of neomedievalism. There was a neomedievalism among romantic gentry who liked to imagine the days when they had been Tory protectors of the poor, Whig defenders of their ancient liberties, and Burkean-Coleridgean upholders of a code of chivalric manners.[188] But this is perhaps of less significance than the opportunity that thinking like Cobbett's supplied to the clerics, academics, and gentlemen who were taking up the role of the clerisy and beginning with the Arnolds to represent culture as the governing class's title to govern. Their thinking could be Tory and even Anglo-Catholic, but it could also be as violently radical as Cobbett's own, and given that a war between classes was always quite as likely in the countryside as in the factory towns, a Tory radicalism remained as lively a possibility in the nineteenth century as it had ever been in the eighteenth and inherited some of its language from the former age. Even today, it might not be impossible to classify English Marxist thinkers as either progressive radical Whigs for whom socialism is the rebellious but natural son of liberalism, or alienated Tory radicals who denounce liberal capitalism, instead of praising it for its revolutionary role, as the destroyer of popular community and moral economy. The difference has something to do with the distribution of emphasis between rural and urban history, more with the view the individual takes of the historic significance of the specialization of labor.

---

[188] Mark Girouard, *The Return to Camelot: Chivalry and the English Gentleman* (New Haven, Conn., 1981).

V.   From Cobbett's *History of the Reformation* to
Macaulay's *History of England*

(*i*)

Where there are Tories there should also be Whigs, but the accidents of nomenclature during the counterrevolutionary wars left the term "Tory" denoting an
inflexible defender of the Revolution-Hanoverian Whig regime, and the term
"Whig" denoting an aristocratic frondeur and member of an antiwar rump, which
had survived from the earlier opposition to George III and become a magnet
attracting a miscellany of ideologies. It was of this "Whig party" that Byron
wrote:

> Where are the Grenvilles? Turn'd, as usual. Where
> My friends the Whigs? Exactly where they were.
> . . . Nought's permanent among the human race
> Except the Whigs not getting into place. [189]

But it has to be reiterated that Grenvilles were Whigs and had never been
anything else. We have to distinguish between the "Whig party" (Burke's "New
Whigs") and the century-old Whig regime that Burke's "Old Whigs" (survivors
of the Old Corps becoming known as "Tories") defended against its enemies.
What of "Old Whig" thought in the very different sense made known to us by
Caroline Robbins? Insofar as there was a continuous rhetoric demanding reform
of the franchise and the electoral system – the "Whig party" tended to avoid
using it – this contained elements as old as the First Whigs if not the New
Model Army: Old Whig in the Commonwealth sense. Insofar as the Whig party
and other radical groups kept up the attack on the king's ministers, in Parliament
and at war, as exponents of Old Corruption, it employed a language as old as
Robert Harley and Charles Davenant: both Commonwealth Whig and country
Tory. By 1832, however, the wars were over and the finances stabilized, Cobbett
was on his gridiron, and something like a "Walpolean moment" had recurred.
But instead of reimposing an oligarchic *governo stretto*, a recombination of Whiggisms, capable of governing and claiming to speak for the mainstream Whig
tradition, reversed the policy symbolized by the Septennial Act and carried a
cautious but at the same time far-reaching measure of parliamentary reform. This
was bitterly opposed by "Tories" who saw themselves as the heirs of Pitt and
Burke, but the greatest of its intellectual apologists presented reform as a Burkean measure. Macaulay declared that because England had enjoyed a "preserving

[189] *Don Juan*, canto XI, stanzas 79, 82.

revolution" in 1688, Britain had escaped a "destroying revolution" in 1848,[190] and it has recently been pointed out how little sympathy he displayed for either the country or the Commonwealth criticisms of what was established in 1688 and after.[191] A revision of ideologies accompanied the formation of Reform Whiggism and the "Whig interpretation of history," and this long essay has been concerned with how we must see history now that this interpretation has been taken apart. It may therefore conclude with a study of how it was put together.

Given that reform was accomplished within the parameters of regime history, we need to ask what role in preparing it was played by the various radicals who during the Napoleonic wars were active in and around the city of Westminster: Burdett, Hobhouse, Cartwright, Cobbett, Hunt, and Place. All of these heartily mistrusted the Whig party as engaged in the aristocratic game of politics it pretended to oppose, and all remembered with pleasure their victory over the aging Sheridan. But it is always difficult to decide when reform ceases to be radical and becomes accommodation, and though they found it easy to denounce the aristocracy in politics as a monolith of Old Corruption, the Westminster radicals could see within their own ranks evidence that gentlemen politicians could demand reform and denounce corruption without ceasing to be what they were; *governo largo* is an aristocratic strategy as well as *governo stretto*. This study has insisted that the roots of radicalism reached far back in history, and it is with satisfaction that one learns that Burdett was recognized as at heart a Queen Anne Tory and used to meet with Byron, Hobhouse, Kinnaird, and Sir Robert Wilson in a Westminster dining club called The Rota.[192] Harringtonian echoes, while they still resounded, placed these radicals not very far left of the heirs of Fox in the Whig party. One is tempted, of course, to say that this was the end of the neo-Harringtonian road; the latest historian of the Philosophic Radicals thinks that the echoes of agrarian radicalism died out during the 1820s and that the future in Westminster belonged to the Benthamite contributions to the *Westminster Review*.[193] These beyond doubt had not a neo-Harringtonian cell in their bodies, and though they became radical democrats in order to do battle with Old Corruption, it was because Mill had convinced Bentham (or Mill and Bentham themselves) that the aristocratic regime would never enact philosophic legislation. But we have to be careful in evaluating their role. Burdett and Hobhouse ended their days as conservatives, which will furnish some with more evidence of the nostalgic and paternalist character of Harringtonian social criticism; yet the attack on aristocratic corruption remained powerful in working-class rhetoric,

[190] Macaulay, *History of England from the Accession of James II*, ed. C. H. Firth (London, 1913).

[191] J. W. Burrow, *A Liberal Descent: Victorian Historians and the English Past* (Cambridge, 1981).

[192] J. Ann Hone, *For the Cause of Truth: Radicalism in London: 1796–1821* (Oxford, 1982), p. 281. See the following note.

[193] William Thomas, *The Philosophic Radicals: Nine Studies in Theory and Practice, 1817–1841* (Oxford, 1979), pp. 47–57, 62 (the Rota Club), 95–6.

and the names of Coleridge and Cobbett ought to remind us that agrarian values remained valid in stating a radical (and in Cobbett's case an authentically populist) criticism of a commercial society that certainly included the ideology of Philosophic Radicalism. Perhaps we should emphasize less the proposition (which is certainly true) that some kinds of radicalism became Tory, and more the proposition (which has been neglected) that some kinds of Toryism remained radical. The hypothesis that at some point in time a liberalism that was nothing but bourgeois must be confronted by a socialism that could only be proletarian is difficult to elaborate without blotting out the rural scene.

It may very well be, however, that such a figure as Cobbett was more effective as a critic of the changing social relations of his age than as a source of the arguments by which parliamentary reform was in fact justified; the Reform of 1832 was not carried by men he admired, nor was it intended to remedy the ills of which he complained, and there are many contemporary radicals of whom the same could be said. It was achieved by parliamentary aristocrats who believed in a deferential society; what was changing rapidly was the understanding of deference itself and of the social, moral, and political framework within which it operated.[194] The ideology of reform was an ideology of modernization, a concept long effective in the vocabulary of the Whig order. This is not the place in which to review the long and complex debate that preceded the Reform Act, but an attempt will be made to place it in the context of the history of Whiggism during the preceding century — a context of which the debaters themselves were acutely aware. We return, then, to the Revolution of 1688 as the point from which regime and radical Whiggism divided, or rather to the seminal debate concerning the relation between 1688 and 1789.

After Paine's *The Rights of Man,* the most significant of the various replies to Burke's *Reflections* is probably Sir James Mackintosh's *Vindiciae Gallicae,* less because of its argumentative content than of the strategic place it occupies in the argument. Mackintosh complained that Burke's appeal to precedent and prescription was so absolute and constricting that it shut out all understanding of what the French had been doing or why a revolution had occurred; it was a scientific necessity, he said, to have some means of understanding these phenomena, which Burke had left to seem a mere mystery of iniquity.[195] The fact that Mackintosh was not able to avoid the double-standard argument, the fact that a few years later he performed what looks like an intellectual capitulation and submission to Burke, should not obscure the further fact that we are listening here to a representative of Scottish scientific Whiggism.[196] Deeply though Burke was allied to

[194] D. C. Moore, *The Politics of Deference: A Study in the Mid-Nineteenth Century English Political System* (New York, 1976).

[195] *Vindiciae Gallicae,* sec. VI.

[196] Lionel A. McKenzie, "The French Revolution and English Parliamentary Reform; James Mackintosh and the *Vindiciae Gallicae,*" *Eighteenth-Century Studies* XIV, 3 (1981), pp. 264–82.

the great Scottish theorists, his appeal to prescription has such roots in English common-law thinking that it was out of place in Scotland; before Sir Walter Scott could achieve a Scottish equivalent to Burke's conservatism he had to achieve a new imaginative vision of the history of Scotland. Yet it has been argued earlier here that the authority of Burke's argument was such that for a time it virtually drove out and replaced the progressive modernisms of the Scottish Enlightenment as a means of authorizing the Whig order; we have to look closely before we can see in how many ways Burke was in fact an ally of the Scottish school.

Burke's was not a mode of thinking that Mackintosh could adopt, even when he was obliged to endorse it; Gibbon, on the other hand, slipped into a Burkean mode almost as soon as Burke himself. The fierceness of intellectual reaction and repression in Scotland, however, was even greater than in England and forced Scotsmen who might otherwise have thought like Burke's "New Whigs" to choose between submission, emigration, and a risky independence. Mackintosh for some years chose submission, and Dugald Stewart's career was a series of retreats from the subversive attitudes of Hume to a sepulcher exalted above his on the Calton Hill. John Millar, on the other hand, a still-youthful representative of the great generation of the 1770s, was shielded by the patronage of opposition Whig nobility in both kingdoms, and his *Historical View of the English Government,* which began appearing in 1787, is dedicated to Charles James Fox, without whose name coming to mind (says Millar) it is impossible to think about the principles of the constitution for very long.[197] This is not enough to make the *Historical View* a radical work, but it does give its author a significant place in the process by which the Whig mind recovered from the French Revolution and from Burke's assaults on it.

Scottish scientific Whiggism – of which Millar's *Origin of Ranks* is an outstanding representative – had employed the notion of a progress of society, from savagery to commerce, as a means of vindicating the Whig order and presenting commercial and specialized society as superior to the classical republics and their ancient virtue. The *Historical View* does not retreat from this position or equate corruption with the loss of classical virtue, but it does emphasize (as Millar was entitled to stress) that corruption is the danger to which government and liberty in commercial societies are peculiarly exposed; this notion is combined with an apparent fear that the privatization of the socially specialized personality may have gone further in England than in still underdeveloped Scotland and may have begun to produce those deleterious effects that had troubled Adam Smith.[198] Millar further made it clear, as Hume would certainly not have done, that the English constitution contained certain principles, built into it at an earlier time,

---

[197] Millar, *An Historical View of the English Government from the Settlement of the Saxons in Britain to the Revolution in 1688,* 4th ed., 4 vols. (London, 1818), vol. I, sig. A2.
[198] *Historical View,* vol. III, pp. 86–94; IV, 151–3, 198–9.

designed to protect political liberty against the effects of corruption and that it was the business of statesmen at all times to see that these principles were preserved. We encounter here the question of Millar's attitude toward the English ancient constitution, which the modernism inherent in Scottish scientific history had hitherto tended to overthrow. As an original theorist of European feudalism, Millar could not deny that English history had passed through a feudal phase, and he made it quite clear that this was incompatible with many of the supposedly immemorial liberties (including the representation of the Commons in Parliament) on which the doctrine of an ancient constitution had rested. But by a variety of moves — of which the hypothesis of a prefeudal phase of allodial property was one[199] — Millar was able to present the key events in the history of medieval institutions as sometimes the recovery of former liberties and sometimes the consolidation of new ones. He vested these tactics with such continuity that by the time he reached the Stuart reigns in England he was able to maintain that there now existed an ancient constitution — a set of rules based on reverence for antiquity and long in the formation — that the kings were seeking to transgress.[200] His account of Charles I is as sternly Whiggish as Hume's had been skeptical of Whiggism, and it would not be unduly difficult for his readers to equate post-1688 attempts to disturb the principles of the constitution by corruption with post-1603 attempts to disturb them by prerogative. What these principles were must be discovered by historical interpretation rather than in legal precedent, but Millar was a scientific Whig and was prepared to construct such interpretations. Addressing himself to Fox, therefore, he supplied a "Whig interpretation of history" that Hume would have denied and the later Burke would not have constructed.

Burke once remarked that even if the constitution were not as ancient as Englishmen had believed, they had always acted on the belief that it was.[201] Millar's reading of history is more sociologically sophisticated than Burke's and less uncompromisingly presumptive, but the two are not at bottom very far apart. Men in history act as the situation requires, and in historically changing situations they act in changing ways; but to act pragmatically is to act in the consciousness of precedent, and if historical change is continuous, precedents from former situations can be applied to the needs of new ones. Innovative reform may in these circumstances be an essentially conservative activity. The belief is as old as Selden and Hale, but it was Millar's task to write a circumstantial history of how old actions could become new ones and could be used to justify them. If this could be done, it could be shown how even a revolution might be an act of conservation. By the time he wrote, English and Scottish historians were agreed that this

[199] *Historical View*, vol. I, pp. 131–4, 171, 185, 200–3, 290–301.
[200] *Historical View*, vol. III, pp. 156–7, 189–92, 220–7.
[201] Pocock, *Politics, Language and Time*, pp. 205–8.

could be done for the English Revolution of 1688 but not for the French Revolution of 1789, and Mackintosh had made, but subsequently withdrawn, the charge against Burke that on his principles it could not be done at all. It seemed to be the position of Burke and his disciples that 1688 was not repeatable and contained no guide to subsequent practice, and this was becoming a ground for holding that the constitution established after 1688 could not be reformed except on principles as dangerous as those the French had followed. If this position were maintained, there would indeed be something in Burke's rejection of theory profoundly constrictive of practice; and Scottish Whiggism respected practice and wished to advance it.

Lord Dacre has proposed ranking Millar, Mackintosh, and Macaulay as a succession of historians through whom Whigs of the Holland House circle effected a reconstruction of the Whig view of politics and history.[202] Details of this continuous activity, if such it was, remain to be worked out. Millar lived out his life in Glasgow, but it was as a Holland House habitué that Mackintosh formed the extensive documentary collection on which Macaulay drew so heavily for his understanding of the seventeenth century, while the Anglo-Saxon and Norman-Angevin periods — the other great focus of Whig historiography since its beginnings — received the attention of Francis Palgrave and of Macaulay's colleague on the *Edinburgh Review,* John Allen.[203] There is reason to speak of a "Holland House" school of historians, who under the patronage of the heirs of Fox engaged in a reconciliation of old and new Whiggisms, blending the spirit of Scottish scientific history with the headier brew of Burke, an enterprise that could be carried on only by reaffirming the mainstream Whig belief in the continuity of English institutions.

In medieval studies, these writers preserved the essence of the ancient constitution through a variety of restatements of the theme of primeval Germanic liberty. From Palgrave and Allen we are taught to look to Kemble and the reception into England of the notion of the mark community,[204] which linked the anthropological scholarship of the nineteenth century with the allodial assemblies of the eighteenth and the Tacitean folkgatherings of the seventeenth-century antiquarians. However scrupulously the newer Whigs might stress the primitive and agnatic character of early German institutions and the depth and abruptness of

---

[202] Lord Macaulay, *The History of England,* ed. and abridged with an intro. by Hugh Trevor-Roper (Harmondsworth, 1979), pp. 12–13. For Scottish responses to both the French Revolution and Burke's *Reflections,* see Stefan Collini, Donald Winch, and John Burrow, *That Noble Science of Politics: A Study in Nineteenth-century Intellectual History* (Cambridge, 1983), especially chaps. I, III, and VI.

[203] P. B. M. Blaas, *Continuity and Anachronism: Parliamentary and Constitutional Development in Whig Historiography and in the Anti-Whig Reaction between 1890 and 1930* (The Hague, 1978), pp. 72–110.

[204] Here and in what follows I am deeply indebted to J. W. Burrow, *A Liberal Descent.*

the feudalizations they had subsequently undergone, any medieval experiment with counsel, assembly, and representation must take on an appearance of a return to old norms: a recovery of the old and its adaptation to the new. And since any departure from a supposed feudal pattern must look like an enlargement of the consultative community beyond the immediate circle of tenants in chief, it could be viewed as part of a transition from closed feudal to open freeholding and commercial society: a liberalization to which the revival of prefeudal and even tribal norms had paradoxically contributed. The equation of old with new certainly did not originate with these historians, but if we may think of them as engaged in a reconciliation of scientific Whiggism with Burke, the importance of that move in this context becomes evident.

Burke had presented the Whig order as a modern commercial society, of the kind celebrated by the Scottish historians, but one that rested on and would not repudiate its medieval, even its chivalric and clerical, foundations. He had presented these foundations as cultural rather than institutional; manners had interested him more than laws. It was not a long step from manners to customs, however, and the ancient constitution had been a cluster of behavior patterns, mentalities, and institutions bound up with perceiving political action as customary and prescriptive. The question was whether the appeal to precedents, and the adherence to a prescriptive manner of political behavior, could be presented as carried over from one stage of social development to another; if it could, the gap between manners and customs might be bridged, and the habit of basing political action on the authority of former usages would appear valid throughout the process of modernization of which the Scots had written. It is this that lends peculiar importance to the studies of the crisis of the seventeenth century conducted by Hallam and Macaulay. The latter in particular employed an analysis as old as that used by Fletcher and Defoe in 1698. The feudal or Gothic mode of asserting the public liberty in arms endured well enough, rough and violent as it was, so long as the military strength of the kingdom consisted of vassals and retainers following their lords; once it came to consist of mercenary or professional standing armies paid out of the public purse, the cause of liberty must depend on whether that purse was to be dispensed and replenished by the king alone or by the representatives of the kingdom giving their consent to the king's actions.[205] Perceiving this crisis before them, the parliaments of Charles I responded not by asserting that new times required that they be vested with new powers, but by reviving and revising such precedents as they could find from feudal times and affirming their validity under postfeudal circumstances. Whether they did so anachronistically or in a conscious updating and translation hardly mattered; the important consideration was that it was they who were acting prescriptively and the king who was either innovating or falsifying the past by

[205] Macaulay, *The History of England*, vol. I, chap. 1, pp. 27–37.

reading his new need of prerogative into the actions of his feudal predecessors. The Commons had placed themselves in the mainstream of postfeudal history, and left the king no option but to act in ill faith – an option that Charles I, in Macaulay's view, had all too readily embraced.[206] It was a neat reversal of Hume's perception that in a time of historical change the constitutional rules by which king or Parliament should act had been underformulated.

When Macaulay arrives at the crisis of 1688 and the reign of William III, there is a sense in which his long-term strategy seems a little less clear. This statement may seem paradoxical. The years from 1688 to 1702 form both the substance of his *History* as we have it and the hinge on which his understanding of English history turns. In his interpretation of the Revolution Settlement he shows himself more Burkean than Burke himself; like him Macaulay never mentions Locke as theorist of the event,[207] but emphasizes the prudential and pre-scriptive character of the acts then taken almost to the exclusion of Burke's near-Tory insistence that they were acts of necessity whose repetition was not to be contemplated. Macaulay's revolution, one feels, could have been played again if some duke of Cumberland had made it unavoidable,[208] but it is of far greater importance to him to confront the issue of reform and explain that a preserving revolution in the seventeenth century has rendered unnecessary a destroying revolution in the nineteenth. However, if Macaulay were to repeat for 1688 the pattern of interpretation he had established for 1641, this would have been the moment to make clear what changes in the structure of society had occurred to call for the updating of ancient precedents; yet, though social-change explanations of political crises had become profoundly Whig, 1688 has never looked like the product of a social transformation in the way that 1641 has – partly because the lower orders were kept in the role of confused noise off.[209] Crisis in this sense followed a few years later, when the demands of William III's wars produced the military, financial, political, and commercial structure to which Commonwealth Whigs and country Tories set themselves in opposition. Macaulay, whose heroes were William III and the conquerors of India, knew well enough that this cleav-

---

[206] Macaulay, "Hallam's Constitutional History," in *Critical and Historical Essays,* vol. I, pp. 316–22, 341–5.

[207] Macaulay considers Locke as exculpated from complicity in Monmouth's rebellion (Firth, ed., *History of England,* vol. II, chap. V, pp. 538–9n.), as author of the *Letters on Toleration* (vol. II chap. VI, p. 670), as dedicator of the *Essay on Human Understanding* (vol. IV, chap. XV, p. 1,806), and as active in the nonrenewal of the Licensing Act (vol. V, chap. XXI, p. 2,482) and the recoinage of 1695 (ibid., p. 2,571).

[208] The unacceptability of the last of George III's sons is a half-buried theme of the history of this period. See Macaulay's memorandum on the assassination attempt against Victoria in 1840 in G. M. Young, sel. and ed., *Macaulay: Poetry and Prose* (Cambridge, Mass., 1967), pp. 799–804: "The King of Hanover cannot be implicated, one would think."

[209] See the ballad *The Orange* reprinted in Goldie, "The Revolution of 1689 and the Structure of Political Argument."

age among Whigs and Tories alike had occurred, and we are not in any ultimate doubt where he stood in regard to it. As J. W. Burrow has pointed out, Macaulay had no sympathy whatever for the neo-Harringtonian critics of oligarchy and corruption.[210] If Somers is his paragon among the Revolution and Junto Whigs, Treasurer Montagu ranks close behind; his labors in setting up the Bank of England are celebrated, the need for a new credit structure is explained, and Macaulay remarks on the paradox that of all the great English social thinkers only Burke — he does not mention Tucker; few people did — has grasped the function of the national debt and refrained from saying that it will ruin the nation.[211] There is hardly a grain of the Old Whig in Macaulay's composition, and this is important to our understanding of his arguments for parliamentary reform.

What we lack is Macaulay's completed interpretation of the eighteenth century, which he intended to bring to the death of George III but did not live to carry past that of William. We must reconstruct, or conjecture, what it would have been from his essays in the *Edinburgh Review*, but it is this that gives his account of the foundations of Whig rule an air of incompleteness. It can be seen that he approved of the Tory opposition to "no peace without Spain"[212] — perhaps because his hatred of Marlborough survived the latter's victories, perhaps as an echo of Holland House disapproval of the war in the Peninsula — and might have done justice to Harley if execution (we may be sure) upon Bolingbroke. For his judgment of Walpole we must rely upon two rather slight essays on Horace Walpole and the earlier career of the elder Pitt,[213] and we are without his sustained interpretation of the Septennial Act and the years between 1714 and 1760. We should like to know how far he would have presented Old Corps rule as a regime of oligarchy, patronage, and restriction, or conceded that the Whig reforms of his time were aimed at Whig foundations laid a century earlier. We should like to know his sustained interpretation of the first half of George III's reign, and whether he would have kept up his early contention that the ministries of Bute (North? Pitt?) were "Tory" and the oppositions of Rockingham (Fox? Grey?) the true heirs of Hampden, Russell, and Somers; for this would have been crucial to his two-party reading of English history, with the Whigs perpetually the party of progress and the Tories that of resistance. We should like to have his study of Pitt, Fox, and Burke in the early years of the revolutionary wars, because without it we do not know how he would have gone about reconciling the sundered fragments of the Whig tradition or how he would have presented the early history of parliamentary reform, and related this theme to those of European,

[210] Burrow, *A Liberal Descent*, pp. 55–60.

[211] Macaulay, *History of England*, vol. V, chap. XIX, p. 2,284.

[212] Macaulay, "Lord Mahon's War of the Succession in Spain," *Critical and Historical Essays*, vol. II, pp. 181–6.

[213] Ibid., pp. 207–24 (for the Septennial Act, see pp. 221–2), 237–9.

imperial, and conservative power, made necessary in English history by the second phase of oligarchic rule. All we are left with is the impression the essays
convey, namely, that Whig oligarchy was a necessary holding action, pending
the rise of the middle class.

The point is not that we know less than we might about Macaulay's historical
intellect, but that the authority — in many ways so great as to remain dominant
— of the "Whig interpretation of history" is in fact deficient to the extent that
we do not have a history of the greatest of Whig centuries by the greatest of
Whig historians. Hume stopped in 1688, and Smollett was a lesser if more
radical continuator. Macaulay did not go beyond 1702, and the Trevelyans and
Hammonds took a sterner view of George III and a more irenic view of the rivalry
between Pitt and Fox than Macaulay might have done. The Whig view of this
reign was a secondary construction, which blurred the answer to the question
Whigs were in fact confronting. In consequence the Whig interpretation has
been found vulnerable at its weakest point, which lies on either side of the year
1760, and has been replaced by an altogether different style of historiography,
which seeks to escape from eighteenth-century rhetoric and its categories. How
far this escape has been effected might be the subject of debate; the view that
there is nothing to government but high politics is profoundly oligarchic, and
Whig discourse can now be seen as a conversation about oligarchy. Against the
emergence of this paradigm Butterfield struggled, in some ways in vain; but if
there had really been an authoritative Whig interpretation of the reign of George
III the history of historiography would have been different.

(ii)

By the time of Macaulay's *History,* however, Whig historiography had a long life
before it. P. B. M. Blaas does not see it undergoing significant modification until
the last years of the century; ideologically speaking, it is tempting to connect
this, somehow, with the watershed of 1886.[214] In the meantime, there was one
major respect in which Macaulay may be said to have perfected the Whig interpretation: He made it possible to see common-law and Burkean adherence to
precedent as compatible with, indeed as an instrument of, Scottish and scientific-
Whig progress and modernization. His view of political action was Burkean to
the point of conservatism; his view of social progress was commercial to the point
of philistinism, and in his minute on Indian education he endorsed the radical
utilitarianism of James Mill, which he had condemned as an approach to English
politics.[215] The idea that a ruling class was charged with and legitimated by the

---

[214] John Roach, "Liberalism and the Victorian Intelligentsia," *Cambridge Historical Journal* XIII, 1
(1957), pp. 37–57. For Blaas, see n. 203.
[215] Macaulay, "Mill's Essay on Government," "The Westminster Reviewer's Defence of Mill," both
in *Critical and Historical Essays.*

maintenance of culture was about to pass from the hands of the heirs of Addison into those of the heirs of Coleridge. But with these paradoxes and the extent to which they could be reconciled in mind, we can now solve (it is hoped finally) what may be termed *das Herbert Butterfieldproblem:* that of seeing how the complacent progesssivism criticized in *The Whig Interpretation of History* could coexist with the complacent antiquarianism admired in *The Englishman and His History.* The Whig historians had at last discovered how to have it both ways, and from this time on the enduring offense of Hume was his love of making the smooth places rough: of insisting on the knots and fractures in what they desired to see as the straight grain of the English oak.[216]

On the other hand, as we have seen, Macaulay left the Whig interpretation weak, in the sense that he did not synthesize the history of the eighteenth century as that of the conflict between the Whig order and its critics, many of whom in America and England were or claimed to be more Whiggish than the Whigs. We can see that Macaulay could and would have written such a history, and we suspect that it would have been strongly supportive of the ruling order and scornful of a quasi-republican criticism, which, whether in Commonwealth or country shape, he visibly disliked. What — we ask yet again — would have been his history of the American Revolution? Yet his ideas were formed in some measure by Holland House and the *Edinburgh Review,* by circles critical of, if not hostile to, the oligarchy in its Pittite form and to its conduct of the wars, and we have to ask (we cannot answer) how far he would have been able to detach himself from the language still traditional with oppositions. His historical intellect took further shape during the debates prior to 1832, when he was advocating in terms reminiscent of Burke a reform of a parliamentary structure essentially Whig, which the heirs of Pitt bitterly opposed and the heirs of Fox had left in the hands of the Westminster radicals. It was one thing to pour the ashes of Burke into the urn of Fox, to marry the historiographical style of Burke with that of Millar; in 1832 Macaulay was faced with the ghost of Burke and a living memory (Grey) of the Society of the Friends of the People. It was an accident, but it was not an accident without meaning, that Macaulay did not write the history of a reform program that had until recently been conducted by Commonwealth Whigs and Tory radicals. Unlike Hume, who had deliberately stopped short of the contests over the character of the Whig regime, Macaulay did not live to write its history; he would not have abstained from doing so. But the fact that his part of his history remained unwritten lent strength to two of the ideological maneuvers with which he was most involved. One is the conflation, under the name of "Tories," of the defenders of the unreformed Whig structure, the King's Friends in the early years of George III, the nostalgic and quasi-Jacobite squires of William III's reign, the more corrupt and sinister figures of Restoration politics, and

---

[216] This is the object of allusion in Duncan Forbes's "terrible campaign country."

– still more remotely perceived in the historical pageant – the churchmen, cav-
aliers, and agents of the prerogative under the early Stuarts. It is hard to believe
that this would have been unmodified by a detailed narrative of Georgian politics.
Macaulay knew that Tories had used radical and republican language, and he
would have had to come to grips with the implications. We may regret that he
did not.

The second maneuver was the advocacy of reform in the terms that Macaulay
and others had employed in the debates preceding 1832. These too remained
unmodified by the *History of England* as published, but we may doubt if they
could have been unaffected had it been carried to completion. They furnish an
interesting blend of arguments emerging from the history of Whig discourse. It
had always been recognized that there was a formidable number of socially active
and conscious persons not represented in Parliament, and discourse had been
faced with the problems of finding terms in which they could be categorized and
arguments in which it could be debated whether they should be represented or
not. It was recognized that the social structure was too complex and the representative structure too random to leave it possible for long to dismiss these persons
merely as "the mob," and the more it was granted that many of them were
"respectable," the more it became necessary to determine in what their respectability consisted and in what ways if any it entitled them to be represented. In
quasi-republican language it was contended that the existing regime was corrupt
because too many of the persons it represented were in various ways dependent
and that the admission to the franchise of large numbers of persons presumed
independent would render it more virtuous. In more Lockean language it was
contended that because these persons were moral individuals, or because they
were in various ways proprietors, they possessed a right to be represented that
ought not to be denied them. There ensued from both arguments a debate regarding what constituted independence and property, and what constituted these things
the prerequisites of either virtue or right; by some it was argued that the possession of a moral personality, and by others that the possession of a capacity to
labor, was enough to make the possessor at least potentially an independent moral
and political being. We have seen, however, how Tucker argued that this was to
misstate the case, because the individual needed a deeper involvement in commercial relations before rights could be generated; we have also seen how Burke
followed the same strategy as Ireton at Putney, in attacking the abstract grounds
of a claim to representation rather than the expediency of granting the claim.

Well before 1832, the practice had developed of referring to the unrepresented
but active sector of the population as "public opinion," not because the represented lacked opinions ("the electors of Liskeard," remarked Gibbon, "are commonly of the same opinion as Mr. Elliott")[217] but because the unrepresented had

---

[217] Gibbon, *Memoirs of My Life*, ed. Georges A. Bonnard (New York, 1966), p. 162.

nothing else by which to make their presence felt. The term "opinion" was of considerable antiquity in Whig political thinking. In Hume's hands it had offered the reassurances of a conservative skeptic, who considered that opinions were on the whole subject to the disciplines of social experience; but if we look back as far as Sir William Temple, writing in 1672, we find it laid down that the authority of rulers can rest upon nothing but opinion, because power (his language has overtones of both Hobbes and Harrington) is invariably in the hands of the ruled.[218] Some of Temple's implications are not reassuring. The state possesses no monopoly of the means of coercion, and opinion emancipated from its discipline can prove wild and ungovernable. The specter of enthusiasm starts from the page, and we recall how Burke attributed the French Revolution to the growth of "middle classes," no longer deferential to their superiors, among whom there was nothing to "resist an opinion in its course" and human energy could break free from all the disciplines of property.

The reformers of 1832 declared that there now existed a "public opinion" and a "middle class" or classes, which required only to be represented in Parliament and did not need that representation mediated through the controls exerted by aristocratic patronage or influence. The antireformers replied that to emancipate parliamentary representation from the discipline, stern or gentle, exercised by the natural superiors of society would be to liberate human energy in just the same way as had happened in France and would infallibly lead to the same results. Some of them seem to have been very much in earnest. To this some reformers responded by drawing a distinction between patronage and deference, arguing that the latter was given freely to natural superiors and need not be controlled or influenced by the former; this opens up the larger question of just where they situated the "public opinion" it was proposed to enfranchise, and how far the 1832 Reform Act was an experiment in the institutionalization of deference. A considerable literature now exists on this subject, but it may be remarked that any aristocratic polity experimenting with a *governo largo* must do so in some degree of expectation that deference will continue to operate. Others again carried the argument in a direction recalling Madison, contending that representation itself ensured the presence of a natural aristocracy, or alternatively that it rendered one unnecessary.[219]

The reformers did not share – though the antireformers in some cases did – Burke's fear that the rule of the middle classes would subject all property to nothing but the mind of desperate men. It is proper to observe that, since they were not proposing to enfranchise numbers of workmen, they had every reason to suppose that those they were enfranchising would be distinguished precisely by the possession of property; but this does not cover every aspect of the case. Burke had imagined the revolutionary middle class less as entrepreneurs and

---

[218] Sir William Temple, "Of Government," *Works*, 3 vols (London, 1770), vol. I, p. 34.
[219] See Weston, *English Constitutional Theory and the House of Lords*, chap. VI.

speculators than as restless and power-hungry men of talent, who wanted to serve an expanding state and seized the state in order to expand it: a Machiavellian and Sorelian vision. There was enough substance left in eighteenth-century notions of *le doux commerce*[220] to make the idea of a middle class engaged primarily in commerce and industry reassuring by comparison, and we can imagine how easily it could be argued that such men would readily defer to their natural superiors if the relationships linking them were not corrupt. The classes enfranchised in 1832 were by no means all of this sort; provincial rentiers and professionals (the so-called pseudogentry) were conspicuous among them, and the debates reflect their presence. Nevertheless there is an ideologue of the period – W. M. Mackinnon– who specifically equates "the history of civilisation" itself with the advent of government by "public opinion," and the latter with a "middle class" whose "personal property" enables it to command the labor of others.[221] It is, of course, the formula for a Marxist bourgeoisie, except that Mackinnon considers this a historically determinant but not a revolutionary class. Where Marx's bourgeoisie captures and conquers the state, Mackinnon's is admitted to the councils of the state by the reforming Whig aristocracy, this bourgeoisie's natural superiors and historic allies. Civilization may be governed by opinion, but governments rule with its consent; it is not incapable of a Bagehotian deference.

Macaulay and Mackinnon lived toward the end of the age of oligarchy, witnessing the reform and partial disestablishment of a system of parliamentary restriction and control set up by a governing aristocracy between one and two centuries earlier. Because that aristocracy was limited in size, scarcely large enough to be called a class, it had felt obliged to rule in this way, fearing rivals and enemies within its own ranks and in urban and rural populations outside them. The coincidence of an expanding commerce, and a rapidly changing financial and military technology, had enabled the aristocracy to preside over a rapid economic modernization, with which it had successfully allied itself. An ideology of modernization had served it very effectively during the age in which it had ruled by restrictive devices, though some of these were ancient and others modern, and continued to serve it during the period in which it was desirable to dismantle these devices and seek a wider circle of allies. In contrast, the groups excluded from power by the oligarchic regime, who were several and diverse, found it appropriate to adopt an ideology of ancient values, those of the classical republic and its virtues; this, as is generally the case with the vocabularies of opposition, served to articulate some highly telling criticisms of the values being rendered dominant by the regime. Neither the republican discourse nor those who adopted it can be written off as reactionary or nostalgic merely because they were opposed

---

[220] Albert Hirschman, *The Passions and the Interests* (Princeton, N.J., 1976).
[221] W. M. Mackinnon, *On the Rise, Progress and Present State of Public Opinion in Great Britain and Other Parts of the World* (London, 1828); *History of Civilisation,* 2 vols. (London, 1846).

by an ideology of modernization, any more than they can be written up as bourgeois and progressive merely because they were opposed by an entrenched aristocracy; the whole point is that they were opposed by both at the same time. The republican discourse enabled some to engage in the pursuit of modernization, others to criticize it, and not a few to engage in it and criticize it at the same time; America, where opposition Whiggism took off into a new theater of world history, is perhaps the supreme example of this duality of mind. But the American Revolution effectively amputated republican rhetoric of the Commonwealth mode from British political discourse. It became clear after that event, if it had not been clear before, that the thrust of radical criticism in British politics must be toward the reform, not the replacement, of a parliamentary system of government, to which an intensely complex and dynamic society was committed. The intellectual debate was correspondingly intense. It has remained unclear to this day how far the growth of class conflict in Britain, bitter and obsessive as it has long been in many ways, originates and continues within, and how far outside, the parameters imposed by a parliamentary structure.

Reform in 1832 was effected by Burke's New Whigs, who had regrouped themselves and become more like his Old Whigs; it was not effected by Old Whigs as we have learned the term from Caroline Robbins, and there is a sense in which it marks the moment of their demise. The Reform Whigs retained the outlook of an aristocracy, but because this was not a *noblesse d'ancienne extraction* there was the less need to write its history, and they were able to ignore those eighteenth-century presentations of history that had emphasized that its rule was little older than 1716 or 1688. The most telling way of undermining the Whig aristocracy's role in history was to emphasize their origins under Henry VIII, but Cobbett's *History of the Reformation* had virtually played itself off the board. The myth of antiquity that best served the reforming aristocracy was that of the ancient constitution, and we have seen how a synthesis of Scottish and Burkean elements could render this compatible with an ideology of progressive modernization. Proposals for reforming the franchise in 1832 went rather better with the belief that the Commons had first been summoned to Parliament in 1265 than with the belief that they had attended in pre-Conquest antiquity; in both cases, it could be said, new and useful classes were being invited to the councils of the realm. But in both cases there must already have existed a realm, governed by counsel and capable of reforming itself within the parameters of its already existing institutions, and there was no reason why that realm's history, and that of its Burkean capacity for self-reform, should not be traced back to the folkmoots of a Teutonic dawn. The ghosts of Petyt and Brady, Bolingbroke and Hume, Cartwright and Tucker might now lie down together under the benignly amused eye of John Selden.

What was being suppressed, but could not altogether be silenced, was the

eighteenth-century radical historiography that averred that constitution and society had begun to be corrupted at a point in past time that could be fixed and
that reform must lie in a reaffirmation of principles (or a balance of principles)
that had existed before corruption set in. This was the reform language of the
Commonwealth Whigs, and there is an obvious sense in which it, and they, must
lose all reason for existence once regime Whiggism discovered a language, as
much its own as theirs, in which to reform itself. The story Caroline Robbins
began to tell therefore comes to an end, as far as Britain is concerned, in 1832;
the American republic has continued to lament the failure of its dream and the
loss of its innocence in every generation since it was founded. But the sociology
of Commonwealth and country criticism outlasts its role in constitutional debate.
The debates over reform in 1867[222] as well as 1832 were debates over the nature
of the property, the independence, and the self and the capacity to respect it that
might qualify new classes for admission to the franchise; and the theme of an
equilibrium or harmony between landed, monied, and laboring interests, or classes,
is by no means absent from the debates. One foundation for franchised independence, of course, was the control over personal property, and the capacity to
employ labor, which permitted the formation of an informed opinion, and it is
down this line that we should look for the emergence of conflict between a class
that employs labor and a class that has labor to sell. What is to be suspected is
the Whiggishness of writing all history as if it were subsumed under this conflict.
Another foundation for social and political personality, much discussed with relation to the clerisies and service gentries of the nineteenth and twentieth centuries, has been the possession and transmission of literate culture, and it is when
we look back from this debate to the ethos of politeness in the eighteenth century
that we catch sight of a major historical fissure. From Addison to Smith it had
been taken for granted that polite culture was the child of commerce and justified
the Whig order, but Burke and Coleridge in one way, Blake and even Cobbett
in others, had opened up serious cracks in this argument, which J. S. Mill,
Carlyle, Arnold, and Morris continued to explore. It is perhaps when the clerisies
– a better word than intelligentsias – both radical and Tory began to denounce
the Whig and Liberal ruling order as irremediably philistine, and seek for communitarian, proletarian, or authoritarian allies against a cultural "bourgeoisie,"
that we may regard the Scottish Enlightenment as effectively dead.

[222] F. B. Smith, *The Making of the Second Reform Bill* (Cambridge, 1966).

Index